Understanding Domestic Violence

Understanding Domestic Violence

Theories, Challenges, and Remedies

Edited by Rafael Art. Javier
and William G. Herron

ROWMAN & LITTLEFIELD
Lanham • Boulder • New York • London

Published by Rowman & Littlefield
An imprint of The Rowman & Littlefield Publishing Group, Inc.
4501 Forbes Boulevard, Suite 200, Lanham, Maryland 20706
www.rowman.com

Unit A, Whitacre Mews, 26-34 Stannary Street, London SE11 4AB

British Library Cataloguing in Publication Information Available

Library of Congress Cataloging-in-Publication Data

Names: Javier, Rafael Art., editor. | Herron, William G., editor.
Title: Understanding domestic violence : theories, challenges, and remedies / edited by Rafael Art. Javier, William G. Herron.
Description: Lanham, Maryland : Rowman & Littlefield, [2018] | Includes bibliographical references and index.
Identifiers: LCCN 2018012525 (print) | LCCN 2018013354 (ebook) | ISBN 9780765709547 (ebook) | ISBN 9780765709530 (cloth : alk. paper) | ISBN 9781538158180 (pbk : alk. paper)
Subjects: LCSH: Family violence. | Family violence—Treatment.
Classification: LCC HV6626 (ebook) | LCC HV6626 .U526 2018 (print) | DDC 362.82/92—dc23
LC record available at https://lccn.loc.gov/2018012525

∞™ The paper used in this publication meets the minimum requirements of American National Standard for Information Sciences Permanence of Paper for Printed Library Materials, ANSI/NISO Z39.48-1992.

Printed in the United States of America

For Margaret Cashin, my son Joshua, my siblings, and my patients
for each found ways to support this endeavor
Rafael Art. Javier

For Mary Jane for her unwavering support in all the years
we had together
Bill Herron

Contents

Preface

The purpose of *Understanding Domestic Violence: Theories, Challenges, and Remedies* is to continue the discussion that we started in our previous book on domestic violence (Javier, Herron, & Bergman, 1996) and to highlight the different challenges that we continue to face in effectively addressing issues of domestic violence in all its forms. There are social, health, moral, and economic benefits for the individuals and society as a whole in being able to address issues of domestic violence in all its permutations and complexities before they reach the boiling point. It is our contention in this book that an effective intervention for domestic violence can only take place by considering this multiplicity of factors in its design, with the understanding that the application of a specific response should be guided first by ensuring the physical safety and psychological need of the victim(s) at the time of the intervention. By victim we are referring to spouses or partners and their children and other vulnerable individuals likely to be victimized in the domestic violence situation.

The chapters included in this volume were selected to provide fundamental information about domestic violence in today's complex society where the definition of family has gone through a major transformation. They were selected (1) to provide a comprehensive discussion of different models utilized to understand domestic violence incidents; (2) to highlight its complexity, usually related to the intersectionality of issues normally present in any domestic violence incident; and (3) to provide explanations that reflect that complexity and that can serve as a guide to the development and designing of more efficient and targeted intervention programs for that population. We recognize that we could not cover all aspects of domestic violence and its consequences on its victims/perpetrators; nevertheless, we have included what we consider the most critical issues that should be examined. When it comes to domestic violence, there is no gender, race, religion, cultural background, social class, political affiliation, or country that has been found to be impervious to that phenomenon and its consequences. We have found, for instance, troubling incidents of domestic violence that involve male, female, and members of the LGBT communities as victims and perpetrators who have different religious affiliations, geographical locations, cultural backgrounds, race, educational levels, and socioeconomic class (Ard & Makadon, 2011; Black et al., 2011; Institute of Medicine, 2011; Ristock, 2005; Swan, Gambone, Caldwell, Sullivan, & Snow, 2008; Vivian & Langhinrichsen-Rohling, 2004).

This book is divided into four parts, each preceded by a short introduction summarizing the major issues addressed in the specific section. It begins with a comprehensive introductory chapter to set the stage for the themes addressed in the rest of the book. Part I addresses the conceptual framework guiding the book (chapters 2–6). Part II focuses on the challenges in addressing issues of domestic violence in ethnic, racial, and cultural contexts (chapters 7–9). The three chapters in part III are specifically dedicated to addressing treatment issues in domestic violence (chapters 10–12). The final chapter is dedicated to bringing together all the major themes of the book, raise additional challenges for further future exploration, and provide intervention recommendations guided by the main thrust of the book.

The reader will find additional comments about the chapters included in this book in the introduction to the different parts. We have also included important information in the appendix and other parts of the book: a list of resources of what may be available in various communities to assist victims/perpetrators of domestic violence that the reader may find helpful in clinical practices; also included is a list of legal cases adjudicated by the court that now serve as precedence and provide the legal context guiding the legal resolutions of domestic violence complaints. Finally, the reader will find a list of concepts that have now become part of the vernacular in domestic violence literature.

Although it was not designed specifically as a treatment and intervention text, the reader will find ample clinical discussions throughout the various chapters featured in the book, and more specifically in part III with the chapters by Martha Banks (chapter 10), Christine Murray and Allison Crowe (chapter 11), and Lenore Walker and Tara Jungersen (chapter 12). These authors address issues of evaluation and treatment and provide specific and thoughtful recommendations and treatment strategies that we hope are of benefit to students and more seasoned clinicians looking for concrete treatment/assessment recommendations. The strength of this book is in its scope and comprehensiveness in the examination of the multiple and fundamental challenges in understanding domestic violence as a complex phenomenon. In that context, we dedicate a great deal of our effort to teasing out the conditions involved in domestic violence incidents and delineate some of the mechanisms that keep this phenomenon so impervious to treatment intervention. An important part of that effort is on making sure that we recognize the different faces of domestic violence victims and to recognize that perpetuators come in different forms. The reader will find in this regard a whole chapter (chapter 6) dedicated to an examination of what makes a woman become a perpetrator in the domestic violence dynamic, an area that has received only limited attention in the literature on domestic violence. We hope that the reader will find that the discussion on the different explanatory models included in the conceptual section helpful and it will encourage new ways of looking at the conditions and factors that make domestic violence so difficult to eradicate; at the same time, armed with a better appreciation of its complexity, we hope that the reader is then emboldened to consider designing treatment interventions that include the most relevant factors required to address the multiplicity of specific issues normally present in any domestic violence incident.

A core focus in this regard is the recognition of the inherent traumatic effects that domestic violence has on its victims. Recognizing the critical importance of trauma in this regard, we dedicate a substantial component of the introductory chapter to the exploration of the various ways trauma is implicated in any experience of domestic violence. We describe the inherent survival mechanism that is triggered and that results in the activation of response schemes that are biologically engrained to protect the individual from danger. We describe in this chapter how the automatic deployment of this mechanism, when not guided by mentation and more appropriate response style, could create a problem for the individual and complicate the domestic violence situation further. It is our contention that it is the blind operation of this mechanism that makes the eradication of domestic violence so challenging. The reader will find ample recommendations in the different chapters included in this book to help address that very challenge. We find that anchoring domestic violence within the trauma framework is not only innovative but more accurate of what we see in clients coming into our offices. We invite the reader to keep in mind the likely involvement of trauma in the different chapters included in this book even when not explicitly referred to in the specific chapter under consideration.

Another crucial issue addressed is the importance of maintaining an open and nonjudgmental mind-set when dealing with domestic violence. There are too many factors usually involved that, if we are not careful, we may end up stepping on land mines. One such instance can be found when dealing with individuals from different cultural and ethnic backgrounds. Making assumptions about homogeneity within different ethnic and cultural groups is one of the greatest obstacles to understanding the uniqueness of the experience of DV in these groups. We address that issue head-on in the chapters included in part II. As El-Jamil and Abi-Hashem eloquently stated in their chapter 7 with regard to individuals coming from the Middle East, not all Middle Easterners are Arabs, not all Arabs are Muslims, not all Arabic speaking people are Middle Easterners, and not all Muslims are Arabs or Middle Easterners. Similar differentiation can be made of all ethnic and racial groups, an issue emphatically made by authors in this section and other chapters included in the book. For instance, the analysis of the impact of sociocultural, socioeconomic, ethnopolitical, religious, and legal factors on the prevalence of DV provide an insightful view and an opportunity for the reader to appreciate the cultural and subtle maneuvering a woman in that society has to engage in to successfully reconcile the public's expectations related to professional career and education with her internal need to ensure her position in that patriarchal society. At the same time, one must recognize that in many homes and communities, the status of the woman can be quite elevated, powerful, and intimidating. How these two views of the woman as the victim and as the one exerting the control over the whole family can coexist in the same society is the subject of El-Jamil and Abi-Hashem's chapter 7. That chapter will challenge the reader to consider the complex nature of how gender roles and relationships are determined in the context of cultural rules and expectations that appear mutually contradictory. Considering the sensitivity of the issues addressed in this chapter, El-Jamil and Abi-Hashem provide the reader sufficient and helpful insights at the end of the chapter to guide the proper intervention for this population.

This emphasis is continued in chapter 8 by Carolyn West, who makes an important argument refuting the perception about Black Americans as being inherently more violent than other ethnic groups. In her analysis, she makes the point that intimate partner violence in the African American community can only be understood by broadening its definition to include the impact of risk factors that are unique to the African American experience. By that she means the influence of historical trauma, institutionalized violence, and coercive control that infiltrate and define the life of the African American individuals in this country. In this context, she uses an ecological model to examine the impact of structural inequalities, such as poverty and neighborhood disadvantage, at the individual, relational, communal, and societal levels. When examining incidents of DV, she found these factors to be involved where poor socioeconomic condition creates the necessary condition for DV, which includes bidirectional intimate partner violence or wife-to-husband abuse. She provides a comprehensive review of these and other risk factors as they interplay in the African American community, contributing to the development of the toxic environment likely to contribute to intimate partner violence.

Clauss-Ehlers, Millán, and Zhao in chapter 9 make a similar point as West with regard to the risk factors involved in incidents of DV within

Latino cultures. These authors found that once socioeconomic variables (such as education and income) are controlled for, intimate partner violence is not found more frequently in the Latino population than other groups, such as African American and White Americans. They highlight the importance of considering the issue of immigration when addressing DV in this population. Also highlighted in this chapter are the unique cultural ways this population attempts to navigate the tremendous stress associated with the immigration experience and its impact in their personal and family life.

In chapter 13, we address issues of future challenges that emerge in the context of the different contributions included in the book. It provides specific recommendations related to the assessment and the specific ingredients an intervention for domestic violence should include.

This is an exciting project that took several years in the making to ensure its comprehensiveness and high level of sophistication. We are honored to have attracted a well-recognized group of scholars with extensive knowledge on the issue to contribute their expertise; the result is the magnificent compendium of the latest perspectives on domestic violence, including the most recent research data and explanatory models. We expect this book to be a great asset to anyone interested in understanding this insidious problem that is affecting so many individuals in our society. *Understanding Domestic Violence* is written with graduate students, researchers, scholars, and practitioners in mind. It is ideal for graduate courses or upper-level undergraduate courses and for those looking for the latest thinking on the subject. To that end, we have included a list of activities/homework after each chapter with an invitation to explore treatment implications related to the theme of the specific chapter under consideration.

Hope that you find this volume professionally rewarding!

REFERENCES

Ard, K. L., and Makadon, H. J. (2011). Addressing intimate partner violence in lesbian, gay, bisexual, and transgender patients. *Journal of General Internal Medicine*, 26(8): 930–933. Published online 2011 Mar 30. doi: 10.1007/s11606-011-1697-6.

Black, M. C., Basile, K. C., Breiding, M. J., Smith, S. G., Walters, M. L., Merrick, M. T., . . . Spivak, H. R. (2011). *The National Intimate Partner and Sexual Violence Survey (NISVS): 2010 summary report*. Atlanta, GA: National Center for Injury.

Institute of Medicine (2011). *The Health of Lesbian, Gay, Bisexual, and Transgender People: Building a Foundation for Better Understanding*. Washington, DC: The National Academies Press. doi: 10.17226/13128.

Javier, R. A., Herron, W. G., & Bergman, A. (1996). *Domestic violence: Assessment and treatment*. Northvale, NJ: Jason Aronson, Inc.

Prevention and Control, Centers for Disease Control and Prevention. Retrieved from http://www.cdc.gov/violenceprevention/pdf/nisvs_executive_summary-a.pdf.

Ristock, J. (2005). Relationship violence in lesbian/gay/bisexual/transgender/queer [LGBTQ] communities: Moving beyond a gender-based framework. *Violence Against Women Online*

Resources. Retrieved from http://citeseerx.ist.psu.edu/viewdoc/download?doi=10.1.1.208.7282&rep=rep1&type=pdf.

Swan, S. C., Gambone, L. J., Caldwell, J. E., Sullivan, T. P., & Snow, D. L. (2008). A review of research on women's use of violence with male intimate partners. *Violence and Victims, 23*, 301–314.

Vivian, D., & Langhincrichsen-Rohling, J. (2004). Are bi-directionality violent couples mutually victimized? A gender-sensitive comparison. *Violence and Victims, 9*, 107–123.

Acknowledgments

The completion of this book is the result of a long and arduous journey that included not only the two co-authors but also a dedicated and determined group of individuals whose contributions are palpable throughout. We are referring to the outstanding chapter contributors whose scholarship has made this book much more relevant to address the fundamental issues normally associated with domestic violence incidents. We thank them for their willingness to share their expertise on the subject in the manner that only dedicated professionals do. Please accept our wholehearted appreciation and gratitude.

The contribution made by a number of graduate students and student workers is also acknowledged, particularly Yosef Amrami, Maria Barlis, Jennifer De Mucci, Marko Lamela, Gerald Pantoja, Michelle Yakobson, and Cindy Yu. They deserve great recognition and our appreciation for their steadfast commitment to the various stages of the book preparation. We particularly recognize the latest addition to our office, Devesh Permanan, for his important contribution in putting together the appendixes included in this book. He is to be commended for his work and invaluable contribution. Finally, our profound thanks and gratitude to Dr. William Chaplin, the department chair, and secretarial staff Evelyn Falcone and Lauren Euell for their unique and unwavering support provided over the years that facilitated the completion of this project. We are also appreciative to the helpful and insightful recommendations made by the reviewers of this book which resulted in a much improved presentation. All and all, it is clear that without their involvement, their careful literature review on the subject, their editorial assistance, their continuous work with the different contributors, and overall support, the final completion of this book project would not have occurred. They were the engine behind the scene that made things happen, and for that we thank them and extend our gratitude.

We recognize also with deep gratitude the support received from Margaret Cashin. She was eager to read early versions of the book and offered numerous suggestions along the way to improve the quality of its content. My gratitude also to my son Joshua and my siblings (in alphabetical order) Ana Espinoza, Rosa Homolka, Marino Javier, Lucy Lopez, Margarita Lugo, and Doris Rodriguez for finding their unique ways to support what I do and for encouraging me to continue in my journey. Even in their physical absence, they continue to be a warm and comforting presence in what I do. My deceased younger brother Luis is also recognized in this context. Finally, my coauthor William Herron has been a godsend and with whom I have been able to complete a number of important book projects that have contributed to a substantial increase in my understanding of various psychological conditions and processes. He has a way to encourage me to take on yet one more important project, and this book is one of these examples. Thank you, Bill, for your friendship and for making me better in what I do.

In the end, I have been given an unusual opportunity to engage in various exploration of domestic violence with many of my patients who have, in the process, provided me with a wealth and depth of information that can only be found when submerged in their unique domestic violence situations. Thank you to all my patients for their courage and for allowing me to be part of such a painful journey but where a sense of hope and recovery was also possible.

A Timeline of Relevant Events of Domestic Violence Regulations in the United States

1848: At Seneca Falls, New York, 300 women and men sign the Declaration of Sentiments, a plea for the end of discrimination against women in all spheres of society.

In the United States, the courts continued to uphold a man's right to punish his wife with violence until **1871**. In a case known as *Fulgam v. the State of Alabama*, the court ruled that, "The privilege, ancient though it may be, to beat her with a stick, to pull her hair, choke her, spit in her face or kick her about the floor or to inflict upon her other like indignities [referring to any act of violence or degradation], is not now acknowledged by our law."

1910: The U.S. Supreme Court ruled that a wife had no cause for action on an assault and battery charge against her husband because it "would open the doors of the courts to accusations of all sorts of one spouse against the other and bring into public notice complaints for assault, slander and libel."

1962: In New York, domestic violence cases are transferred from Criminal Court to Family Court where only civil procedures apply. The husband never faces the harsher penalties he would suffer if found guilty in Criminal Court for assaulting a stranger.

1966: Beating, as cruel and inhumane treatment, becomes grounds for divorce in New York, but the plaintiff must establish that a "sufficient" number of beatings have taken place.

1967: The state of Maine opens one of the first domestic violence shelters in the United States.

1968: The Harris poll interviews 1,176 American adults in October. They find that 1/5 approve of slapping one's spouse on "appropriate occasions."

Before the 1970s, judges and police officers still saw wife beating as a trivial offense—policemen would tell husbands to calm down and wives to stop annoying them, and cases rarely came to court. Popular culture depicted wife beating as a joke, and psychiatrists saw it as a pathology of the underclass or of individual women. In general, the problem was denied or explained away.

Early 1970s: Throughout many cities, married battered women who leave their husbands are denied welfare due to their husbands' income.

1972: In June, the first emergency rape crisis line opens in Washington, D.C.

1973: From 1968 to 1973, the crime of rape increased 62% nationwide.

Mid-1970s: "We will not be beaten" becomes the mantra of women across the country organizing to end domestic violence. A grassroots organizing effort begins, transforming public consciousness and women's lives.

1975: Most U.S. states allow wives to bring criminal action against a husband who inflicts injury upon her. In New York, Abused Women's Aid in Crisis is formed after a domestic violence conference held in January. The AWAIC offers referral service and group counseling sessions to wives who need help breaking out of the victim syndrome.

1976: In November, the New York City Council passes Resolution 491, introduced by Council Member Miriam Freidlander, urging city agencies to make concrete plans for providing specialized assistance to battered women. The first domestic violence shelter in New York City opened as well.

1977: New York State funding was provided for shelters and victims of domestic violence. A law was passed allowing married victims of domestic violence to file criminal charges against a spouse.

As recently as **1977**, the California Penal Code stated that wives charging husbands with criminal assault and battery must suffer more injuries than commonly needed for charges of battery.

1978: The New York State Coalition Against Domestic Violence (NYSCADV) was established.

1979: The New York State Governor's Task Force on Domestic Violence was created.

In the **1970s**, feminists documented the widespread incidence of wife beating and asserted that it was not just working-class husbands who assaulted their wives, but all classes of men. They defined wife beating as one extreme in a spectrum of male efforts to dominate women, and argued that rape was a crime of violence, not sex. Feminists founded shelters where women could take refuge, demanded that the police do more to protect women, and advocated for battered women in the courts. The Gay Liberation Movement paved the way for the creation of mainstream feminist groups like the National Organization for Women (NOW). Gatherings such as women's music concerts, bookstore readings, and lesbian festivals well beyond the United States were extraordinarily successful in organizing women to become activists; the feminist movement against domestic violence also assisted women to leave abusive marriages, while retaining custody of children became a paramount issue for lesbian mothers.

1981: The New York State Domestic Violence Hotline was established and the first annual Domestic Violence Awareness Week is celebrated.

1982: The Human Resource Administration (HRA) establishes one shelter for battered women in each borough. Over 700 women were served.

1985: The New York State Spanish Domestic Violence Hotline was established, the first in the nation.

A New York Asian Women's Center is also formed in New York City. It sponsors programs to combat violence against Asian women.

For children, the National Assault Prevention Center is formed by Sally Cooper, which helps youths deal with different forms of abuse.

1986: In *Meritor Savings Bank v. Vinson*, 477 U.S. 57 (1986), the U.S. Supreme Court held that a hostile or abusive work environment can prove discrimination based on sex.

1987: The Domestic Violence Prevention Act permanently funded emergency shelters for victims through local Departments of Social Services. Additionally, the New York State Coalition Against Sexual Assault (NYSCASA) was established.

In Vermont, violation of a protection order became a crime with the passage of a law to that effect in **1990**. Police officers are authorized to enforce orders, and the law outlines penalties for violations.

In the **1990s**, welfare reform tried to get women to become economically independent, but also subjected poor women to surveillance and regulation. As feminist activists and shelters became co-opted by the state, policy focused on treating women and transforming their lives as individuals.

1992: The New York State Office for the Prevention of Domestic Violence (OPDV) was created by statute, replacing the Commission. New York became the only state with an executive level state agency dedicated to addressing the issue of domestic violence. The American Medical Association releases guidelines suggesting that doctors screen women for signs of domestic violence.

1993: The United Nations recognizes domestic violence as an international human rights issue and issues a Declaration on the Elimination of Violence Against Women. A similar resolution is issued by the Organization of American States. Manhattan Borough President Ruth Messinger and New York City Council Member Ronnie Eldridge co-chaired the Task Force on Family Violence.

1994: The federal Violence Against Women Act (VAWA) created the first legislation acknowledging domestic violence and sexual assault as crimes and provided federal resources to encourage coordinated community responses to domestic violence.

New York follows Florida in recognizing that rapists cannot claim that the victim's dress provoked their crime. New Jersey and Pennsylvania add stalking to definitions of abuse.

1995: Governor Pataki made prevention of domestic violence a priority, declaring a policy of "zero tolerance" for domestic violence in New York State.

1999: *United States v. Morrison*, 527 U.S. 1068 stated that the Violence Against Women Act of 1994, 42 U.S.C. § 13981, is unconstitutional as exceeding congressional power under the Commerce Clause and under section 5 of the Fourteenth Amendment to the Constitution.

2000: The average number of New York City families served by HRA per day was nearly 400. The DV shelter capacity increased from 871 beds in 1994 to 1,365 in 2001, serving nearly 2,000 families. In addition to HRA residential services, HRA provided oversight for 11 contracted nonresidential DV service providers, which served more than 15,000 victims during FY 2000.

The Sexual Assault Reform Act (SARA) was passed, enacting sweeping changes in New York State's rape, sexual assault, and child sexual abuse laws.

2002: A New York State law requiring all current and new Child Protective Service workers to be trained on domestic violence issues was passed.

2005: Reauthorization of the Violence Against Women Act. The 2005 reauthorization allocated federal funds to aid victims, provided housing to prevent victims from becoming homeless, and ensured victims had access to the justice system, and created intervention programs to assist children who witnessed domestic violence and to those at risk of domestic violence.

2010: The United Nations defines violence against women as "any act of gender-based violence that results in, or is likely to result in, physical, sexual or mental harm or suffering to women, including threats of such acts, coercion or arbitrary deprivation of liberty, whether occurring in public or in private life." Legislation to prevent and address domestic abuse through civil lawsuits, family law, and asylum law is discussed.

2011: A report by the Institute of Medicine acknowledges the impact of intrafamily and domestic violence in the life course of LGBT persons.

2013: The CDC released the results of a 2010 study on victimization by sexual orientation, and admitted that "little is known about the national prevalence of intimate partner violence, sexual violence, and stalking among lesbian, gay, and bisexual women and men in the United States." The report found that bisexual women had an overwhelming prevalence of violent partners in their lives: 75% had been with a violent partner, as opposed to 46% of lesbian women and 43% of straight women. For bisexual men, that number was 47%. For gay men, it was 40%, and 21% for straight men.

President Obama reauthorized the Violence Against Women Act. While the law still focuses on women in heterosexual relationships, it has a new section that includes coverage of same-sex partners.

2016: Analysis by the World Health Organization found that women who had been physically or sexually abused were 1.5 times more likely to have a sexually transmitted infection and, in some regions, HIV, compared to women who had not experienced partner violence. They are also twice as likely to have an abortion.

Today, women have the ability to obtain protection orders through the court. However, in almost half of our states, the police are not empowered to enforce these orders, nor is there any penalty for the men who violate them.

REFERENCES

Clark, A. (2011, September 03). Domestic Violence, Past and Present. Retrieved September 27, 2017, from https://muse.jhu.edu/article/449295.

Committee on Lesbian, Gay, Bisexual, and Transgender Health Issues and Research Gaps and Opportunities, Populations, Board on the Health of Select, and Medicine, I. O. (2014). *Health of Lesbian, Gay, Bisexual, and Transgender People: Building a Foundation for Better Understanding*. Washington, DC: National Academies Press.

Duquette-Hoffman, K. (n.d.). Overview of Historical Laws Supporting Domestic Violence. Retrieved September 27, 2017, from http://www.womensafe.net/home/index.php/domesticviolence/29-overview-of-historical-laws-that-supported-domestic-violence.

Fulgham v. The State (June, 1871) (Flaglerlive.com, Dist. file). Supreme Court of Alabama.

Morris, B. J. (n.d.). History of Lesbian, Gay and Bisexual Social Movements—American Psychological Association. Retrieved September 27, 2017, from http://www.apa.org/pi/lgbt/resources/history.aspx

Nations, U. (2010). *Handbook for Legislation on Violence against Women*. New York: United Nations Publications.

Shwayder, M. (2013, November 05). A Same-Sex Domestic Violence Epidemic Is Silent. Retrieved September 27, 2017, from https://www.theatlantic.com/health/archive/2013/11/a-same-sex-domestic-violence-epidemic-is-silent/281131/.

Timeline of Legal History of Women in the United States. (n.d.). Retrieved September 27, 2017, from http://www.nwhp.org/resources/womens-rights-movement/detailed-timeline/ National Women's History Project.

Timeline of the Battered Women's Movement. (2008). Retrieved September 27, 2017, from http://www.ncdsv.org/images/NYCHRADSS_TImelineBWM_2008.pdf NYC Human Resources Administration.

World Health Organization—Violence Against Women. (2016, November). Retrieved September 27, 2017, from http://www.who.int/mediacentre/factsheets/fs239/en/.

Chapter One

A Look at Domestic Violence through the Trauma Lens

An Introduction

Rafael Art. Javier and William G. Herron

Domestic violence appears to have always been with us and despite considerable effort to understand and prevent such behavior, it has remained unstoppable. We have targeted this problem before (Javier et al., 1996), as have many others, but as viable solutions have remained elusive, the situation urgently needs further exploration. We recognize domestic violence as a paradoxical type of aggression because it occurs in a setting that is supposed to represent the very opposite of any type of abuse. The words "domestic" and "violence" should not belong together, but for centuries they have existed together as a confounding syndrome of the cultures of the world. Now there is a high level of awareness of this coupling, and depending on the society and the culture, a growing level of outrage about the presence of domestic violence.

Despite such awareness, and numerous efforts to both understand and ameliorate domestic violence, it remains a significant and very disturbing problem. The physical and mental/emotional health of all involved is at risk, and that includes not only the victims and the perpetrators (Ard & Makadon, 2011; Institute of Medicine, 2011; WHO, 2013), but the very integrity of the social order of the culture where it occurs. As a result, basic trust, security, self-worth, and consideration for others are dismembered with the attackers forever tainted and the victims left physically and emotionally devastated. Added to this injury and trauma is the poor or lack of responses received from the same social institutions that are supposed to provide protection and secure one's safety.

Domestic Violence (DV) and Intimate Partner Violence (IPV) are not unique to a particular country or region of the world. It is a worldwide phenomenon (World Health Organization, 2005/2013) that continues to be of great concern to behavioral and social scientists. This concern is justified even in view of the seemingly downward fluctuation in the rate of intimate partner abuses reported in some of the countries. Such a declining statistic was reported in recent years in the United States (Crowe et al., 2009). According to these statistics, there was a decrease in the rates of fatal and nonfatal violence crimes against women by men from 1.1 million to 588,490 reported in the United States between 1993 and 2001 (Crowe et al., 2009); there was also a decrease in 2005 reported in the domestic violence statistics to 1,181 females and 329 males killed by an intimate partner, from a previous statistic of 1,218 women and 424 men in 1999 (CDC, 2009).

However, later statistics reported by the National Coalition Against Domestic Violence (2017) summarizing several sources, including the 2010 CDC report, presents a much more alarming picture. According to that report, 1 in 3 women and 1 in 4 men experience intimate partner physical violence, intimate partner sexual violence, and/or intimate partner stalking in their lifetime. It is reported that 1 in 4 women and 1 in 7 men experience severe physical intimate partner violence in their lifetime; that 1 in 6 women and 1 in 19 men have been stalked by an intimate partner during their lifetime to the point in which they felt very fearful or believed that they or someone close to them would be harmed or killed; and that on average, nearly 20 people per minute are being physically abused by an intimate partner in the United States. During one year, this equates to more than 10 million women and men. Finally, when looking at the frequency we find that among victims of intimate partner violence, more than 1 in 3 women experienced multiple forms of rape, stalking, or physical violence; 92.1% of male victims experienced physical violence alone, and 6.3% experienced physical violence and stalking (Black et al., 2011).

These estimates vary by states for the most part across all types of violence examined in this report. We find in this report that the lifetime estimates for women ranged from 11.4% to 29.2% for rape; 28.9% to 58% for sexual violence other than rape; and 25.3% to 49.1% for rape, physical violence, and/or stalking by an intimate partner. For men, lifetime estimates ranged from 10.8% to 33.7% for sexual violence other than rape; and 17.4% to 41.2% for rape, physical violence, and/or stalking by an intimate partner (Black et al., 2011).

The 2010 report by CDC suggests that these statistics differ for different racial and ethnic groups with regard to experiencing violence in general and more specifically domestic violence (Black et al., 2011). For instance, it is reported that approximately 4 in 10 women of non-Hispanic Black or American Indian or Alaska Native race/ethnicity (43.7% and 46.0%, respectively), and 1 in 2 multiracial non-Hispanic women (53.8%) have experienced rape, physical violence, and/or stalking by an intimate partner in their lifetime. Forty-five and three-tenths of American Indian or Alaska Native men and almost 4 in 10 Black and multiracial men (38.6% and 39.3%, respectively) reported having experienced rape, physical violence, and/or stalking by an intimate partner during their lifetime (Black et al., 2011).

Similar findings are emerging in nontraditional family contexts, such as gay and lesbian relationships. A 2013 CDC report indicated in this regard that 26% of gay men and 44% of lesbians surveyed experienced intimate partner violence (Heavey, 2013). This is an increase from findings in 2003 that reported the rates for lesbians by their partners as 11% and 15% for gay men by their partners, respectively (Tjaden, 2003). Same-sex cohabitants reported significantly more intimate partner violence than did opposite-sex cohabitants at some time in their lifetime (39.2% among women and 15.4% of men with same sex cohabitants vs. 21.7% with opposite-sex cohabitants) (Tjaden & Thoennes, 2000). These estimates are likely to be much lower than the reality on the ground due to underreporting of domestic violence by LGBT community (Ard & Makadon, 2011).

Because of the multiplicity of possible victims and perpetrators, we will use "he" or "she" interchangeably when appropriate throughout this volume, with the understanding that the issue under discussion may also apply to the other genders and sexual orientations. The perpetrator is the aggressor in the transaction whether male or female or member of the LGBT, while the target of the act is the victim, whether a female or a male or member of the LGBT (Ard & Makadon, 2011; Heavey, 2013; Ristock, 2005; Walters, Chen, & Breiding, 2013).

There are multiple factors involved in domestic violence incidents that tend to complicate the picture of domestic violence and how solutions are negotiated. These complications vary depending on whether one is dealing with domestic violence situations in heterosexual or LGBT relations, religious orientations, socioeconomic levels, presence of children, and so on (Institute of Medicine, 2011). For instance, there is evidence that disclosing IPV in an LGBT relationship becomes more complicated because it also involves discussing one's identity at a time when such identity is kept secret for fear of judgment and discrimination from many sectors of our society. Within the LGBT community, there is evidence that transgender members tend to experience higher rates of violence than other members of the LGBT community (Ard & Makadon, 2011). In cases of children, we also see that domestic violence tends to increase during certain critical periods, such as early childrearing and childbearing. This period appears to be a particularly vulnerable time, according to a 2006 report by the United Nations General Assembly (Agenda Item 61/143). Women are three times more likely to be killed by their partners, particularly during pregnancy (Bailey, 2010; Gielen,

O'Campo, Faden, Kass, & Xue, 1994). Violence also tends to increase in severity and frequency even more during the postpartum period (Finnbogadóttir & Dykes, 2016; Harrykissoon, Rickert, & Wiemann, 2002).

CRUCIAL ELEMENT IN THE DEFINITION OF DOMESTIC VIOLENCE

At the heart of the problem is the issue of defining domestic violence to allow for better and more effective ways to address it. By some definitions, not all acts of violence that occur in the context of the family environment would be considered part of the domestic violence syndrome. Intimate partner violence (IPV) should also include different ways in which relationships are established, given the fact of gender fluidity and the variety of gender identities of many individuals (Ard & Makadon, 2011; Flake & Forste, 2006; Wheeler et al., 2014). The Institute of Medicine refers to the confluence of all these factors as "intersectionality" and describes in its 2011 report the various gender identities related to sexual orientations that are involved in the LGBT acronym: lesbians, gay men, bisexual men and women, transgender, male-to-female transgender, transgender females or transwomen, female-to-male transgender, transgender males or transmen, and individuals with same-sex-attractions or behaviors but who do not adopt a non-heterosexual identity (Ristock, 2005). The reader is encouraged to become familiar with that extensive document and Ristock's earlier work to appreciate the multiple ways domestic violence could manifest in that population and the added complexities that these permutations normally bring about. What becomes clear is that in each of these possible permutations, the nature of the motivation behind the violent act, the extent of severity, and the impact should be closely assessed and addressed.

Johnson and his colleagues have taken the lead in attempting to provide a useful typology that could guide researchers and practitioners alike in differentiating different types of IPV (Johnson, 2008; Johnson & Ferraro, 2000; Johnson & Leone, 2005). We discuss these categories with the understanding that these different manifestations of domestic violence may vary in different gender identities involved in domestic violence; we discuss them also with the understanding that we are left with a number of questions as to how these typological transformations are formed and then activated by and in these individuals (Wangmann, 2011). To illustrate this very point, we have included some case examples in this chapter that are meant to help the reader appreciate more fully the human faces and suffering likely to be experienced by victims of domestic violence.

There are crucial elements that have consistently emerged in the literature as part of defining domestic violence definition, namely, (a) that it has to be a pattern of abuse against a member or members of the family or intimate partner; and (b) that there has to be an explicit intention to exert control and power over the intended victim(s). These critical elements are found in the definition of domestic/intimate partner violence advanced by the U.S. Office of Violence against Women (Crowe et al., 2009). It has also been found to be similar, for the most part, among the gender nonconformist communities (Ard & Makadon, 2011; Institute of Medicine Report, 2011). It is defined in these documents as a "pattern of abusive behavior in any relationship that is used by one partner to gain or maintain control over another intimate partner." It is considered a "criminal and noncriminal behavior in which one person in an intimate relationship misuses his or her power to control or coerce the other partner" (Crowe et al., 2009, p. 14). These behaviors are repeated by individuals in current or former intimate heterosexual or same-sex partners and gender-nonconformists for the purpose of creating a violent context and an atmosphere of fear "in which the victims are coerced, intimidated, degraded, and exploited" (Crowe et al., 2009, p. 14).

Following this definition, a single act of violence would not be considered domestic violence if perpetrated in the context of a heated argument or under conditions where the intention is not to exert power and control over the victim. Nevertheless, these types of situations may become complicated when trying to ascertain clearly the true intention of the perpetrator.

A case in point is of a 50-year-old man with a sporadic history of demanding and belligerent behavior when he felt his needs were not being met. He had never engaged in physical abuse previously. "I will never put my hands on my wife and children," he would say proudly, stating that he loved his family and was very proud of being able to provide for them. Violent outbursts began to emerge after he was laid off when the company he was working for downsized. After several attempts at looking for a job and not being able to find one, he saw his savings dwindling rapidly, and his wife and children began to voice their discontent and anxiety with the whole situation. They were afraid that once his unemployment checks ran out, the whole family would be doomed and would become destitute.

He became progressively more despondent and reclusive, preferring to spend his time in the bedroom, partly in his attempt to escape the questioning and disapproving eyes of his family. He began to have trouble sleeping and felt that he was beginning to lose his grip with reality when he began to feel "phony sensations" and hearing voices. He began to suspect that his wife and family were plotting to do him in so that they could cash in his life insurance check. He fought this thought intensely because deeply in his heart he did not feel that that could be the case. He started to drink and smoke heavily and it was on one of these occasions when he confronted his wife about what she and the children were plotting. She responded with her concern that "we need to get help," because he was falling apart and the whole family was suffering.

He became quite belligerent and accused her of secret meetings with the children and "making secret phone calls" behind his back. In exasperation, she screamed at him, "Don't you see what this is doing to you and to us?" He responded by slapping his wife so strongly that he broke her nose and dislocated her jaw. By the time the police arrived he was back in his bedroom crying and talking to himself, asking for her forgiveness. He was taken into custody for assault. His children were not home at the time of the incident but reported to the police that they were not surprised to hear that it had progressed into physical abuse, considering his deteriorating condition.

Characterizing this incident simply as a case of domestic violence misses a number of critical elements referred to in the above definition; namely, that it has to be a *repeated abusive condition* with the intended purpose *to gain power and control* over the victim. This was not clearly the case, especially at the time of the physical assault. The most we can venture to say is that striking his wife was indeed a violent act, but the explanation for which, however, seems to involve his attempt to get control over the situation at a time when he was under a poor and seriously compromised mental condition. However, the violent physical act, albeit being the first time that it happened, in the context of the sporadic history of his being demanding and belligerent might have been felt by his wife and family as the last straw that finally poisoned the family well. Ultimately, this left a lingering sense of intimidation in the family interaction and a fear of a future reoccurrence.

There are several types of intimate partner violence (IPV) that have been identified and that can help us recognize different manifestations of DV: *Intimate Terrorism*, *Violence Resistance*, *Common Couple Violence*, and *Mutual Violent Control*. The term *Intimate Terrorism* is used to distinguish domestic violence from other forms of violence. The essential characteristic of this type of violence is a pattern of ongoing use of physical, emotional, economic, and sexual forms of violence to exert control over the victims.

A case in point is one that captured the imagination of many in the United States and most likely around the world at the end of 1980s and early 1990s. This is the case of a six-year-old girl called Lisa who was killed in 1987 by Joel Steinberg who was reported to have illegally adopted her. Prior to her death there is a report that she was subjected to a period of continuous physical and emotional abuse and neglect, even in the presence of her adopted mother, Hedda Nussbaum (Kilgannon, 2006; McQuiston, 2000). There were also indications that the girl had been sexually abused. The other adopted child (a boy) also showed signs of neglect. Hedda was reported to have suffered serious physical harm as well that required immediate medical attention once the authorities became involved. When she was found, her face was somewhat deformed by the continuous beating she had received, she was physically disheveled, and was in poor hygiene and health. According to the report, she was found to be anemic, malnourished, and suffered from broken bones and chronic infections. Her coworkers at Random House Publishers, where she was an editor and author of children's books, had noticed that she was progressively showing physical signs of abuse (i.e., obvious bruises), which she always tried to explain away. Her performance at her job was characterized by serious absenteeism and deterioration of her overall functioning. In view of her poor performance and attendance, her employer decided to place her on a consulting editor status rather than the full-time job she had been holding. This new assignment allowed her to make her own schedule until eventually she stopped going to the workplace altogether.

A lot of mistakes were made along the way with this case that suggested failures at all levels. We are now able to deconstruct these failures because so much was revealed in court when the case was finally adjudicated. Ms. Nussbaum explained her inability to protect her children as due to intimidation by her husband. She claimed that she felt totally paralyzed by the frequency and intensity of the abuse that it rendered her a victim suffering from a Stockholm-like syndrome condition. She testified then against her ex-husband and was given immunity because the court also saw her primarily as a victim.

Her ex-husband was described as a man who used all kinds of strategies (e.g., intimidation, threat, isolation, physical and sexual assault, deprivation of food, coercion, and economic control) to maintain full control over his victims. She described her ordeal more fully in her book *Surviving Intimate Terrorism* (Nussbaum, 2005). But not everybody has been sympathetic to her situation, as evidenced by a number of demonstrations that blocked her from speaking in public arenas and from selling her story unquestioned. In the view of the demonstrators, Ms. Nussbaum had numerous opportunities to seek the best interests of her children but instead was more concerned with protecting herself (McQuiston, 2000).

The term *intimate terrorism* is to be distinguished from violence exerted in self-defense, referred to as *Violence Resistance* perpetrated by the victims against their abusive partners. Another type is *Common Couple Violence* where both partners become engaged in domestic violence; in this situation, it is not clear who the perpetrator or the victim is because these roles can become interchangeable. Finally, in the case of *Mutual Violent Control*, both partners act in a violent manner battling for control (Johnson & Ferraro, 2000).

Not satisfied with the level of specificity offered by the above categories, Kelly and Johnson (2008) provided further refinement and expansion of the previous typological set by including three additional types of IPV, namely *Coercive Controlling Violence*, *Separation-Instigated Violence*, and *Situational Violence*. In *Coercive Control Violence*, referred to earlier as Intimate Terrorism, the authors try to highlight an important distinction that this type of violence is not exclusively perpetrated by men or rooted in a patriarchal paradigm, which is implied in the previous category. They refer to *Separation-Instigated Violence* to highlight a specific IPV that is confined primarily to the period of separation when violence can erupt as a result of tension related to that specific condition. Finally, *Situational Couple Violence* refers to violence that is not motivated by control but in response to a particular situation and not likely to occur in any other situation.

These distinctions in the definition could provide an important assessment tool that may allow for more targeted intervention. Also, clarifying the issues involved in domestic violence further the understanding of the multiplicity of factors (or intersectionality) normally involved in any incident of domestic violence. We are referring to (1) the source(s) involved in any aggressive act, (2) the individual psychology of the perpetrator and the victim, and (3) the specific context where it occurs.

The discussion about typologies is designed to facilitate understanding of the fundamental, profound, and multiple factors normally involved in the dynamic of domestic violence. It is designed to provide important perspectives to guide clinical practices. An example of that is the finding that *situational violence* is the most prevalent type in the general population and in couples seeking conjoint therapy (Stith et al., 2012). The core problem for these couples tends to focus on communication skill deficiencies, which gets compensated with verbal aggression and violence. Similarly, there are perpetrators who could be described as *characterological* and others as *situational,* based on the work of Babcock and colleagues (Babcock, 2003; Badcock, Canady, Graham, & Schart, 2007). In the case of characterological perpetrators "violence is part of an overall effort to dominate and control a partner and violence is not necessarily limited to the family" (Stith et al., 2012, p. 6). For *situational perpetrators*, violence tends to occur in relationships "in which there is more likely to be reciprocal . . . where violence serves to exert control over specific interactions, rather than as part of an overarching pattern of domination" (p. 6).

Other findings point to the characteristics of female offenders, suggesting that women engaging in violence can be categorized as *General Violent (GV)* or as *Partner Only Violent (PO)*. GV were reported to perpetrate "more psychological and physical abuse, causing more injury in the past year, and a higher frequency of severe violent acts (e.g., 'beating up' a partner) than did PO women" (Stith et al., 2012, p. 7). Motivation for engaging in violence was also found to be different, with GV more likely to become violent because "he was asking for it," "they lost control," "were frustrated," or just "to push his buttons." For women in the PO category, violence was more likely to be part of self-defense.

Findings by Neal, Dixon, Edwards, and Gidycz (2014) also suggest the need to consider motivation components that may be involved in violence behavior. They found that women who engaged in psychological and physical IPV typically reported anger, retaliation for being hit first, or for emotional hurt, and an inability to express themselves verbally as the main motives to engage in abuse. On the other hand, women who engaged in sexual penetration gave sexual arousal as motives to prove love and a sense of loss of control.

Stith and colleagues suggest that being able to distinguish the different typologies and motivations in both male and female perpetrators calls for different treatment approaches. For instance, in the case of those "with characterological violence or intimate terrorism, or a history of violence outside the family, individual and gender-specific group treatments may be more appropriate." This is the case because of the "safety concerns regarding the existence of more severe forms of violence and patterns of coercive control in those experiencing intimate terrorism" (2012, pp. 7–8).

Other findings looking at the relationship between interpersonal victimization and emotional dysregulation also suggest the importance of distinguishing types of abuse (Kraft et al., 2014). They found that emotional clarity, awareness, and impulsivity accounted for a significant amount of variance in the relationship between child emotional abuse and adult emotional abuse. On the other hand, non-acceptance was found to account for significant variance in the relationship between child physical abuse and adult physical abuse.

TRAUMA IN DOMESTIC VIOLENCE: ITS CONTEXTS, PRECURSORS, AND CONSEQUENCES

We have seen in many of our patients how the experience of domestic violence reverberates at so many levels of their lives and has such a devastating effect on their overall functioning, including at the neurological level (Campbell, 2002; Murray, Lundgreen, Olson, & Hunnicutt, 2016; Center for Disease Control and Prevention, 2003, 2009; Reich, Blackwell, Simmons, & Beck, 2015; Smith & Stover, 2016; WHO, 2013). It is clear that IPV has all the trappings of what we normally refer to as trauma, and that may have propelled Walker and Jungersen (chapter 12 in this book) to develop a trauma-informed domestic violence intervention model.

What makes something traumatic is the fact that it causes pain and injury. According to Russell, it results in a traumatic condition where "there is an encroachment on the capacity to see things as they are, partly due to seeing the present in terms of the past"in which "memory is confused with perception" (1998, p. 3). There is a disturbance of the normal capacity to process information, particularly the ability to perceive and process motivation from others. This comes about because trauma tends to place the individual in a state of high alert where even the minimum similarity to the traumatic event tends to trigger the entire defensive maneuver required for protecting oneself. We often see in these cases high levels of hypervigilance, anxiety, depressive symptomatology, emotional numbness, difficulty concentrating, cognitive confusion, restrictive affect, withdrawal, and so forth. We also see hyperactivity, promiscuity, externalizing disorders (including disruptive behavior disorders, high use of alcohol and other substances, etc.) (Courtois & Ford, 2009; Reich et al., 2015; Stith, McCollum, Amanor-Boadu, & Smith, 2012). That is, the individual finds her/himself in the grip of what Russell refers to as "affective incompetence." In this state of affairs, the individual tries desperately to repair the disruption in the relationship that, although abusive, may be experienced by the individual as providing a sense of safety and predictability, and a sense of connection even in the midst of emotional disconnectedness. It is quite paradoxical and dangerous because what appears to be harming the individual (robbing them of their humanity) seems to serve also an important function for that individual—the glue that keeps her engaged and connected to the situation, as if immobilized by a mysterious force. The content of that force could be related to the often related fear of abandonment and of being alone that we hear from some victims of domestic violence. It is this very interconnection that makes domestic violence so difficult to address.

Russell (1998) speaks about the process generated by the trauma as part of a compulsion where a person repeats and engages in the same script (personal scheme), as if expecting a different result. The goal of this maneuver is to make sure that the relationship (even if abusive) is preserved because the alternative is felt as too devastating to consider. As stated earlier, this process is made possible because the person is dealing with an injury (physical and/or psychologically) that has left the person wounded and with a scar that recalls the event and/or condition that caused the injury and how the person felt (incompetent, overwhelmed, hopeless, terrified, etc.) when it happened; it recalls what the person did or didn't do (became paralyzed and acquiescent, run away, or engaged in any other protective maneuvering). How the person responds to the traumatic event will determine what kind of injury will be left in the individual's psyche and what will be the prominent affect associated with the experience (as defeated and violated and thus a victim; or as someone who, although injured, fought back to protect herself).

That concept of injury is of crucial importance because it explains the fact that once injured, that will never fully go away (remaining organized in sensory memory mode). The complication is that this way of organizing the experience is not always consciously present in one's mind, until it is triggered by something in the environment. We see similar reactions in veterans suffering from PTSD as a result of combat exposure, and other individuals who have suffered trauma (Courtois & Ford, 2009; Garbarino, 2015; Richardson, Freeh, & Acierno, 2010; Veterans and PTSD Statistics, 2016). The details of that memory and its affective components may vary in scope and clarity, but generally, it tends to have sufficient elements to remind the individual of the event and condition that caused him the injury even years later. Solms and Turnbull (2002) tell us that there is an evolutionary reason for that, namely, to ensure that the individual never totally forgets the condition that caused him injury and that created a threat to that person's survival. In keeping with this perspective, we will now attempt to describe the inherent mechanism that we consider to be involved in all incidents of domestic violence.

DESCRIBING THE STUBBORN MECHANISM IN DOMESTIC VIOLENCE

The central point that we want to make here is that domestic violence, and what it triggers in the individuals involved, represents a condition for which the organism has been prepared from time immemorial to respond to in ways that are motivated and guided by basic biologically given principles (operating automatically). That is, it has an evolutionary reason for being, with the ultimate goal to ensure the individual's physical (and by extension, psychological) survival. The negative affects normally associated with an experience of domestic violence (i.e., fear, terror, anxiety, etc.) provide the necessary condition for the individual to trigger responses already anchored in the basic structure of the brain that get automatically mobilized to ensure the individual's basic survival. The result of this process is the creation of organizing patterns or script structures in the individual that are normally interconnected with other specific sets of associated affects. An example of that is when we clinch our eyes or duck automatically when an object is getting too close to us and likely to hurt us. These are response patterns that are so ingrained in the individual's behavioral repertoire that mentation is at its minimum (if at all) and that can be inappropriately utilized (like when a victim fails to respond to the need to flee before more serious injury can befall upon her) under certain conditions. It is this inappropriate utilization of scripts that is normally associated with the development of psychological problems and that is involved in the process of becoming a victim and/or perpetrator of DV.

Describing the development of affects and different script structures along with their specific evolutionary function is one of the main points made by Tomkins (1962/1978), and Solms and Turnbull (2002) in their books. Both of these authors emphasize in different ways that we are born and wired with the capacity to experience the full range of basic affects (Demos, 1998; Tomkins, 1962). The function of these affects is to provide essential information about our experience in the world (something to enjoy, to fear, to treat tentatively, to get close to, to run away from, etc.) and that are then organized as "affect programs," or what Solms and Turnbull refer to as "basic emotional command systems" (2002, p. 113). These are interconnected sets of responses that include "facial expressions, vocalizations, respiratory patterns, autonomic responses (heart rate, skin temperature, viscera), and skeletal responses" (Demos, 1998, p. 75). These are the elements that, in their totality, provide all the components of what we refer to as "an experience." These affect programs include important information about the conditions that become inherently rewarding or punishing. It is a sophisticated structure that allows for each discrete affect to become activated by a particular pattern of stimulation, depending upon the nature of the events being experienced (Demos, 1998).

Tompkins identified eight basic affects that are involved in most human interactions that he believes become activated in various situations. These are: enjoyment, interest, distress, anger, fear, startle, disgust, and shame. In the case of domestic violence, it is more likely that affects with negative valence (e.g., distress, anger, fear, etc.) will predominate.

Solms and Turnbull (2002) anchor their view in findings from neuroscience research to describe how and the extent to which our existence is guided by the presence of affects. They suggest that it is trouble with affects that our patient reports when seeking treatment (e.g., I feel anxious, depressed, and angry), and that there is a good reason for that. Affect is what makes the person comfortable or uncomfortable, what the person feels about a situation, and that the person coming for treatment is trying to address when dealing negative affects. Ultimately, people tend to organize transactions with the world in search of feeling good and that feeling serves an important motivating force for what we do and how we organize our lives (Sullivan, 1953). Feeling good means not feeling the tension associated with negative emotions. In the end, we always seek to increase the conditions under which an experience of enjoyment and sense of safety and well-being become the prominent valence of our experience. This basic thrust in the individual's existence has been an important component in theories of personality formation that features prominently in the seminal work of Freud, Sullivan, Maslow, Klein, Winnicott, Rogers, Skinners, Bowlby, Ellis, and many of the authors whose contributions have been included in this book.

Affect provides the individual with crucial information about the state of affairs affecting him which requires a response (an action). Solms and Turnbull (2002) identified four clusters of affects that explain most activities the individual is faced with and that are organized into specific categories or "basic-emotion command systems": seeking, rage, fear, and panic. According to these authors, these systems operate neurologically with clear interconnected representations in the brain. These are "phylogenetically ancient structures that lie in deep regions of the brain, in the middle and upper zones of the brainstem . . . (that) include the hypothalamus, ventral tegmental area, parabrachial nuclei, periaqueductal gray, raphe nuclei, nucleus locus coeruleus complex, and classical reticular formation" (pp. 107–108). These structures have been found to be implicated in the processing of affects, or the monitoring and regulation of visceral (emotional) states or conditions that require and demand from the individual a response in order to ensure her biological, and psychological, survival. In the case of domestic violence, the activation of these structures, triggered by the emergence of powerful negative affects (e.g., feeling overwhelmed, profound fearful, feeling stunned and confused, anxious, angry, etc.), is what makes it possible for those individuals who finally decide to seek a solution to their dilemma to be able to do so. For instance, there is some evidence suggesting that victims of domestic violence who are able to experience anger are more likely to leave the abusive relationship (WHO, 2005).

In Tomkins's view, these emotions tend to function as an "amplifier" that highlights the importance of what is occurring at a particular moment and time to alert and propel the individual for action. But how is that done? It happens (1) when specific sets of affects that trigger the same/or similar emotional valence are sufficiently magnified; and (2) when the situation at hand rises to an urgent and critical level. At this point, the affects generated by the situation are organized into classes or scripts that become automatically activated when similar condition in the environment occur (Demos, 1998). So, one may develop pleasant scripts, or scripts that are more frightening and fearful, or may develop other affect programs that organize experience where affects related to happiness and sense of safety and fulfillment predominate. Under the best of circumstances, one's life is equipped with a combination of scripts with various affective valences to ensure that we can distinguish experiences that will create happiness from those that are likely to create problems for us.

In essence, scripts are "sets of ordering rules for the interpretation, evaluation, prediction, production, or control of scenes," or experiences in the world (Demos, 1998, p. 82). Inherent in the script is the specific way of responding to the demands of the scene (e.g., run away, get ready to fight back, or to remain quiet) that the individual has already incorporated into her repertoire and that tends to guide that individual's behavior when relating in her surroundings. In a final analysis, the purpose of these scripts (or schemas) is to allow and guide the organism to respond to the environmental demands in a parsimonious, efficient, and historically contextual manner, the ways that are consistent with one's past history.

According to Tomkins, the number and types of scenes included in the specific script are initially incomplete and inaccurate and the criteria for inclusion quite selective. However, with repeated experiences with similar qualities (e.g., verbal and physical abuse, bullying, sexual abuse, and harassment) the number of connected scenes tends to include any scene (experience) in which the individual feels uncomfortable. By so doing, it results in an expansion of the range of experiences that are included (Demos, 1998) and become part of the individual's behavioral and attitudinal repertoire, even when not totally justified. For instance, once traumatized by abuse, the individual may not only feel threatened by the components of the event related to the abuse (e.g., the actual physical/verbal abuse: being punched, slapped, sexually assaulted, and stabbed); by the memory of the physiological state of the perpetrator (if she was breathing heavily and sweating or trembling); by remembering the content of the communication surrounding the event and/or other components of the abusive experience, such as the music that may have been playing at the time of the event. He may be threatened by and may remember also the quality of the perpetrator's voice preceding the abuse (if she spoke in a loud or low and raspy voice), and the perfume and color of the clothing the perpetrator was wearing. The victim may remember as well the items of clothing he was wearing, the time and place of the occurrence, or even the fact that he may have been thinking something unpleasant about the perpetrator preceding the event (e.g., wishing her dead).

The victim's involvement in all these activities can be seen as a desperate attempt to search for any clue that can be used and helpful to control future scenes. In the process, it is likely that this will include a larger number of individuals and scenes (e.g., members of the helping profession responding to domestic violence incidents) that will be seen initially and responded to indiscriminately with suspiciousness, although ultimately not clearly justified by the condition on the ground. This could be particularly the case when the violent situation was profoundly traumatic.

According to Demos, it is in this context that the nature of scripts once formed begins to determine the nature and quality of the scenes (experience) and that "most scripts become more self-validating than self-fulfilling" (1998, p. 83). This is the inherent process involved in the development of prejudice, discrimination, and bigotry (Lichtenberg, van Beusekom, & Gibbons, 1997) that become part of the person's overall demeanor. Once reaching this level of transformation, it can become problematic for the individual if these scripts are applied indiscriminately to other interpersonal relations/interactions that happen to have some of these same characteristics. An example of that is of a victim of domestic violence responding negatively to men with beards or wearing glasses because they remind her of the abuser who used to wear glasses and had a beard. In the end, the individual may paradoxically contaminate and destroy the potential for future and healthier encounters with others in an attempt to protect herself from future abuses.

CONCLUSION

Domestic violence continues to be a major issue throughout the world. We are still confronted with the fact that over 1,259,390 domestic violence incidents still take place per year (Truman, Langton, & Planty, 2013). We are also still confronted with the fact that, on average, more than three women are murdered by their husbands or boyfriends every day (Catalano, 2012); that one woman is beaten by her husband or intimate partner every 9 seconds in the United States and 24 every minute; and that 1 in 4 or 1 in 3 women is likely to experience domestic violence in her life time, with an estimate of 1.3 million women being the victims of physical assault by an intimate partner every year (Black et al., 2011; Tjaden & Thornnes, 2000). We are also still confronted with the serious problem of underreported incidents of domestic violence among members of the LGBT communities for fear of incurring additional trauma/rejection from a society that is unprepared to address issues of domestic violence from individuals with multiple gender identities (Institute of Medicine, 2011; Ristock, 2005). At the international level, we see how many regions of the world are still actively engaged in violent treatment of intimate partners, with prevalence ranging from 30–40% (in some Latin American countries, North Africa/Middle East, south Asian regions, and East/West Sub-Sahara Africa) to as high as 65.64% in some African countries (Central/South Sahara Africa) (World Health Organization, 2013).

Thus, we are left with the realization that domestic violence has no boundaries and affects all genders, religions, cultural and racial groups, and different socioeconomic and sociopolitical classes. We are also left with the poignant question as to why we have not been able to be more effective in addressing the issue of domestic violence in our midst, considering the serious consequences for its victims and the society at large (Black et al., 2011; CDC, 2003, 2014). Finally, we are left with an urgent need to reexamine the obstacles and leading assumptions and explanatory models that have guided our approach to the understanding of domestic violence, as well as its assessment and interventions.

It is clear that in spite of our advances, we are still limited in the development of comprehensive, timely, and effective prevention and intervention strategies. As suggested by Meichenbaum (2007), an effective approach should actively incorporate all the components of our society that are of crucial importance in the lives of the individuals mired in the domestic violence dilemma. Following Meichenbaum's recommendations, this book is guided by the recognition that an effective prevention and intervention program for domestic violence can only be adequately developed in the context of a comprehensive model of domestic violence that includes (1) the extent to which external factors related to sociohistorical, sociopolitical, sociocultural, socioeconomic, and legal and law enforcement systems are involved; (2) examination of factors related to the individual's psychology that are forged in the context of early experience; and (3) biological and evolutionary factors related to mechanism of survival, as described by Solms and Turnbull (2002). This confluence of factors is aptly captured in chapter 4 by Warburton and Anderson and chapter 3 by Herron and Javier. The emphasis on such a view is meant to encourage practitioners to take all of these components into consideration when assessing the presence and extent of domestic violence; it is also meant to ensure that the prevention and intervention approaches resulting from this examination include elements that are appropriate and organic for the particular situation and individuals involved. In keeping with Meichenbaum's recommendations, the reader is encouraged to look into the work on an integrative family therapy approach developed by Patricia Pitta (2014), although not yet systematically applied to cases of domestic violence.

Our aim is to interest the reader in becoming more actively involved in thinking about the various issues of domestic violence beyond what it is covered in the book. For that purpose, we pose a series of questions at the end of each chapter to encourage discussions on the issues addressed in the specific chapters or that readers could explore in their own writings or class assignments. The more we are able to engage the larger community in understanding what group of individuals are more likely to be victims, survivors, and/or perpetrators, and why domestic violence occurs, the more likely finding more effective treatment intervention will become a priority. In the end, the ultimate goal is to reduce the rate and extent of domestic violence and its devastating consequences. It is a win-win situation for potential future victims, perpetrators, and the society at large.

DISCUSSION QUESTIONS

1. Provide examples of the different types of domestic violence suggested by Johnson and colleagues.
2. Discuss some of the challenges in defining domestic violence in general.
3. Looking at the clinical examples presented in the text, discuss the specific complications in the selected clinical case in terms of the inherent mechanism involved in domestic violence incidents described in this chapter.
4. Discuss similarities and differences in how domestic violence affects the LGBT communities, particularly members of the transgender community.

5. Discuss the differences and similarities in how and the extent to which early trauma may be implicated in domestic violence experiences among the heterosexual and gender nonconformist communities.
6. Explore how domestic violence is addressed in the media and films and the impact on the societal/legal responses to specific incidents of domestic violence.
7. Explore how technology could complicate the picture of domestic violence incidents and their consequences both for the victims and perpetrators with regard to its assessment and response.

REFERENCES

Ard, K. L., & Makadon, H. J. (2011). Addressing intimate partner violence in lesbian, gay, bisexual, and transgender patients. *Journal of General Internal Medicine., 26*(8), 930–933. Published online 2011 Mar 30. doi: 10.1007/s11606-011-1697-6.

Babcock, J. C. (2003). Toward a typology of abusive women: Differences between partner-only and generally violent women in the use of violence. *Psychology of Women Quarterly, 27*(2), 153.

Babcock, J. C., Canady, B. E., Graham, K., & Schart, L. (2007). The evolution of battering Interventions: From the dark ages into the scientific ages. In J. Hamel & T. L. Nicholls (Eds.), *Family Interventions in Domestic Violence: A Handbook of Gender-Inclusive Theory and Treatment* (pp. 215–244). New York, NY: Springer Publishing Company.

Bailey, B. A. (2010). Partner violence during pregnancy: prevalence, effects, screening, and Management. *International Journal of Women's Health, 2*: 183–197. Published online 2010 Aug 9. PMCID: PMC2971723.

Black, M. C., Basile, K. C., Breiding, M. J., Smith, S. G., Walters, M. L., Merrick, M. T., & Spivak, H. R. (2011). *The National Intimate Partner and Sexual Violence Survey (NISVS): 2010 summary report.* Atlanta, GA: National Center for Injury Prevention and Control, Centers for Disease Control and Prevention. Retrieved from http://www.cdc.gov/violenceprevention/pdf/nisvs_executive_summary-a.pdf.

Campbell, J. C. (2002). Health consequences of intimate partner violence. *The Lancet, 359*(9314), 1331–1336.

Catalano, S. M. (2012). *Intimate partner violence, 1993–2010.* Retrieved from http:/www.bjs.gov/index.cfm?ty=pbdetail&iid=4536.

Centers for Disease Control. (2003). *Costs of intimate partner violence against women in the United States.* Retrieved from http://www.cdc.gov/violenceprevention/pdf/ipvbook-a.pdf.

Centers for Disease Control and Prevention. (2009). *Injury-intimate partner violence consequences.* Retrieved from http://www.cdc.gov/violenceprevention/intimatepartnerviolence/consequences.html.

Centers for Disease Control and Prevention. (2014). *Intimate partner violence: Consequences.* Retrieved from http://www.cdc.gov/violenceprevention/intimatepartnerviolence/consequences.html.

Courtois, C. A. & Ford, J. (Eds.). (2009). *Treating complex traumatic stress disorders: An evidence-based guide.* New York: The Guilford Press.

Crowe, A. H., Sydney, L., DeMichele, M., Keilitz, S., Neal, C., Frohman, S., & Thomas, M. (2009). *Community corrections response to domestic violence: Guidelines for practice.* Retrieved from http://www.appa-et.org/eweb/docs/appa/pubs/ccrdv.pdf.

Demos, E. V. (1998). Differentiating the repetition compulsion from trauma through the lens of Tomkins's script theory: A response to Russell. In J. G. Teicholz & D. Kriegman (Eds.), *Trauma, repetition & affect regulation: The work of Paul Russell* (pp. 67–104). New York: The Other Press.

Finnbogadóttir, H., & Dykes, A. K. (2016). Increasing prevalence and incidence of domestic violence during the pregnancy and one and a half year postpartum, as well as risk factors: A longitudinal cohort study in Southern Sweden. *BMC Pregnancy and Childbirth—BMC series*—open, inclusive and trusted. 16:327 https://doi.org/10.1186/s12884-016-1122-6.

Flake, D., & Forste, R. (2006). Fighting families: Family characteristics associated with domestic violence in Five Latin American Countries. *Journal of Family Violence, 21*(1), 16–39.

Garbarino, J. (2015). *Listening to killers: Lessons learned from my twenty years as a psychological expert in murder cases*. Los Angeles: University California Press.

Gielen, A. C., O'Campo, P. J., Faden, R. R., Kass, N. E., & Xue, X. (1994). Interpersonal conflict and physical violence during the childbearing year. *Social Science and Medicine, 39*, 181–187.

Harrykissoon, S. D., Rickert, V. I., & Wiemann, C. M. (2002). Prevalence and patterns of intimate partner violence among adolescent mothers during postpartum period. *Archives of Pediatrics & Adolescent Medicine, 156*, 325–330.

Heavey, S. (2013). *Data show domestic violence, rape an issue for gays*. Retrieved from http://www.reuters.com/article/2013/01/25/us-usa-gays-violence-id.

Institute of Medicine (2011). *The Health of Lesbian, Gay, Bisexual, and Transgender People: Building a Foundation for Better Understanding*. Washington, DC: The National Academies Press. doi: 10.17226/13128.

Javier, R. A., Herron, W. G., & Bergman, A. (Eds.) (1996). *Domestic violence: Assessment and treatment*. Northvale, NJ: Jason Aronson, Inc.

Johnson, M. (2008). *A typology of domestic violence: Intimate terrorism, violent resistance and situational couple violence*. Lebanon, NH: Northeastern University Press.

Johnson, M., & Ferraro, K. (2000). Research on domestic violence in the 1990s: Making distinctions. *Journal of Marriage and the Family, 62*, 948–963.

Johnson, M., & Leone, J. (2005). The differential effects of intimate terrorism and situational couple violence. *Journal of Family Issues, 26*, 322–349.

Kaur, R., & Garg, S. (2008). Addressing violence against women: An unfinished agenda. *Indian Journal of Community Medicine 33*, 73–76. doi: 10.4103/0970-0218.40871.

Kelly, J. & Johnson, J. (2008). Differentiation among types of intimate partner violence: Research update and implications for intervention. *Family Court Review, 46*, 476–499.

Kilgannon, C. (April 6, 2006). Hedda Nussbaum promotes her memoir of life with an abuser. Retrieved from http://www.nytimes.com/2006/04/06/nyregion/06hedda.html?ref=heddanussbaum&_r=0-

Kraft, K., Menatti, A., & Gidycz, C. A. (2014). Examining the relationship between interpersonal victimization and emotion dysregulation. Paper presented at the International Family Violence and Child Victimization Research Conference, Portsmouth, New Hampshire, July 13–15, 2014.

Lichtenberg, P., van Beusekom, J., & Gibbons, D. (1997). *Encountering bigotry: Befriending projecting persons in everyday life*. Northvale, NJ: Jason Aronson, Inc.

McQuiston, J. T. (2000, April 8). Hedda Nussbaum cancels speech after protest at college. Retrieved from http://www.nytimes.com/2000/04/08/nyregion/hedda-nussbaum-cancels-speech-after-prot-

Meichenbaum, D. (2007). *Family violence: Treatment of perpetrators and victims*. Retrieved from www.melissainstititute.org.

Murray, C. E., Lundgreen, K., Olson, L., & Hunnicutt, G. (2016). Practice update: What professional who are not brain injury specialists need to know about intimate partner violence-related traumatic brain injury. *Trauma Violence, & Abuse, 17*(3), 298–305.

National Coalition Against Domestic Violence (2017). Retrieved from http://ncadv.org/learn-more/statistics.

Neal, A., Dixon, C., Edwards, K. M., & Gidycz, C. A. (2014). College women's motives for perpetrating intimate partner violence. Paper presented at the International Family Violence and Child Victimization Research Conference, Portsmouth, New Hampshire, July 13–15, 2014.

Nussbaum, H. (2005). Surviving intimate terrorism. PublishAmerica.

Pitta, P. (2014). *Solving modern family dilemmas: An assimilative therapy model*. New York: Taylor & Francis.

Reich, C. M., Blackwell, N., Simmons, C., & Beck, J. G. (2015). Social problem solving strategies and posttraumatic disorder in the aftermath of intimate partner violence. *Journal of Anxiety Disorders, 32*, 31–37.

Richardson, L., Freeh, B. C., & Acierno, A. (2010). Prevalence estimates of combat-related PTSD: A critical review. *Australian and New Zealand Journal of Psychiatry, 44* (1), 4–19.

Ristock, J. (2005). Relationship violence in lesbian/gay/bisexual/transgender/queer [LGBTQ] communities: Moving beyond a gender-based framework. *Violence Against Women Online Resources*. Retrieved from http://citeseerx.ist.psu.edu/viewdoc/download?doi=10.1.1.208.7282&rep=rep1&type=pdf.

Russell, P. L. (1998). The role of paradox in repetition compulsion. In J. G. Teicholz & D. Kriegman (Eds.), *Trauma, repetition compulsion, and affect regulation: The work of Paul Russell* (pp. 1–22). New York: The Other Press.

Smith, L. S., & Stover, C. S. (2016). The moderating role of attachment on the relationship between history of trauma and intimate violence victimization. *Violence Against Women, 22*(6), 745–764.

Solms, M., & Turnbull, O. (2002). *The brain and the inner world: An introduction to the neuroscience of subjective experience*. New York: Karnac Books.

Stith, S. M., McCollum, E. E., Amanor-Boadu, Y., & Smith, D. (2012). Systemic perspectives on Intimate Partner Violence treatment. *Journal of Marital and Family Therapy, 38*(1), 220–240.

Sullivan, H. S. (1953). *The interpersonal theory of psychiatry*. New York: Norton.

Swan, S. C., Gambone, L. J., Caldwell, J. E., Sullivan, T. P., & Snow, D. L. (2008). A review of research on women's use of violence with male intimate partners. *Violence and Victims, 23*, 301–314.

Tjaden, J. (2003). Symposium on integrating responses to domestic violence: Extent and nature of intimate partner violence as measured by the National Violence Against Women Survey, *47 Loy, L. Rev. 41, 54*.

Tjaden, P., & Thoennes, N. (2000). *US Department of Justice: Full report of the prevalence, incidence and consequences of violence against women*. Retrieved from. http://www.ncjrs.gov.

Tomkins, S. (1962). *Affect, imagery, consciousness (vol. 1): The positive affects*. New York: Springer.

Tomkins, S. (1978). Script theory: Differential magnification of affects. In H. E. Howe Jr. & R. A. Dunstbier (Eds.), *Nebraska Symposium on Motivation* (pp. 201–236). Lincoln: University of Nebraska Press.

Truman, J., Langton, L., & Planty, M. (2013, October). *Criminal victimization, 2012*. Retrieved from http://www.bjs.gov/content/pub/pdf/cv12.pdf.

United Nations General Assembly Report (2006). *Intensification of efforts to eliminate all forms of violence against women. Agenda Item 61/143*. Retrieved from hppt://www.daccess-dds-ny.un.org/doc/UNDOC/GEN/N06/503/01/PDF/NO650301.pdf?Open Element.

Veterans and PTSD Statistics (2016). Retrieved from www.veteransandptsd.com/PTSD-statistics.html

Vivian, D., & Langhincrichsen-Rohling, J. (2004). Are bi-directionality violent couples mutually victimized? A gender-sensitive comparison. *Violence and Victims, 9*, 107–123.

Walters, M., L. Chen, J., & Breiding, M. J. (2013). *The National Intimate Partner and Sexual Violence Survey*. Retrieved from http://www.cdc.gov/violenceprevention/pdf/nisvs_sofings.pdf.

Wangmann, J. (2011). Different types of intimate partner violence. An exploration of the literature. *Australian Domestic & Family Violence Clearinghouse, Issues Paper 22*, 1–25. Retrieved from hppt://www.ncbi.nlm.nih.gov/pubmed/16180370.

Wheeler, J., Anfinson, K., Valvert, D., & Lungo, S. (2014). Is violence associated with increased risk behavior among MSM? Evidence from a population-based survey conducted across nine cities in Central America. *Journal of GlobalHealth Action. 7:* 10.3402/gha.v7.24814. Published online 2014 Oct 23. doi: 10.3402/gha.v7.24814.

World Health Organization. (2005). *Summary report: Multi-country study on women's health and domestic violence against women. Initial results on prevalence, health outcomes and women's responses.* Geneva, Switzerland: World Health Organization.

World Health Organization (2013). *Global and regional estimates of violence against women: Prevalence and health effects of intimate partner violence and non-partner sexual violence.* Retrieved from www.who.int/reproductive_health.

I

Conceptual Framework

We begin in chapter 2 by contextualizing domestic violence (DV) as a worldwide phenomenon and how it is influenced and guided by the cultural, social, and economic contexts where it takes place. The chapter presents relevant statistics from around the world on DV to demonstrate the pervasive nature of the phenomenon. Our goal is to provide the reader with sufficient information about its prevalence to encourage a renewed appreciation and understanding of DV as not just a function of a poor socioeconomic status, but as an intersectional phenomenon that cuts across socioeconomic class, religion, educational level, gender and sexual orientations, and political affiliations. This book also discusses what we know about risk and causal factors, including characteristics of the victims and perpetrators (particularly personality characteristics). The reader will find the chapters in this section to be particularly illuminating on those factors. These chapters are rich with important conceptual information and ample clinical examples meant to bring the point home more poignantly.

A crucial issue tackled by all of these authors is the definition of what should be considered DV and how it can be distinguished from any other act of aggression. What emerges from these discussions is that DV is an aggressive behavior where the perpetrator intentionally harms the victim to exercise power, and where the victim is motivated to avoid such a behavior (chapters 2–6). What follows is a sophisticated and critical review of various theoretical formulations of DV that have attempted to explain the phenomenon, some with strong empirical support. The prominent framework that comes across in these chapters, and particularly in chapter 4, is the recognition that there are many dimensions involved in the actual act of DV that create the necessary condition for the phenomenon to occur. These include biological-based dimensions (or biological modifiers), individual dimensions related to personality characteristics, environmental modifiers, and social factors that can function as triggers of DV expression under certain conditions. It is in this context that scripts, or acquisition of schemas (or knowledge structures/organizing schema) that then serve as cognitive structures, are developed. Once established, they are used to process, organize, understand, and respond to the person's reality. The role of attribution bias and belief structures, as well as specific personality characteristics of those involved (aggressive personality style and traits, etc.), become crucial to understand violent behavior. These dimensions are also amply described in chapter 5 in terms of what psychoanalytic conceptualizations can provide regarding the individual's psychology.

The reader is directed to the work of Tomkins (1992; Demos, 1998) for further discussion as to how scripts are formed and how, once established, they become anchored in the person's behavioral repertoire. According to Tomkins's script theory, scripts emerge in the context of the evolutionary process to provide the individual with the necessary information to help him/her negotiate the challenges normally found in the environment (1962). These scripts are compressed sets of ordering rules for the interpretation, evaluation, prediction, production, and management of scenes (experiences), and include strategies to be used in the future (Demos, 1998; Tomkins, 1992). This issue is discussed in the introduction (chapter 1) and further elaborated in the last chapter of the book (chapter 13).

Warburton and Anderson's conceptualization about scripts also emphasizes similar developmental or evolutionary patterns. According to these authors, aggressive behaviors are acquired and operationalized through associative conditioning, instrumental conditioning, and social learning that can become generalized to a range of other situations that trigger similar associations. The associative activation depends upon unique personality characteristics and mental resources of the perpetrator. The authors also come from the perspective that it is possible for an individual with the necessary psychological and mental resources to use strategies (ability to assess and examine the consequences of the aggressive behavior or reappraisal of consequences) to find alternative courses of action that do not involve the use of DV. According to these authors, such an acquisition, which can be learned through therapeutic intervention, makes it possible to alter the nature of the connections within a neural network and thus making it less likely for the individual to respond violently to a situation that in the past may have provoked such a reaction. In this context, new and more appropriate scripts and cognitions can then be developed, thus making the old structures obsolete and less automatically triggered. These are the fundamental factors of the

General Aggression Model put forward by Anderson and Bushman (2002) that Warburton and Anderson used to explain the many factors involved in the DV phenomenon.

We find these types of analyses quite helpful from the perspective of providing a better understanding of the complexity of factors contributing to DV. Our greatest concern is the need to find more practical and immediate guidance to assist those in the front line who try to prevent DV, and where there is "limited time and methods to use diagnostic signs" for risk assessment. You will also find in the latter part of chapter 4 very concrete recommendations geared specifically at deescalating and containing the situation, while also providing an understanding of the larger picture of the factors involved.

Chapter 6 offers an important and sobering analysis of how pervasive aggression and violent outbursts are in our midst, cutting across gender and class. These authors raised important issues related to the implications of our failure to recognize violence in women, although there are ample examples through history and cultures affirming otherwise. The problem, as they see it, is that such neglect has resulted in inadequate attempts to develop the necessary prevention and intervention programs that are unique to the psychology of women. We expect the reader to come out of this chapter with a new understanding of the various ways women are involved and actively contribute to violence and DV, for whom the motivational explanation for engaging in violence acts tends to differ from men.

At the end of each of these chapters the reader will find a list of questions and activities meant to encourage further exploration of the issues addressed in the specific chapters.

Chapter Two

Domestic Violence in all Its Contexts

An Issue for all Cultures, Races, Genders, and Classes

Rafael Art. Javier, William G. Herron, Gerald A. Pantoja, and Jennifer De Mucci

In the previous chapter, we attempted to provide a general framework of this book and in that context provided some statistics in order to highlight the urgent and pervasive nature of domestic violence. In this chapter, we provide a more systematic review of these statistical findings to highlight further the various and insidious forms of domestic violence affecting all phases of our society and individuals across many nations, cultures, religions, and sexual orientations. This fact was clearly documented in most recent reports by the World Health Organization (2005, 2013), which provided an account of findings from a broad range of violence research surveys conducted in various regions of the world. Recognizing the importance of socioeconomic and cultural factors in the prevalence of violence, these studies juxtapose low-, middle-, and high-income regions in order to evaluate noteworthy trends. The following are areas and countries included in these reviews:

- *Latin American and Caribbean countries* (e.g., Bolivia, Brazil, Chile, Colombia, Costa Rica, Dominican Republic, Ecuador, El Salvador, Haití, Honduras, Jamaica, México, Nicaragua, Paraguay, and Perú)
- *Africa* (e.g., Cameroon, Democratic Republic of Congo, Ethiopia, Kenya, Liberia, Mozambique, Namibia, Rwanda, South Africa, Tanzania, Uganda, Zambia, and Zimbabwe)
- *Eastern Mediterranean* (e.g., Egypt, Iran, Iraq, Jordan, and Palestine)
- *Europe* (e.g., Albania, Azerbaijan, Georgia, Lithuania, Moldova, Romania, Russian Federation, Serbia, Turkey, and Ukraine)

- *Southeast Asia* (e.g., Bangladesh, East Timor, India, Myanmar, Sri Lanka, and Thailand)
- *Western Pacific* (e.g., Cambodia, China, Philippines, Samoa, and Viet Nam)
- *High-income countries* (e.g., Australia, Canada, Croatia, Czech Republic, Denmark, Finland, France, Germany, Hong Kong, Ireland, Israel, Japan, Netherlands, Norway, Poland, South Korea, Spain, Sweden, Switzerland, the United Kingdom of Great Britain and Northern Ireland, and the United States)

Taken together, these findings provide a comprehensive picture of the prevalence of domestic violence around the world, as well as the physical and psychological damage victims endure. We should keep in mind that the findings provided by these reports *only* reflect statistics that have been self-reported and that the reality of domestic violence may be worse in some of these regions. This is particularly the case because of the unwillingness by many to report incidents of domestic violence out of fear and intimidation (WHO, 2005, 2013), an issue predominantly for members of the gender nonconformists or individuals with multiple gender identities (Institute of Medicine, 2011). The statistics reported by these findings focus primarily on violence against women, leaving unanswered the rate of violence against men and the LGBT communities (Ard & Makadon, 2011). Nevertheless, although there are differences in the rate, sources, and consequences of domestic violence between the LBGT communities and violence against women in general, there are also a great deal of similarities (Ard & Makadon, 2011; Institute of Medicine, 2011). "The findings send a powerful message that violence against women is not a small problem that occurs in some pockets of society, but rather is a global public health problem with epidemic proportions" (WHO, 2013, p. 3). The fact that there is a high percentage of intimate partner homicide in various regions of the world shows high risk of many intimate partners for severe injury, with serious repercussion to the physical and mental health outcomes, including disability and death from homicide or suicide (Ard & Makadon, 2011; Institute of Medicine, 2011; White Hughto, Pachankis, Willie, & Reisner, 2017; WHO, 2013). This makes it urgent for the professional community to focus concentrated efforts to find more effective responses to the issue of domestic violence in all its forms.

A LOOK AT THE LANDSCAPE OF DOMESTIC VIOLENCE

Taking a closer look at the data provides the reader with more specific information of the pervasiveness and severity of the problem throughout the world, leaving us with the poignant and disturbing realization that this problem has remained practically unchallenged even into the twenty-first century. We see in table 2.1 that the lifetime prevalence estimates are quite disturbing even in the high-income countries, with the highest rates found in Southeast Asia, East Mediterranean, and Africa (at 37.7%, 37.0%, and 36.6%, respectively). The lowest rate, but still alarming, is found in high-income countries (23.2%), the Western Pacific (24.2%), and Europe (25.8%), suggesting that socioeconomic status alone does not function as a buffer against becoming a victim and/or perpetrator of domestic violence.

When examining the data by age groups, we find that the lowest rates of violence prevalence in these regions are found in the 55–59 and 60–64 age groups (15.1% and 19.6%, respectively). By contrast, the highest rates (36.6%–37.8%) are found in the 35–44 age groups, followed by the 25–29 (32.3%), 20–24 (31.6%), 30–34 (31.1%), and 15–19 (29.4%) age groups, respectively. So the trajectory is quite alarming if we consider that the violence exposure is already high in the 15–19 age group and even earlier by other reports (Tjaden & Thoennes, 2000a/2000b), and if we consider the findings that those who have been victims of abuse are more likely to be victims of physical assaults and rape as adults (National Coalition Against Domestic Violence, 2017; National Institute of Justice, 2011). Moreover, there are some findings that suggest a possible linkage between early violence exposure and future involvement in domestic violence behavior. According to these statistics, adolescents and men exposed to child abuse and sexual abuse and/or domestic violence earlier in life are found to be four times more likely than other men to engage in domestic violence as adults and three-fifths times more likely to engage in juvenile violent behaviors (Gilbert, El-Bassel, Wu, & Chang, 2007; National Institute of Justice, 2011; Tjaden & Thoennes, 2000a/2000b; Whitfield, Anda, Dube, & Felitti, 2003).

Table 2.1. Lifetime prevalence of physical and/or sexual intimate partner violence among ever-partnered women (95% CI, %)

Low- and middle-income regions	Prevalence, %
Southeast Asia	37.7
Eastern Mediterranean	37.0
Africa	36.6
Latin American and Caribbean	29.8
Europe	25.4
Western Pacific	24.6
High Income	23.2

A more specific analysis is found in the 2005 WHO Report of the prevalence of domestic violence broken down by specific countries (rather than regions), and looking at factors related to gender, age, and marital status that have been found to be involved in prevalence of domestic violence in a number of representative countries. This report includes information from countries such as Peru, Ethiopia, the United Republic of Tanzania, Bangladesh, Samoa, Thailand, Brazil, Namibia, Serbia and Montenegro, and Japan. What becomes clear from the findings in this report is the following:

1. Although the nature of the prevalence of domestic violence differs from country to country, we find incidents of domestic violence even in countries where the prevalence of the phenomenon is considered to be very low. This is the case in Japan, which reported the lowest prevalence level of sexual violence (6%) and physical violence (13%) reported. The highest prevalence of physical abuse reported is found in provincial Peru (61%), followed by provincial Ethiopia and Peru city (both 49%), and United Republic of Tanzania province (47%), with the other countries falling in the middle range. With regard to the prevalence of sexual violence, it was found to be most prevalent in provincial Ethiopia (59%), Bangladesh (50%), and Peru (47%). These findings suggest that the problem is more severe in the provinces and that physical and sexual violence are of concern in many of these regions.
2. Regarding the nature of violence perpetrated against women, the most common act was being slapped (ranging from 9% in Japan to 52% in provincial Peru). The next most common act was being struck with a fist (ranging from 4% in Japan city to 49% in provincial Peru, with most countries falling between 13–26%). Such violence was considered severe physical abuse because of the amount of physical damage that can be caused is along the same range as being kicked, dragged, and being threatened with a weapon.
3. Most of the more severe cases of physical violence are reported to have occurred over a year ago in most countries. Exceptions to that are the domestic violence incidents occurring in urban Bangladesh, Ethiopia, Namibia, and Samoa, where more recent occurrences (within the past 12 months of the time of the report) are reported.
4. Women ages 15–19 are most vulnerable to physical and sexual violence in all settings, with the exception of Japan and Ethiopia, as compared to women 45–49 years old.
5. Separated or divorced women and women living together with their partners are more likely to be victims of domestic violence than married women and women with higher education.

6. The most frequently reported emotional abuse incidents were insults, belittling, and intimidation.
7. Physical or sexual violence was found to be accompanied by more controlling behavior by the intimate partner.
8. Women's attitudes toward partner violence tended to vary, with a significant number in urban settings of Brazil, Japan, Namibia, and Serbia and Montenegro taking the position that there was no justifiable reason for domestic violence. This same position was also taken by a smaller number in the provincial settings of Bangladesh, Ethiopia, Peru, and Samoa. This notwithstanding, domestic violence was prevalent in many of these countries.
9. There were two reasons most widely accepted in almost all settings to justify violence: One was infidelity on part of the woman, and two, disobeying a husband.
10. Acceptance of wife beating was higher among women who have already been victims of abuse as compared to those who have not. It was less common among women with higher education, particularly beyond secondary school.
11. Most of the abuse perpetrated by non-partners included fathers and other family members. In some settings (Bangladesh, Namibia, Samoa, and the United Republic of Tanzania), teachers are also included in that list.
12. A large proportion of women reported being abused during pregnancy in 11 of the 15 settings studied. The lowest was in Japan (1%) and the highest (28%) in provincial Peru; between a quarter and half of these women reported that the abuse consisted of being kicked and punched in the abdomen. Ninety percent reported being abused by the biological father of the child the woman was carrying; between 13% (Ethiopia) and about 50% (urban Brazil and Serbia and Montenegro) reported that they were beaten for the first time during pregnancy.
13. Abused women in all settings were more likely to report poor health, mostly associated with lifetime experience of violence, than women who have never been abused. More reports of miscarriage were also found among abused women when compared with non-abused women.
14. Women who experienced more severe abuse were more likely to seek help from outside authorities and institutions than women who only experienced mild, albeit chronic, intimate partner violence. The more the severity of the physical abuse the more likely that the victim opted to leave the relationship.
15. Although most physical abuse is initiated by males, some women who reported ever being physically abused were the ones who initiated violence against their partner at some point (15% in Thailand).

Statistics from the 2010 CDC (Black et al., 2011; CDC, 2013) focusing more specifically on the United States corroborated similar findings: It was reported that about 1 in 3 women (35.6%) have experienced violence in their lifetime; that 1 in 5 women reported being raped at some point in their lives; and that about half of these women reported being raped by an intimate partner and 40.8% by an acquaintance. Also 79% of female rape victims reported experiencing their first rape before the age 25, with 40% experiencing it before the age of 18 and 21.6% before age 12 (Tjaden & Thoennes, 2000a/2000b).

Regarding the rate of domestic violence in the LGBT communities, findings from a survey of 3,000 gay men found five-year rates of physical and sexual abuse of 22% and 5.1%, respectively. According to Ard and Makadon (2011), these five-year rates are similar to the lifetime rates of 20.4% for physical assault and 4.4% for sexual assault for opposite-sex cohabitating women in the NVAW survey reported by Tjaden and Thoennes (2000a/2000b). In another survey of 1,600 people by the Massachusetts Department of Public Health (Landers & Gilsanz, 2009), transgender respondents reported lifetime physical abuse rates by a partner of 34.6%, versus 14% for gay or lesbian individuals. As stated earlier, we need to consider these statistics with caution and very tentatively because of the additional difficulty in gathering such information from communities that include multiple gender identities. The most relevant obstacle is their fear of additional discrimination and judgment by a society that is still not ready to recognize their unique experiences (White Hughto et al., 2017).

SEXUAL VIOLENCE: A CLEAR EVIDENCE OF DOMINANCE

In reporting incidents of domestic violence, we often combine the various forms that violence takes. However, we believe that it is important to recognize that not all violence has the same effects on its victims. Sexual violence is one of the most utilized forms of violence of one partner against another; the fact that such a form of violence is so pervasive in our society reflects the social and individual views and attitudes toward victims (particularly toward women and members of the LGBT communities). This contributes to making the eradication of this phenomenon much more difficult. We see, for instance, high prevalence of sexual violence in the various regions of Sub-Sahara Africa, Andean regions in Latin America, in various regions of Australasia, and even Western Europe and in the United States. Much lower estimates (below 6%) are found in South and Southeast Asia, southern Latin America, North Africa, and the Middle East. The lowest estimate is found in South Asia (3.35%). With the exception of South Asia, North Africa, and the Middle East with relatively lower although still substantial rates, all the countries that reported high intimate partner violence estimates listed in table 2.2 also showed the highest non-partner sexual violence rates.

The fact that similar findings have been reported with regard to members of the gender nonconformist communities (Institute of Medicine, 2011; NCADV, 2017) provides the clearest evidence that intimate and non-partner violence are more likely to occur in societies with tolerance of such aggressive behavior and where the view of women and spouses (regardless of whether we are referring to a heterosexual or multiple gender identities) is as property. In the case of the traditional heterosexual relationships, males are afforded much more preferential treatment at all levels of society. It reflects a fundamental power and control condition, where an entrenched gender and social inequality dynamism provides the necessary fueling for the maintenance of that type of violence against another.

As stated earlier, in the case of individuals with multiple gender identities (LGBT), the situation becomes more complicated with the victims not feeling comfortable reporting the domestic violence incident for fear of additional discrimination and judgment; the other issue likely to impact on reporting is the concern of outing the perpetrator in the process whose non-traditional relationship(s) may still be widely unknown to families, friends, places of employment, and so on (Ard & Makadon, 2011; Institute of Medicine, 2011). According to Ard and Makadon, "outing may constitute both a tool of abuse and a barrier to seeking help. LGBT individuals often hide outward expression of their sexual orientation or gender identity for fear of stigma and discrimination; abusive partners may exploit this fear through the threat of forced outing." They went on to say that "victims' reluctance to out themselves may hinder them from turning to family, friends, or the police for support, further isolating them in abusive relationships" (p. 930). Added to that are the various direct and/or indirect forms of rejections and discrimination experienced from family of origins, bullying, hate speech, and hate crimes frequently encountered in their communities, that leave them with a strong feeling of alienation and being marginalized and the sense that there is no feasible solution. This realization becomes particularly poignant with not being able to find even shelter services available in many communities where they are desperately needed, particularly for transgender individuals (Ard & Makadon, 2011).

The mental set of seeing the spouse as a possession and viewing a woman as subservient to the whimsical will of a patriarchal society may be the main factor behind the perpetuation of the female genital circumcision procedure that more than 125 million women and girls alive today have endured, particularly in 29 African countries (such as Egypt, Guinea, Sierra Leon, Somalia, Northern Sudan, Mali, and Eritrea). A rate >85% of the women have received the procedure in these countries. A lower rate (<30%) is found in Senegal, Ethiopia, Central Africa Republic, Ghana, Cameroon, and Nigeria, as well as in the Middle East (e.g., Yemen, Kurdish communities, Oman, Iraq, Saudi Arabia, Palestine, and Israel), some Asian countries (e.g., India, Indonesia, Malaysia, Pakistan, and Sri Lanka), South America (e.g., Columbia, Ecuador, and Peru), and Western countries (e.g., Australia, Canada, Europe, the United Kingdom, and the United States, mostly practiced among the diaspora populations) (United Nations Population Fund or UNFPA, 2015; WHO, 2014).

While this procedure is normally performed by community elders specifically assigned for this task, it can be performed by traditional health professionals, particularly in Egypt, Sudan, Kenya, Nigeria, and Guinea. It includes complete or partial removal of the clitoral hood (Type I or clitoridectomy), complete or partial removal of the lit or labia minora (Type II or excision), and complete removal of all external genitalia and fusing of the wound (Type III or infibulation). In this procedure, a small hole is left for the passage of the urine and menstrual blood. The last form of genital mutilation (Type IV) consists of nicking the clitoris, piercing, scraping the tissue from around the vagina, scarring and/or burning the genitals, and even the removal of the hymen (UNFPA, 2015; WHO, 2014, 2015). The first two procedures are the most common and are performed as early as a couple of days after birth, during childhood, and even at the time of the marriage and first pregnancy. In the United States and Western Europe, clitoridectomy was performed until 1950s as a medical procedure to treat epilepsy, hysteria, and other mental disorders (UNFPA, 2015).

Although the genital mutilation is banned by law in many of the countries where the procedure is practiced (UNFPA, 2015), several reasons have been given to justify the procedure, all wrapped in a combination of cultural, religious, and social causes (Gruenbaum, 2006; Johnson, 2007; WHO, 2008; 2014):

- It is considered a necessary part of raising a girl properly to prepare her for marriage; it is a prerequisite for marriage and the right to inherit in some communities.
- It is a way to ensure premarital virginity and marital fidelity by reducing the women's libido and thus presumably helping her to resist "illicit" sexual acts and restrain sexual desire. There is a belief held by some women in these communities that genital mutilation enhances men's sexual pleasure.
- It is associated with the cultural ideals of femininity and modesty and the idea that a woman should be cleaned and beautiful. By removing body parts that are considered male in appearance and unclean, the procedure is meant to make the woman clean.
- It is considered a cultural tradition that helps define the very core of what it is meant to be a full member of that society. It is an important part of the

cultural identity that provides those receiving the procedure a sense of pride and feeling of community membership.

- There is a fear of stigmatization and rejection by their communities if the practice is not followed. Those departing from the tradition may face condemnation, harassment, and ostracism, while those who follow it receive public recognition and rewards.
- It is upheld by local power structures in these societies, including by older women who have been given the task as gatekeepers of the practice, making them responsible for the practical arrangements of the ceremony.

CONSEQUENCES OF DOMESTIC VIOLENCE ON ITS VICTIMS

There is an extensive list of direct and indirect health and mental health consequences of exposure to violence that have been documented in the literature (Institute of Medicine, 2011; Ristock, 2005; Tjaden & Thoennes, 2000b; Walters, Chen, & Breiding, 2013; Wheeler, Anfinson, Valvert, & Lungo, 2014; White Hughto et al., 2017; WHO, 2010, 2013) that includes impacting women's physical (sexual and reproductive) and mental health, sometimes resulting in an increased morbidity and mortality rate. The more indirect consequence of violence exposure is related to the increase in the stress level in the abused women and members of the LGBT communities, which, when prolonged or too acute, has been associated with a compromised immune system. This association has been linked to cardiovascular disease, hypertension, gastrointestinal disorders, chronic pain, low birth weight rate, somatoform disorders, anxiety, and depression. It has also been linked to other risks factors, such as increased use of alcohol and drugs (Campbell, 2002; Institute of Medicine, 2011; Miller, 1998; Wadhwa, Entinger, Buss, & Lu, 2011; Wheeler et al., 2014; White Hughto et al., 2017; WHO, 2013). The countries where these effects are found most prominently for women surveyed by the World Health Organization are listed in table 2.2 in descending rate order of disease burden. In these statistics, central Sub-Saharan Africa leads the pack with an estimate of 65.64% with health consequences (WHO, 2013).

According to these data, the following are the countries where the health consequences of the exposure to intimate partner violence and non-partner sexual violence are found to be most pronounced: Central and West Sub-Sahara Africa, South Asia, the Andean region of Latin America, East Africa and Middle East, and Oceania with at least 35% prevalence of health consequences as a result of in intimate partner violence. The only regions with prevalence of 26% or below (but still alarming) were Southern Latin America (23.68%), Central Asia (22.89%), North America (21.32%), and Western Europe (19.3%), with the lowest found in East Asia (16.3%). All the other

Table 2.2. Prevalence of intimate partner violence and non-partner sexual violence by Global Burden of Disease regions

Region	Prevalence % of intimate partner violence in descending order (95% CI)	Prevalence % of non-partner sexual violence (95% CI)
Central Sub-Sahara Africa	**65.64**	**21.05**
West Sub-Sahara Africa	**41.75**	9.15
South Asia	**41.73**	3.35
Latin America Andean region	**40.63**	**15.33**
East Sub-Sahara Africa	**38.83**	**11.46**
North Africa/Middle East	**35.38**	4.53
Oceania	**35.27**	**14.86**
Southern Sub-Sahara Africa	29.67	**17.41**
Central Latin America	29.51	**11.88**
Asia Pacific (high-income region)	28.45	**12.20**
Australasia (a region of Oceania, comprises Australia, New Zealand, the island of New Guinea, and neighboring islands in the Pacific Ocean)	28.29	**16.46**
Southeast Asia	27.99	5.28
Central Europe	27.85	10.76
Tropical Latin America	27.43	7.68
Caribbean	27.09	10.32
Eastern Europe	26.13	6.97
Southern Latin America	23.68	5.86
Central Asia	22.89	6.45
North America (high-income region)	21.32	**13.01**
Western Europe	19.30	**11.50**
East Asia	16.30	5.87

countries fell between 29.67% and 27.03% in sexual violence estimate of health consequences.

We found that although there are negative health consequences for both genders (Anderson, 2004; Black et al., 2011; Tjaden & Thoennes, 2000a/2000b; Walter, Chen, & Breiding, 2013), DV tends to affect males and females differently. For instance, male victims of IPV were more likely to experience externalizing disorders, including disruptive disorders and substance use disorders when compared with males in nonviolent relationships. Female victims in violence relationships also reported more externalizing disorders than females in nonviolent relationships but also more internalizing disorders (anxiety) and suicide ideation (Afifi et al., 2009; Black et al., 2011; Institute of Medicine, 2011; Stith et al., 2012). In another major study, women were found to suffer from more depression and substance abuse as compared to males (Anderson, 2004). Gay and bisexual men who experience domestic violence were found to be more prone to abuse alcohol and other substances (Ard & Makadon, 2011). In general, depression, anxiety, and suicide were found to be high among the transgender populations (Institute of Medicine, 2011; White Hughto, Pachankis, Willie, & Reisner, 2017).

DOMESTIC VIOLENCE KNOWS NO GENDER, RACE, ETHNICITY, OR RELIGION BOUNDARIES

It is clear from the findings discussed earlier that the issue of domestic violence is present and permeates all aspects in most societies, cutting across various religions, socioeconomic classes, race, genders, and levels of education (Alkhateeb & Abagideiri, 2007; Anderson, Simpson-Taylor, & Herman, 2004; Ard & Makadon, 2011; Viki & Abrams, 2002). An example of that is the fact that domestic violence and female genital mutilation are found among Christians, Jews, and Muslims alike, although none of the religious texts of these religions prescribe female genital mutilation or openly endorse violence against the spouses (UNFPA, 2015; WHO, 2008). Evidence of domestic violence was found among Seventh Day Adventists (46%), Jews (19–25%), and American Muslims (10%). The estimates in this latter group could be much higher if emotional and verbal abuse had been included in the survey (Alkhateeb, 1999, 2002; Drumm et al., 2006; Graetz, 2004; National Resource Center on Domestic Violence, 2007). Findings from Ellison, Trinitapoli, Anderson, and Johnson (2007) suggest that it is not a question of what religious denomination a perpetrator may belong to but the extent of religious involvement (church attendance) that serves as a protection against domestic violence. This is particularly the case among the African American and Hispanic men and women in their study.

In terms of racial and ethnic groups, we find in the recent report by the CDC (Black et al., 2011; Tjaden & Thoennes, 2000a/2000b) that violent victimization among American Indian/Alaskan Native male and female as well as other racial and ethnic groups remains a fundamental problem in our society. Findings from this report highlight a cultural and ethnic difference in reported incidents of sexual assaults. For instance, we find that Hispanic women were significantly less likely to report being raped at some time in their lives than non-Hispanic women, suggesting that the findings from Hispanic women are likely to be an underrepresentation of the problem. We also find that American Indian/Alaskan Native women were more likely (26.9%) than White non-Hispanic women (18.8%), Black (1 in 5 or 22%), and Hispanic women (1 in 7 or 14.6%) to be the victim of rape at some point in their lives. One in 3 women (33.5%) who identified as multiracial non-Hispanic in the United States also reported to have experienced being raped at some point in their lives (Black et al., 2011).

This same pattern is seen in the rate of stalking among these groups. About 1 in 4 (22.7%) of American Indian/Alaska Native women, 1 in 5 Black non-Hispanic women (19.6%), and 1 in 7 Hispanic women (15.2%) reported being stalked at some point in their lives. This rate is much higher for multiracial non-Hispanic women (1 in 3 or 30.6%) and when the violence is perpetrated by an intimate partner where it was found that 43% of non-Hispanic Black, 46% of American Indian/Alaskan Native women, and 53.8% of multiracial non-Hispanic women reported having experienced rape, physical violence, and/or stalking by an intimate partner in their lifetime.

Violence was also found to be high in several other countries in Latin America not included in the WHO reports discussed earlier, where estimates of physical abuse ranged from 16% to 39% across five countries (Flake, 2006). Although not clearly referred to as intimate partner violence, these statistics also provide a window to understand the increase in violence experienced by members of the LGBT communities. For instance, in Guatemala 24.5 and 12.3% of women reported ever being physically or sexually abused; 16% of men reported engaging in physical violence within a marital relationship (Wheeler et al., 2014). Studies focusing on MSM (men having sex with men but who do not identify as homosexual) and TW (MSM who identify as transgender women) found that violence is particularly high among that population. The greatest violence is experienced by MSM and TW. This latter group (TW) reported experiencing greater levels of violence in Mexico in a study by Betron (reported by Wheeler et al., 2014), which also included a Thailand sample. The reason given for this endemic violence is the culture of "machismo" that prevails in most Central America countries that promotes an insidious and pervasive intolerance against members of multiple gender identities. This culturally based intolerance was supported by a report of a regional study that close to 40% of respondents believe that "God" punishes homosexuals and sex workers with AIDS for their way of life; 38.5% of these respondents agree that people have the right to assault transgender and transvestite individuals (Wheeler et al., 2014).

The importance of considering these cultural and racial characteristics in domestic violence becomes particularly relevant when determining treatment intervention strategies. This was demonstrated by findings emerging from Sarah Ullman's lab at the University of Illinois at Chicago that provide crucial information about sexual minority and race status variables as they relate to recovery following sexual assault incidents. It was found that although bisexual women and Black women reported greater recovery problems, Black women tended to improve more quickly in depression symptoms than non-Black women. Also, it was found that repeated victimization undermined survivor's recovery, even when controlling for child sexual abuse. The conclusion from these findings is that "sexual minority and race status variables and their intersections with revictimization play roles in recovery and should be considered in treatment protocol for sexual assault survivors" (Sigurvinsdottir & Ullman, 2015, p. 1).

MALE VICTIMIZATION

We are also getting better reporting on the extent of male violence victimization, primarily from United States samples. There was an attempt in the 2005 WHO Report to begin including violence information about male victims in its survey but it was decided against for "fear of putting women at risk of future abuse" (p. 2); it is not clear how surveying the rate of male victimization translates necessarily into putting women at risk of future violence. However, CDC reports in 2000 and 2010 (Black et al., 2011) provide us with one of the first glimpses of prevalence rate of domestic violence in male, primarily from the United States, and it is disturbing. It was found that 66.4% of the men surveyed reported having been physically assaulted as children, with an estimate of 3.2 million men reporting having been physically assaulted and 371,000 having been stalked annually in the United States (Black et al., 2011). One in 71 men reported having been raped at some point in their lives, and more than half (52.4%) reported having been raped by an acquaintance and 15.1% by a stranger; 27.8% experienced their rape at the age of 10 years or younger. With regard to intimate partner violence, the 2010 CDC Report (Black et al., 2011) revealed that an estimated 92.1% of males in the survey experienced physical violence, with 13.8% reporting the physical violence to be severe (i.e., hit with a fist, beaten, and slammed against something). Fifty-three percent of the male victims reported having experienced some form of intimate partner violence before the age of 25.

Other interesting statistics regarding male violence among various ethnic and racial groups seem to follow the same pattern as the women in these groups with regard to intimate partner violence. It was found that 45.3% of American Indian/Alaskan Native men, 38.6% of Black men, and 39.3% of multiracial men reported experiencing rape, physical violence, and/or stalking by an intimate partner at some point in their lifetime (Black et al., 2011).

These statistics do not indicate who the perpetrators are (male to male or female to male partner violence) in these incidents of intimate partner violence, but it tends to be about dominance, power, and control, three important motivations that seem to emerge in all incidents of violence that we have discussed in this chapter. It is likely that the victims have wittingly or unwittingly incorporated and assumed a traditional submissive role in the relationship. In the end, it reflects a view of the perpetrator toward the victim as a possession, property, and the one in the lowest position in the equality–inequality dimension. In the case of male to male or female to male violence, a clear identification with a traditional male psychology seems to be present in the perpetrators in some of these situations but not in all. For instance, there is evidence suggesting that women tend to display physical violence against a violent partner under very specific conditions. It tends to occur if they experience severe abuse by their partners and that is done in the presence of their children (Fanslow et al., 2014). It was also found that the experience of men who identified as victims of domestic violence to be similar to women who were victims but also to have some commonalities with men who used violence (Jones, 2014). In general, it reflects a culturally sanctioned atmosphere that directly or indirectly allows as normative these types of behavior toward the recipient of the violence to occur. This issue is more amply discussed in many of the chapters in this book, particularly in chapter 3.

UNDERSTANDING DOMESTIC VIOLENCE IN CULTURAL CONTEXTS

There are several ingredients that are involved and determine the basic dynamic of the domestic violence syndrome when looked at from a cultural and global perspective. It deserves the term "domestic violence syndrome," considering the multiplicity of factors that tend to be involved directly or indirectly in producing the phenomenon. To begin with, what emerges from the WHO report is the importance of recognizing that there is a "cultural, social, and economic context" where violence takes place (WHO, 2005). This context influences and is influenced by explicit or implicit "laws and procedures" enacted by the specific society to dictate and guide the relationships of its members with one another. This includes the (a) "view of male privilege," (b) the "role of patriarchal society principles," (c) "view and attitude toward individuals with multiple gender identities," and (d) "sociopolitical and socioeconomic factors" that guide one's behavior toward others in that society. Those views and principles are more clearly evident in provincial settings but also exist in city settings. In this context, a male offender of domestic violence in some traditional cultures finds justification to kill a domestic partner that he feels has violated the basic honor code enforced by their cultures. This is the case of bride burning and honor killing in a patriarchal country like India where there is a report of a bride burning every two hours (Kristof & WuDunn, 2009). Social context also explains the reluctance of members of the LGBT community to report incidents of intimate partner violence particularly related to their concerns about having to reveal their sexual preferences.

There are also a number of incidents of male partners engaged in domestic violence who feel compelled by cultural expectations to resort to physical means in order to defend their family's honor. In the context of that society, these individuals feel that they have no choice or they will be judged as not respected family men and as poor providers for the safety and well-being of their families. One such an incident with a Latino man is described in chapter 3 of this book.

The high incidence of domestic violence throughout the world suggests that the perpetrator of domestic/intimate partner violence does not function in a vacuum, as depicted in figure 2.1. This is an issue that will be elucidated further in subsequent chapters in this book. We need to understand how the phenomenon continues to haunt us even today, what makes some individuals

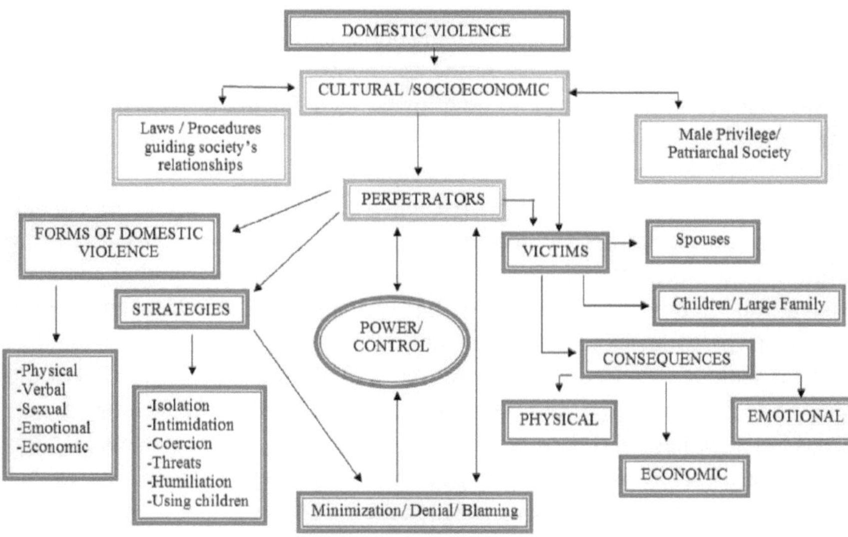

Figure 2.1. Dynamic of domestic violence and its consequences: This figure depicts the trajectory of domestic violence with the ultimate goal of exerting power and control over their victims by the perpetrators. Created by the authors

resort to the different forms of abuses found in the WHO reports (e.g., physical, verbal, sexual, emotional, and economic) and types of strategies (e.g., isolation, intimidation, coercion, and humiliation) to accomplish their ultimate goal: The *absolute power* and psychological, physical, and economic *control* and *dominance* over the victims (see figure 2.1). Minimization and blaming are normally used by the perpetrator to deflect the responsibility for the violent and abusive behavior toward the victim. Also, not infrequently, the perpetrator finds an "unwitting/willing" participant in this regard as the victim may also blame herself (WHO, 2005, 2013) for triggering the violent act by not doing a specific act (that is not always clear to the victim) required by the perpetrator to ensure a different outcome.

There are several models that we and other scholars have discussed previously in an attempt to provide some explanations for the conditions that make domestic violence possible (Javier et al., 1996; Meichenbaum, 2007; Twohey, 2009). It is clear from these discussions that we will only be able to shed additional light on the phenomenon in all its complexity and to come up with more effective prevention and intervention approaches by considering the interplay of the operation of multiple factors. As more fully discussed in subsequent chapters 3–6, these include the individual psychology of the victim and the perpetrator, gender issues, and the cultural, socioeconomic, and sociopolitical contexts in which domestic violence occurs.

A case in point is of Mrs. S., a woman from a South Asian community who lived with her family in the United States for many years. The product of an arranged marriage, she was the mother of several children before reaching her thirties. Her husband, although not a chronic physical abuser, was described as a womanizer and prone to intense jealousy. He held strong beliefs that he, as a man, should be allowed to roam freely with friends and other women as long as he took care of his family and was discreet about his affairs, which was not always the case. For his affairs, he was attracted to women from other ethnic groups, particularly Hispanics, whom he considered exotic. Mrs. S. was an attractive and feisty young woman with strong religious and moral convictions. She was aware of her patriarchal society's expectation of being submissive to the husband, but she also had strong beliefs that such an expectation did not have to include being subjected to physical violence. Her convictions were tested several times when he would threaten to hit her in the middle of an argument and would venture a slap across her face here and there when she was least expecting it. This was the case on several occasions, particularly when she was feeding one of her several young children or taking care of their other needs. On one of these occasions, he came in at midday looking for his lunch, as was customary. It was, however, not ready because she did not have time to prepare it. Her morning had been very hectic, and she was sitting at a chair by the kitchen breastfeeding her newborn child when her husband arrived. An argument ensued when he demanded his meal. She tried desperately to explain her day, pleading for his understanding; but he would have none of that. The exchange became more and more heated. Exasperated, he finally slapped her across the face because she was not supposed to talk back to him and because she did not just stop what she was doing to attend to his demand. As soon as he hit her, she reacted by jumping off her seat as if she had been waiting for such an occasion. Putting her newborn child down for safety, she went after him with whatever she was able to grab to defend herself. He quickly retreated, left the house in a hurry, and did not return for a few days. Her family and her husband's were living nearby and were conflicted about how to respond to the situation. Calling the police was out of the question because "this was a private family matter." She and members of her family struggled with strong feelings of shame and embarrassment at the realization of what the situation would mean for her and her family. She felt acutely her parents' (and her own) accusation that she had failed as a wife for the situation to reach this level. The husband was accused of abandonment by her family, an accusation that was initially rejected by his family. His own family later turned against him when he refused to return to his wife and children. He eventually returned home, but the relationship between them was never the same as the possibility for violence was always in the background.

It is a stubborn dynamic to overcome in an atmosphere that often maintains a view that domestic violence is a private matter (Douki, Nacef, Behadj, Bouasker, & Ghachem, 2003), of women or the "other" in the relationship as property and subject to the dominance and socioeconomic control of the perpetrator, and where the victim (male or female, or with multiple gender identities) is seen as dependent and submissive, voluntarily or by force. This dynamic follows the rationale put forward to justify wife-beating given by even the victims of domestic violence in the WHO report, particularly from the provincial sites (WHO, 2013):

- Failure to complete housework adequately
- Refusing to have sex
- Disobeying her husband
- Being unfaithful

It is the internalization and incorporation of these beliefs in self-definition and personal identities along with the acceptance of these prescriptions of behavior that make the eradication of domestic and intimate partner violence such a formidable challenge. But even in this culturally bound family dynamic there are opportunities for a different outcome when certain shift in the personal dynamic takes place. For instance, although violence had happened before in the case of Ms. S., something different happened with her on that occasion. She came to an important realization that she no longer believed that he had her and her children's best interests in mind. The relationship eventually became unsustainable, leading to a final break many years later when she became financially independent. That took several years because, in the meantime, she decided to keep the family together by allowing him to remain involved with the children for financial reasons, which was particularly important once her parents died. She took seriously her role that she had the responsibility, as the wife, to preserve the family unit and to do anything possible to keep the family together, regardless of the various ways her husband behaved to sabotage that.

Another component to consider in understanding and intervening in domestic violence generally is the nature of early attachment in those involved in domestic violence as victim or perpetrator. According to some findings, the extent to which a person develops a secure attachment with primary people in her life may protect her from the impact of intimate partner violence (Smith & Stover, 2016). When attachment experience is fraught with high anxiety (resulting in insecure attachment), trauma history was found to be positively associated with intimate partner victimization and use of violence. That is, these individuals were more likely to end up as a victim and/or perpetrator of violence. This suggests that it is "fear of abandonment" that becomes the most powerful motivation for staying in the abusive relationship and/or engaging in abuse. This applies to both the victim and the perpetrator and to people with different gender and religion orientations. Related to that is when the individual is exposed to repeated conditions of abuse and maltreatment (e.g., bullying/cyberbullying in school, in the community, from older siblings, from friends and/or early romantic relationships, in the workplace) that may have resulted in a complex trauma condition or posttraumatic stress condition (Courtois & Ford, 2009). There is some evidence indicating that severity of child sexual abuse history in adult sexual assault victims was related to greater PTSD and depression indirectly through maladaptive coping and decreased emotional regulation, but not self-blame. Other traumas were found to be related to self-blame (Ullman, Peter-Hagene, & Relyea, 2014). However, suffering from PTSD alone was not enough of a predictor for the likely use of aggression against an intimate partner, at least among women, until alcohol was also involved (Weiss & Sullivan, 2014).

Substance abuse, particularly alcohol use, has been found to be significantly implicated and a strong predictor of IPV perpetration and victimization in men and women (Campbell, 2002; Miller, 1998; Smith, Stover, Meadows, & Kaufman, 2009; Wadhwa, Entinger, Buss, & Lu, 2011; WHO, 2013). This fact has been systematically supported by various research findings discussed by Stith and colleagues (2012) and highlights the importance of urgently addressing that behavior. Similar findings are reported for members of the LGBT communities with regard to the rate of alcohol and other substances use in cases of IPV (Ard & Makadon, 2011). In Korvo's view

(2014), domestic violence is considered a maladaptive and destructive coping method, reflecting disorders of impulsivity, impaired by executive function deficits and psychopathology that worsen by substance abuse. Findings from another somewhat related study provided further support to that view. It was found that those with substantiated history of child maltreatment and a moderate to high degree of dysregulation problem were more likely to engage in later substance abuse, while for those with low dysregulation problem the link was not as strong. PTSD did not emerge as a mediator, suggesting the role of self-regulation as a risk or protective factor is the link between child maltreatment and later substance abuse through its influence on externalizing behaviors (Kaufman, Wright, Allbaugh, Folger, & Noll, 2014).

CONCLUSION

In this chapter we discussed the issue of domestic violence as a worldwide phenomenon that affects many aspects of our society, producing an inordinate amount of physical and psychological health consequences to its victims. The statistics presented are quite convincing that we cannot afford to remain passively on the sidelines as social and behavioral professionals and thus motivates our decision to engage not only in attempting to elucidate the phenomenon further but also to offer suggestions for more effective interventions. There is too much at stake for the individual and society to do otherwise. It is clear that more attention should be focused on elucidating the basic dynamic of domestic violence that is influenced and guided by the cultural, racial, social, and economic context where it takes place. The perpetuator finds justification in these influences as well in what is explicitly and implicitly condoned in that context. It is important to recognize in this regard that although cultural factors (including class, race, ethnicity, and other forms of social difference) contribute to the development of attitudes toward violence against women and members of the LBGT communities (Ard & Makadon, 2011; Flood & Pease, 2009; Wheeler et al., 2014), a more sophisticated lens needs to be applied in order to appreciate the extent to which these factors apply to the specific situation under consideration. We know from experience that it does not apply in the same way to all individuals within the same culture, gender orientations, race, and socioeconomic and sociopolitical contexts.

This issue will be further elucidated in different chapters included in this book with the goal of adding a more sophisticated appreciation as to why one person in the relationship engages in harming another. There are important treatment implications that derive directly from our analysis also highlighted in this chapter. We are venturing into this important project with the understanding that our attempt to explain reasons behind the behavior should not be used as justification for harming another person in the relation. Ultimately, there is no justification for that.

DISCUSSION QUESTIONS

1. Explore the rate of domestic violence incidence in your own community by cultural/gender/socioeconomic status.
2. Compare/contrast the rate of domestic violence incidence in the different groups found in your community.
3. Provide your understanding of the rationales given by the different ethnic, cultural, and gender groups to justify domestic violence in their midst.
4. Could you identify other more symbolic examples of female genital mutilation still present in our society?
5. Are there conditions/groups for which using violence against other members of the family are more acceptable or justified in the eyes of the law?
6. Are there specific types of interventions that these groups find most helpful when in the midst of a domestic violence incident?
7. List differences and similarities in cases of child abuse and elder abuse. How can that be explained within the group culture?
8. Looking more specifically to members of the LGBT communities and elements identified in figure 2.1, list/discuss the most crucial factors that contribute to increase in intimate partner violence incidents among those communities.
9. Interview a victim and/or perpetrator of domestic violence and identify the specific factors from what is described in figure 2.1 that may be involved in his/her particular circumstances.

REFERENCES

Afifi, T. O., MacMillan, H., Cox, B. J., Asmundson, G. J. G., Stein, M. B., & Sareen, J. (2009). Mental health correlates of intimate partner violence in marital relationships in a nationally representative sample of males and females. *Journal of Interpersonal Violence, 24*(8), 1398–1417.

Alkhateeb, S. (1999). Ending domestic violence in Muslim families, *Journal of Religion and Abuse, 1(44)*, 49–59.

Alkhateeb, S. (2002). Who has the right to save Muslim women from abuse? *Journal of Religion and Abuse, 4,* 7–20.

Alkhateeb, M. B., & Abagideiri, S. E. (2007) *Changes from within: Diverse perspectives on domestic violence in the Muslim communities*. Herndon, VA: Peaceful Family Project.

Anderson, K. L. (2004). Perpetrator or victim? Relationships between intimate partner violence and well-being. *Journal of Marriage and Family, 64*(2), 851–863.

Anderson, V. N., Simpson-Taylor, D., & Hermann, D. J. (2004). Gender, age, and rape supportive rules. *Sex Roles: A Journal of Research, 50*, 77–90.

Ard, K. L., & Makadon, H. J. (2011). Addressing intimate partner violence in lesbian, gay, bisexual, and transgender patients. *Journal of General Internal Medicine, 26*(8), 930–933. Published online 2011 Mar 30. doi: 10.1007/s11606-011-1697-6.

Babcock, J. C. (2003). Toward a typology of abusive women: Differences between partner-only and generally violent women in the use of violence. *Psychology of Women Quarterly, 27*(2), 153.

Babcock, J. C., Canady, B. E., Graham, K., & Schart, L. (2007). The evolution of battering interventions: From the dark ages into the scientific ages. In J. Hamel & T. L. Nicholls (Eds.), *Family Interventions in Domestic Violence: A Handbook of Gender-Inclusive Theory and Treatment* (pp. 215–244). New York: Springer Publishing Company.

Black, M. C., Basile, K., Breiding, M. J., Smith, S. G., Walters, M. L., Merrick, M. T., et al. (2011). *The National Intimate Partner and Sexual Violence Survey: 2010 Summary Report.* Atlanta, GA: National Center for Injury Prevention and Control, CDC. www.cdc.gov/violenceprevention/pdf/nisvs_executive_summary-a.pdf. Retrieved 6/28/2014.

Campbell, J. C. (2002). Health consequences of intimate partner violence. *The Lancet, 359* (9314), 1331–1336. CDC (2013). *National Intimate Partner and Sexual Violence Survey.* Retrieved from http://www.cdc.gtov/reproductivehealth/global/surveys.htm, 1/30/2014.

Courtois, C. A. & Ford, J. (Eds.). (2009). *Treating complex traumatic stress disorders: An evidence-based guide.* New York: The Guilford Press.

Douki, S., Nacef, F., Belhadj, A., Bouasker, A., & Ghachem, R. (2003). Violence against women in Arab and Islamic countries. *Archives of Women's Mental Health, 6,* 165–171.

Drumm, R., McBride, D., Hopkins, G., Thayer, J., Popescu, M., & Wrenn, J. (2006). Intimate partner violence in the conservative Christian Denomination: Prevalence and types. *Social Work & Christianity, 33* (3), 233–251.

Ellison, C., Trinitapoli, J. A., Anderson, K. L., & Johnson, B. R. (2007). Race/ethnicity, religious involvement, and domestic violence. *Violence Against Women, 13* (11), 1094–1112.

Fanslow, J., Gulliver, P., Dixon, R., & Ayalo, I. (2014). Exploring factors associated with women's use of physical violence against a violent partner. Paper presented at the International Family Violence and Child Victimization Research Conference, Portsmouth, New Hampshire, July 13–15, 2014.

Flake, D. & Forste, R. (2006). Fighting families: Family characteristics associated with domestic violence in Five Latin American Countries. *Journal of Family Violence, 21*(1), 16–39.

Flood, M., & Pease, B. (2009). Factors influencing attitudes towards violence against women. *Trauma, Violence & Abuse, 10* , 125–142.

Gilbert, L., El-Bassel, N., Wu, E., & Chang, M. (2007). Intimate partner violence and HIV risks: Longitudinal study of men on methadone. *Journal of Urban Health, 84*(5), 667–680.

Graetz, N. (2004). The battered women in Jewish tradition: See no evil, hear no evil, and speak no evil. *Journal of Religion and Abuse: Advocacy, Pastoral Care and Prevention, 6* (3/4), 31–48.

Gruenbaum, E. (2006). Sexuality issues in the movement to abolish female genital cutting in Sudan. *Medical Anthropology Quarterly, 20,* 121.

Institute of Medicine (2011). *The Health of Lesbian, Gay, Bisexual, and Transgender People: Building a Foundation for Better Understanding.* Washington, DC: The National Academies Press. doi: 10.17226/13128.

Javier, R. A., Herron, W. G., & Bergman, A. (Eds.) (1996). *Domestic violence: Assessment and treatment.* Northvale, NJ: Jason Aronson, Inc.

Johnson, M. (2007). Making mandinga or making Muslims? Debating female circumcision, ethnicity, and Islam in Guinea-Bissau and Portugal. In Y. Hernlund & B. Shell-Duncan (Eds.), *Transcultural bodies: female genital cutting in global context* (pp. 202–223). New Brunswick, NJ: Rutgers University Press.

Johnson, M. (2008). *A typology of domestic violence: Intimate terrorism, violence resistance and situational couple violence*. Lebanon, NH: Northeastern University Press.

Johnson, M. P., & Ferraro, K. J. (2000). Research on domestic violence in the 1990s: Making distinctions. *Journal of Marriage and the Family, 62*, 948–963.

Jones, C. (2014). Men who identified as victims of domestic violence. Paper presented at the International Family Violence and Child Victimization Research Conference, Portsmouth, New Hampshire, July 13–15, 2014.

Kaufman, J., Wright, M. O., Allbaugh, L. J., Folger, S. F., & Noll, J. (2014). The impact of child maltreatment on maturing self-regulatory systems and later substance use. Paper presented at the International Family Violence and Child Victimization Research Conference, Portsmouth, New Hampshire, July 13–15, 2014.

Korvo, K. (2014). The role of executive function deficits in domestic violence perpetration. Paper presented at the International Family Violence and Child Victimization Research Conference, Portsmouth, New Hampshire, July 13–15, 2014.

Kraft, K., Menatti, A., & Gidycz, C. A. (2014). Examining the relationship between interpersonal victimization and emotion dysregulation. Paper presented at the International Family Violence and Child Victimization Research Conference, Portsmouth, New Hampshire, July 13–15, 2014.

Kristof, N. D., & WuDunn, S. (2009). *The women's crusade*. www.nytimes.com/2009/08/23/magazine/23Women-t.html. The *New York Times*. Retrieved January 1, 2014.

Landers, S., & Gilsanz P. (2009). *The health of lesbian, gay, bisexual, and transgender (LGBT) persons in Massachusetts.* Massachusetts Department of Public Health, 2009. Available at: www.masstpc.org/wp-content/uploads/2012/10/DPH-2009-lgbt-health-report.pdf. Accessed August 21, 2017.

Meichenbaum, D. (2007). *Family violence: Treatment of perpetrators and victims*. Retrieved from: www.melissainstititute.org. December 20, 2013.

Miller, A. H. (1998). Neuroendocrine and immune system interactions in stress and depression. *Psychiatric Clinics of North America, 21* (2), 443–463. *National Coalition Against Domestic Violence* (2017). Retrieved from http://www.ncadv.org on August 31, 2017.

National Coalition Against Domestic Violence (2017). Retrieved from http://ncadv.org/learn-more/ statistics.

National Institute of Justice (2011). *Impact of child abuse and maltreatment on delinquency, arrest and victimization*. Retrieved from htpp://www.nij.gov on August 31, 2017.

National Resource Center on Domestic Violence (NRCDV) (2007). *Religion and domestic violence: Information and resources*. Retrieved from www.nrcdv.org/topics/crime/child-abuse/pages/impact-on-arrest-victimization.aspx, on June 28, 2015.

Neal, A., Dixon, C., Edwards, K. M., & Gidycz, C. A. (2014). College women's motives for perpetrating intimate partner violence. Paper presented at the International Family Violence and Child Victimization Research Conference, Portsmouth, New Hampshire, July 13–15, 2014.

Ristock, J. (2005). Relationship violence in lesbian/gay/bisexual/transgender/queer [LGBTQ] communities: Moving beyond a gender-based framework. *Violence Against Women Online Resources.* Retrieved from http://citeseerx.ist.psu.edu/viewdoc/download?doi=10.1.1.208.7282&rep=rep1&type=pdfAugust 29, 2017.

Sigurvinsdottir, R., & Ullman, S. E. (2015). Sexual orientation, race, and trauma as predictors of sexual assault recovery. *Journal of Family Violence,* 1–9. Doi:10.1007/s10896-015-9793-8.

Smith, L. S., & Stover, C. S. (2016). The moderating role of attachment on the relationship between history of trauma and intimate violence victimization. *Violence Against Women, 22*(6), 745–764.

Smith, C. W., Stover, C., Meadows, A. L., & Kaufman, J. (2009). Interventions for intimate partner violence: Review and implications for evidence-based practice. *Professional Psychology: Research and Practice, 40*, 223–233.

Stith, S. M., McCollum, E. E., Amanor-Boadu, Y., & Smith, D. (2012). Systemic perspectives on Intimate Partner Violence treatment. *Journal of Marital and Family Therapy, 38*(1), 220–240.

Sullivan, T. P., Weiss, N., & Price, C. (2014). Coping with individual PTSD symptoms: The unique experience of victims. Paper presented at the International Family Violence and Child Victimization Research Conference, Portsmouth, New Hampshire, July 13–15, 2014.

Tjaden, P., & Thoennes, N. (2000a). *Extent, nature and consequences of intimate partner violence: Findings from the National Violence Against Women Survey*. National Institute of Justice and the Centers for Disease Control and Prevention. Atlanta, GA.

Tjaden, P., & Thoennes, N. (2000b). *US Department of Justice-Full report of the prevalence, incidence and consequences of violence against women*. National Institute of Justice, United States Department of Justice. http://www.ncjrs.gov, retrieved January 30, 2014.

Twohey, M. (2009). *How can domestic violence be stopped?* Chicago Tribune, January 2, 2009, p. 2. www.chicagotribune.com/news/local/chi-abusers-02-jan02,0,1147422.story?page=2. Retrieved December 20, 2013.

Ullman, S., Petter-Hagene, L. C., & Relyea, M. (2014). Coping, emotion regulation, and self-blame as mediator of sexual abuse and psychological symptoms in adult sexual assault. *Journal of Child Sex Abuse, 23*(1): doi:10.1080/10538721.2014.864747.

United Nations Population Fund (UNFPA) (2015). *Female genital mutilation (FGM) frequently asked questions*. Retrieved from http://www.unfpa.org/sources/female-genital-mutilation-fgm-frequently-asked-questions. on November 14, 2015.

Viki, G. T., & Abrams, D. (2002). But she was unfaithful: Benevolent sexism and reactions to rape victims who violate traditional gender role expectations. *Sex Roles, 47*, 289–293.

Wadhwa, P. D., Entinger, S., Buss, C., & Lu, M. C. (2011). The contribution of maternal stress to preterm birth: Issues and considerations. *Clinical Perinatology, 2011, 39*, 351–384.

Walters, M. L., Chen, J., & Breiding, M. J. (2013). *The national intimate partner and sexual violence survey (NISVS): 2010 findings on victimization by sexual orientation.* National Center for Injury Prevention and Control, Centers for Disease Control and Prevention, Atlanta, Georgia. Retrieved from https://www.cdc.gov/violenceprevention/pdf/nisvs_sofindings.pdf

Weiss, N., Duke, A. A., & Sullivan, T. P. (2014). Posttraumatic stress disorder and women's use of aggression in intimate relationships: The moderating role of alcohol dependence. Paper presented at the International Family Violence and Child Victimization Research Conference, Portsmouth, New Hampshire, July 13–15, 2014.

White Hughto, J. M., Pachankis, J. E., Willie, T. C., & Reisner, S. L. (2017). Victimization and depressive symptomology in transgender adults: The mediating role of avoidant coping. *Journal of Counseling Psychology, 64*(1), 41–51. doi: 10.1037/cou0000184.

Wheeler, J., Anfinson, K., Valvert, D., & Lungo, S. (2014). Is violence associated with increased risk behavior among MSM? Evidence from a population-based survey conducted across nine cities in Central America Journal of Global Health Action. 7: 10.3402/gha.v7.24814. Published online October 3, 2014. doi: 10.3402/gha.v7.24814.PMCID: PMC4212078

Whitfield, C. L., Anda, R. F., Dube, S. R., & Felitti, V. J. (2003). Violent childhood experiences and the risk of intimate partner violence in adults. *Journal of Interpersonal Violence, 18*, 166–185.

World Health Organization (2005). *Summary report: Multi-country study on women's health and domestic violence against women. Initial results on prevalence, health outcomes and women's responses*. Geneva, World Health Organization.

World Health Organization (2008). *Global and regional estimates of violence and health effects of intimate partner violence and non-partner sexual violence*. Geneva, Switzerland. (www.who.int)

World Health Organization (2010). *Preventing intimate partner violence and sexual violence against women. Taking action and generating evidence*. Geneva.

World Health Organization (2013). *Global and regional estimates of violence against women: Prevalence and health effects of intimate partner violence and non-partner sexual violence*. www.who.int/reproductivehealth.

World Health Organization (2014). *Female Genital Mutilation*. Retrieved from http://www.who.int/mediacentre/factsheets/fs241/en/: April 11, 2015.

World Health Organization (2015). *Sexual and reproductive health. Female genital mutilation and other harmful practices*. Retrieved from http://www.who.int/reproductivehealth/topics/fgm/prevalence/en/, November 14, 2015.

Chapter Three

Overview-Aggression, Domestic Violence, and Risk Factors

William G. Herron and Rafael Art. Javier

In this chapter we will address a fundamental issue in understanding domestic violence, which we consider as one form of the larger domain of aggression. It is our contention that in order to understand domestic violence, a type of violence that is particularly disturbing in its rupture of interpersonal connections within the home, it is necessary to first understand aggression. In attempting to do this we have to begin with a disclaimer: all theories of aggression have existing limitations. The current state of knowledge regarding aggression and violence is minimal and therefore subject to further exploration. However, these approaches provide direction for the socially desirable goal of reducing human violence and suffering. Regretfully, acts of violence continue to happen. The evidence is clear that we must continue to seek better solutions and change the ways in which we rectify this global problem.

DEFINITIONS OF AGGRESSION

The first challenge to our endeavor is the complexity of delineating aggression because it is a complicated and multifaceted concept. Usually it is thought of as destructive action, although there are forms of aggression that are not destructive. The basic concept refers to the capacity of the self to take action: the self-as-agent. The concept is based on the "invasion" of space, physical or psychological, that was not previously occupied by the invader. However, this is too broad an approach to be operational in regard to a more consensual meaning of aggression. It is necessary to consider both the motives for the action and the accompanying effects. The aggressor needs a reason to act, namely a desire to get something that the person believes will be attained by the action, and affects, such as anger and satisfaction, are part of the action sequence.

Various theories have attempted to elucidate these core components of aggression that have guided the discussion on aggression and domestic violence for years. It is instructive to revisit some of these discussions so as to anchor our understanding of domestic violence in terms of its core motivating factors, aims, and consequences, which then can provide the fundamental framework for a better intervention. We will begin with psychoanalytic formulations (albeit only briefly, with a more comprehensive discussion included in another chapter dedicated exclusively to this discussion) because it is the first theoretical articulation that attempts to provide a comprehensive explanatory model of the presence of aggression in human behavior. This framework is anchored in biological sciences, evolutionary theory, as well as developmental and attachment theories. We will also discuss social learning theories, particularly the General Aggression Model (GAM) (with a more comprehensive chapter by Warburton and Anderson to follow), highlighting the points of convergences and differences between these two important frameworks. The importance of these two frameworks is that they provide separately and in combination the best opportunity to understand and appreciate more fully internal (individual) and external factors discussed in the introductory chapter and that have been found to contribute to the presence of violence in general and domestic violence in particular. In the final analysis, we are looking for a reasonable explanation as to why people engage in violent behavior even to the point of doing serious physical and psychological harm to those who are closer to the abuser, and thus paradoxically poisoning the very environment that it is needed for the individual's survival.

PSYCHODYNAMIC THEORIES

Psychoanalytic theory defined aggression as "The manifest strivings, either physical or verbal, to subjugate or prevail over another" (Moore & Fine, 1990, p. 10). Aggression can be direct, indirect, indirect and disguised, passive, or against the self. The usual intent is destructive, but aggression also includes acts that are not destructive, such as self-assertion. Motivation can be both conscious and unconscious, and affect can be felt even when it is not displayed. The most frequent motive is destruction and the most frequent affect is anger.

Pine (2005) provides more details regarding aggression, considering it biologically based and having the quality of a drive, a type of energy that is a strong motivational force, suggesting that it is an innate force and necessary for the survival of the individual. Aggression is seen as *primarily reactive to frustrations and deprivations* that are inevitable aspects of life and hence part of the normal human condition. Another aspect of aggression is highlighted by Parens (1979) who separates aggression into non-hostile (as exploratory activity), non-hostile destructiveness, and hostile destructiveness (the type of aggression that causes the most concern).

Rizzuto, Meissner, and Buie (2004) provide an important refinement of aggression, described as a *mental capacity* to act to overcome obstacles blocking an intended action. In this context, they distinguish between a *cause* and a *motive*, considering aggression to be a motive, with causality and agency coming from the self-as-agent.

With the advent of relational theory, which emphasized the importance of connecting to others as the primary motivational force, there has been movement away from defining aggression as an innate drive even though a tie to a biological base often remains. For example, Mitchell (1993) considers aggression to be a primarily hostile biological response to self-endangerment. He sees aggression as reactive: a biological potential for destruction activated by relational conditions that pose a threat to the self. The view of aggression as a reactive condition is emphasized by early Object Relations theoreticians such as Fairbairn (1963), who viewed aggression as a reaction to frustration, and Guntrip (1969), who considered it to be a reaction to fear and isolation. In their formulations, the biological, energetic aspect of aggression is retained, but the instinctual drive element is downplayed or removed. Winnicott (1974), another major Object Relations theoretician, on the other hand, focused on the positive aspects of aggression, namely considering it to be a self-assertive developmental force involving biological energy with a constructive aim.

Continually moving further from the singularity of destructive aggression, Lichtenberg, Lachmann, and Fossaghe (2011) proposed seven motivational systems, only two of which seem to be considered as a form of aggression, namely exploratory, which could be considered positive aggression; the other one is aversive, which could be viewed as negative. What is important here is that they do not use the term *aggression* for any of the systems. They make a point of motivational systems not being derived from drives. Instead they hypothesize that the systems are due to experience and are both self-organized and self-stabilized. They admit to some innate influence, but suggest that early values are learned and the combinations remain as life span dispositions. Motivational systems are considered as intrinsic parts of a creative developmental process.

Lichtenberg (1991) described two major psychodynamic views that remain active at the present time. One is that there is a primary aggressive drive, with derivatives that can be shaped to modulate destructiveness. The other is that there is a primary assertiveness that is learned from experience and can also be shaped into functional pleasure or, if frustrated, can result in destructive aggression. Viewed either way, aggression is a product of a developmental process throughout the life cycle.

Our concern in this book is with destructive aggression. While not agreeing on its origins, psychodynamic descriptions view it as a strong motivational force, implying some type of energy and action that is predisposed and heightened by experience and can result in violence. Aggression appears to be present in everyone but varies in form and expression. Psychological development includes a series of triggers for aggressive reactions, with the family a likely situation for various forms of aggression, such as violence in general and domestic violence in particular, as described in figure 2.1.

SOCIAL LEARNING THEORIES

The view of the social learning theories with regard to aggression is not much different than other views with regard to its manifestation. For instance, interpersonal aggression is described as "any behavior involving an intent to harm another person" (Felson, 2002, p. 12). A more recent description by Shaver and Mikulincer (2011) is also in accord with the "intent to harm." Felson elaborates further, depicting aggression as "coercive behavior in which an actor deliberately harms another person" (2002, p. 13). He notes that one approach is to see aggression as a reaction to frustration, such as when goals are blocked or aversive stimuli are experienced (Berkowitz, 1993). In this approach, aggression is considered an innate drive. When the aggressor is frustrated the aim is to hurt others. Aversive stimuli result in negative affect, such as anger and rage, and these affects stimulate destructive aggression, either directly expressed or displaced to an available other. However, this appears to be true only when the aggressor perceives negative intentions on the part of the person creating the frustration. So the issue of intentionality or attribution of specific intent governing the action of the person creating the frustration becomes central. The motivational power of affect is similar to a psychodynamic conception of aggression suggested by Kernberg (1992). There is also a connection to his broader conception of the psychological function of aggression, namely "to assert autonomy, to eliminate an obstacle or barrier to a desired degree of satisfaction, or to eliminate or destroy source of profound pain or frustration" (1992, p. 22).

However, Felson favors what he calls an "instrumental" approach, based on the rewards or costs of the action rather than aggression being a biological force, or innate. Biology is seen as having an indirect infusion through types of temperament. An example of this is impulsivity increasing the probability of aggression. Aggression is seen as motivated by a number of possibilities, such as control, retribution, self-image protection, and excitement. In this context, violence is divided into two categories, *dispute-related*, where aggressors are responding to what they believe is provocation, and *predatory*, where the victim is used for the personal desire of the attacker. Aggression is considered to involve a reasoned approach, even when it is impulsive. The basic motivation for aggression is to get something the attacker believes he or she will value.

In a similar vein, Anderson and Bushman (2002) summarize five theories of aggression and subsequently propose what they consider to be a unified model, the General Aggression Model (GAM). They define aggression as behavior toward another with the intent to harm that person, who in turn is motivated to avoid the harm. Violence is seen as the extreme form of aggression. The five theories are *cognitive neoassociation theory* (Berkowitz, 1990), *social cognitive theory* (Bandura, 2001), *script theory* (Huesmann, 1988), *excitation theory* (Zillmann, 1983), and *social interaction theory* (Tedeschi & Felson, 1994).

The first theory (*cognitive neoassociation*) postulates that unpleasant events result in the linking of aggressive thoughts, feelings, and behaviors in an associative memory structure likely to be reactivated in similar situations. There is a similarity to the psychodynamic concepts of the motivation involved in the pleasure principle (geared at ensuring the attainment of personal satisfaction, sense of well-being, and personal affirmation) and the idea of repetition compulsion (where behaviors are compulsively repeated, which is linked to frustration and the resulting unresolved unconscious aggression).

Social cognition emphasizes learning aggressive behavior either by experiencing or observing it, while *script theory* provides the patterns of learned aggression that have been conceptualized and coded in memory and are available for activation. This is an important concept because it has to do with the process by which we develop experience in the context of our developmental trajectory. This process is internalized in what the psychodynamic formulation refers to as identification in object relations, particularly identification with the aggressor, though masochistic identification (identification with the victim) is also possible. Thus, the individual engaged in a violent act against another may be expressing an early acquired behavior resulting from early identifications learned/acquired in the primary environment. In this context, attachment theory that describes the different bonds developed by the child influenced by the nature and quality of the early relationships with the primary object, the mother, and how that tends to influence the nature and quality of future relationships also fits in with these two social learning theories.

Excitation theory uses the idea that physiological arousal dissolves slowly, so in the case of anger, once felt, it may be still present for another situation through the transfer of excitation. The emphasis here is the idea that intense emotions are coded sensorially and become part of the sensory memory that is expressed through other situations that trigger its expression. Such a view reflects an overlap to an earlier psychodynamic idea related to the economic principle of the role of psychic energy in mental life and the development of psychological disorders, including domestic violence. Finally, *social interaction theory* sees aggression as a behavior designed to influence interpersonal situations with a rational goal filtered through evaluation of costs and rewards, also basic components highlighted in aspects of object-relations theory.

In general we can conclude that these are essentially partial theories of aggression viewed primarily as a learned response. They provide building blocks for a more comprehensive approach such as that attempted in the GAM (DeWall & Anderson, 2011). The most crucial part of this model is that it provides an integration of probable environmental, psychological, biological, and social factors that can foster aggressive behavior. These are classified as either *person* or *situational* factors: (a) Person factors highlight individual-specific components involved in the preparedness to act aggressively (i.e., attitudes, personality traits, and genetic predispositions). An example is a personal tendency toward hostile attribution and expectation. (b) Situational factors involve provocation and noxious stimuli. Both person and situational factors influence aggression by stimulating arousal, cognition, and affect. These are input variables creating an internal state that moves a person toward aggression. Examples include having hostile thoughts or feeling pain.

The GAM focuses on a current specific social interaction (family transaction), in which there are personal and situational stimuli as well as cognitive, arousal, and affective paths through which the stimuli have an impact. This is followed by potential outcomes (an increase/decrease of the possible violent behavior) based on appraisal and subsequent decisions about the value of acting aggressively. Although there is an emphasis on the present episode, past and future states are also involved so that information emerging from these different states are involved in and determine the final outcome. The overall thrust is to understand knowledge structures constituting aggression that are learned and constructed from experience. This approach is akin to the instrumental aggression described earlier, except that it is more inclusive of a possible genetic predisposition.

There is also considerable similarity, despite the different language, to the model of pathological psychic development proposed by psychodynamic theories. For example, aggression considered as a drive is a significant force in personality development where it is shaped through the influence of structural factors in the context of the interaction with the environment. According to the relational approach, instrumental aggression originates in this context. Manifestations of aggression include both conscious and unconscious components and range in intensity, violence being the extreme. The GAM takes notice of possible unconscious motivation as well.

It is clear from our discussion thus far that a more comprehensive understanding of how violence occurs, what factors are involved, and through what mechanisms, is possible if we consider what the GAM model and psychoanalytic theories have delineated regarding individual/person and structural/environmental factors. The GAM considers violence to be the result of inputs from the person and the situation resulting in a decision by the person to take aggressive action. In psychodynamic terms this would involve superego distortions (or distortions in one's moral values) as well as possible ego misconceptions. Person factors operating in service of destructive aggression, as abusing a domestic partner, would involve a paranoid set to be convinced of provocation serious enough to justify a violent reaction. There would be a projection of hostility now seen as coming from the partner, as well as a possible type of narcissism that combines high unwarranted self-esteem with unconscious low self-esteem, attachment insecurity, and any other attitudes and beliefs involving violent solutions deemed necessary by the attacker. Situational variables involve the presence of some behavior by the partner that can be considered a provocation, as well as less immediate variables such as exposure to violent video games or assault weapons.

Person and situational factors are starting points in predicting aggression as well as describing the components of an aggressive act. These factors create interactive internal states, namely affect, cognition, and arousal. They underlie a relationship between person-situational variables and the outcomes of appraisal and decision making. Appraisals can be immediate and impulsive, or involve reappraisals and thoughtfulness. The latter requires the ability to overcome aggressive impulses, in essence a good blend of ego and superego. However, in line with a psychodynamic economic view, reappraisal in this theory is also considered as possibly depending on a limited energy resource which can be depleted by a number of factors, as repeated perceived provocation leads to an appraisal justifying aggressive action as the most satisfactory personal outcome. The behavior enacted can be reused by the inputs in subsequent episodes, so when it is destructive aggression the result can be a cycle of escalating violence.

The comprehensiveness of the GAM model is both an asset and a problem. The asset is the identification of inputs that can serve as assessment markers for the probability of violence in specific situations. They are supported by research evidence, but none are universal predictors. For example, it would be inaccurate to say that growing up in an atmosphere of violence means that all involved will be violent. However, it does mean that such exposure increases the probability that one or more of the family members will frequently resort to violent solutions (Gilbert, El-Bassel, Wu, & Chang, 2007; National Institute of Justice, 2011; Tjaden & Thoennes, 2000; Whitfield, Anda, Dube, & Felitti, 2003). Also, given that possibility, a preventative avenue is opened. There can be a reduction of "enhancements," as exposure to violent media, or making actual changes in the social environment, including problem-solving behavior in families. Based on identified contributing factors, the model illustrates how a violent episode is likely to develop and how violence can escalate. Risk factors for aggression can be categorized as *instigating*, *impelling*, or *inhibiting* (Slotter & Finkel, 2011). Instigators are provoking others to be aggressive, and also can feel they have reasons to respond aggressively. Those who are directly impelled express destructive aggression. In combating this, interventions aimed at improving self-regulation, a type of ego-strength as well as effective superego operation, are promising in behavioral inhibition of aggression (Baumeister, 2005).

The problem is that, from the perspective of developing easy-to-use assessment tools, the number of risk factors is very large and the factors are often interactive, so diagnostic evaluation becomes quite complicated. Accuracy requires considerable time, and knowledge about each person, but in clinical situations such an approach often would not be possible. As an example, consider the complexity of person factors such as narcissism (Herron, 1999), relying for comprehension on unconscious factors as well as conscious behavior. In that regard, as noted earlier there is evidence that a combination of high (exaggerated) self-esteem and low implicit (unconscious underestimation) self-regard is related to aggressive actions (Thomaes & Bushman, 2011). However, this also indicates that the complexity of causality requires greater exploration of developmental factors as well as factors delineated by Dodge (2011), who depicts a model where genes and an early traumatic environment predict risk for chronic violence. To add to the complication, with situational factors, the impact on each individual tends to be variable and difficult to assess.

The GAM appears to emphasize social factors in primarily conscious experience in the creation of a predisposition to violence, particularly the deprivation of basic needs, and downplays innate factors. The etiology of the "violent person" remains elusive, suggesting it involves a multiplicity similar to risk factors. Slotter and Finkel note the need for "interventions designed to help individuals manage their aggressive impulses in a constructive manner" (2011, p. 48), but do not indicate the origins of the impulses.

The use of the term *impulse* suggests the possibility that people have innate aggression, but it could be that the impulses are learned in the process of psychic development. At the same time, considering aggression to be primarily instrumental, it is still possible that an innate predisposition is necessary to learn to act in an aggressive manner, particularly to be destructive. Social learning theories do not directly state that all individuals are aggressive, though this is suggested in early development. Relational theorists also deemphasize the powerful role of aggression, but their descriptions of interpersonal interactions also suggest this. Added to these inferences is the prevalence of aggression worldwide. As to its origins, Rhee and Waldman conclude, "there are moderate additive genetic and nonshared environmental influences and modest shared environmental influences in aggression" (2011, p. 158).

In conclusion, the GAM is clear on what it is not trying to do, and it is certainly to be valued for the large territory it does cover, as well as its attempt at integrating theories of aggression. It contributes an improved understanding of the enactment, or inhibition, of violence and the need for appropriate self-regulation.

Psychodynamic theories have significant commonalities with social learning theories, a number of which have already been noted. Both point to the contribution of experience, particularly the individual developmental process taking place within the family structure as well as the influence of significant others. Dysfunctional families are major contributors to the formation of violent people. Attachment theory, originally a psychoanalytic product, has been integrated into social learning theory (Mikulincer & Shaver, 2011). The psychoanalytic concept of narcissism has also been explored as a risk factor (Thomaes & Bushman, 2011). Social learning has been considered both an ego function and a significant aspect of interpersonal connection in psychodynamic theories, so there are significant points of integration.

Although both theories in their more contemporary forms emphasize instrumental aggression and deemphasize the idea of a universal drive continually seeking discharge (Freud, 1920), they seem to acknowledge the probability of an innate psychobiological disposition in the formation of an aggressive character. A major difference is the emphasis on unconscious motivation that characterizes psychodynamic approaches, though that idea does get some consideration in social learning theories. Psychodynamic theories also focus more distinctly on object-relations and the agency of the self, and far less on situational and cultural variables. Such a focus has limitations, certainly when it comes to domestic violence. For example, in domestic violence the person-agents of the violence will get prime consideration, but the "domestic" aspect will not. Also, in the relational mode, destructive aggression can be sidestepped. For example, Winnicott (Winnicott, Shepherd, & Davis, 1984) describes aggression as an energy source for the mastery of developmental tasks rather than being primarily destructive.

Two major views appear in psychodynamic theories. One is that aggression is instinctual with a destructive aim. The other is that aggression is reactive, and may or may not become destructive. Blanck and Blanck (1994) have attempted a type of marriage of viewpoints by postulating that aggression as a destructive force refers to the severing of connections that powers the movement of developmental phases, but that does not account for the strong presence of destructive aggression. In the case of destructive aggression, the superego has a major task of appropriate mastery of desires in relation to reality, but the relational approach moves away from the emphasis on the force of destructive aggression to focus primarily on making connections. Further detachment from the drive model appears in the work of Lichtenberg, Lachmann, and Fossaghe (2011). They propose a number of motivational systems, none of which are called aggression, though it is possible to view aggression as a component of all of them. However, rather than considering motivation in terms of drives, they focus on inter-subjective factors whereby developmentally there is interactive organization and self-stabilization.

The different views in psychodynamic theory as to how aggression originates make it difficult to present a unified concept of aggression. This is in contrast to approaches such as the GAM. At the same time, psychodynamic concepts have considerable potential in developing a consensual view of aggression. Although the situational emphasis in social learning theory offers a broader view than psychodynamic theory, at present it does not appear that there is a satisfactory comprehensive theory of aggression.

DOMESTIC VIOLENCE

We described domestic violence earlier as referring to the use of violence against one or more members of a domestic living situation. The questions here are how can we understand violence in a situation where the opposite is the norm, and how can we evaluate the possibility of such violence happening?

The GAM offers some possible answers in that some of the inputs have been shown to be significant risk factors. Examples are hostile attribution by the aggressor, male gender, which increases the potential for physical aggression, a belief in the supremacy of the father, and excessive use of alcohol and/or drugs. Structural factors would include provocation, an unpleasant environment, and excessive noise. The affect could be anger, the arousal could be to strike out, and the cognition could be a belief in the validity of violence as a solution. The outcome is likely to be an immediate appraisal of intentional justification in the use of violence.

Felson (2002) has provided valuable data facilitating an appropriate perspective on domestic violence. In terms of risk factors, most of the research has focused on men who are more likely than women to use physical aggression. The exception is parental aggression toward children (like in child abuse), which may be because women generally spend more time with children than men in domestic situations. In single-parent families, men are more likely to use violence. Men generally are more violent than women, and this appears to be true whether partners are heterosexual or homosexual. However, it would be inaccurate to classify domestic violence, particularly the use of physical force, as only a male, sexist issue. We are more aware of, and familiar with, male offenders, but there are violent women as well as it is discussed more fully by Chisholm and Magee in chapter 6 of this book. While domestic violence is relatively low compared to the overall level of violence in the world, there is no question that it is a serious problem for all societies. As we indicated earlier, incidence in the United States, where it is viewed as unacceptable and, in many instances, criminal, nonetheless remains markedly high (Tjaden & Theonnes, 2000).

Although earlier we introduced one working definition, it is important to keep in mind that the issue of definition has not been solved. The fact is that the study of domestic violence is complicated by the lack of a standardized functional definition of violence (White, Koss, & Kazdin, 2011). Two possible approaches tend to be used. One is considering the issue as a consensus based on extremes that hit a point of agreement by authorities that intervention is necessary to stop it. The other is that there is sufficient empirical evidence that harm is being inflicted. Both involve the perceptions of people other than the violent person and the victims. The two possibilities do not automatically coincide because harm can be inflicted prior to identifying extremes of the problem.

Felson has also pointed out the frequency of verbal disputes within families relative to physical violence, as well as many people having special inhibitions against physically assaulting a partner. It is both difficult to conclude when verbal disputes constitute abuse, as well as to know when they may turn into physical violence. Felson also brought attention to men being more prone to injure their partners and violence between partners often being reciprocal (Felson, 2002).

There is also a need for including and integrating individual and cultural differences. All societies create rules enabling their members to function in an orderly manner. These are *cultural* syndromes (Triandis, 1994) that are organizing principles forming a cultural logic of scripts, behaviors, values, and personalities defined by behavioral signatures (Mendoza-Denton & Mischel, 2007) that become individualized behaviors varying within a society. Cohen and Leung (2011) describe a model focusing on variations between and within cultural behaviors as well as individual differences. Although not explored in this model, there is the possibility of individual differences operating across cultures as well. This view suggests the existence of an *aggressive character*, possibly instinctual, linked to a genetic predisposition and honed by environmental developmental factors. The importance of childhood development affecting subsequent expressions of violence is consistent with clinical and research findings. Violent people are often products of dysfunctional, conflict-prone families, but that is not always the case, nor do all children growing up in such environments become violent.

Take, for instance, the case of a young Latino man living in a poor sector of one of the Caribbean islands who grabbed a young woman by her hair, pulling her head down while kicking her mouth and punching her on the head. He was furious in the delivery of his punishment while screaming at her "to shut up and stop divulging wrong information" about him and his family. Concerned neighbors gathered around and became alarmed when he grabbed a stone and was about to smash her head with it. They tried to reason with him from a distance because he was in the grip of a blind rage to which he felt justified. She was now bleeding profusely from her mouth and looked quite dizzy from the beating she was receiving on her head. "Compadre, that's enough!" they yelled urgently. "You are about to kill her and you don't want to end up disgracing yourself and your family." With his voice altered in a growl by his rage he responded that "she has done enough damage with her mouth" and that he'd had enough. Although some of the onlookers were saying openly that she finally got what she deserved, others, frightened by the feeling that the situation was getting out of hand, managed to stop him by telling him that he was going too far and that he is disgracing himself and bringing trouble to his family if he is put in prison.

There are many ways in which the preceding scenario can be explained. For example, there are very clear scripts that the perpetrator, the victim, and the onlookers in this scenario may have been following; perhaps the perpetrator and victim may come from a dysfunctional and conflict-prone family history; perhaps there may be something fundamentally wrong with the perpetrator and the victim; or perhaps the community culture is one of permissiveness toward violence, as suggested by Cohen and Leung's model. The fact that not everyone seems to have the same attitude about what was taking place between the perpetrator and the victim in this scenario makes the understanding of that and any violent incident more complex. That was also the finding in a study by Yoshioka, DiNoia, and Ullah (2001) where they found that attitudes toward violence vary not only between cultures but also within cultural groups. They found differences between East Asians and South Asians pertaining to acceptance of domestic violence, with South Asians found to be more likely to endorse male privilege pertaining to violence against women. Differences found within seemingly related cultural groups seem to be affected by variables such as gender, socioeconomic and immigration status, degree of acculturation, education, and strength of religious beliefs (WHO, 2005, 2013).

Flood and Pease (2009) identified three domains in reference to attitudes toward violence: (a) the perpetration of violence against women, (b) women's response to victimization, and (c) community and institutional responses toward violence. Attitudes such as those fostering beliefs in more traditional male roles have often been attributed as a main factor contributing to the perpetration of violence toward women. Related to that is the consistently positive relationship found between patriarchal beliefs and domestic violence (Anderson, Simpson-Taylor, & Hermann, 2004; Murnen, Wright, & Kaluzny, 2002). Women who adhere to traditional beliefs regarding gender roles have been found to be less likely to report instances of violence and more likely to assign blame toward themselves for having been assaulted (Frias & Angel, 2012; WHO, 2005), a behavior also found in university-educated women (Ewoldt, Monson, & Langhinrichsen-Rohling, 2000; Nayak, Byrne, Martin, & Abraham, 2003; Sakalh, 2001; Tang & Cheung, 1997).

We have previously noted the apparent relationship between certain types of narcissism and an inclination to violence that includes domestic violence. Different theories are offered as developmental explanations. Social learning theory targets parental overvaluation of children's achievements (Twenge, 2001). Psychodynamic theory targets parental rejection (Rizzuto et al., 2004). Empirical studies support both views (Thomaes & Bushman, 2011), so that more than style of parental malfunctioning contributes to the development of overly hostile children, which is not a surprise, given the complexity of the problem. The result is that it is difficult to provide an assessment that will accurately predict the probability of violence.

Domestic violence is a particular conundrum in understanding the cause of aggression because of the love-hate intermingling that can exist in a domestic situation. Felson has noted the high level of contact between family members that offers opportunities for conflict that are often more frequent than found in life outside the family, and these conflicts serve as origins for domestic violence.

Mikulincer and Shaver (2011) use attachment theory (Bowlby, 1988) to explore causes of domestic violence. Two different types of anger are suggested based on different attachment strategies. The attachment system is considered innate, psychobiological motivation for attachment to a protective other, usually a parent. Attachment security exists when others are available and supportive, but attachment anxiety or avoidance occurs when secure attachment is not achieved.

Anger in this context may appear as a reaction to separation, with two forms as possibilities, namely constructive and destructive. The latter can intensify into violence. Domestic violence is conceptualized as an angry protest against a partner's oppositional behavior. Anxious attachment correlates with violence, and in some instances, so does avoidant attachment (Melody, 2002). Thus insecure attachment can be added to some types of narcissism as risk factors for domestic violence.

The domestic situation offers the possibility of security and positive self-esteem for all involved, but when this is experienced as missing, the path is opened to violent reactions. The key issue is the *perception* of the person who becomes violent. Another person may or may not be provocative, but is perceived as instigating the violent reaction. Such a perception may result from character or environmental predispositions supporting a violent reaction based on imagined slights and injuries. Alcohol and drugs are also frequently contributing factors that cloud the discernment of motivation due to induced distorted perception and sense of reality.

Added to these factors are the interactions between the attacker and the rest of the household. Arriaga and Capezza (2005) suggest that if the commitment to the aggressor is strong enough, victims will downplay the aggression. This happens most often with verbal abuse, but also occurs in regard to physical abuse. Attachment insecurity both puts people at risk for abuse and abuse in turn can increase the insecurity. At the same time there are relationships that seem to be held together by reciprocal violence (Bartholomew & Allison, 2006), raising questions regarding the identity of perpetrators and victims in domestic situations.

The starting point appears to be a confluence of factors, some theorized based on experiential evidence, others having empirical support. All of the evidence suggests a multidimensional approach. An interesting model in this regard, in addition to the GAM, is the multivariate model proposed by Harway and O'Neill (1999). This theory focuses on men's violence against women and highlights seven risk factors, namely macrosocietal, relational, biological, psychological, socialization, psychosocial, and the interaction among these factors. Specifically, societal factors refer to institutional structures discriminating against women that are internalized by men. Relational factors involve partner interactions that provoke violence. Biological factors are physiological and genetic predispositions. Socialization refers to learned gender roles, and psychosocial refers to the interaction of psychological factors and socialization. All of the factors both overlap and interact, resulting in a complex set of risk factors which the authors have operationalized as testable hypotheses of specific variables. The result is 40 hypotheses with 60 independent variables involving 60 risk factors. This approach is certainly comprehensive but unwieldy in clinical situations.

Kurst-Swanger and Petcosky (2003) reviewed theoretical models and suggested four possibilities. The first, a psychopathological model, has two categories. The first category is a psychological emphasis on inherent personality characteristics that predispose a person to be violent. The second category, termed psychodynamic, emphasizes individual internal conflicts in managing aggression. These may be due to relational failures or interactive genetic and biological predispositions. Victim characteristics that could be perceived as inviting abuse are also considered, which fit with previously noted findings of reciprocal domestic violence. However, they comment that such theorizing has not developed sufficient research evidence and has not developed an accurate "abuser profile."

The second model is called sociopsychological. This broadens the explanation beyond the individual to family patterns and interaction with family members as well as the outside environment. The GAM fits in this category but is not discussed in this review. Nine other theories are evaluated of some relevance to the sociopsychological model. These are traumatic bonding, stress, social conflict, power, resource, exchange/social control, symbolic interactions, sociobiological/evolutionary, and social learning theories. These are considered an improvement over the psychopathological model, but still limited in explaining the totality of variables involved in family violence.

The third group is sociocultural models explaining domestic violence in terms of social structures that would foster such aggression. They include patriarchal/feminist, culture of violence, political economy, and environmental stress/strain theories. Although providing more understanding of the entangled interactions in violent homes they are better at explaining how violence occurs than what causes the occurrence in one home, but not in another.

The final grouping, favored by Kurst-Swanger and Petcosky, are multidimensional theories, namely general systems/global and ecological, which are thought to account for all variables involved. As noted earlier, comprehensiveness is of interest, but the complexity limits the operational value of such theories.

A Closer Look at the Perpetrator of Domestic Violence

In this book, we recognize that more attention and focus should be placed on understanding factors involved with the one individual who is producing most of the violence. As an attempt to shed some more light on the psychology of the perpetrator, some explanatory models of domestic violence have examined factors such as the role of empathy in violence. Schweinle and Ickes (2007) found that men who were prone toward domestic violence were more likely to maintain their bias toward overattributing criticism and rejection. The findings examined the cognitive mechanisms underlying abuse and revealed that men within the study were found to display contemptuous feelings and disengagement whenever their wives expressed emotions. That is, that they had trouble processing negative emotions and could not give themselves the opportunity to understand and appreciate what their wives were expressing. Similar findings have found that violent men exhibited poor empathetic accuracy when attempting to understand their female partner's thoughts and feelings (Clements, Holtzworth-Monroe, Schweinle, & Ickes 2007). Recent studies have also found that intimate partner abuse, emotion dysregulation, and the specific masculine norms of dominance, emotional control, and self-reliance were associated (Tager, Good, & Brammer, 2010).

Of significant interest on a clinical level, namely working with families in conflict in attempting to prevent domestic violence, are predictive indicators. The majority of evidence in this area has been gathered about men. A summary of the evidence suggests high risk factors are relationships with high conflict levels, emotional abuse and verbal aggression, male dominance and forced sex, limited communication and limited problem-solving skills, and a lack of emotional and material resources. In terms of the broader society, greater risk occurs where communities are characterized by poverty, low levels of trust, limited human support, and few sanctions for domestic violence, as well as gender and economic divisions and acceptance of violence as a solution to disputes. On an individual level, at least for men, risk factors include histories of aggression in the family of origin, and against female partners, personal psychopathology, histories of violence, substance abuse, low levels of academic achievement, low income, and traditional sex-role expectations with negative attitudes about women, as well as intolerance of others' views of the world. However, in utilizing the risk factors as predictive, it is suggested that the availability of protective factors, as personal and social support as well a sense of personal control and motivation to change, also need to be considered (White, Koss, & Kazdin, 2011).

Meichenbaum's (2007) list of predictive risk factors for domestic violence is also of interest in this regard because it is more detailed in identifying specific psychological characteristics that should be considered in the perpetrator as someone likely to have serious problems with impulse control, aggression and aggressive and disruptive behaviors, poor frustration tolerance, strong sense of entitlement, concrete and rigid cognitive process, problems with affect regulation (with strong tendency to anxiety/depressive mood, easily irritable), tendency to externalize and ruminate, feeling easily threatened and hurt, feeling insecure and argumentative, poor communication skills, struggling with strong sense of inadequacy, hold rigid suspiciousness about the motivation of others, and show tendency to develop dependent attachment pattern.

CONCLUSION

There is a great amount of information regarding domestic violence. Most of the theoretical conceptions are derived from research carried out by social scientists rather than clinicians. The results are multidimensional theories with so many variables that the risk factors are not of practical value in clinical situations. In addition, there is a lack of agreement as to the cause of domestic violence, other than more than one variable is involved. Also, White et al. (2011, pp. 297–299) have provided an excellent summary of the methodological issues affecting the research supporting the numerous theories. As for the infamous question posed by children in car trips (domestic violence research), "Are we there yet?" The answer is, "No."

Given that, where are we? The clinical issue is, what is it within the people involved that causes them to act in a violent way in domestic situations? Consider the following sequence: A man arrives home after a day of work. His wife asks, "What did *you do* today?" In his perception her manner implies that he did very little of value, which may or may not have been her intention. Regardless, he experiences the question as a provocation, but what causes him to react to that with violence, and if she was trying to be provocative, what was the cause of that action? We can supply various answers, using at least some of the risk factors cited in the literature. For example, he comes from an environment in which the male is valued as a worker, regardless of his degree of success, so he feels a lack of regard on her part. Understandable, but what leads to violence as the solution? Let us also suppose that he comes from a dysfunctional family where he was exposed to violent solutions to disputes, so he is accustomed to that method. Familiar certainly, but not every person with such exposure chooses it. Nor does every wife disillusioned with her husband decide to be provocative, if that was the case.

We remain with the basic question of what causes people to be violent. The risk factors are triggers that have been uncovered to some extent, and which get pulled in some situations. Some of these factors, as a history of violence, are useful in clinical situations, but often to limit further damage. Earlier intervention would be more useful, but the etiology of individual violence remains in the hypothetical realm with limited empirical support. The latter is not for lack of trying, but it is a difficult question to both pose and answer in a research format. Clinical impressions are the most frequent source for making judgments in situations of potential violence. They have a validity based on being in "real time," but also are subject to individual impressions, so theoretical constructions are useful accompaniments, along with empirical support where available.

Also at present, identification of risk factors via research appears to be aimed primarily at influencing policy, as gun control and media content, regarding domestic violence. Such an approach is certainly useful and valuable, but the social environment is only part of the solution and is open to subversion. Clearly, if a person wishes to be violent, there is always a way to display this in domestic situations. There is a need for the refinement of risk factors to fit clinical situations where people directly trying to prevent an incident of domestic violence have limited time and methods to use diagnostic signs. Even without knowing the cause of predispositions for violence in two people in a domestic argument, it would be very helpful to have practical methods of risk assessment. Practical questions for the clinician are: how angry are these people, and how will they display their anger? Theory and research that moves in this practical direction is needed. We have some of it that can be taken from the broader policy research, but we need more of the type that will be of immediate help "in the situation."

Violence escalates, and the home is often the crucible for it. The issues of domestic violence are not only the direct harm that is experienced by those who are attacked, but also the developmental examples of violence as an acceptable form of problem solving. The probability of a "spread effect" makes it very important to understand the probable causes of such violence as well as providing interventions to decrease it significantly. This book is offered in the spirit of continuing to move forward to ameliorate the appalling problem of domestic violence.

DISCUSSION QUESTIONS

1. How does development influence aggressors' internalization of experiences? How is this particularly shaped by early environment—specifically childhood relationships?
2. How might excitation theory overlap with psychodynamic theory?
3. Distinguish between person and situation factors. In what way does each influence aggression?
4. What are some of the problems inherent in the GAM model? Do any other models or theories have strengths where the GAM exhibits potential weaknesses?
5. Aggression is a global, not local, phenomenon. What does this tell us about the origins, cause, and trajectory of aggressive impulses and violent behavior?
6. How does narcissism influence a person's proneness toward aggression, in particular its expression as domestic violence?
7. Following the different models discussed in this chapter, how do you explain domestic violence among members of the LGBT?

REFERENCES

Ainsworth, M. (1982). Attachment: Retrospective and prospective. In C. M. Parkes & J. Stevenson-Hinde (Eds.), *The place of attachment in human behavior* (pp. 3–30). New York: Basic Books.

Andersen, C. A., & Bushman, B. I. (2002). Human aggression. *Annual Review of Psychology, 53*, 27–51.

Anderson, V. N., Simpson-Taylor, D., & Hermann, D. J. (2004). Gender, age, and rape supportive rules. *Sex Roles: A Journal of Research, 50*, 77–90.

Arriaga, B., & Capezza, N. M. (2005). Targets of partner violence: The importance of understanding coping strategies. *Journal of Interpersonal Violence, 20*, 89–99.

Bandura, A. (2001). Social cognitive theory: An agentic perspective. *Annual Review of Psychology, 52*, 1–20.

Bartholomew, K., & Allison, C. J. (2006). An attachment perspective on abusive dynamics in intimate relationships. In M. Mikulincer & G. S. Goodman (Eds.), *Dynamics of romantic love* (pp. 102–127). New York: The Guilford Press.

Baumeister, R. F. (2005). *The cultural animal. Human nature, meaning, and social life*. New York: Oxford University Press.

Berkowitz, L. (1993). *Aggression: Its causes, consequences, and control*. Philadelphia: Temple University Press.

Berkowitz, L. (1990). On the formation and regulation of anger and aggression: A cognitive neoassocianistic analysis. *American Psychologist, 45*, 491–503.

Blanck, G., & Blanck, R. (1994). *Ego psychology: Theory and practice* (2nd ed.). New York: Columbia University Press.

Bowlby, J. (1988). *A secure base: Clinical applications of attachment theory.* London: Routledge.

Bowlby, J. (1969). *Attachment and loss (Vol. 1)*. New York: Basic Books.

Bowlby, J. (1973). *Attachment and loss (Vol. 2)*. New York: Basic Books.

Bowlby, J. (1980). *Attachment and loss (Vol. 3)*. New York: Basic Books.

Child Welfare Information Gateway (2009). Domestic violence and the child welfare system Retrieved from http://www.childwelfare.gov/pubs/factsheets/domesticviolence.cfm.

Clements, K., Holtzworth-Monroe, A., Schweinle, W., & Ickes, W. (2007). Empathic accuracy of intimate partners in violent versus nonviolent relationships. *Personal Relationships, 14*, 369–388.

Cohen, G., & Leung, A. K.-y. (2011). Violence and character: A CuPS (culture x person x situation) perspective. In P. R. Shaver & M. Mikulincer (Eds.), *Human aggression and violence: Causes, manifestations, and consequences* (pp. 187–200). Washington, DC: American Psychological Association.

DeWall, C. N., & Anderson, C. A. (2011). The general aggression model. In P. R. Shaver & M. Mikulincer (Eds.), *Human aggression and violence: Causes, manifestations, and consequences* (pp. 15–33). Washington, DC: American Psychological Association.

Dodge, K. (2011). Social information processing patterns as mediators of the interaction between genetic factors and life experiences in the development of aggressive behavior. In P. R. Shaver & M. Mikulincer (Eds.), *Human aggression: Causes, manifestations, and consequences* (pp.165–185). Washington, DC: American Psychological Association.

Ewoldt, C. A., Monson, C. M., & Langhinrichsen-Rohling, J. (2000). Attributions about rape in a continuum of dissolving marital relationships. *Journal of Interpersonal Violence, 15* 1175–1182.

Fairbairn, W. R. D. (1963). Synopsis of an object-relations theory of the personality. *International Journal of Psychoanalysis, 44,* 224–225.

Felson, R. D. (2002). *Violence and gender reexamined.* Washington, DC: American Psychological Association.

Flood, M., & Pease, B. (2009). Factors influencing attitudes towards violence against women. *Trauma, Violence & Abuse, 10*, 125–142.

Freud, S. (1920). Beyond the pleasure principle. *Standard Edition, 18*, 1–64.

Frias, S. M., & Angel, R. J. (2012). Beyond Borders: Comparative quantitative research on partner violence in the United States and Mexico. *Violence Against Women, 18*, 5–29.

Gilbert, L., El-Bassel, N., Wu, E., & Chang, M. (2007). Intimate partner violence and HIV risks: A longitudinal study of men on methadone. *Journal of Urban Health, 84*(5), 667–680.

Greenberg, J. R., & Mitchell, S. A. (1983). *Object relations in psychoanalytic theory.* Cambridge: Harvard University Press.

Guntrip, H. (1969). *Schizoid phenomena, object relations and the self.* New York: International Universities Press.

Harway, M., & O'Neil, J. M. (1999) (Eds.). *What causes men's violence against women?* Thousand Oaks, CA: Sage.

Herron, W. G. (1999). *Narcissism and the relational world.* Lanham, MD: University Press of America.

Huesmann, L. R. (1988). An information-processing model for the development of aggression. *Aggressive Behavior, 14*, 13–24.

Kernberg, O. F. (1992). *Aggression in personality disorders and perversions.* New Haven, CT: Yale University Press.

Kurst-Swanger, K., & Petcosky, J. (2003). *Violence in the home: Multidisciplinary perspectives.* New York: Oxford University Press.

Lichtenberg, J. D. (1991). *Psychoanalysis and infant research.* Hillsdale, NJ: The Analytic Press.

Lichtenberg, J. D., Lachmann, F. M., & Fossaghe, J. L. (2011). *Psychoanalysis and motivational systems. A new look.* New York: Routledge.

Mahler, M. S. (1979). *Selected papers of Margaret S. Mahler* (Vols. 1–2). New York: Jason Aronson.
Mendoza-Denton, R., & Mischel, W. (2007). Integrating systems approaches to culture and personality. In S. Kitayama & D. Cohen (Eds.), *Handbook of cultural psychology* (pp. 175–195). New York: The Guilford Press.
Meichenbaum, D. (2007). Family violence: Treatment of perpetrators and victims. Retrieved from www.melissainstititute.org.
Mikulincer, M., & Shaver, P. R. (2011). Attachment, anger, and aggression. In P. R. Shaver (Eds.), *Human aggression and violence: Causes, manifestations, and consequences* (pp. 241–257). Washington, DC: American Psychological Association.
Melody, J. R. (2002). *Violent attachments*. Northvale, NJ: Jason Aronson, Inc.
Mitchell, S. A. (1993). Aggression and the endangered self. *Psychoanalytic Quarterly, 62*, 351–382.
Moore, B. E., & Fine, B. D. (Eds.). (1990). *Psychoanalytic terms and concepts.* New Haven, CT: Yale University Press.
Murnen, S. K., Wright, C., & Kaluzny, G. (2002). If "boys will be boys," then girls will be victims? A meta-analytic review of the research that relates masculine ideology to sexual aggression. *Sex Roles, 46*, 359–375.
Nayak, M. B., Byrne, C. A., Martin, M. K., & Abraham, A. G. (2003). Attitudes towards violence against women: A cross-nation study. *Sex Roles, 49*, 333–342.
Parens, H. (1979). *The development of aggression in early childhood.* Northvale, NJ: Jason Aronson.
Pine, F. (2005). Theories of motivation in psychoanalysis. In E. S. Person, A. M. Cooper, & G. O. Gabbard (Eds.), *Textbook of psychoanalysis* (pp. 3–20). Arlington, VA: American Psychiatric Publishing.
Rhee, S. H., & Waldman, T. D. (2011). Genetic and environmental influences on aggression. In P. R. Shaver & M. Mikulincer (Eds.), *Human aggression and violence: Causes, manifestations, and consequences* (pp. 143–163). Washington, DC: American Psychological Association.
Rizzuto, A. M., Meissner, W. W., & Buie, D. H. (2004). *The dynamics of human aggression: Theoretical foundations, clinical applications.* New York: Brunner-Routledge.
Sakalh, N. (2001). Beliefs about wife beating among Turkish college students: The effects of patriarchy, sexism, and sex differences. *Sex Roles, 44*, 599–610.
Schweinle, W., & Ickes, W. (2007). The role of men's critical/rejecting over-attribution bias, affect and attentional disengagement in marital aggression. *Journal of Social and Clinical Psychology, 26*, 173–198.
Shaver, P. R., & Mikulincer, M. (2011). Introduction. In P. R. Shaver & M. Mikulincer, (Eds.), *Human aggression and violence: Causes, manifestations, and consequences* (pp. 5–11). Washington, DC: American Psychological Association.
Shaver, P. R., & Mikulincer, M. (Eds.) (2011), *Human aggression and violence: Causes, manifestations, and consequences* (pp. 203–219). Washington, DC: American Psychological Association.
Slotter, E. B., & Finkel, E. J. (2011). I3 Theory: Instigating, impelling, and inhibiting factors in aggression. In P. R. Shaver & M. Mikulincer (Eds.), *Human aggression and violence: Causes, manifestations, and consequences* (pp. 35–52). Washington, DC: American Psychological Association.
Sullivan, H. S. (1953). *The interpersonal theory of psychiatry*. New York: W.W. Norton & Company, Inc.
Tager, D., Good, G. E., & Brammer, S. (2010). Walking over 'em: An exploration of relations between emotion dysregulation, masculine norms and intimate partner abuse in a clinical sample of men. *Psychology of Men and Masculinity, 11*, 233–239.
Tang, C. S.-K., & Cheung, F. M.-C. (1997). Effects of gender and profession type on definitions of violence against women in Hong-Kong. *Sex Roles, 36,* 837–849.
Tedeschi, J. T., & Felson, R. B. (1994). *Violence, aggression, and coercive actions.* Washington, DC: American Psychological Association.

Thomaes, S., & Bushman, B. J. (2011). Mirror, mirror, on the wall, who's the most aggressive of them all? Narcissism, self-esteem, and aggression. In P. R. Shaver & M. Mikulincer (Eds.), *Human aggression and violence: Causes, manifestations, and consequences* (pp. 203–219). Washington, DC : American Psychological Association.

Tjaden, P., & Thoennes, N. (2000). *Prevalence, incidence, and consequences of violence against women: Findings from the National Violence Against Women Survey.* Washington, DC: National Institute of Justice.

Triandis, H. C. (1994). *Culture and social behavior.* New York: McGraw-Hill.

Twenge, J. M. (2001). Changes in women's assertiveness in response to status and roles: A cross-temporal meta-analysis, 1931–1993. *Journal of Personality and Social Psychology, 81*, 133–145.

Twenge, J. M. (2006). *Generation me: Why today's young Americans are more confident, assertive, entitled—and more miserable than ever before.* New York: Free Press.

Wadhwa, P. D., Entinger, S., Buss, C., & Lu, M. C. (2011). The contribution of maternal stress to preterm birth: Issues and considerations. *Clinical Perinatology, 2011, 39*, 351–384.

White, J., Koss, M. P., & Kazdin, A. E. (Eds.) (2011). *Violence against women and children: Mapping the terrain* (Vol. 1) (pp. 297–299). Washington, DC: American Psychological Association.

Whitfield, C. L., Anda, R. F., Dube, S. R., & Felitti, V. J. (2003). Violent childhood experiences and the risk of intimate partner violence in adults. *Journal of Interpersonal Violence, 18,* 166–185.

World Health Organization (2005). Summary Report: Multi-country Study on Women's Health and Domestic Violence Against Women. Initial results on prevalence, health outcomes and women's responses. Geneva, World Health Organization.

World Health Organization (2013). Global and regional estimates of violence against women: Prevalence and health effects of intimate partner violence and non-partner sexual violence. www.who.int/reproductivehealth.

Winnicott, C., Shepard, R., & Davis, M. (Eds.) (1984). *Deprivation and development.* London: Tavistock.

Winnicott, D. W. (1974). *The maturational processes and the facilitating environment.* New York: International University Press, Inc.

Yoshioka, M. R., DiNoia, J., & Ullah, K. (2001). Attitudes toward marital violence: An examination of four Asian communities. *Violence Against Women, 7*, 900–926.

Zillmann, D. (1983). Arousal and aggression. In R. G. Green & E. Donnerstein (Eds.), *Aggression: Theoretical and empirical reviews* (Vol. I) (pp. 75–102). New York: Academic Press.

Chapter Four

On the Clinical Applications of the General Aggression Model to Understanding Domestic Violence

Wayne Warburton and Craig A. Anderson

> "It just seems to happen the same way over and over. It usually happens on the same days of the week and follows the same pattern. He will come home drunk and I will say something and he will get angry and things escalate from there. Before you know it, he has hit me and I am calling the police. I know if I don't respond a certain way or just walk away, things will be different, but he pushes my buttons and then I push his and it all seems so inevitable, so hard to stop the pattern from repeating. . . ."—Domestic violence victim AB during counseling.

A key aim of this book is to shed light on domestic violence (DV) by examining ways that relevant models of aggression and violence can help us to understand this phenomenon. Two key approaches have been targeted—the psychodynamic perspective, which emphasizes the drive-related and motivational aspects of aggressive behavior (see chapter 5), and the social cognitive approach, which emphasizes the activation of learned patterns of aggressive behavior when specific environmental triggers are present. In terms of the latter, the most current and most comprehensive model is the General Aggression Model (GAM) by Anderson and Bushman (2002a), the focus of this chapter.

The GAM, although just over a decade old, is now supported by a large body of evidence suggesting it can explain a wide range of aggressive phenomena (for reviews, see Anderson & Barlett, 2016; Anderson & Groves, 2013; DeWall & Anderson, 2011), as well as a wide range of violent behaviors (DeWall, Anderson, & Bushman, 2011; Gilbert & Daffern, 2011).

More importantly, the GAM appears to have utility in both explaining domestic violence and formulating practical remedies for it. For example, when applied to individual instances of DV, the GAM would emphasize factors within the perpetrator that predisposes him or her to aggression, triggers and cues in the environment that would activate existing patterns of violent behavior, and factors that would increase the likelihood of aggression in that instance (e.g., high levels of emotional arousal and the disinhibiting role of alcohol).

The key focus within this chapter will be the clinical applications of the GAM to domestic violence. In it, we will describe theories of neural connectivity and behavior that underpin the GAM and theories of aggression that have predated and been incorporated into the GAM. The GAM itself will be described in detail, along with insights into how the GAM can assist practitioners to understand and respond to instances of domestic violence. Before then, however, we need to be clear about how aggression, violence, and domestic violence will be defined in this chapter.

DEFINING AGGRESSION AND VIOLENCE

Aggression

Producing a definition of aggression that captures most behaviors considered as instances of aggression, that excludes behaviors which should not be, and that is also parsimonious, is a very difficult task (Baron & Richardson, 1994; Berkowitz, 1993; Geen, 2001; Krahe, 2013). However, at its simplest level, aggression involves behaviors intended to hurt others. To this end, we will use the definition formulated by Anderson and Bushman (2002a) that aggression is "any behavior directed toward another individual that is carried out with the proximate (immediate) intent to cause harm" and further specify that "the perpetrator must believe that the behavior will harm the target, and that the target is motivated to avoid the behavior" (p. 28). The latter is to rule out consensual harm, such as the hurt caused by dentistry.

A key point is that aggression is behavior, not a feeling such as anger nor a hostile mind-set. Aggression is an act (Warburton, 2013; Warburton & Anderson, 2015). Also key is that the nature of the harm is not restricted to physically hurting another (*physical aggression*), but may also involve other modes of harm such as hurting another with words (*verbal aggression*), hurting a person's relationships (*relational aggression*), or hurting a person from a distance (*indirect aggression*) (Warburton, 2013; Warburton & Anderson, 2015). This seems to accord better with more recent conceptualizations of domestic violence that emphasize multiple forms of harm to the victim, not just physical violence. A third key point is that the act need not succeed in order to be considered aggression; shooting a gun at someone with the intent to kill is an act of aggression, even if the shot misses the target.

When conceptualizing aggression it is also important to distinguish the function of the aggression (Warburton & Anderson, 2015). One way to do this is to locate aggressive acts on three dimensions—the "degree to which the goal is to harm the victim versus benefit the perpetrator; the level of hostile or agitated emotion that is present; and the degree to which the aggressive act was thought-through" (Warburton & Anderson, 2015, in press; see also Anderson & Huesmann, 2003; Bushman & Anderson, 2001). Some aggressive acts are carried out simply to benefit the perpetrator (for example, a violent robbery), whereas others are motivated primarily by a desire to hurt the victim (for example, beating an unfaithful partner). Aggression may be fueled by high levels of anger and arousal (such as DV that occurs during a fight) or may be cold and instrumental (enacted in the absence of strong emotion). Sometimes aggressive responses are automatic and reflexive (such as instinctively responding with aggression when one's children are threatened), but aggression can also be planned and thought through (such as carefully planning revenge against a violent partner).

Violence

Unfortunately, the term aggression is often, and incorrectly, used interchangeably with the term violence, leading to considerable confusion among researchers, public policy makers, and the general public (Warburton & Anderson, 2015, in press). However, whereas aggression refers to a wide group of acts where the levels of harm can range from mild to extreme, the term violence refers only to a smaller subset of aggressive behaviors that are intended to cause harm extreme enough to require medical/therapeutic attention or to cause death (Anderson & Bushman, 2002a; Warburton & Anderson, 2015, in press). Many psychologists extend this definition to include acts that can cause severe emotional harm (Warburton & Anderson, 2015, in press), a factor relevant to recent formulations of domestic violence. Thus, all violent behavior is aggression, but most aggression is not violence. In the domestic situation the same principles apply: mild and mild-moderate acts of aggression would be seen as more within the normal range of behaviors between family members, but aggressive acts that cause moderate to extreme hurt/harm would be seen as within the spectrum of violence.

Domestic Violence

We will not give a highly detailed definition of domestic violence here—various approaches and definitions are provided elsewhere in this book—but instead merely highlight that, for the purposes of this chapter, domestic violence includes behaviors that meet the criteria for violence noted above, and which form an ongoing pattern of abuse to the victim. The perpetrators may be male or female, and the same principles apply to both heterosexual and homosexual intimate relationships.

Also relevant to our definition of domestic violence is the definition of intimate partner violence (IPV). Definitions and formulations of IPV have been also well covered earlier in this book, but for the purposes of this chapter we take particular note of the four World Health Organization (WHO, 2010) categories of IPV. Physical violence includes all undesired physical contact (e.g., pushing, hitting, hair pulling, beating, burning). Sexual violence refers to any coerced sexually related act (e.g., taking revealing photographs or sexual intercourse). Psychological abuse represents threats to harm the victim, take away children, intimidation (e.g., destroying property), insults, and humiliation. Finally, controlling behaviors (social abuse) include restricting access to food, shelter, financial resources, friends or family, employment, and education. Other controlling behaviors include the restriction of liberty and independence and the monitoring of the victim's movements. Thus we define IPV as an aggressive behavior or a threatened aggressive behavior, to a current or former intimate partner, that has the goal of inflicting severe physical, sexual, psychological, or social harm. Because this chapter will focus on IPV exemplars of DV, we will use the term *domestic violence* to describe IPV that occurs repeatedly across time.

BASIC PRINCIPLES THAT UNDERLIE THE GAM

Because the GAM is a bio-social cognitive theory of aggression that incorporates an information-processing substrate, it is important here to note the basic principles of neural connectivity that underlie this approach, as well as earlier theories of aggression that have been incorporated into the GAM.

The key assumption is that human beings learn through creating a set of associations in their neural network, as suggested by Collins and Loftus (1975). When a new perceptual experience occurs, or a new concept is experienced, it is assumed that a node of specific neurons is set aside in the brain to recognize that thing/concept and to fire when it is experienced again. When two things are experienced together, the two nodes are not only activated at the same time; they start to become *neurally connected.* The more often these two things are activated together, the stronger this neural connection becomes, with some nodes becoming strongly associated (for example, the concepts of blood and red). Further, if two nodes develop a significant connection, activating one will begin to activate the other through *spreading activation* (Collins & Loftus, 1975). In this way, activating one concept (such as blood) will also start the process of activating neurally linked concepts (such as red)—thus, the adage that "neurons that fire together, wire together."

Crucially, from the toddler years on, patterns of connections develop from experience. These can involve multiple nodes arranged into a complex network of stable links called *knowledge structures*, some of which become discrete entities known as *schemas*. Schemas contain strongly linked thoughts, feelings, concepts, and memories related to specific aspects of experience that have in the past occurred regularly and played out similarly. *Schemas* typically include knowledge about a particular facet of experience, related attitudes, beliefs, expectations, and memories, links to typical feelings, and *scripts* for how to behave. Because a schema is a discrete entity, activating one component will activate or partially activate (prime) the whole schema, and the schema will then impact the way the holder perceives the world, as well as his or her expectations and behavior. For example, a child may have a schema about his or her bedtime routine that includes the typical script of events (after dinner, Mother asks me to brush my teeth and go to the toilet, and then Dad takes me into my room, tucks me into bed, and takes a book off the shelf. He starts to read and I start to feel sleepy). It will also include other information about the routine (I will be in my pajamas; it may or may not be dark, etc.), as well as links to specific memories (Dad read, *The Tiger Who Came to Tea* two nights ago), past feelings (secure, warm, sleepy, happy), beliefs and expectations (this will happen every night that Dad is home) and action tendencies (I go straight to the bathroom when asked and brush my teeth, etc.). When activated by a trigger such as Mother saying "bed time," the script will remind the child of what normally happens next and what can be expected and will guide their behavior.

Once knowledge structures such as scripts, schemas, and cognitive biases become well established, they can be both helpful and unhelpful. Holders may be spared the need to learn information over and over again (such as where items are usually located at the local supermarket), and can follow a script for behavior automatically or with minimal conscious thought, thus freeing up memory and cognitive capacity for other tasks. However, if the patterns of behavior linked with these knowledge structures are maladaptive, they can often continue unchallenged because the impact of activated knowledge structures on behavior is often automatic and non-conscious.

Conceptualizing human response in terms of the activity of a person's associative neural network allows researchers to theorize about how people acquire a repertoire of aggressive or violent behaviors through actual or vicarious learned experience. They may associate aggressive responses to particular cues in the environment through *associative learning*, learn that aggressive behavior is rewarded more than it is punished through *instrumental conditioning* (Eron, Walder, & Lefkowitz, 1971), or simply copy the behavior of others (Bandura, 1973, 1983; Bandura, Ross, & Ross, 1961,

1963). Environmental cues may trigger aggression-related concepts, schemas, or scripts for behavior, and, if frequently enacted, aggressive responses included within knowledge structures may operate automatically and without the holder being aware of what has driven that response.

THEORIES OF AGGRESSION THAT UNDERLIE THE GAM

Early theories of aggression reflected current knowledge about behavior acquisition. The frustration-aggression hypothesis of Dollard, Doob, Miller, Mowrer, and Sears (1939) was the first systematic theory of aggressive behavior and, with roots in psychoanalysis, emphasized the frustration felt when people are thwarted from attaining goals. It was theorized initially that all aggression stems from the anger produced when one is frustrated, but because it became quickly clear that not all aggression can be traced back to anger or to frustration, the formulation was later revised to allow for alternate responses to frustration.

In the 1950s and 1960s, when much research was taking place on associative and instrumental conditioning, it was demonstrated that these learning principles applied to the acquisition of aggressive behaviors as well (Eron et al., 1971). Further, in the 1960s it became clear that people could also learn aggressive behavior through simply observing the behavior of aggressive models. Such behaviors are particularly likely to be imitated if the models are heroic, admired, high status, attractive, similar to the observer, and are rewarded for their aggressive behavior (see Bandura, 1973, 1983; Bandura et al. 1961; 1963).

Another approach emerged in the late 1970s. It had become known that the cognitive labels people give to emotions and states of physiological arousal are crucial in determining their behavior (e.g., Schachter & Singer, 1962). Building on these findings, Zillmann (1979) proposed an Excitation Transfer theory of aggression. Zillmann noted that physiological arousal is slow to dissipate and theorized that when two arousing events are separated by a short period of time, arousal from the first event will be added to arousal from the second. Crucially, there may be a misattribution whereby the cause of the second event is assumed to be responsible for all of the arousal. So, for example, if a person has sex (or takes a bike ride, or runs up a flight of stairs) and shortly afterward has a conflict with their partner, the person may become disproportionately angry, assuming that their strong feelings and high levels of physiological arousal are all due to the argument. Such anger, along with the misattribution for what caused the anger, may last long after the physiological arousal itself has dissipated.

In the 1980s, with the cognitive revolution and bourgeoning knowledge about neural networks and cognitive processes, some earlier models were revised. Bandura's theory of social learning was extended to become Social Cognitive theory (Bandura, 1986) and Berkowitz (1989, 1990, 1993) reformulated the frustration-aggression hypothesis of Dollard et al. (1939) into the Cognitive Neo-Association Theory (CNT).

In Berkowitz's formulation, aversive events such as frustrations, provocations, or unpleasant physical environments (e.g., hot temperatures, foul odors) produce negative affect, which is neurally linked to various thoughts, feelings, and behavioral tendencies that are themselves linked to fight and flight tendencies. One response type (fight or flight) will become more activated than the other, depending on the characteristics of the person and the specifics of the situation. Dominant fight responses are linked with anger and are thus more likely to elicit aggression. Although aggression in this formulation can always be traced back to an increase in negative feelings/affect, the CNT allows for higher order processes such as making attributions about another's motives or thinking through the consequences of an aggressive response. Such processes may cause a person to moderate an initial aggressive impulse.

Also in the 1980s, some scholars started to conceptualize the acquisition of social behavior in terms of computer-like processes—inputs, outputs, and information processing. From this endeavor came two influential approaches to understanding aggression—Script Theory from Huesmann (1988, 1998) and the Social Information Processing Model of Crick and Dodge (1994, 1996).

Huesmann's Script Theory of Aggression (based in part on Abelson's work on scripts, see Schank & Abelson, 1977) emphasizes the learning of behavioral scripts (conceptualized as similar to the sorts of scripts an actor might use in playing a role), which might be acquired through direct experience or through vicariously seeing such scripts enacted either in the mass media or in real life. Once encoded in semantic memory, scripts define particular situations and provide a guide for how to behave in them. Script Theory assumes a progression of steps that would typically occur. When faced with a particular situation the person would retrieve a script relevant to that situation from memory, assess the appropriateness or likely outcome of enacting the script (if the script is unacceptable the person would retrieve further scripts until an acceptable script is retrieved), and once a script is judged appropriate, behave in accordance with that script. When people respond to conflict by habitually retrieving and acting on aggressive scripts for behavior, these scripts may become chronically accessible (more easily brought to mind). Aggressive responses to certain triggers may then become more and more automatic, and generalize to a wider and wider range of situations.

Another tenet of Script Theory is that beliefs which normalize and approve the use of aggressive behavior decrease resistance to the enactment of aggressive scripts and increase the likelihood that an aggressive script will be chosen, enacted, repeated, and, eventually, become chronically accessible. In a sense, beliefs about the appropriateness and the likely outcomes of scripts become decision rules that help determine whether a particular script will be enacted or rejected. And of course, with practice these "decisions" tend to become automatized, requiring little or no thought, and little or no awareness by the person that a decision has been made.

Social Information Processing (SIP) theory emphasizes the way people perceive the behavior of others and make attributions about their motives. Like Script Theory, it posits a progression of steps in processing and interpreting cues from the environment. A key construct in SIP theory is the hostile attributional bias—a tendency to interpret ambiguous events (such as being bumped in a corridor) as being motivated by hostile intent.

CNT, SIP, and Script Theory have a number of common elements.

- They are based on neural processing of information;
- They assume that aggressive patterns of behavior can be acquired through associative conditioning, instrumental conditioning, and social learning;
- They emphasize the role of triggers and cues in the environment that then activate learned patterns of aggressive behavior that are stored in a person's neural network, often in larger knowledge structures such as schemas and scripts;
- They acknowledge that each person holds a different set of such knowledge structures;
- Evaluations take place during appraisal processes. For example, if people have the time and mental resources they will typically make decisions as to whether aggressive behavior is appropriate in the situation (i.e., normative) and will achieve the desired outcome. They will likely also evaluate whether they have the self-efficacy to aggress successfully (e.g., Boxer & Dubow, 2001);
- Many of these processes can become so over-learned that they become automatic, and therefore somewhat difficult to disrupt or stop.

THE GENERAL AGGRESSION MODEL

The General Aggression Model (GAM; Anderson & Bushman, 2002a) incorporates key elements from these recent social cognitive and information processing approaches, along with elements of learning theories and arousal-based theories. It assumes the neural substrate already noted, and incorporates findings from a wide range of psychology disciplines (Warburton & Anderson, 2015, in press).

The core of the model explains the psychological processes involved in a single instance of aggressive behavior. Such an instance involves a person, with all of his or her characteristics (including biological attributes, genetic predispositions, personality, attitudes, beliefs and learned behavioral scripts), responding to an environmental trigger such as a provocation, an aversive event, or an aggression-related cue (see figure 4.1). The person factors, together, impact the degree to which the person is likely to respond to particular triggers with aggression.

The environmental trigger impacts the person's current internal state in three key areas: their activated cognitions (e.g., knowledge structures), their current affective (emotional) state, and their level of physiological arousal. All three areas interact, as well as exerting a direct effect on the individual. If the activated cognitions include beliefs, and attitudes approving aggression, hostile biases, scripts that involve aggressive behavior, or other concepts/ideas/tendencies that facilitate an aggressive response, then the likelihood of

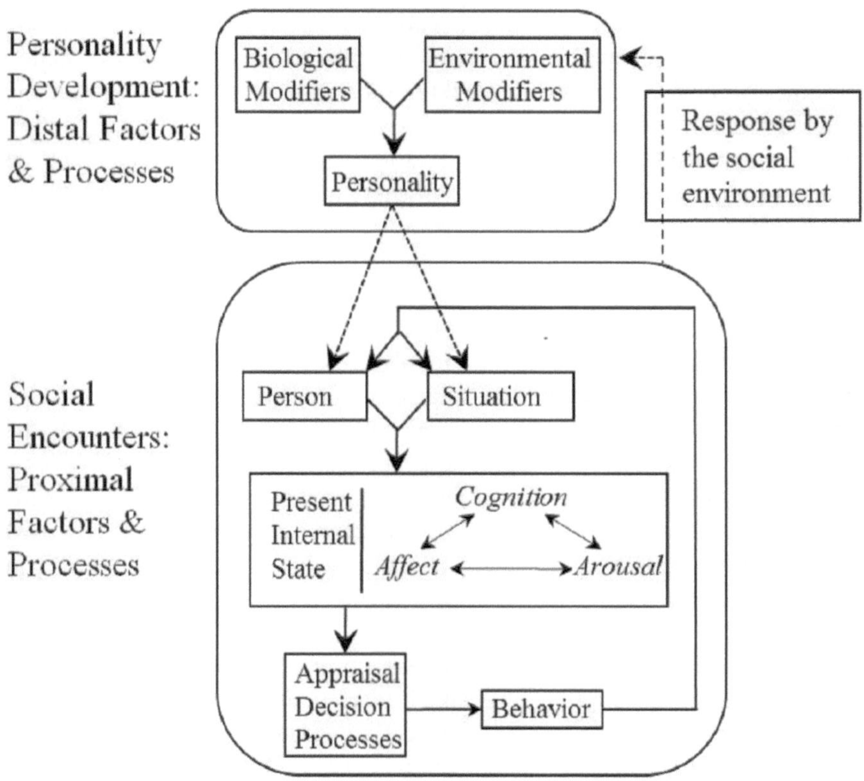

Figure 4.1. General Aggression Model Created by the authors

aggressive response is increased. The same is true when hostile emotions, such as anger, are active. Increases in physiological arousal do not alone increase the likelihood of aggression; they increase the likelihood that the person will act on an impulse or enact a dominant action tendency. However, if a person is feeling angry and inclined to aggress, and is also physiologically aroused, this arousal will increase the likelihood that the person will act on that inclination rather than think through the consequences of his or her actions and thus moderate his or her behavior. Of course, if nonaggressive cognitions and emotions are activated, then the likelihood of aggressive action declines.

During the appraisal stage, an immediate response to the situational trigger is formulated, based on the influence of the activated cognitions and feelings. This immediate response may be to aggress. However, other factors may come into play. If the person is highly stressed or aroused, needs to act quickly, does not have the cognitive resources to think through action or is not much concerned about the impact of that response, he or she may respond aggressively, and, in such a case, impulsively. However, if the person has the time and psychological resources to do so, and the immediate scripted response is deemed likely to have negative consequences, then the person would engage in reappraisal processes whereby alternate courses of action are quickly considered and discarded until a suitable response is chosen and enacted. This may or may not be aggressive. Often (but not always), higher levels of appraisal reduce the likelihood that an aggressive impulse will be acted on. This is one point in the cycle where impulse control and cognitive capacity play a large role.

In any case, it is important to note that each such instance of social behavior is also a learning experience. That is, whatever behavior is enacted feeds back into the current situation, influences what the other person does, and has consequences for everyone involved. What is learned from the encounter is accommodated and assimilated into and with existing knowledge structures, thus impacting attitudes and beliefs, and becoming part of the person's psychological makeup. These changes impact subsequent events because they impact the "person" factors that increase or decrease the likelihood of responding to certain triggers with aggression. In this way, the GAM can explain the long-term acquisition of aggressive patterns of behavior. In short, this is how experience produces fairly stable long-term changes in personality.

Although the GAM looks deceptively simple as a diagram, the model includes detailed assumptions that take into account a wide range of within-person factors, possible triggers for aggression, known internal psychological processes, and the means by which behavior is reinforced and learned. These latter processes include many that have been described earlier in previous aggression models—the acquisition of schemas, scripts, and learned behaviors through changes to a person's neural network.

In the following section we will examine factors that fall within each part of the GAM and note known or potential links with domestic violence.

DOMESTIC VIOLENCE THROUGH THE LENS OF THE GAM

Person Factors

There are hundreds of possible within-person factors that may contribute to domestic violence. Although a small number of key variables are noted here, clinicians who use the GAM to inform their understanding of DV should be vigilant for and flexible in discovering and using factors not listed here.

Biology and Genetics

Both biological and genetic characteristics can impact aggression and thus domestic violence. For example, increases in hormones such as testosterone can increase the likelihood of both aggression (Archer, 1994) and domestic violence (e.g., McKenry, Julian, & Gavazzi, 1995), especially in DV perpetrators who also have alcohol problems (George et al., 2001). In terms of managing domestic violence, it is important to note that testosterone levels can increase and decrease in response to environmental factors (Archer, 1994).

In relation to genetics, it is currently thought that inherited characteristics probably account for perhaps a quarter to a third of an aggressive predisposition (Tuvblad, Raine, Zheng, & Baker, 2009). A number of genes have been identified, but the effect on aggressive or violent behavior is mostly indirect, with holders of genetic markers typically having higher levels of aggression-related temperament factors such as impulsivity. Two genetic markers have attracted the most attention in the field of aggression research—a polymorphism in the promoter of the monoamine oxidase A gene (MAOA) and a variation in the 5-HT serotonin transporter gene. Importantly, for children in families where there is domestic violence, the effects of the MAOA gene polymorphism are epigenetic (i.e., caused by an interaction between the genetic predisposition and environmental factors that impact the action of the gene). Those who have this genetic polymorphism are most likely to become aggressive and engage in antisocial behaviors if they also experience childhood maltreatment (Kim-Cohen et al., 2006). Thus, this genetic factor has the potential to underlie some of the intergenerational family violence noted by Widom, Szaja, and Dutton (2014), whereby child maltreatment predicts the most serious forms of later domestic violence.

It is important to keep in mind that even though these genetic risk factors influence brain function, they eventually operate through the psychological processes outlined in GAM. This means that DV or other forms of violence are not inevitable but can be moderated by interventions that operate more directly on the psychological factors known to be involved in promoting and inhibiting violent behavior. For example, certain biological factors may influence a person's impulse control system, but one can improve impulse control through practice, and other aspects of the aggression/violence system can also be modified (e.g., beliefs about the appropriateness of DV, accessibility of non-violent solutions to conflict).

Gender

Gender issues around DV are currently contentious and we do not wish in this chapter to become part of this debate. However, there seems to be evidence that DV that results in severe physical or emotional harm can be perpetrated by both males and females (e.g., Dobash & Dobash, 2004; Zanoni, Warburton, Bussey, & McMaugh, 2014), but that males are responsible for a greater proportion of serious physical injuries and higher level IPV such as behavior that could be categorized as "intimate terrorism" (Johnson, 1995, 2006, 2011). For example, data from the US (Catalano, 2013), the UK (Smith et al., 2012), and Australia (Australian Bureau of Statistics, 2013) all suggest that women report considerably more violent behavior and injuries perpetrated by their partner than men do, and that the majority of victims of sexual violence are women. This is also reflected in homicide statistics. The World Health Organization (2013) notes that globally, IPV homicides constituted 38% of all female homicides, compared to just 6% of all male homicides. 2002–2011 US data analyzed by Catalano (2013) revealed that 39.3% of female homicides were related to IPV compared to just 2.8% of male homicides, and that in the same period, non-fatal violent victimizations stood at 805,700 for women versus 173,960 for men.

This has two important implications for clinical practice. First, practitioners should be aware that severe domestic violence is more often perpetrated by men. Second, this information should not cause practitioners to overlook the possibility of female to male domestic violence, especially given the reluctance of males to admit to being badly hurt by females in most cultures, and the severe physical and psychological harm that can be caused to male victims (Zanoni et al., 2014).

Personality Traits

Personality characteristics essentially refer to those psychological parts of a person that remain somewhat stable across situations (such as a tendency toward shyness) and across time. Although much personality research currently conceptualizes personality as a set of stable traits (e.g., Costa & McCrae, 1994), it is relevant for DV practitioners that the GAM assumes a much wider conceptualization of personality that emphasizes the contribution of scripts, schemas, beliefs, and attitudes to a person's stable personality (Anderson & Carnagey, 2004; Warburton & Anderson, in press; see also Mischel 1999; Mischel & Shoda, 1995). Thus, a person whose personality incorporates a lot of aggressive schemas and scripts, or a belief system that normalizes aggressive responding to conflict, will have a higher predisposition to aggress. This does not mean the GAM makes no allowance for the impact of traits—the GAM also assumes that high levels of personality traits linked with aggression (most notably high trait anger, high trait aggression, low agreeableness and high neuroticism) would also predispose a person toward aggression and DV (e.g., Barlett & Anderson, 2012; Caprara, Barbaranelli, Pastorelli, & Perugini, 1994; Graziano & Eisenberg, 1997). Further, longitudinal studies have shown that repeated environmental experiences (e.g., high exposure to media violence) can create systematic changes in trait aggression (e.g., Anderson et al., 2010; Gentile et al., 2014; Moller & Krahe, 2009).

Also germane to the GAM are personality styles linked with aggressive behavior. These include the narcissistic personality (Warburton, Edwards, Hossieny, Pieper, & Yip, 2008), the shame-prone personality (Tangney, Wagner, Hill-Barlow, Marschall, & Gramzow, 1996), the psychopathic (antisocial) personality (Reidy et al., 2007), and the Machiavellian personality (Kerig & Stellwager, 2010).

Another relevant within-person variable is the presence of a personality disorder. It has been shown that IPV perpetrators and repeat violent offenders are more likely to have a personality disorder, most notably a Borderline Personality Disorder or Antisocial Personality Disorder (Gilbert & Daffern, 2011; Holtzworth-Munroe & Stuart, 1994; Ross & Babcock, 2009; South, Turkheimer, & Oltmanns, 2008). However, other personality disorders have also been linked with aggression and with domestic violence, including the Narcissistic Personality Disorder and Dependent/Compulsive Personality Disorders (Hamberger & Hastings, 1986).

In terms of the GAM and domestic violence, the most relevant components of personality, whether they are parts of traits, personality styles, or clinical disorders, are those that influence the way a person thinks and feels. People with personalities that include more hostile cognitions and/or a tendency toward negative affective states are more likely to hurt an intimate partner.

Beliefs, Attitudes, and Attributions

Beliefs, attitudes, and values underlie many of the personality components noted earlier. Most relevant to the GAM and to understanding domestic violence are those beliefs and attitudes that approve aggression and violence. Normative beliefs that approve of aggression (Huesmann, 1998) are particularly relevant. Such beliefs tend to be stronger and better elaborated in violent populations (Gilbert & Deffern, 2010), and the strength of such beliefs predicts levels of violent behavior in criminals (Polaschek, Calvert, & Gannon, 2009; Polaschek, Collie, & Walkey, 2004).

More specific to domestic violence, Sugarman and Frankel's (1996) meta-analytic review of studies of IPV perpetrators' attitudes revealed that this group is far more predisposed to have positive attitudes toward using physical aggression in relationships. In addition, a prospective study by Fincham, Cui, Braithwaite, and Pasley (2008) found that people with attitudes that are more positive toward IPV were more likely to physically assault or regularly abuse their current intimate partner in the following 14 weeks. Interestingly, tests of implicit attitudes have shown that relationally violent men may not be consciously aware of holding such attitudes, but still unconsciously pair the concepts of women and violence (Eckhardt, Samper, Suhr, & Holtzworth-Munroe, 2012). Also relevant is the robust finding that IPV perpetrators tend to attribute the cause of violent incidents to their partners rather than themselves (Murphy & Eckhardt, 2005).

Schemas and Scripts

Aggression-related knowledge structures are central to both the GAM and to understanding violence (including domestic violence) through the lens of the GAM (Gilbert & Daffern, 2010; Gilbert, Daffern, Talevski, & Ogloff, 2013). In this approach, domestically violent men and women would be expected to have a neural network that includes many concepts around aggressive behavior and many knowledge structures with aggression-related and/or violent content. When considering instances of domestic violence, evidence that aggressive/violent schemas and scripts are causing patterns of behavior that are repeated would be seen as highly important and instructive. Also important are the sorts of cues, triggers, and situations that would typically activate those schemas and scripts. In the first author's clinical experience with victims of domestic violence, such patterns are often apparent once specific examples of IPV are described in detail by victims.

Another type of schema also seems relevant here. Young and colleagues (e.g., Young 1999; Young, Klosko, & Weishaar, 2003) describe 18 *early maladaptive schemas* (EMS), each of which comprises a constellation of unhelpful beliefs, attitudes, and feelings about key aspects of life. For example, those with *entitlement* schemas tend to see themselves as above the law, entitled to treat others as they see fit, and not accountable for their actions. Those with *subjugation* schemas believe they must surrender control of their life to others in order to avoid that person's anger, retaliation, or abandonment. Not only are those with maladaptive schemas more likely to be more aggressive (Warburton & McIlwain, 2005), but exposure to "toxic" and traumatizing experiences (such as violence and abuse in the home) has also been linked to the development of a range of maladaptive schemas (Young et al., 2003). Once developed, these EMSs may underlie a range of personality disorders (Giesen-Bloo et al., 2006; Young & Flanagan, 1998; Young & Lindemann, 1992, 2002) that are, in turn, linked with domestic violence (e.g.. Holtzworth-Munroe & Stuart, 1994). Thus, an intergenerational cycle of abuse, psychological damage, and later interpersonal violence seems likely in some families. *Schema therapy*, which challenges the cognitive substrate of EMSs (e.g., Young et al., 2003), has been incorporated into some treatment programs for abusive partners (e.g., Murphy & Eckhardt, 2005).

Impulsivity and Self-Regulation

There are clear links between impulsivity and aggression, especially when the impulsive person is provoked (e.g., Bettencourt, Talley, Benjamin, & Valentine, 2006). This link is probably mediated by a number of other factors such as inadequate self-restraint against aggressive impulses (Berkowitz, 2008), failure to properly think through the consequences of actions (Joireman, Anderson, & Strathman, 2003) and emotional arousal linked to anger and negative thoughts (e.g., Gilbert & Daffern, 2010).

In addition, both impulsive and non-impulsive people can have failures of self-regulation that lead to aggression and violence (DeWall et al., 2011). This may especially occur when the person is physically tired, mentally exhausted, or under time pressure to respond to a situation. Finkel and colleagues (2009) investigated associations between IPV and self-regulation failure, and concluded (1) that self-regulatory failure is an important predictor of IPV and (2) that conditions which reduce the capacity for self-control (such as mental exhaustion) increase the risk of IPV. Alcohol also interferes with self-control, which is one reason (but not the only one) why it is so highly associated with DV.

Needs

It is clear that much aggression and violence stems from a perceived deprivation of physical, psychological, emotional, and social needs, and represents an attempt to satisfy these needs (e.g., DeWall & Anderson, 2011). One key need is to have control over one's world and one's relationships. Aggression may be one way of reasserting control over one's environment (Warburton & Williams, 2005; Warburton, Williams, & Cairns, 2006) and over one's intimate partner (e.g., Stets, 1988). Indeed, it is possible that feeling powerless may be the catalyst for violence that serves to "restore control" in both intimate relationships (Petrik, Petrik, Olson, & Subotnik, 1994; Rosenbaum & Leisring, 2003) and parent-child relationships (Bugental & Johnson, 2000; Bugental & Schwartz, 2009).

There is also evidence that other key needs—to feel autonomous and have positive self-esteem—may be implicated in domestic violence. One study has shown that partner-assaultive men had lower self-esteem and greater spouse dependency than partner non-assaultive men (Murphy, Meyer, & O'Leary, 1994) and another has replicated the finding of greater spouse dependency (Kane, Staiger, & Ricciardelli, 2000). Thus, it is possible that some IPV perpetrators use verbal, psychological, and physical abuse to restore depleted self-esteem and feelings of autonomy.

SITUATION FACTORS

Provocation

Perhaps the single biggest trigger for aggression is being provoked by another (Bettencourt et al., 2006). This is important in domestic violence, where many perpetrators believe that the causes of most domestically violent interactions involve the provoking actions of their partner (Murphy & Eckhardt, 2005). It is important to remember that such provocations do not have to be proximal and direct to elicit aggression and violence (Warburton & Anderson, 2015, in press). For example, they may involve feeling ostracized, excluded, or rejected by one's partner, or being the subject of hurtful rumors and gossip. Furthermore, provocation may not even be real, but simply imagined by the perpetrator, or exaggerated by a hostile attribution bias.

Aggressive Cues and Triggers

This is a central factor in the GAM. At the beginning of any episode of aggression (and thus domestic violence), there needs to be some sort of cue or trigger in the environment that then causes various thoughts and feelings to be activated in the perpetrator. Crucially, this trigger does not have to be consciously thought of. Some aspects of life are strongly linked to concepts of violence for almost all people. These cues, such as seeing a gun or a depiction of a gun, or reading weapon-related words, can prime aggressive thoughts and increase the likelihood of aggressive behavior, even when the exposure is so brief that the person cannot recollect it (Anderson, Anderson, & Deuser, 1996; Anderson, Benjamin, & Bartholow, 1998).

One possible cue that is commonly found in most homes is media with violent content. There is now considerable consensus around the notion that watching violent television or movies (Anderson et al., 2003; Anderson & Bushman, 2002b; Krahe et al., 2012; Warburton, 2012a), listening to violent music (Anderson, Carnagey, & Eubanks, 2003; Brummert-Lennings & Warburton, 2011; Warburton, 2012b; 2014a; Warburton, Gilmour, & Laczkowski, 2008; Warburton, Roberts, & Christenson, 2014), or playing violent video games (Anderson et al., 2004, 2010; Anderson, Gentile, & Buckley, 2007; Anderson & Warburton, 2012; Warburton, 2014b) has an immediate impact on aggressive cognitions and feelings and increases the likelihood of aggressive behavior.

Importantly, those with more aggression-related concepts and knowledge structures in their neural network, and those predisposed to aggressive affects such as anger, are likely to also have more cues and triggers for aggressive thoughts and feelings (Anderson & Bushman, 2002a). Thus, there is a greater range of situations that may lead to that person becoming aggressive or violent.

Interestingly, a stimulus that cues aggression in most people may not do so in others. For instance, although seeing a hunting weapon cues aggressive thoughts and increases aggressive behavior in most people, hunting weapons cue a very different set of thoughts among people who grew up as hunters. For them, hunting guns (e.g., rifles with wood stocks) remind them of family hunting trips with their father and brothers, thereby reducing or eliminating the standard weapons effect. Interestingly, these same hunters show the standard weapons effects on aggressive thoughts and behavior when the weapon is clearly an assault-type weapon or a handgun (Bartholow, Anderson, Carnagey, & Benjamin, 2005).

Aversive Environment

A wide variety of aversive experiences or stimuli in the environment are known to increase the likelihood of aggression and violence. The most notable are high temperatures (Anderson & Anderson, 1998; Anderson et al., 2005), physical pain (Berkowitz, Cochran, & Embree, 1981), loud or aversive noises (Glass & Singer, 1972), foul odors (Jones & Bogat, 1972), and exposure to another's tobacco smoke (Zillman, Baron, & Tamborini, 1981). The impact of such stressors on aggressive behavior is much greater when the individual has no control over them (Donnerstein & Wilson, 1976; Warburton et al., 2006).

In terms of domestic violence, it is helpful to know that these environmental factors can exacerbate aggressive responding. If the potential perpetrator is in pain, if the day is very hot, if there is a lot of tobacco smoke, if loud music is playing, or if the environment is unpleasant in some other way, then this may influence the likelihood of violence occurring. Clearly, an effective strategy for reducing domestic violence should take into account minimizing the impact of aversive experiences or environments.

Alcohol and Other Substances

There are clear links between aggression and substances that cause either disinhibition (such as alcohol) and/or an increase in physiological arousal (e.g., stimulants, amphetamines, and methamphetamines) (Warburton & Anderson, 2015). This is most true for those with an existing predisposition to aggress, because this aggressive tendency is more likely to be the automatic response to a perceived provocation, and substances that promote impulsivity or impede self-control (i.e., that reduce the likelihood to reappraise) thereby increase the likelihood of impulsive aggression and thus DV (e.g., Giancola, 2000).

Being intoxicated or having alcohol abuse problems is among the most robust predictor of IPV (Murphy & Eckhardt, 2005). Studies consistently find a significant linear relationship between alcohol consumption and intimate partner violence (Kantor & Straus, 1987) and between alcohol-related problems and IPV (Cunradi, Caetano, Clark & Schafer, 1999). Indeed, one study by Murphy and O'Farrell (1996) found that over half of the female partners of men receiving treatment for alcohol problems had experienced IPV from that person in the prior 12 months. However it should be noted that use of alcohol increases the risk of IPV for both females and males (see Foran & O'Leary, 2008, for a review).

CURRENT INTERNAL STATE: HOSTILE THOUGHTS AND BIASES

The role of existing hostile cognitions (including knowledge structures, normative beliefs, and attributional biases) has been noted in some detail above. Here we examine factors relevant to the person's current internal state. Some key assumptions derived from the GAM are that:

1. The more hostile the content within a person's neural network, the greater the likelihood of aggression in the moment;
2. The greater the activation of aggression-related cognitions (in terms of both the number and the level of activation), the greater the risk of aggression in the moment;
3. Concurrent activation of aggressive cognitions and aggressive feelings will increase the risk of aggression in the moment;
4. Greater arousal will increase the likelihood of a person acting on an aggressive impulse in the moment.

In terms of habitually violent people, it has been established that this group has more developed and more extensive cognitive networks and knowledge structures linked to aggression as hypothesized by the GAM (e.g., Gilbert & Daffern, 2010; Gilbert et al., 2013). Although this aspect of the GAM has not been tested specifically in a domestically violent population, this group has been represented within existing offender studies that have been tested, and it seems logical that the same principles would apply to this group. Findings related to the attitudes, biases, and attributions of IPV perpetrators are certainly congruent with this notion, as are studies finding links between hostile cognitions about one's partner and increased levels of IPV (e.g., Fincham et al., 1997). This higher level of existing aggressive cognitions increases the likelihood of aggressive schemas and scripts being activated in the moment. Studies of aggressive cognitions activated in the moment (i.e., of current internal state) show that, in line with the GAM, concurrent activation of multiple aggressive cognitions (i.e., aggressive scripts as well as normative beliefs approving aggression) increases violent inclinations (Gilbert et al., 2013).

CURRENT INTERNAL STATE: HOSTILE FEELINGS AND AFFECT

Hostile feelings can have a direct effect on aggression, but can also play a part in activating aggression-related concepts and knowledge structures (Gilbert & Daffern, 2010). For example, Gilbert and colleagues (2013) found that the inclination to be violent increases when both aggressive cognitions and feelings of anger are activated together. It should be noted that although the emotion most linked with aggression is anger (Howells, 1998; Novaco, 1997), those with a general tendency toward negative affective states also are more likely to be aggressive (Bettencourt et al., 2006), and other negative emotions such as jealousy and shame are also linked with aggression (e.g., Mescher & Rudman, 2014; Tangney et al., 1996).

In terms of domestic violence, the effect of anger has been well researched. Although this research often has issues with both measuring and defining anger (e.g., Murphy & Eckhardt, 2005), a review of findings by Holtzworth-Munroe and Clements (2007) suggests that perpetrators of IPV are more likely to have high levels of trait anger, and that high levels of state anger increase the likelihood of IPV occurring. They note, however, that perpetrators of IPV are a heterogenous group. Some are much more likely than others to have high levels of trait anger (e.g., those with posttraumatic stress issues and those with a "fearful" attachment style), and some will be more prone to explosive anger in the moment (for example, those with borderline traits).

CURRENT INTERNAL STATE: HIGH LEVELS OF AROUSAL

Although it has been shown that high levels of physiological and emotional arousal increase the likelihood of aggression and violence, this is one of the least well researched facets of both aggressive behavior and the GAM (Anderson & Bushman, 2002a). Nevertheless, a number of facts are known. The original source of the arousal is largely irrelevant to whether it impacts aggression or not. In addition, the impact on aggression may be through a range of processes. Arousal increases the likelihood that a person will act on an aggressive impulse and reduces the likelihood they will think through the consequences of an aggressive action. Also, high levels of arousal can feel unpleasant, thus becoming an aversive experience that can elicit aggression. Sometimes arousal is part of a fight or flight response that impels people straight into an aggressive action. Arousal may also be cognitively labeled as being due to anger, and excitation transfer may compound this effect, leading to a disproportionately aggressive response. At the other end of the arousal spectrum, low levels of arousal may facilitate aggression if people lack the energy and motivation to inhibit aggressive impulses or if chronic low arousal is experienced as a negative state. It seems likely that arousal would impact instances of IPV in similar ways to those noted above; however, to date there is very little research on arousal and IPV (DeWall et al., 2011).

OPPORTUNITY FOR REAPPRAISAL

Overall, it seems that the risk of aggression (and for domestic violence) increases as risk factors accumulate: those within the person's psychological makeup, those related to currently activated cognitions and emotions, and those related to levels of arousal. In the final phase of the GAM, there is further opportunity for the risk of aggression and domestic violence to be reduced or increased. At this point in the model, the person has already formulated an immediate (automatic) response to some perceived threat or provocation. In a domestically violent person with an accumulation of personal risk factors, the likely immediate response is to hurt their partner. However, at this point, the person has the chance to evaluate and think through the consequences of such an action. For this to occur, the conditions for an automatic response must be absent, and the requirements for reappraisal to occur must be present. The person should have sufficient mental resources to reappraise (including not being under the influence of disinhibiting substances), the immediate response should be unsatisfactory in some way (for example, have perceived negative consequences), and there should be no time urgency. In most cases, reappraisal would be expected to reduce the risk of subsequent domestic violence.

In terms of domestic violence and reappraisal, the findings of Finkel and colleagues (2009) are instructive. Their studies on self-regulatory strength and IPV suggested that people who do not have sufficient mental resources to engage in reappraisal processing (i.e., are mentally exhausted) are more likely to be aggressive to intimate partners.

Of course, in some cases reappraisal can increase both the likelihood and the severity of an aggressive response. For example, reappraisal may lead the person to decide that the provocation was even more severe than initially thought, and that it warrants even more severe punishment or retaliation. The research literature on how rumination increases aggression is particularly relevant here (e.g., Denson, Pederson, & Friese, 2011; Denson, White, & Warburton, 2009).

THE GAM AND THERAPEUTIC INTERVENTIONS FOR DOMESTIC VIOLENCE

Principles from the GAM that Could Inform Treatment Approaches

A number of the principles that underlie the GAM, or that can be derived from the model, has relevance to the treatment and management of domestic violence. First, although many domestic violence programs based on social learning principles are group-based interventions, therapists who use GAM principles as a basis for treatment would also need to take an individualized approach, as the GAM emphasizes so strongly the unique factors in each person that predispose a person to domestic violence in particular situations. Such a dual approach would allow the therapist to take advantage of the economy of group-based approaches to help change risk factors that are common among most DV perpetrators, while also capitalizing on the power of individualized approaches to discover and change risk factors that are fairly unique to the individual. For example, two such risk factors that seem common among many DV perpetrators are poor reappraisal skills and normative beliefs about physical aggression. A recent experimental study has shown that a classroom-based reappraisal intervention can reduce aggression by college students (Barlett & Anderson, 2011). Nonetheless, because the specific set of knowledge structures and cognitive/affective abilities and tendencies that are involved in DV vary across individuals, careful idiographic assessment of which ones are most relevant for a particular client is needed to allow individualized treatment plans to be created.

Second, in order to understand and treat DV, the therapist needs to obtain quite a detailed understanding of both the DV client and the situation factors that contribute to their DV episodes. There will be risk factors, protective factors, and a range of triggers that are important for the therapist to understand.

Third, patterns of behavior can be changed by altering the content of, and triggers for, cognitions and knowledge structures learned over time. It is harder to change the sorts of emotions that might be activated in a particular situation (emotions are deeper in the brain and patterns of activation are more change-resistant; e.g., see Panksepp, 2008), however people can also be taught more adaptive ways to manage their emotions (McMain, Korman, & Dimeff, 2001). Overall, because neural plasticity occurs throughout the life-span (Gutchess, 2015), a person's neural network is able to be changed in ways that facilitate significant decreases in aggressive and violent behavior (e.g., through modifying aggressive cognitions—see Polaschek & Collie, 2004).

Finally, the same principles that underlie aggressive behavior in the GAM also work to establish prosocial behavior. For example, the General Learning Model (GLM), a modification of the GAM (Buckley & Anderson, 2006; Barlett & Anderson, 2013; Gentile et al., 2009), emphasizes that exactly the same processes ensure that prosocial person factors interact with cues and triggers to activate prosocial cognitions and feelings, and ultimately prosocial behaviors.

Assessing the DV Client and Typical Instances of DV

If therapists use the GAM to inform their practice with domestically violent clients, they would need to gather a range of information. The facets of the GAM, as well as its underlying assumptions, suggest enquiries in several fields, discussed below.

Function of Violence

First, it would be important to understand the function of the aggression on the three aggression domains.

1. What needs does each violent instance meet for the DV client? Does the violence serve the purpose of benefiting the perpetrator or hurting the other? How? Why?
2. Are DV instances typically affectively charged or cold and calculated? What are the emotions that are aroused? How does violence satisfy these emotions?
3. How thought-through is each instance? Is there a pattern? Do episodes play out automatically, almost like scripts? Are there opportunities to think-through responses? If violent responses are thought-through, what goals does the violence achieve?

Within-Person Factors

It would also be important to get some understanding of the relevant within-person factors. For example, what components of the DV client's personality are relevant to their domestic violence?

- Are there aggressive traits? High trait anger, high trait aggression, high neuroticism, low agreeableness?
- Is there low empathy; low emotional intelligence?
- Does the DV client have an aggressive personality style (e.g., narcissistic or psychopathic), or is there evidence of a personality disorder?
- Is there a tendency to interpret others' behaviors negatively? Is there a hostile attributional bias? Does the DV client tend to blame their partner for instances of domestic violence?
- Is there a tendency to interpret the outcomes of aggression positively? Are there normative beliefs approving aggression?
- Is there evidence of the presence of aggressive schemas and scripts? Is there evidence of the presence of early maladaptive schemas?

Also relevant within the DV client are their affective tendencies. Are they emotionally labile? Is there a tendency toward negative affectivity? Are they prone to depression, jealousy, and anger?

It is also helpful to know a little about the DV client's executive functioning. Are they impulsive? Are they skilled at self-control and emotional regulation?

In terms of motivational influences, what needs are met by being violent? Is the DV client feeling powerless or dependent and exerting control through violence? Does the DV client have low self-esteem that is bolstered by hurting their partner? Are they fearful of abandonment and using violence to ensure their partner stays?

Finally, does the DV client have skill deficits in key areas such as communication, problem solving, stress management, assertiveness, and emotion regulation?

A Strengths-Based Approach: Assessing Positive Characteristics

Although it is important to understand the negative characteristics that contribute to domestic violence, the GAM and GLM emphasize that there is "another side to the coin." DV clients also have strengths and abilities and memories of when they managed to avoid violence during domestic conflicts. They should be able to increase the impact of positive influences on positive behaviors and to change the contingency between cues and behaviors, so that triggers for aggression can start to elicit a more positive response (for example, to use the cue of acute feelings of dependence on a partner as a trigger to take independent action in a predetermined area rather than as a way to hurt the partner). Thus, the GAM and GLM support a *strengths-based approach* whereby the therapist is aware of negative personal characteristics, but works to build on the DV client's strengths, to assist them to develop positive skills in communication, active listening and managing conflict, to foster positive attitudes toward others, and to find positive ways to deal with traditional precursors of domestic violence.

For this reason, it is important to also discover the DV client's *positive within-person characteristics*. What are their positive traits? What are they good at? What cognitive approaches are helpful and/or can be built on? Do they have empathy and can it be strengthened? Are they able to take another person's perspective in role plays, and does a change of perspective elicit helpful changes to thinking? Can self-regulation be strengthened? Are there types of aggression and violence that the DV client disapproves of? Are there positive role models in the DV client's life? Are there people the DV client cares for greatly or would like to protect? Are there positive emotional tendencies, or have there been times in the DV client's life when they felt calm and happy, and which they can draw on for inspiration? Are there ways in which key needs can be met in a positive way? Were there times when the DV client better controlled their aggressive impulses or better managed their substance issues, and can those memories become a base from which to build a more positive response repertoire?

A good understanding of the DV client's strengths can help the therapist understand likely protective factors for domestic violence. In addition, working from a strengths-based approach is more likely to gain the DV client's cooperation and reduce the sort of resistance and defensiveness the therapist might experience if the client feels judged or shamed. Finally, it provides a basis from which to change the impact of environmental factors, so that, within the DV client's neural network, they trigger positive rather than negative cognitions and feelings. However, to achieve this, the therapist first needs to know what the relevant environment factors are.

Environmental Factors

The best way to ascertain violence-relevant factors in the DV client's environment is to look at the circumstances that have led to domestic violence across a number of instances. What are the most common provocations? Are there cues for aggression in the environment? Are there weapons or depictions of weapons nearby? Are there other aggressive people present? Has the DV client been exposed to violent media (e.g., news, movies, TV, etc.) or been playing a violent video game? Is there violent music playing in the background? Is the person aware of violence occurring in the streets or homes nearby? Remember that the DV client does not need to be aware of such cues for them to impact on their behavior.

Also important is to identify any aversive experiences or environments that may exacerbate aggressive tendencies. Is the home often hot or noisy? Is the DV client often in physical pain? Is the family home in an area where there are foul odors or high levels of pollution? Is the DV client a non-smoker in a house where there is a lot of tobacco smoke? Are other people in the house intoxicated or using substances, with their behavior impacting the DV client?

Finally, it is important to know if alcohol or other substances are involved in the behavior of the DV client. Do they have alcohol or other substance abuse issues? Are they usually intoxicated during episodes of domestic violence? Is the victim?

Using GAM-Relevant Information to Establish Intervention Protocols

Once the therapist, through talking to the DV client and possibly administering relevant testing instruments, has a good understanding of the client's strengths and weaknesses, and of relevant environment factors, they will have a good understanding of risk factors and protective factors for domestic violence that can form the basis for reducing the risk of DV.

When considering interventions and treatments through the lens of the GAM/GLM, however, it is crucial to make one point. These tools can help the therapist but are not sufficient basis for therapy alone. When applying the GAM/GLM to therapeutic interventions, it is important to also adhere to a range of therapeutic practices not linked to these models of aggressive and prosocial behavior. For example, the therapist will get best results if they have unconditional positive regard for their client, develop an empathic and connected client-therapist relationship, strive for client-directed change, and use key skills such as active listening (e.g., Murphy & Eckhardt, 2005).

Having said this, the GAM/GLM indicates a number of therapeutic approaches that should be helpful.

Reducing Person Risk Factors and Bolstering Protective Factors

The underlying principle here is that each person's neural network is plastic, and can thus be changed. What is already present in a person's network cannot be simply erased—humans cannot "unlearn" things—but the nature of the connections within a neural network can be altered. For example, if two new things are activated together often, they will develop a strong new neural connection. Old connections that become unused begin to fade and become less strong. Knowledge structures can incorporate new knowledge and triggers for one thing can become triggers for another, with the old connections fading if they are not used. In this way, positive schemas and scripts can be augmented, and negative ones restructured to include more helpful content.

With this in mind, practitioners can address risk and protective factors in the three GAM domains—cognitions, affects, and arousal (Gilbert & Daffern, 2011). Most amenable to change, but often underemphasized in treatment are aggressive cognitions (Gilbert & Daffern, 2010). Cognitive restructuring will not be unfamiliar to most therapists, and involves gently challenging the attitudes, beliefs, values, and attributions that have already been noted as contributing to domestic violence. In this way, new information can be accommodated and assimilated into schemas and scripts, and biases can be subtly altered in more positive directions.

In terms of domestic violence, this restructuring may involve:

- De-normalizing and devaluing aggressive and violent behavior; this may include making the DV client aware of the full range of consequences both to their partner, to others (such as their children), and to themselves;
- Examining social norms around aggression and violence to provide a wider perspective;
- Revaluing others and relearning trust. Challenging hostile attributions about others and the world around. Emphasizing the good in others and the positive benefits of mutually supportive relationships;
- Helping the DV client to take personal responsibility for those actions for which it is appropriate to do so, and gently challenging unhelpful attributions about their partner;
- Challenging the core beliefs underlying early maladaptive schemas.

Also helpful will be assisting the client to develop better emotion regulation and self-regulation skills. More recent formulations of self-regulation processes (e.g., Vohs & Baumeister, 2011) have emphasized that people self-regulate better when they practice it, and when they are not too mentally fatigued. The same principles seem to apply to aggressive and violent behavior (DeWall et al., 2011). Thus, DV clients may benefit from both working consistently at self-regulation, and understanding that failures of self-regulation occur when they are fatigued.

In terms of emotion regulation, many programs for DV clients include anger management. Such techniques are somewhat controversial (e.g., Murphy & Eckhardt, 2005) and some approaches work better than others. Space precludes a detailed analysis here, but clearly, people who can regulate their emotions better and who can channel the energy from anger into positive pursuits are less likely to be domestically violent.

One key issue that is perhaps not as often addressed is the issue of managing physiological arousal. According to GAM principles, techniques that reduce arousal will help reduce the likelihood of domestic violence. This may involve teaching clients relaxation, inner calmness and/or mindfulness techniques, helping them learn their own triggers for arousal, and helping them establish patterns for lessening arousal during stressful situations (such as leaving the situation and having a cup of tea). In addition, some environments are more arousing than others. Noise, heat, parties, busy places, homes with many occupants, and threatening situations would all be expected to increase arousal levels. Having an advance plan about how to relax in such situations may also be very helpful to DV clients.

Another important facet of the GAM is the acquisition and maintenance of learned behaviors. Thus, skills training and the opportunity to practice new skills would be seen as crucial to any effective domestic violence intervention. Key new skills may include better couple communication, active listening, non-aggressive assertiveness, perspective-taking, relaxation, and mindfulness. The more that therapy sessions offer the opportunity to practice these skills and to role play situations where the skills are used, and the more that clients can build the practice of such skills into their everyday lives, the greater the likelihood of positive change and a real reduction in domestic violence potential.

Reducing Risk Factors in the Environment

Changes within the DV client are important to reducing domestic violence, but take time. Changes to their environment are also important, and, crucially for therapeutic interventions, some can be instituted fairly quickly. Easiest to approach is identifying aversive experiences and environmental factors that may increase the potential for violence and looking for ways they can be managed. For example, can chronic pain be alleviated better or could the sufferer enter a program to manage chronic pain? Can sources of noise be quieted? Is it possible to air condition a room in the house or find a way to reduce the temperature on hot days?

More challenging but definitely possible is identifying environmental cues and triggers for violence and finding ways to remove them or change what they mean to the person. Perhaps the DV client could make sure there are no weapons around, play fewer violent video games, listen to less aggressive music, or store their samurai memorabilia where it can't be seen. With cognitive restructuring, it may also be possible to link old triggers to new behaviors. For example, coming home to a frowning partner may once have been the trigger for a cutting comment or the start of a conflict, but with practice could become the trigger for a concerned enquiry as to how their day was.

In the first instance, those predisposed to domestic violence can be taught to walk away from provoking situations. In the longer term, helping the person to develop conflict resolution skills may assist them to manage provoking situations better, and the learning of relaxation and calming techniques may reduce their predisposition to be provoked by or overreact to minor irritations. Cognitive restructuring around hostile biases will also help reduce the range of situations they find provoking.

Managing substance use will also be relevant for a great many DV clients. Usually, comorbid problems such as substance abuse would require separate treatment because therapy for domestic violence is less likely to be successful when those issues are not being specifically addressed (see Fals-Stewart, 2003).

Opportunities for Reappraisal

Another key tenet of the GAM is that maximizing the opportunities for reappraisal, in most cases, will reduce the likelihood of aggression. In practice, this means making sure that during conflicts the DV client has the time and the mental resources to think through the consequences of each possible response and to choose the most adaptive one. Being intoxicated or under the influence of stimulants will disinhibit immediate responses and undermine such processes, so sobriety during conflicts will be important. Also important will be managing levels of emotional and physical arousal. In addition, the DV client, especially if male, will need a way of backing down from an aggressive response without "losing face."

To facilitate reappraisal during conflicts, the therapist might run through role plays of various conflict scenarios and have the DV client practice strategies that increase their time and mental resources for reappraisal. Various alternate scripts for behavior and their consequences might be discussed, along with strategies for backing down from conflict without feeling a loss of self-esteem.

CONCLUSION

The General Aggression Model provides a helpful lens through which practitioners can understand both instances of domestic violence and the long-term acquisition of domestically violent behaviors. Although the GAM and the GLM are not a sufficient resource for therapy alone, they provide a range of principles and concepts that can guide the therapist as to what information is important to know from their client, and what types of interventions may be effective in reducing the risk of DV in clients. It is hoped that future research on the GAM extends to include findings that specifically examine the way that key tenets of the GAM underlie the behaviors of those who are domestically violent, and the efficacy of intervention approaches based on GAM principles.

DISCUSSION QUESTIONS

1. How is the General Aggression Model (GAM) useful in explaining the domestic violence? How can it be used to formulate ways to end patterns of DV?
2. What are some factors that might increase the likelihood of aggression in a perpetrator?
3. Are these factors different for members of the LGBT communities?
4. What types of interventions might be supported by the GAM?
5. Distinguish between aggression and violence. What are some of the challenges inherent in coming up with a universal definition of aggression?
6. Based on Warburton and Anderson's "three dimensions" model, what would the functions of domestic violence be?
7. What are the basic principles of neural connectivity that underlie the GAM approach?
8. Describe how theories of aggression have changed over time to result in today's approach to the GAM. What do CNT, SIP, and Script Theory share in common, and how are they different?

ACKNOWLEDGMENTS

The authors would like to thank Dorothy Curtis for her assistance in researching the background information for this chapter.

REFERENCES

Anderson, C. A., & Anderson, K. B. (1998). Temperature and aggression: Paradox, controversy, and a (fairly) clear picture. In R. G. Geen & E. Donnerstein (Eds.), *Human aggression: Theories, research, and implications for social policy* (pp. 247–298). San Diego, CA: Academic Press.

Anderson, C. A., Anderson, K. B., & Deuser, W. E. (1996). Examining an affective aggression framework: Weapon and temperature effects on aggressive thoughts, affect and attitudes. *Personality and Social Psychology Bulletin, 22*, 366–376.

Anderson, C. A., Anderson, K. B., Dorr, N., De Neve, K. M., & Flanagan, M. (2000). Temperature and aggression. In R. F. Baumeister & M. R. Leary (Eds.), *Advances in experimental social psychology* (Vol. 32, pp. 63–133). New York: Academic Press.

Anderson, C. A., & Barlett, C. P. (2016). The general aggression model. In H. Miller (Ed.) *Encyclopedia of theory in psychology*. Thousand Oaks CA: Sage.

Anderson, C. A., & Bushman, B. J. (2002a). Human aggression. *Annual Review of Psychology, 53,* 27–51.

Anderson, C. A., & Bushman, B. J. (2002b). The effects of media violence on society. *Science, 295,* 2377–2378.

Anderson, C. A., Benjamin, A. J., & Bartholow, B. D. (1998). Does the gun pull the trigger? Automatic priming effects of weapon pictures and weapon names. *Psychological Science, 9,* 308–314.

Anderson, C. A., Berkowitz, L., Donnerstein, E., Huesmann, L. R., Johnson, J., Linz, D., Malamuth, N., & Wartella, E. (2003). The influence of media violence on youth. *Psychological Science in the Public Interest, 4*, 81–110.

Anderson, C. A., & Carnagey, N. L. (2004).Violent evil and the general aggression model. In A. Miller (Ed.), *The social psychology of good and evil* (pp. 168–192). New York: Guilford Publications.

Anderson, C. A., Carnagey, N. L., & Eubanks, J. (2003). Exposure to violent media: The effects of songs with violent lyrics on aggressive thoughts and feelings. *Journal of Personality and Social Psychology, 84,* 960–971.

Anderson, C. A., Carnagey, N. L., Flanagan, M., Benjamin, A. J., Eubanks, J., & Valentine, J. C. (2004). Violent video games: Specific effects of violent content on aggressive thoughts and behavior. *Advances in Experimental Social Psychology, 36,* 199–249.

Anderson, C. A., Gentile, D. A., & Buckley, K. E. (2007). *Violent video game effects on children and adolescents: Theory, research, and public policy*. Oxford: Oxford University Press.

Anderson, C. A., & Groves, C. (2013). General aggression model. In M. S. Eastin (Ed.), *Encyclopedia of Media Violence* (pp. 182–187). Los Angeles, CA: Sage.

Anderson, C. A., & Huesmann, L. R. (2003). Human aggression: A social–cognitive view. In M. A. Hogg & J. Cooper (Eds.), *Handbook of social psychology* (pp. 296–323). London, UK: Sage.

Anderson, C. A., Shibuya, A., Ihori, N., Swing, E. L., Bushman, B. J., Sakamoto, A., Rothstein, H. R., & Saleem, M. (2010). Violent video game effects on aggression, empathy, and prosocial behavior in Eastern and Western countries. *Psychological Bulletin, 136,* 151–173.

Anderson, C. A., & Warburton, W. A. (2012). The impact of violent video games: An overview. In W. A. Warburton & D. Braunstein (Eds.), *Growing up fast and furious: Reviewing the impacts of violent and sexualised media on children* (pp. 56–84). Sydney: The Federation Press.

Archer, J. (1994). Testosterone and aggression. *Journal of Offender Rehabilitation, 21*, 3–25.

Australian Bureau of Statistics (2013). *4906.0—Personal Safety, Australia, 2012.* Available online at: http://www.abs.gov.au/AUSSTATS/abs@.nsf/DetailsPage/4906.02012.

Bandura, A. (1973). *Aggression: A social learning analysis*. Englewood Cliffs, NJ: Prentice Hall.

Bandura, A. (1983). Psychological mechanisms of aggression. In R. G. Geen & E. Donnerstein (Eds.), *Aggression: Theoretical and empirical reviews* (pp. 1–11). New York: Academic Press.

Bandura, A. (1986). *Social foundations of thought and action: A social cognitive theory.* Englewood Cliffs, NJ: Prentice Hall.

Bandura, A., Ross, D., & Ross, S. A. (1961). Transmission of aggression through imitation of aggressive models. *Journal of Abnormal and Social Psychology, 63*, 575–582.

Bandura, A., Ross, D., & Ross, S. A. (1963). Imitation of aggression through imitation of film-mediated aggressive models. *Journal of Abnormal and Social Psychology, 66,* 3–11.

Barlett, C. P., & Anderson, C. A. (2011). Re-appraising the situation and its impact on aggressive behavior. *Personality and Social Psychology Bulletin, 37*, 1564–1573. doi: 10.1177/0146167211423671.

Barlett, C. P., & Anderson, C. A. (2012). Direct and indirect relations between the Big 5 personality traits and aggressive behavior. *Personality and Individual Differences, 52,* 870–875.

Barlett, C. P., & Anderson, C. A. (2013). Examining media effects: The general aggression and general learning models. In E. Scharrer (Ed.), *Media effects/media psychology* (pp. 1–20). Boston: Blackwell-Wiley.

Baron, R. A., & Richardson, D. R. (1994). *Human aggression (2nd Ed.)*. New York: Plenum Press.

Bartholow, B. D., Anderson, C. A., Carnagey, N. L., & Benjamin, A. J. (2005). Interactive effects of life experience and situational cues on aggression: The weapons priming effect in hunters and nonhunters. *Journal of Experimental Social Psychology, 41,* 48–60.

Berkowitz, L. (1989). Frustration-aggression hypothesis: Examination and reformulation. *Psychological Bulletin, 106*, 59–73.

Berkowitz, L. (1990). On the formation and regulation of anger and aggression: A cognitive-neoassociationistic analysis. *American Psychologist, 45*, 494–503.

Berkowitz, L. (1993). *Aggression: Its causes, consequences, and control.* New York: McGraw Hill.

Berkowitz, L. (2008). On the consideration of automatic as well as controlled psychological processes in aggression. *Aggressive Behavior, 34*, 117–129.

Berkowitz, L., Cochran, S. T., & Embree, M. C. (1981). Physical pain and the goal of aversively stimulated aggression. *Journal of Personality and Social Psychology, 40*, 687–700.

Bettencourt, B. A., Talley, A., Benjamin, A. J., & Valentine, J. (2006). Personality and aggressive behavior under provoking and neutral conditions: A meta-analytic review. *Psychological Bulletin, 132*, 751–777.

Boxer, P., & Dubow, E. F. (2001). A social-cognitive information-processing model for school-based aggression reduction and prevention programs: Issues for research and practice. *Applied and Preventive Psychology, 10,* 177–192.

Brummert-Lennings, H. I., & Warburton, W. A. (2011). The effect of auditory versus visual violent media exposure on aggressive behavior: The role of song lyrics, video clips and musical tone. *Journal of Experimental Social Psychology, 47,* 794–799.

Buckley, K. E., & Anderson, C. A. (2006). A theoretical model of the effects and consequences of playing video games. In P. Vorderer & J. Bryant (Eds.), *Playing video games: Motives, responses, and consequences* (pp. 363–378). Mahwah, NJ: LEA.

Bugental, D. B., & Johnston, C. (2000). Parental and child cognitions in the context of the family. *Annual Review of Psychology, 51*, 315–344.

Bugental, D. B., & Schwartz, A. (2009). Cognitive approach to child mistreatment prevention among medically at-risk infants. *Developmental Psychology, 45,* 284–288. doi: 10.1037/a0014031.

Bushman, B. J., & Anderson, C. A. (2001). Is it time to pull the plug on the hostile versus instrumental aggression dichotomy? *Psychological Review, 108*, 273–279.

Caprara, G. V., Barbaranelli, C., Pastorelli, C., & Perugini, M. (1994). Individual differences in the study of human aggression. *Aggressive Behavior, 20*, 291–303.

Catalano, S. (2013). *Intimate partner violence: Attributes of victimization, 1993–2011.* Washington, DC: Bureau of Justice Statistics. Available online at: http://www.bjs.gov/index.cfm?ty=pbdetail&iid=4912.

Collins, A. M., & Loftus, E. F. (1975). A spreading activation theory of semantic processing. *Psychological Review, 82,* 407–428.

Costa, P. T., & McCrae, R. R. (1994). "Set like plaster?" Evidence for the stability of adult personality. In T. Heatherton & J. Weinberger (Eds.), *Can personality change* (pp. 21–40). Washington, DC: American Psychological Society.

Crick, N. R., & Dodge, K. A. (1994). A review and reformulation of social information processing mechanisms in children's adjustment. *Psychological Bulletin, 115*, 74–101.

Crick, N. R., & Dodge, K. A. (1996). Social information-processing mechanisms in reactive and proactive aggression. *Child Development, 66*, 993–1002.

Cunradi, C. B., Caetano, R., Clark, C. L., & Schafer, J. (1999). Alcohol-related problems and intimate partner violence among White, Black and Hispanic couples in the US. *Alcoholism: Clinical and Experimental Research, 23*, 1492–1501.

Denson, T. F., Pederson, W. C., & Friese, M. (2011). Understanding impulsive aggression: Angry rumination and reduced self-control capacity are mechanisms underlying the provocation-aggression relationship. *Personality and Social Psychology Bulletin, 37*, 850–862.

Denson, T. F., White, A. J., & Warburton, W. A. (2009). Psychopathy and trait displaced aggression differentially moderate the effects of rumination and acute alcohol intoxication on triggered displaced aggression. *Journal of Research in Personality, 43*, 673–681.

DeWall, C. N., & Anderson, C. A. (2011). The general aggression model. In P. R. Shaver & M. Mikulincer (Eds.), *Human aggression and violence: Causes, manifestations, and consequences* (pp. 15–33). Washington, DC: American Psychological Association.

DeWall, C. N., Anderson, C. A., & Bushman, B. J. (2011). The General Aggression Model: Theoretical extensions to violence. *Psychology of Violence, 1*, 245–258. doi: 10.1037/a0023842.

Dobash, R. P., & Dobash, R. E. (2004).Women's violence to men in intimate relationships: Working on a puzzle. *British Journal of Criminology, 44,* 324–349. http://dx.doi.org/10.1093/bjc/azh026.

Dollard, J., Doob, L. W., Miller, N. E., Mowrer, O. H., & Sears, R. R. (1939). *Frustration and aggression.* New Haven, CT: Yale University Press.

Donnerstein, E., & Wilson, D. W. (1976). The effects of noise and perceived control upon ongoing and subsequent aggressive behavior. *Journal of Personality and Social Psychology, 34,* 774–783.

Eckhardt, C. I., Samper, R., Suhr, L., & Holtzworth-Munroe, A. (2012). Implicit attitudes toward violence among male perpetrators of intimate partner violence: A preliminary investigation. *Journal of Interpersonal Violence, 27,* 471–491.

Fals-Stewart, W. (2003). The occurrence of partner physical violence on days of alcohol consumption: A longitudinal diary study. *Journal of Consulting and Clinical Psychology, 71,* 41–52.

Fincham, F. D., Bradbury, T. N., Arias, I., Byrne, C. A., & Karney, B. R. (1997). Marital violence, marital distress, and attributions. *Journal of Family Psychology, 11,* 367–372.

Fincham, F. D., Cui, M., Braithwaite, S. R., & Pasley, K. (2008). Attitudes towards intimate partner violence in dating relationships. *Psychological Assessment, 20,* 260–269.

Finkel, E. J., DeWall, C. N., Slotter, E. B., Oaten, M., & Foshee, V. A. (2009). Self-regulatory failure and intimate partner violence perpetration. Journal of Personality and Social Psychology, *97,* 483–499.

Foran, H. M., & O'Leary, K. D. (2008). Alcohol and intimate partner violence: A meta-analytic review. *Clinical Psychology Review, 28,* 1222–1234.

Geen, R. G. (2001). *Human aggression (2nd Ed.).* Buckingham, England: Open University Press.

Gentile, D. A., Anderson, C. A., Yukawa. S., Ihori, N., Saleem, M., Ming, L. K., Shibuya, A., Liau, A. K., Khoo, A., & Sakamoto, A. (2009). The effects of prosocial video games on prosocial behaviors: International evidence from correlational, experimental, and longitudinal studies. *Personality and Social Psychology Bulletin, 35,* 752–763.

Gentile, D. G., Li, D., Khoo, A., Prot, S., & Anderson, C. A. (2014). Mediators and moderators of long-term violent video game effects on aggressive behavior: Practice, thinking, and action. *JAMA Pediatrics,168,* 450–457. doi:10.1001/jamapediatrics.2014.63.

George, D. T., Umhau, J. C., Phillips, M. J., Emmela, D., Ragan, P. W., Shoaf, S. F., & Rawlings, R. R. (2001). Serotonin, testosterone and alcohol in the etiology of domestic violence. *Psychiatry Research, 104,* 27–37.

Giancola, P. R. (2000). Executive functioning: A conceptual framework for alcohol-related aggression. *Experimental and Clinical Psychopharmacology, 8,* 576–597.

Giesen-Bloo, J., van Dyck, R., Spinhoven, P., van Tilburg, W., Dirksen, C., van Asselt, T., Kremers, I., Nadort, M., & Arntz, A. (2006). Outpatient psychotherapy for borderline personality disorder: A randomized trial of schema-focused therapy versus transference-focused therapy. *Archives of General Psychiatry, 63,* 649–658.

Gilbert, F., & Daffern, M. (2010). Integrating contemporary aggression theory with violent offender treatment: How thoroughly do interventions target violent behavior? *Aggression and Violent Behavior, 15,* 167–180. doi: 10.1016/j.avb.2009.11.003.

Gilbert, F., & Daffern, M. (2011). Illuminating the relationship between personality disorder and violence: Contributions of the General Aggression Model. *Psychology of Violence, 3,* 230–244. doi: 10.1037/a0024089.

Gilbert, F., Daffern, M., Talevski, D., & Ogloff, J. R. P. (2013). The role of aggression-related cognition in the aggressive behavior of offenders: A general aggression model perspective. *Criminal Justice and Behavior, 40,* 119–138. doi: 10.1177/0093854812467943.

Glass, D. C., & Singer, J. E. (1972). *Urban stress: Experiments on noise and social stressors.* New York: Academic Press.

Graziano, W. G., & Eisenberg, N. (1997). Agreeableness: A dimension of personality. In R. Hogan, J. A. Johnson, & S. R. Briggs (Eds.), *Handbook of personality psychology* (pp. 795–824). San Diego, CA: Academic Press.

Gutchess, A. (2015). Plasticity of the aging brain: New directions in cognitive neuroscience. *Science, 346,* 579–582.

Hamberger, L. K., & Hastings, J. E. (1986). Personality correlates of men who abuse their partners: A cross-validation study. *Journal of Family Violence, 1,* 323–341.

Holtzworth-Munroe, A., & Clements, K. (2007). The association between anger and male perpetration of intimate partner violence. In T. A. Cavell & T. Malcolm (Eds.), *Anger, aggression and interventions for interpersonal violence* (pp. 313–348). Mahwah, NJ: Lawrence Erlbaum and Associates.

Holtzworth-Munroe, A., & Stuart, G. L. (1994). Typologies of male batterers: Three subtypes and differences among them. *Psychological Bulletin, 116,* 476–497.

Howells, K. (1998). Cognitive-behavioral interventions for anger, aggression and violence. In N. Tarrier, A. Wells, & G. Haddock (Eds.), *Treating complex cases: The cognitive behavioral therapy approach* (pp. 295–318). Chichester: Wiley.

Huesmann, L. R. (1988). An information processing model for the development of aggression. *Aggressive Behavior, 14,* 13–24.

Huesmann, L. R. (1998). The role of social information processing and cognitive schema in the acquisition and maintenance of habitual aggressive behavior. In R. G. Geen & E. Donnerstein (Eds.), *Human aggression: Theories, research and implications for social policy* (pp. 73–109). San Diego, CA: Academic Press.

Johnson, M. P. (1995). Patriarchal terrorism and common couple violence: Two forms of violence against women. *Journal of Marriage and the Family, 57,* 283–294.

Johnson, M. P. (2006). Conflict and control: Gender symmetry and asymmetry in domestic violence. *Violence Against Women, 12,* 1003–1018.

Johnson, M. P. (2011). Gender and types of intimate partner violence: A response to an anti-feminist literature review. *Aggression and Violent Behavior, 16,* 289–296. http://dx.doi.org/10.1016/j.avb.2011.04.006.

Joireman, J., Anderson, J., & Strathman, A. (2003). The aggression paradox: Understanding links among aggression, sensation seeking, and the consideration of future consequences. *Journal of Personality and Social Psychology, 84,* 1287–1302.

Jones, J., & Bogat, K. (1972). Air pollution and human aggression. *Psychological Reports, 43,* 721–722.

Kane, T. A., Staiger, P. K., & Ricciardelli, L. A. (2000). Male domestic violence: Attitudes, aggression, and interpersonal dependency. *Journal of Interpersonal Violence, 15,* 16–29.

Kantor, G., K., & Straus, M. A. (1987). The "drunken bum" theory of wife beating. *Social Problems, 34,* 213–230.

Kerig, P. K., & Stellwager, K. K. (2010). Roles of callous-unemotional traits, narcissism, and Machiavellianism in childhood aggression. *Journal of Psychopathology and Behavioral Assessment, 32,* 343–352.

Kim-Cohen, J., Caspi, A., Taylor, A., Williams, B., Newcombe, R., Craig, I. W., & Moffitt, T. E. (2006). *MAOA*, maltreatment, and gene-environment interaction predicting children's mental health: New evidence and a meta-analysis. *Molecular Psychiatry, 11,* 903–913.

Krahé, B. (2013). *The Social Psychology of Aggression, 2nd Edition.* London: Psychology Press.

Krahé, B., Berkowitz, L., Brockmeyer, J. H., Bushman, B. J., Coyne, S. M., Dill, K. E., . . . Warburton, W. A. (2012). Report of the media violence commission. *Aggressive Behavior, 38,* 335–341.

McKenry, P. C., Julian, T. W., & Gavazzi, S. M. (1995). Toward a biopsychosocial model of domestic violence. *Journal of Marriage and Family, 57,* 307–320.

McMain, S., Korman, L. M., & Dimeff, L. (2001). Dialectical behavior therapy and the treatment of emotion dysregulation. *Journal of Clinical Psychology, 57,* 183–196.

Mescher, K., & Rudman, L. A. (2014). Men in the mirror: The role of men's body shame in sexual aggression. *Personality and Social Psychology Bulletin, 40,* 1063–1075. doi:http://dx.doi.org/10.1177/0146167214535641.

Mischel, W. (1999). Personality, coherence and dispositions in a cognitive-affective personality (CAPS) approach. In D. Cervone & Y. Shoda (Eds.), *The coherence of personality: Social-cognitive bases of consistency, variability, and organization* (pp. 37–60). New York: The Guilford Press.

Mischel, W., & Shoda, Y. (1995). A cognitive-affective system theory of personality: Reconceptualizing situations, dispositions, dynamics, and invariance in personality structure. *Psychological Review, 102*, 246–268.

Moller, I., & Krahe, B. (2009). Exposure to violent video games and aggression in German adolescents: A longitudinal analysis. *Aggressive Behavior, 35,* 75–89.

Murphy, C. M., & Eckhardt, C. I. (2005). *Treating the abusive partner: An individualised cognitive-behavioral approach.* New York: The Guilford Press.

Murphy, C. M., Meyer, S. L., & O'Leary, K. D. (1994). Dependency characteristics of partner assaultive men. *Journal of Abnormal Psychology, 103*, 729–735.

Murphy, C. M., & O'Farrell, T. J. (1996). Marital violence amongst alcoholics. *Current Directions in Psychological Science, 5*, 183–186.

Novaco, R. W. (1997). Remediating anger and aggression with violent offenders. *Legal and Criminological Psychology, 2*, 77–88.

Panksepp, J. (2008). The affective brain and core consciousness: How does neural activity generate emotional feelings? In M. Lewis, J. M. Haviland-Jones, & L. F. Barrett (Eds.), *Handbook of emotions (3rd ed.)* (pp. 47–67). New York: The Guilford Press.

Petrik, N. D., Petrik Olson, R. E., & Subotnik, L. S. (1994). Powerlessness and the need to control: The male abuser's dilemma. *Journal of Interpersonal Violence, 9*, 278–285.

Polaschek, D. L., Calvert, S. W., & Gannon, T. A. (2009). Linking violent thinking: Implicit theory-based research with violent offenders. *Journal of Interpersonal Violence, 24*, 75–96.

Polaschek, D. L., & Collie, R. (2004). Rehabilitating serious violent adult offenders: An empirical and theoretical stocktake. *Psychology, Crime and Law, 10*, 321–334.

Polaschek, D. L., Collie, R. M., & Walkey, F. H. (2004). Criminal attitudes to violence: Development and preliminary validation of a scale for male prisoners. *Aggressive Behavior, 30*, 484–503.

Reidy, D. R., Zeichner, A., Miller, J. D., & Martin, M. A. (2007). Psychopathy and aggression: Examining the role of psychopathy factors in predicting laboratory aggression under hostile and instrumental conditions. *Journal of Research in Personality, 41,* 1244–1251.

Rosenbaum, A., & Leisring, P. A. (2003). Beyond power and control: Towards an understanding of partner abusive men. *Journal of Comparative Family Studies, 34*, 7–22.

Ross, J., & Babcock, J. (2009). Proactive and reactive violence among intimate partner violent men diagnosed with antisocial and borderline personality disorder. *Journal of Family Violence, 24,* 607–617.

Schachter, S., & Singer, J. (1962). Cognitive, social, and physiological determinants of emotional state. *Psychological Review, 69*, 379–399.

Schank, R. C., & Abelson, R. P. (1977). *Scripts, plans, goals, and understanding: An inquiry into human knowledge structures.* Hillsdale, NJ: Erlbaum.

Smith, K. E., Osborne, S., Lau, I., & Britton, A. (2012). *Homicides, firearm offences and intimate violence 2010/11: Supplementary Volume 2 to crime in England and Wales 2010/11.* Available online from: https://www.gov.uk/government/uploads/system/uploads/attachment_data/file/116483/hosb0212.pdf.

South, S., Turkheimer, E., & Oltmanns, T. (2008). Personality disorder symptoms and marital functioning. *Journal of Consulting and Clinical Psychology, 76,* 769–780.

Stets, J. E. (1988). *Domestic violence and control*. New York: Springer-Verlag.

Sugarman, D. B., & Frankel, S. L. (1996). Patriarchal ideology and wife assault: A meta-analytic review. *Journal of Family Violence, 11*, 13–40.

Tangney, J. P., Wagner, P., Hill-Barlow, D., Marschall, D. E., & Gramzow, R. (1996). Relation of shame and guilt to constructive versus destructive responses to anger. *Journal of Personality and Social Psychology, 70*, 797–810.

Tuvblad, C., Raine, A., Zheng, M., & Baker, L. A. (2009). Genetic and environmental stability differs in reactive and proactive aggression. *Aggressive Behavior, vol. 35* (pp. 437–452).

Vohs, K. D., & Baumeister, R. F. (2011). *Handbook of self-regulation: Research, theory, and applications (2nd Ed.)*. New York: The Guilford Press.

Warburton, W. A. (2012a). Growing up fast and furious in a media saturated world. In W. A. Warburton & D. Braunstein (Eds.), *Growing up fast and furious: Reviewing the impacts of violent and sexualised media on children* (pp. 1–33). Sydney: The Federation Press.

Warburton, W. A. (2012b). How does listening to Eminem do me any harm? What the research says about music and antisocial behavior. In W. A. Warburton & D. Braunstein (Eds.), *Growing up fast and furious: Reviewing the impacts of violent and sexualised media on children* (pp. 85–115). Sydney: The Federation Press.

Warburton, W. A. (2013). Aggression: Definition and measurement of. In M. Eastin (Ed.), *Encyclopedia of media violence* (pp. 10–14). Thousand Oaks, CA: Sage.

Warburton, W. A. (2014a). Violence and aggression. In W. F. Thompson (Ed.), *Music in the social and behavioral sciences: An encyclopedia* (pp. 1168–1171). Thousand Oaks, CA: Sage.

Warburton, W. A. (2014b). Apples, oranges and the burden of proof: Putting media violence findings in context. *European Psychologist, 19,* 60–67. doi: 10.1027/1016-9040/a000166.

Warburton, W. A., & Anderson, C. A. (2015). Social psychological study of aggression. In J. Wright (Ed.), *International encyclopaedia of social and behavioral sciences (2nd ed.)*. Oxford, UK: Elsevier.

Warburton, W. A., & Anderson, C. A. (in press). Aggression. In T. K. Shackleford & P. Zeigler-Hill [Eds.], *The SAGE handbook of personality and individual differences: Vol. 3 Applications of personality and individual differences* (pp. 183–211). Thousand Oaks CA: Sage.

Warburton, W. A., Edwards, P., Hossieny, T., Pieper, L., & Yip, T. (2008). Factors that mediate the narcissism-aggression link. In S. Boag (Ed.), *Personality down under: Perspectives from Australia* (pp. 215–233). New York: Nova Science Publishers.

Warburton, W. A., Gilmour, L., & Laczkowski, P. (2008). Eminem v. Rambo: A comparison of media violence effects for auditory versus visual modalities. In S. Boag (Ed.), *Personality down under: Perspectives from Australia* (pp. 255–273). New York: Nova Science Publishers.

Warburton, W. A., & McIlwain, D. (2005). The role of early maladaptive schemas in adult aggression. *Psychology, Psychiatry and Mental Health Monographs, 2,* 17–34.

Warburton, W. A., Roberts, D. F., & Christensen, P. G. (2014). The effects of violent and antisocial music on children and adolescents. In D. Gentile (Ed.), *Media violence and children (2nd ed.)* (pp. 301–328). Westport, CT: Praeger.

Warburton, W. A., & Williams, K. D. (2005). Ostracism: When social motives collide. In J. P. Forgas, K. D. Williams, & S. M. Laham (Eds.), *Social motivation: Conscious and unconscious processes* (pp. 294–313). London: Cambridge University Press.

Warburton, W. A., Williams, K. D., & Cairns, D. R. (2006). When ostracism leads to aggression: The moderating effects of control deprivation. *Journal of Experimental Social Psychology, 42,* 213–220.

Widom, C. S., Czaja, S., & Dutton, M. A. (2014). Child abuse and neglect and intimate partner violence victimization and perpetration: A prospective investigation. *Child Abuse and Neglect, 38,* 650–663.

World Health Organization (WHO). (2010). *Preventing intimate partner and sexual violence against women: Taking action and generating evidence*. Geneva, Switzerland: World Health Organization. Available online at: http://apps.who.int/iris/bitstream/10665/44350/1/9789241564007_eng.pdf?ua=1.

World Health Organization (WHO). (2013). *Global and regional estimates of violence against women: prevalence and health effect of intimate partner violence and non- partner sexual violence.* Geneva, Switzerland: World Health Organization. Available online at: http://apps.who.int/iris/bitstream/10665/85239/1/9789241564625_eng.pdf?ua=1.

Young, J. E. (1999). *Cognitive therapy for personality disorders: A schema focused approach* (Rev. ed.). Sarasota FL: Professional Resource Exchange.

Young, J. E., & Flanagan, C. (1998). Schema focused therapy for narcissistic patients. In E. Ronningstam (Ed.), *Disorders of narcissism: Diagnostic, clinical and empirical implications* (pp. 239–268). Arlington, VA: American Psychiatric Publishing.

Young, J. E., Klosko, J. S., & Weishaar, M. E. (2003). *Schema therapy: A practitioner's guide.* New York: The Guilford Press.

Young, J. E., & Lindemann, M. D. (1992). An integrative schema-focused model for personality disorders. *Journal of Cognitive Psychotherapy, 6*, 11–23.

Young, J. E., & Lindemann, M. D. (2002). An integrative schema-focused model for personality disorders. In R. L. Leahy & E. T. Dowd (Eds.), *Clinical advances in cognitive psychotherapy: Theory and application* (pp. 93–109). New York: Springer.

Zanoni, L., Warburton, W. A., Bussey, K., & McMaugh, A. (2014). Child protection fathers' experiences of childhood, intimate partner violence and parenting. *Children and Youth Services Review, 46,* 91–102. doi: 10.1016/j.childyouth.2014.08.009.

Zillmann, D., 1979. *Hostility and aggression.* Hillsdale, NJ: Erlbaum.

Zillmann, D., Baron, R., & Tamborini, R. (1981). Social costs of smoking: Effects of tobacco smoke on hostile behavior. *Journal of Applied Psychology, 11*, 548–561.

Chapter Five

A Psychodynamic Theory of Domestic Violence

William G. Herron and Rafael Art. Javier

Our concern is with domestic violence, a targeting form of aggression, violence within a specific context, the family. The family members are the targets for at least one member who dominates the structure through his aggression. Up to this time such aggression has drawn very limited attention in psychodynamic theorizing. It has been overshadowed by a broader interrelated issue, namely the origins of aggression.

We touched on this encompassing issue earlier in the book. The basic question is whether aggression is to be considered as instinctual or derived from the interpersonal environment. Knowing the answer would certainly assist in explorations of targeting aggression, both in terms of understanding origins and providing effective treatment. In regard to origins, innate aggression means that the observable behavior is primarily a product of instinctual forces that use the social environment for an outlet. In this model everybody is aggressive by nature so the focus is on the person's use of aggression. In contrast, if aggression is a reaction to a provocative environment then people are not aggressive by nature. This puts the focus on the environment. Treatment would be in line with the determination of origins.

In both models the person is interactive with the environment. However, in the case of instinctual dominance manipulating the environment would alter the timing and manner of expression, but would not change the desire to be aggressive. Focusing on personal characteristics would be necessary to facilitate the use of methods other than indiscriminate or unjustified discharge. In the second model the person's interaction with others becomes the focus. The aim would be to develop situations facilitating accommodation and cooperation, thereby avoiding the need for aggression.

Aggression has been viewed from both conceptions, and treated accordingly. This suggests the question of origination has been definitively answered, although as we will demonstrate, it has not. Nonetheless opinions have been formed and theories about aggression formulated, leading to methods of treatment. In addition the *type* of aggression, including context, as targeting, has had limited exposure. Our interest, specific directed aggression, family violence, has not appeared as a significant concern within the spectrum of psychodynamic theories of aggression.

However, there have been recent explorations of other types of directed aggression, as racism, sexism, and homophobia (Sue, 2010). This is a start to fill the need for looking at specific aggressions. Related possibilities for theorizing are studies of revenge (LaFarge, 2006; Lansky, 2007; Rosen, 2007). Given this lack of previous studies on psychodynamic theories of domestic violence, our approach becomes a new extension of understanding the activation of aggression. This is built upon the existing theories of aggression, so our first step is to revisit the psychodynamic views of the origins, development, and activation of aggression.

PSYCHOANALYTIC CONCEPTIONS OF AGGRESSION

The current psychoanalytic definition of aggression is "the wish to subjugate, prevail over, harm or destroy others, and the expression of any of these wishes in action, words or fantasy" (Auchincloss & Samberg, 2012, p. 11).

The description is basic, but has qualifiers, such as that aggression can also appear in a disguised form, can be turned against the self, and can involve constructive behavior, such as assertion. Also, aggression originated in psychoanalytic theory along with libido as primary motivation. Domestic violence is an example of the pathological expression of aggression. The origins of such aggression appear to be multiple, including genetic and developmental stimuli. Our focus with domestic violence is on experiential events, such as disturbed developmental phases that may have included frustrations, deprivations, and other forms of abuse.

As noted there is considerable controversy about the formation of aggression. Many theorists, beginning with Freud, view it as an instinctual drive that is destructive, but can also be used adaptively. Domestic violence represents a failure in adaptation. Such a failure is congruent with viewing aggression as a reaction to developmental deprivations, but also fits with it being an innate drive. Given the probability of multiple causal factors it seems prudent to consider the coexistence of instinctual and environmental stimuli.

The drive emphasis has an intriguing history that has been described by Mitchell (1993). Adler in 1908 appears to have been the initiator of conceptualizing aggression as instinctual, with Freud at first arguing the aggression was a reaction to frustration. In 1920 Freud changed his view and proposed the concept of an aggressive drive. This view continued with both ego psychologists and Kleinian analysts, though the former included the neutralization of drives as a way to limit destructive aggression. The latter saw aggression as a lifelong force to be struggled with by separation cycles countering its perpetual presence.

A slightly different view has been suggested by Schmidt-Hellerau (2002) who proposes two drives, libidinal and self-preservative (instead of aggressive). Aggression is seen as a reaction to a threat involving the intensification of one of the drives. At the same time she considers aggression to be biogenetically based, a reaction to frustration and to a danger to the self.

Mitchell (1993) considers hostile aggression to be generally conceptualized either as instinctual or as a secondary defensive reaction. "Aggression is an extremely powerful, universally wired (although individually varied), biological response to the subjective experience of endangerment" (p. 8). He attempts to bridge the two positions by including features of each one. Drive models emphasize the importance of aggression in the development of the self, whereas nondrive models see destructiveness as a subjective experience in a relational context. However, he believes that both perspectives, while noting positive aspects of aggression, such as assertion, neglect the positive qualities of destructive aggression. He suggests that it is natural to have a destructive self that is one of a person's many self-organizations. This hostile self has useful energizing features and that self is always present to some degree.

The ongoing existence of a destructive self is consistent with the metaphor of the *dark side*, "that aspect of human nature that has the potential to lead people to behave in destructive ways" (Bohart, 2013, p. 3). What remains at issue is whether people are innately destructive or their potential for evil is enacted only when given the appropriate stimulating experiences (Hollis, 2013).

Either way there is agreement in psychoanalysis that a therapeutic goal is the reduction of destructive actions that are inappropriate and harm others. Therapists who see destructiveness as innate tend to focus on aggression as a drive requiring some form of neutralization and diversion of energy into more positive behavior. Therapists who see hostility as an acquired reaction to developmental frustrations focus on increasing the constructive motivation that they believe is released through empathy and understanding.

Attempts at bridging the gap are apparent and usually involve the delinking of aggression from its origins as a primary drive. In the work of Rizzuto, Meissner, and Buie (2004) aggression remains a biological force, but not a drive. It is seen as a mental capacity exercised in overcoming obstacles. It is defined as an action, not as a motivating force or in terms of accompanying affects such as rage and hate. This view is reflective of Schmidt-Hellerau

(2002) who also strives to eliminate the concept of an aggressive drive. She wishes to make room for a self-preservative drive instead of an aggressive one. For Rizzuto et al., it is an attempt to emphasize the self-agency that they believe is being eliminated by drive theory.

These approaches are of interest, but the need to recategorize aggression is not particularly convincing. For example, in a review of the book by Rizzuto et al., Rosenblum (2006) notes that drive theorists do not have their patients avoid personal agency. Mitchell (1993) also removed aggression from the drive category, but retained some of the flavor of a drive by considering it to be biologically based. His aim was to emphasize that aggression is a response to endangerment. All of these variations seem possible while retaining the instinctual nature of aggression. Schmidt-Hellerau concedes that aggression can correctly be seen as inherent, a response to danger within a relational framework, and both destructive and nondestructive.

It would certainly be helpful to resolve the drive-nondrive controversy so that we could formulate theories of specific instances of destructive aggression with certainty regarding the origins of aggression, but the certainty does not exist. Multiple causation is most probable. Based on our own clinical experience we would lean toward viewing aggression as innate, but also consider aggression as customized through interpersonal developmental experience.

DYNAMICS OF DOMESTIC VIOLENCE

Our initial assumption is that all individuals have genetic and constitutional propensities for aggression. We base this view on both the material supporting innate aggression, and on the idea that if aggression needs a facilitating environment, as obstacles to overcome, expression requires a capacity for aggression. In essence, an action cannot be learned if there is no constitutional ability to perform it. However, we have limited ability to either assess or control genetic predispositions, but they usually require "triggers" for activation. These provide opportunities for observation and alteration once the stimuli are identified. This premise is in accord with the "dark side" metaphor representing an apparent prevalent tendency in humanity.

Added to this are environmental forces that result in a tendency to engage in *microaggressions* (Sue, 2010), frequently common unconscious aggressive behavior toward others that is hostile, but not viewed as such by the aggressor. These have their basis in a culture of distrust regarding gender, race, and sexual orientation. The microaggressions have a strong possibility of remediation, but often lack recognition to the point of feeling factual, normal, and necessary.

The underpinning is a distorted defensive structure in which the self is on permanent alert to the possibility of damage. The most likely culprits are the family, particularly designated caretakers, though the social, educational, and vocational environment are also possible contributors.

In a family structure the potential abuser tends to have been developmentally stunted through abuse and neglect having a major impact on ego functions, particularly self-understanding and perception of the intentions of others. The interpersonal surroundings, starting at home, are hostile and other environments may also be that way, or perceived as such. Mastering this type of situation requires abnormal adaptation such as passive acceptance of unwarranted criticism. Doing this stifles both assertion and direct aggression against tormentors who are seen as more powerful, and often are that for some significant period of time.

Chronicling the situation fostering this repressed cradle of anger is complex. Individuals have a differential reaction to seemingly equivalent deprivations due to a variety of intervening factors. These include constitutional components, as temperament and physical strength, as well as environmental possibilities, as social support from outside the family. These intervening possibilities also get differential usage. The result is the impossibility of identifying universal direct causality of psychopathology from child abuse. It is also not possible to have universal offsets to the effects of poor parenting and socioeconomic deprivation. At the same time, as noted in our earlier chapter, there are "markers" in the history of abusers, and a high-frequency marker is a history of damaged self-esteem.

As a result we have a viable hypothesis that when the conditions for adaptation are not facilitating normal developmental growth, the subject of such conditions often feels compelled to seek alternatives. These are defensive maneuvers designed to satisfy the basic motivation of self-organization. People are always motivated by a type of narcissism, namely a personal perspective that may be healthy, pathological, or some mixture of the two (Herron, 1999). Narcissism is used here as a descriptive term devoid of moral or evaluative aspects.

When one is abused the self-image is attacked and weakened. There is a loss of respect coming from both the abuser who disregards appropriate interpersonal boundaries, and from the abused, who is left with regret, guilt, and anger at not being able to maintain a self robust enough to avoid abuse. There is likely to be a mixture of feelings, an ambivalence about the cause of what is happening as well as what to do about the situation. Since abuse is coming from a person who is usually depicted as an object of love, both to be given and gotten from, it is usually difficult for the abused to have a firm sense of assigning blame. Moral masochism may pervade a pattern of abuse so that the abuse remains in the situation for some relatively lengthy duration. The time becomes necessary for the person to resolve a conflict as to whom the fault belongs.

Another possibility is that the abused is a child or marital partner who lacks the resources to get out of the home. Then adaptation means blunting the attacks with what frequently turns out to be false hope of a reprieve. Displacement is also possible, with the abused expressing hostility toward others who can be victimized. Other possibilities are being emotionally rescued by understanding others who promote self-esteem, as a relative, teacher, or peers. Also, an abused person may have interests or abilities that are self-affirming as well as providing an emotional outlet, such as musical ability or athleticism. It is also possible that an understanding of irrational behavior and an ability to forgive its effects may take place through exposure to certain philosophical or moral concepts. Abusers often embrace their own view of righteousness through distorting religious concepts of justice, but in the process may involve their family in religion, inadvertently providing an opportunity for a differing view of a moral code.

While all who are abused are left with the fact of having received such distorted care, some escape its more negative impact through various positive alternative adaptations, but many do not. The most damaged survivors are particularly limited in their ability to relate to others. Some of these people avoid relationships, and within this group some are aware of the reasons for their avoidance while others are not. Those who are aware are more likely to seek therapeutic help and make good use of it. They are motivated to get what they missed, so despite their adaptation anxieties, they can work in therapy to restore self-esteem and be able to express both love and aggression in constructive ways.

This can also happen to those who are unaware of what is determining their isolation and potential for unwanted aggression. Unfortunately they are less likely to seek help, but through avoidance and rationalization they may not become involved in domestic violence.

We are left with a rather large group of people, more males than females, who move into adulthood with a desire to relate, but without having learned effective relationship skills. Their models, previously their families, involved a hierarchy of status built on apparent strength that could, and would, be demonstrated through physical force if verbalization was not sufficient. Although not pleased with being the objects of violence, the process of identification nonetheless has its genesis in limited opportunities. Whether male or female, the parents are gender models for personal development. Thus it may be difficult to alter beliefs that although differing from other possibilities in the environment, are ingrained and more influential than suspected by those experiencing such family situations. The potential unconscious influence, given the degree of exposure, is very strong. Extensive damage happens, but those damaged may be both unaware of the impact and the need for appropriate remediation.

Mentalization

Abuse by love objects, particularly family members, engenders suspicion, anxiety, avoidance, anger, guilt, remorse, and self-doubt, among other disturbing affects. There is plenty of reality to support defensive positions, as paranoid, schizoid, depressed, resentful, any and all of them that are likely to disrupt interpersonal relations. A basic underlying defect is apparent in all of this which can be viewed structurally as a limitation in ego functioning as well as accompanying distortions of the superego and the expression of libido and aggression. Self-structure, attachment, and connection to others are all distorted, with one result being the misuse of aggression in domestic situations.

This can occur through difficulty in developing an effective process of mentalization, which is a theory of the mind that explains to one person the intentions of another (Fonagy, Gergeley, Jurist, & Target, 2002). The mentalization system is part of the normal developmental process. It is implicit at about 18 months and explicit between four and six years (Josephs & McLeod, 2014). False beliefs that may develop include insistence on only one interpretation of behavior, denial of self-deception, anger at differing viewpoints, projection of anger in others, and justification of the "correct" view based on apparent objectivity. Such distortion of mentalization is aimed at diminishing or obliterating the appreciation of diverse perspectives.

How does this come about? The self perceives threats to secure attachment and social standing (Fonagy et al., 2002) and defensively becomes angry. There is a repetitive circular process of distorted mentalization, anger, increased distortion, and increased anger (Josephs & McLeod, 2014). Empathy disappears in a preoccupation with being correct and others being wrong. Physical force is viewed as necessary to make one's point, and it often matters little what the other *really* thinks or does. The other is perceived as being wrong and so must be punished in order to be put on the right path. A pattern of domestic violence begins through identification with a pathological theory of the mind (deficient mentalization) involving a false sense of reality (limited ego function) terminating in hostile aggression supported by superego distortion, e.g., "I hit you for your own good."

There is evidence that abused children opt out of attempting to reflect on the mental status of their abusers as a defense against the paradoxical loss of love they are experiencing (Fonagy & Target, 1995) and in so doing limit their mentalization. A developmental pattern of perceived abuse is actualized in the family situation, introjected, and subsequently carried forward when the abused has the opportunity to become the abuser. The theory of the mind that develops restricts intersubjectivity and the appreciation of different perspectives. A dominance hierarchy supported by the expression of anger is considered necessary for self-preservation.

Anger in the domestic abuser appears to be an attempt to maintain or increase status in the family relationship. The need to do this seems to come from feeling downgraded and emotionally injured by the partner or other family members. The engendered feelings remind the abuser of similar prior relational experiences. Reactive anger crystallizes as justification for violence.

"In enraged states the intentions of others are apprehended in terms of psychic equivalence and the teleologic stance as though the intentions of others are physical obstacles to be overcome with brute force rather than as motives to be understood through empathic identification" (Josephs & McLeod, 2014, p. 71).

Tracing patterns of developmental disturbances suggests that children growing up in an atmosphere that they perceive as degrading and dismissive of their needs are likely to feel very angry about their situations. Given their relative lack of power to directly gain satisfaction they are prone to handle their anger defensively rather than by direct confrontation. The defensive avenues chosen, as repression, displacement, or denial, appear to depend on the possibilities offered by abusers, as "just keep your mouth shut." The lack of potential mutuality results in a disruption and distortion in reflective functioning, the capacity to mentalize in a relational context (Slade, 2005). Reflective functioning is facilitated by parents mirroring infant affects, a process aiding the development of self-understanding and the ability to understand the mental states of others. Appropriate mentalizing is most likely to appear in an environment of secure attachment. In contrast, where there is abuse there is limited ability to differentiate emotions of others that could be due to adverse life experiences rather than personal distaste for another person. Such a lack of adequate functioning tends to lead to adverse relational experiences, as domestic violence.

At the same time, it is necessary to keep in mind the broad scope of behavior included in parental neglect, namely the failure to care adequately for children's physical needs and/or a lack of emotional responsiveness. Such neglect is child abuse, but its presence is not an automatic indicator of the neglected child's potential development of maladaptive anger that will be displayed in domestic situations. Abuse has a variable impact depending on its intensity, frequency, and other qualities as well as how the behavior is perceived and the defensive possibilities open to and/or used by the victim. For example, some abused children have been found to possess reflective functioning that appeared to operate as a buffer against future psychopathology (Borrelli, Compare, Snevely, & Decio, 2015).

Reflective functioning, mentalization, empathy, and intersubjectivity are often used interchangeably. The concepts are correlated and focus on the capacity to consider the other as well as the self as parts of an interpersonal field, with an aim of valuing cooperative behavior. Such capacities can also be distinguished in terms of specific definitions, developmental timetables, and motivational origins (Liljenfors & Lundh, 2015). For example, mentalization can be viewed along the four dimensions of cognitive-affective, implicit-explicit, self-other, and internal-external (Fonagy & Bateman, 2012). Intersubjectivity involves both recognition of the experiences of others and sharing personal experiences with others (Brinck, 2008). These distinctions suggest that abuse may in one instance negatively affect one dimension, not another, or one capacity, not another, or all to a different extent. There is also the possibility of reparative work among dimensions resulting in a varying impact from childhood neglect.

Our focus is not on the intricacies of mentalization, its correlates or components, but on the different probabilities limiting prediction from a concept as broad as child abuse. The perception of such abuse is not an automatic predictor of psychopathology such as domestic violence. The perception itself varies along its own dimensions of significance to the victim and these dimensions vary with genetic loads and biological capacities.

A moral dimension is also involved. Once an act is defined as *abuse* it is also defined as *bad*, meaning the outcome is likely to be bad for the abused and indicative of "badness" in the abuser. Such badness is the "dark side," the improper use of aggression. In turn there is a normative use of aggression, neither sadistic or masochistic, but the norm is complex. Struggle with an unknown intruder in your home, hit him hard with anything even if it kills him, and you are still within the norm because you feared he would kill you. Feel the same degree of anger at your small child, and express it verbally or physically, and you are bad. The norm does have a logic and most people follow it, even when frustrated. Not all though and given the often damaging consequences, we have to attempt to sift through the specifics to seek remedies. Treatment is good, prevention, better, but its accuracy rests on accepting the complexity of possible causality.

Causal Pathways

In a domestic situation the desired relationship is one in which both partners have developed their mentalization to a level of discerning, containing, and integrating personal feelings and beliefs with the feelings of the other person. This fosters collaborative relationships rather than hierarchical dominance. Domestic violence involves a failure to achieve this goal on the part of one of the partners. The result is tyrannical control through both emotional and physical force.

In order for intersubjectivity to be operational the mentalization capacities of individuals attempting relationships needs to be nurtured. This means developmental sequences that emphasize understanding cognitive and emotional states of the self and others. Such understanding involves "psychic enrichment of preformed capacities," as thoughts and affects by caretakers. Holding environments do tend to be imperfect so there has to be an acceptable degree of parental failure, but note needs to be taken of potential damage.

It is possible to foster cognitive appreciation while neglecting the emotional component of ideation, as well as fostering affects over thoughts. Thus "different forms of psychopathology may be distinguished in terms of the inhibition, deactivation or simply dysfunction of one or both systems involved, leading to potential *dissociation* between both systems or difficulties in *integrating* cognitive and affective aspects of mentalization" (Fonagy, Bateman, & Luyten 2012, p. 30).

An abuser with overdeveloped cognitive mentalization is attuned to the recognition of apparent false beliefs of another (false based on a mismatch with the abuser's beliefs). Such recognition is congruent with a personal belief in the importance of correcting falsehoods. Force will be used if deemed necessary (in case the other person continues to hold the "false" belief"). The moral imperative is to make certain a partner "thinks right" to the point of "helping" the other forcibly.

If affective mentalization is overdeveloped the intellectual belief used to justify force is replaced by a feeling of justification. In essence "it just feels right" to punish the other for not being synchronized with the punisher. The "right thing" is making sure the other thinks and acts correctly, namely the way that suits the abuser.

It has been suggested that mentalization in an implicit form begins as an innate process. Implicit affective mentalization proceeding to explicit is seen as markedly influenced by caretakers (Liljenfors & Lundh, 2015). The capacity for mentalization could vary from the start. This bears consideration in understanding subsequent development. Significant psychopathology lies in the development of false representations of others, as well as of the self, based on a distorted organization of unconscious self and object representations. This organization is reliant on both the composition of the innate implicit mentalization and false representations from caregivers. The result can be a large supply of misinformation.

Another issue is the relative balance of the internal–external dimension of mentalization. The former emphasizes mental processes of the self, while the external focuses on visible features and observable actions of others. In the first instance self-absorption makes it difficult to recognize the acceptable perspective of another who may often be viewed as an intruder, and in turn, dangerous. In the second case, the subject views the other as an apparent judge who is likely to disapprove and unsettle the subject. As such it is difficult to appreciate the possibility of acceptance despite differences.

The dimensions noted do overlap so there is relative differentiation. Also, these are described in the categorical language accompanying and including mentalization. They can be described in other psychoanalytic language as well. For example they could be considered as ego functions (thought, perception), superego functions (correctness, accuracy) and id functions (desire, wish). Another possibility is viewing them as relational functions (the self as an agent in action with others). Mentalization language seems to add details to the understanding of self and object perceptions, and in turn facilitates the comprehension of the complex development of psychopathology. This is particularly true in regard to domestic violence where people lose their way in terms of appreciating and respecting others, turning supposed loved ones into enemies with an intent to destroy them.

Revenge

The path to becoming an abuser starts with narcissistic injury. We have described being abused in childhood by one or both parents as an example. However, childhood abuse does not automatically result in becoming an abuser or developing significant psychopathology, though it is a likely source. The narcissistic injury is such that due to reparative ineffectiveness it is not healed, and often instead it is reinforced as a negative self-representation. Rosen (2007) notes the probability of a cumulative accretion through the psychosexual stages. In essence, it is likely to get worse, with the probability of the victim becoming either a primarily sadistic or masochistic character. Within the frame of domestic violence the dynamics of the sadistic abuser have drawn the most interest. Such a person has suffered narcissistic injury that diminishes their sense of self. They are in a painful state of shame that feels unbearable and must be defended against by a fixation on getting even for the injury. The result is a vengeful obsession that obscures their shame. Splitting offers a way to avoid a state of mind that seems unbearable. The shame of living within a diminished self is replaced with empowering rage at the offender with projective identification used to relocate the shame. The shamed victim becomes endowed with the power of rage at the offender and seeks revenge (LaFarge, 2006; Lansky, 2007; Rosen, 2007).

The focus of revenge research had not been on domestic violence, although Lansky mentions it as an example of overt vengefulness, and the dynamics fit the profile of many domestic abusers. The emphasis on narcissistic injury is particularly appropriate. LaFarge sees narcissistic injury as "meaning-disrupting" with revenge as the perceived way to restore both the story of personal meaning and an audience for the story. There are fantasies of the imaginer and the imagined that often have been formed through parent-child relationships that initiated the narcissistic injuries. She states "the fantasy of a sadistic imaginer and its mirror image, the fantasy of revenge, are fundamental ways that we represent and manage pain and rage that are felt to intrude on the representations of a continuous self and a benevolent imagining other" (p. 473).

This explanation can be applied to domestic violence. The abuser has experienced narcissistic injury, namely a damaged sense of individual meaning, and seeks revenge as restoration that includes being valued by the other person. Narcissism, shame, and rage are all involved. LaFarge also notes the relative difficulty of ameliorating vengefulness and illustrates that with a clinical example that emphasizes the repetitive pull to the fantasy of revenge.

Lansky emphasizes the shame that is involved in narcissistic injury. The injured person defends against shame by splitting off a revenge linkage to the offender from customary obligations to the social order. Treatment attempts to restore the connection to shame, the resolution of splitting, and a type of self-forgiveness involving a modification of the ego-ideal. Lansky also acknowledges the difficulty of working this out successfully and demonstrates the problem with clinical material.

Rosen adds a relational component, the connection to the "exciting/rejecting object." The reference is to the mother, both needed and resented, loved and hated, the incipient source and target of ambivalence that can involve an array of differentiated resolutions. He postulates that "the disappointments and betrayals of exciting/rejecting form the nexus of a revenge orientation made stronger with each compulsive repetition . . . with persons who . . . stand as displaced surrogates for the original participants in the primary drama" (p. 608).

The depiction of the revenge state of mind could also be described as a failure in mentalization. This view has been used by Josephs and McLeod (2014) in conceptualizing and treating anger management problems. In domestic violence the inability and unwillingness to see the viewpoint of the other is used by one partner as a justification for violence.

THEORETICAL SYNTHESIS

Domestic violence is likely to take place when the abuser has a history of narcissistic injuries that shame the hurt person to the point that he feels it is unbearable and must be relieved. The shame is defended against by having an available target, a domestic partner, who based on mutual interactions requires punishment as the ultimate symbol of the source of all the abuser's terrible feelings. Anger at perceived psychic wounds turns into rage and is expressed in physical action against the partner. This is empowering for the abuser and at the time of expression has become justified through splitting.

However, there is a frequent pattern of cyclical rage and remorse as the violence alternates between good and bad selves of the abuser. The shame of narcissistic injury that has been split off and justified is replaced by the shame of injuring a loved one. Thus a broader superego activates the incongruity of self as a good person turning into self as a bad person, regardless of the real or imagined provocation. The expectation of the self-representation is that anger will be contained, or, if there is a need to express rage, that it will not be so lethal, particularly toward a partner.

In the revenge model the design is not specifically for the domestic abuser, but applicable to a point, the difference being that in domestic abuse the splitting is a more limited defense that has its weak moments. The revenge model emphasizes both an obsessive rage and the denial of shame that are applicable to chronic, unrelenting abusers. More common are acute, intermittent abusers who alternate abuse with regret, both intense but appearing to be episodes of ambitendency, the precursor of ambivalence, that remains unresolved. Thus abusers appear to have borderline traits, particularly making the object, and the self, all good or all bad.

The abuser lacks the ability for object constancy and self-constancy. It is a shifting landscape of relations. Mentalization plays a role, appearing in fragmented form as an underdeveloped capacity. Full development involves the ability to understand and appreciate the motives of the self and others at the same time and in a consistent adaptable manner. The abuser is limited in this area. Fluidity is replaced with erratic perception and behaviors that eventuate in cyclical behavior aimed at restoration of a continuous self-representation that seems capable of only an imaginary existence. Sadism or masochism dominate, become excessive, replace each other, but on a temporary basis. The abuser cannot get a fix on himself, and as a result is seen by others as at best erratic and hypersensitive. He is difficult to be around and it is very difficult for him to relate to others because of his dubious identity.

A major problem in understanding the dynamics of abusers is the complexity and extent of instances that are considered by each person as narcissistic injuries. Added to this is the problem of attempting to anticipate, or track, the patterns of behavior that will take place as defensive maneuvers to alleviate psychic wounds, and to sort out successful adaptations from tentative pathological efforts. We are usually left with introspective possibilities undoubtedly containing inaccuracies. At the same time, these hypothesized explanations can contain at least possible correlates that border on causality.

The basic etiology of abusers appears to be the personal perception of psychic injury inflicted by others that results in the self-perception of being victimized. The "true" intentions of others may never be known, but the therapeutic situation provides a window into current situations that are likely to be reflective of the past. Such a view is most available in the therapist–patient relationship and in the patient's description of interpersonal activities. Both instances are likely to provide the therapist with the impression that the patient frequently misunderstands the intentions of others. The misunderstanding is in the direction of seeing others as malevolent to varying degrees. The patient often feels victimized, shamed in some manner so that the self is weakened. This feeling is defended against with "soft" moves, such as avoidance, mistaken impressions, but if the shame becomes unbearable, which happens often enough to be a problem, there are more intense inappropriate responses. In the domestic situation this can mean rage and violence directed toward a partner and other household members.

Acting upon rage becomes justified for the abuser in the moment. This justification is usually "carried" as accurate at the same time that there may be an apology and remorse for the action. Self-recrimination, disavowal of the action, and a stated resolution to never do it again also may occur. The switching of sadistic and masochistic positions represents an attempt to unify the self and regain a sense of wholeness after having a hole punched into the self-representation. The ability to maintain and contain contradictory desires is deficient. There is no unifying position because they both represent in some form the loss of the ability to protect against narcissistic injury. No position can be maintained without a firm belief in their justification as the only means of adaptation. In more extreme pathological abusers a single-minded approach may appear without masochistic pauses. These are examples of obsessive revenge and are acted out in relationships as a form of absolute control of the other where the mentalization of the abuser is obsessively preoccupied with a very personal viewpoint that must be in force for both parties in a relationship.

However, most of the domestic abuse cases that involve the abuser being in treatment on a voluntary basis involve the sadistic-masochistic pattern that keeps a tie to the target. This indicates at least an awareness of the "not-right" behavior although not an eradication of the possible correctness of the abuser's original opinion and behavior. Often the awareness of the social and moral incorrectness is temporarily diminished by drugs and/or alcohol use by the abuser. Victims also can say or do enough to be viewed as provocative. Recognition of the consequences of the abuse nonetheless awaits. In today's "no secrets" environment it is very likely to happen. What might have passed for "microaggressions in everyday life" in the past are no longer so likely to be ignored.

Nonetheless there are instances where probable negative consequences are ignored with grandiosity triumphing so that the abuser feels safe, powerful, in command, and acts out. These situations are more likely to occur when the abuser has achieved some status that can become congruent with pathological narcissism. The remediation of abuse is more difficult because of previous social support for the person being "special," so the abuser thinks of himself as "untouchable."

The more prevalent pattern is the cyclical switching that we have described. In this abusers who have a need to go too far and have an awareness of this are more likely to accept treatment. That does not mean they will be easy to treat or that treatment will be effective. Despite their attempts to undo their actions, sadism dominates the cycle. They "carry" their dynamics of perceiving injury from another, loss of status, need for restoration, and violent enactment that seems justified at a particular time. They often do not relinquish the idea that in a relationship a point may come where violence is the only solution to the perceived personal injury being inflicted on them. Although a masochistic attitude may follow vengeful action it operates more as a way out of being deprived of the "exciting/frustrating" object who usually forgives them and continues the relationship.

Why do people get into such relationships and why do they allow them to continue when they become dangerous for both parties? The partners bring unresolved narcissistic injuries to the relationship and are seeking resolution, although the motivation may be unconscious and may not surface unless they get into a therapeutic situation. The abuser wants a target for his unacceptable rage. He seeks a woman who is vulnerable to his apparent attributes, the most enticing being whatever she feels she needs based on her history. Examples are perception of strength suggesting a good provider and caretaker, or perceptions of warmth suggesting consistent intimacy, provided the woman feels a need for one or more of those. Her need will cause her to overlook at least some contradictions in his behavior. Once violence occurs, his subsequent contrition will keep her in the loop for some time as she justifies her masochism as necessary for her survival.

The abuser will be looking for someone who he believes will enhance his self-image. Possibilities include perceived care-taking characteristics, as tolerance of behavior, relatively unqualified acceptance, physical attractiveness, whatever he views as indications of taking care of him. Much of this motivation will be unconscious and operates as a standard the woman is unlikely to be able to meet. As a result he will be disappointed, as she will be with the extent of his narcissism. She is likely to be resentful, but is usually less powerful and more dependent, so he has an edge. His rage will be tolerated while her anger will be felt by him as a provocation. If she is prone to blaming herself for failed relationships this may continue and facilitate his continuing abuse. At some point the "exciting/frustrating" object may see the risk of enduring the relationship and either threaten to withdraw or withdraw. That is usually met with a non-enduring contrition.

We have already noted the difficulty of treating obsessive rage, which is often seen in domestic violence. If there is no recognition by the abuser of responsibility for the violence, the person tends to avoid treatment, or to be uncooperative if it is forced on him. Thus for treatment to have any positive effect it is necessary for the abuser to have, or gain, some awareness of the meaning and consequences of physical and mental abuse. Most abusers who come for treatment do have such awareness, but are prone to splitting off the negativity. Justification remains an available and enduring idea. In addition, their partners often accept an inordinate amount of blame, keeping themselves at risk.

The dyad described here, male abuser, female abused, is the most frequent combination. The reverse is possible, as are other variations, as male-male, female-female, or a disturbed child terrorizing an entire family. We are focusing on the situation most often encountered by therapists. This reflects the gender differences still present in society. Men are more socially dominant, have more power, and are less motivated to understand the feelings of others (Benbassat & Priel, 2015). Their limited reflective functioning is in accord with the role of an abuser.

Achieving a therapeutic effect rests upon achieving some major changes in the dyad. The first is getting each partner to understand the sources of the role they are enacting. This can be brought about through the reconstruction of the narcissistic injuries involving shame and the loss of status and self-integrity. There is a cathartic element and an opportunity for insight and the opportunity to reframe the situation. The individual can understand that past shaming does not have to be an automatic reaction to current situations. Similar feelings may arise based on memory connections, but greater understanding can lead to different relational patterns. Other changes involve assisting in the interpersonal shifts both through the medium of the therapeutic relationship and experimenting with different interpersonal reactions to potentially injurious relational situations. The major analytic tools, emotional insight and new relational experience, can be used to create the possibility of a more collaborative domestic situation.

CLINICAL EXAMPLES

We will use therapeutic encounters where we were supervisors of the therapists who were involved. We are doing this to keep patient identities confidential and to increase objectivity by having less direct involvement with the patients described.

Our first example is a man in his forties, married with two young children and a wife who no longer worked, instead doing most of the child and household care. He sought therapy for both anxiety and depression. He had been raised by an overprotective mother and it became apparent that he viewed his wife as a replacement for his mother. His transference with the therapist put her in the same category. While successful at his work, he felt compelled to pay attention to it as if he was again relating to his mother who had demanded his attention in return for shielding him from many of the struggles of ordinary life. His difficulties at work began with a female superior whom he experienced as excessively demanding. Wanting his wife to be an eternally sympathetic ear, he continually demanded her attention in listening to his problems in the office. He operated in a similar way in therapy, leaving the therapist struggling to get more personal material. His wife had her own difficulties in regard to the children and the home, so she wanted him to listen to her problems, but her issues held little interest for him. Her reaction was to give him some time and move on to her concerns, which annoyed him.

He experienced his superior as dismissing him, his wife doing this as well, and although not directly stated, he seems to have viewed the therapist that way. The original patterns of narcissistic injury involved in the suggestion of weakness requiring maternal protection and a failure to achieve adequate separation-individuation were reactivated. The repetition was in a different form, failure to acknowledge him as an individual deserving positive recognition that he needed to feel adequate.

He felt ashamed and angry. Restricted at work by the possibility of a negative evaluation, he displaced the force of his anger on his wife. She resented this and reacted with her own anger. His rage escalated and began shoving and hitting her. She was furious and threatened separation. He apologized and attempted to both modulate his reactions and be more understanding of her need to talk to him about her issues. However, he was unsuccessful as he considered her problems minor compared to his. They appeared locked in an ever-increasing hostile relationship where at times he continued to use physical force to attempt to make his point. She continued to pose the threat of separation, but did not act upon it, instead using repeated recriminations to make her needs known. Finally, in what seemed to be a desperate act on his part, he made a disastrous move at the office, getting fired. He then used that as a sadistic maneuver to show her how she had driven him and the entire family into financial ruin. He completed the picture by dropping out of treatment, thereby showing his female therapist how inadequate a mother she was.

In reviewing the course of the therapy it seemed that not enough time had been given to developing an understanding of the impact on his ego functions of his involvement with his mother. His attempt at separating and individuating by getting married appeared to have caused his mother to move away from him so he needed more from his wife, and his therapist. The wife did not listen in the right way, and the therapist concluded that she may have had the same problem from his viewpoint. Also, the marital relationship heated up before the therapist expected it and her reaction was to focus on the consequences of that for the man. She told him he could not express his rage through physical violence, an understandable concern on her part. He let her know he was aware of that, but in retrospect she felt her manner had been such that he may have felt his anger and frustration were not being understood. He appears to have ultimately tried to destroy his wife, himself, and the therapist by failing at his work, but the personal consequences were secondary to getting the attention of the women that he craved. In his transference he merged the therapist and his wife to reflect his rage at his mother for not loving him in the way he wanted, and he turned the therapeutic situation into yet another narcissistic injury.

The therapist subsequently realized that the extent of this man's rage frightened her to the point of limiting her capacity for empathy. She stopped becoming the mother of a holding environment where she would not be destroyed by anger. Once recognizing that she was able to reach out to him and restart the therapy with a better understanding of his needs and capabilities, which did include a willingness to begin again with this therapist, his wife, and a new employer, also female.

Our second example focuses on the victim of abuse. She is 30 years old and suffered a childhood of repeated narcissistic injuries. Her parents were always fighting, including physical violence, and they divorced. Her father was given to outbursts of anger and her mother was always critical of her. She feared her father and wanted to marry someone who was different, calmer, less volatile. She was particularly interested in feeling secure. Her mother and father were never able to do this for her. She met a man who appeared both calm and warm and whose family was intact and radiated security as far as she could tell. Also, her husband was not a drinker, an appealing contrast to her father.

Once she was married the picture changed. Although her husband's mother and father lived together they spent most of their time apart. Her husband had an older married brother whom the mother favored. She focused on helping them care for their children. The brother's wife was openly critical of the patient while the brother ignored her. Her husband was assertive, but more demanding than supportive. He was a diligent worker, but over time that required a drinking habit to handle the stress of his job. Soon he was coming home and taking out his repressed hostility on his wife by pushing her around. She began to fear him as she had her father. She turned to her mother for support and instead received advice on how to improve herself.

Therapy involved a detailed examination of her history of narcissistic injuries. She was vulnerable to the opinion of others, particularly her mother, whom she tried to have as an ally, but failed to gain acceptance. It was difficult for the therapist to get her to understand how her mother undermined the patient's self-confidence and how that led her into the search for security that had such a problematic outcome.

Fortunately the violence at home, while repetitive, was neither extreme nor so frequent that there was an imminent crisis. It was possible to spend considerable time understanding the deprivations of childhood. The patient was not adept at empathizing with others due to a preoccupation with her own damaged self, so her relationships were limited and she kept a safe distance from others. She had the potential to be a capable person, but self-doubt usually appeared when she had to make personal choices.

She did feel supported by the therapist, but remained fixated on trying to get her mother's love. She developed a false empathy for her husband using her mother's guidelines, despite such an approach being suspect given that her mother had failed in her marriage. The couple had a tolerable relationship as the patient toned down her expressions of hostility. They had a child, which provided a sufficient diversion for both of them to focus their energies. This also got her mother more involved with her as she allowed her mother to be involved in the care of the child. She admitted to the therapist that she did not feel loved by the mother or her husband, who now placated and diverted, stopped physical abuse and kept verbal abuse at a minimum. She did feel loved by the child, although she wondered how long that would last and if the child really loved the grandmother more. She decided the existing situation was good enough, thanked the therapist for his support, and terminated. For the therapist, too much was unresolved, so it was not good enough. The potential for subsequent violence did remain, as well as the potential for the woman to continue her victimization.

CONCLUSION

We began this chapter with a focus on domestic violence as a directed type of aggression targeting family members. The lack of psychoanalytic studies in this area was noted, as well as the controversy regarding the origins of aggression. Definitive evidence is not available as to the genesis of aggression, so at the moment the most probable solution is a multiple causality model involving both instinctual and interpersonal factors. Within that model we focused on developmental difficulties, as mentalization involving reflective functioning. This provided a foundation for exploring causal pathways for the expression of domestic violence. Possibilities included the overdevelopment of either cognitive or affective mentalization, false representations of the self and others, and an imbalance of internal-external mentalization.

In general the pathways to violence for both abusers and the abused begin with narcissistic injuries inflicted early in life and continuing throughout the life span. These are "perceived" injuries so there are many possibilities based on the innate characteristics as well as the life circumstances of each person. The reliability of any narcissistic injury is in turn variable, but it is always worth consideration. Pathological narcissism, shame, and rage are usually involved as well as revenge fantasies and a connection to an "exciting/rejecting" object. For the abuser there tends to be a cyclical process of rage and shame, each a temporary defense against the other. Such a process can also be found in the abused, but with masochism dominating as opposed to sadism in the abuser.

Narcissistic injuries create fixations of shame that reappear in situations that revive memories that are defended against by extreme reactions of sadistic rage toward a partner in domestic situations as well as shifts into reparative masochism, or embracing victimization as the path to love not received alternating with efforts at self-assertion. The former is the path of the abuser, the latter the way of the abused. These relationships are difficult to alter through therapeutic interventions due to both partners' need for the exciting/frustrating object that began in early life and remains as an unsatisfied quest. Clinical examples were cited to illustrate the therapeutic difficulties, although interpretation and differentiated interpersonal experience have therapeutic value. Psychotherapy can be more effective when both abuser and abused recognize the personal consequences of their roles.

DISCUSSION QUESTIONS

1. What is the major issue regarding the origin of domestic violence?
2. What are the differences between psychodynamic and social learning theories of domestic violence?
3. What are the similarities in psychodynamic and social theories of domestic violence?
4. What are the major differences?
5. Are there specific factors to consider in this regard when considering individuals with multiple gender identities?

REFERENCES

Auchincloss, E. L., & Samberg, E. (2012) (Eds.). *Psychoanalytic terms and concepts.* New Haven, CT: Yale University Press.

Benbassat, N., & Priel, B. (2015). Why is fathers' reflective function important? *Psychoanalytic Psychology, 32,* 1–22.

Bohart, A. C. (2013). Introduction: The dark side metaphor. In A. C. Bohart, B. S. Held, E. Mendelowitz, & K. J. Schneider (Eds.), *Humanity's dark side. Evil, destructive experience, and psychotherapy* (pp. 3–13). Washington, DC: American Psychological Association.

Borelli, J. L., Compare, A., Snavely, J. E., & Decio, V. (2015). Reflective functioning moderates the association between perceptions of parental neglect and attachment in psychopathology. *Psychoanalytic Psychology,* 32, 23–35.

Brinck, I. (208) The role of intersubjectivity in the development of intentional communication. In J. Zlatev, T. P. Racine, C. Sinha, & E. Itkomen (Eds.), *The shared mind: Perspectives in intersubjectivity* (pp. 115–140). Amsterdam: Benjamin Publishing.

Fonagy, P., & Bateman, A. (2012) (Eds.). *Handbook of mentalizing in mental health practice.* Arlington, VA: American Psychiatric Publishing, Inc.

Fonagy, P., Bateman, A. W., & Luyten, P. (2012). Introduction and overview. In P. Fonagy and A. W. Bateman (Eds.), *Handbook of mentalizing in mental health practice* (pp. 3–41). Arlington, VA: American Psychiatric Publishing, Inc.

Fonagy, P., Gergely, G., Jurist, E., & Target, M. (2002). *Affect regulation, mentalization, and the development of the self.* New York: Other Press.

Fonagy, P., & Target, M. (1995). Understanding the violent person. The use of the body and the role of the father. *The International Journal of Psychoanalysis, 77,* 217–233.

Herron, W. G. (1999). *Narcissism and the relational world.* Lanham, MD: University Press of America.

Hollis, J. (2013). Theogonies and therapies: A Jungian perspective on humanity's Dark side. In A. C. Bohart, B. S. Held, E. Mendelitz, & K. J. Schneider (Eds.), *Humanity's dark side. Evil, destructive experience, and psychotherapy, (pp. 83–97).* Washington, DC: American Psychological Association.

Josephs, L., & McLeod, B. A. (2014). A theory of mind-focused anger management. *Psychoanalytic Psychology, 31,* 68–83.

LaFarge, L. (2006). The wish for revenge. *Psychoanalytic Quarterly,* 75, 447–476.

Lansky, M. R. (2007). The resolution of vengefulness. *Journal of the American Psychoanalytic Association, 55,* 571–594.

Liljenfors, R., & Lundh, L-G. (2015). Mentalization and intersubjectivity towards a theoretical integration. *Psychoanalytic Psychology, 32,* 36–60.

Mitchell, S. A. (1993). Aggression and the endangered self. *Psychoanalytic Quarterly, 62,* 351–382.

Rizzuto, A. M., Meissner, W. W., & Buie, D. H. (2004). *The dynamics of human aggression.* New York: Brunner-Routledge.

Rosen, I. (2007). Revenge: A psychoanalytic experience. *Journal of the American Psychoanalytic Associaion,* 55, 595–620.

Rizzuto, A. M., Meissner, W. W., & Buie, D. H.. The dynamics of human aggression. New York: Brunner-Routledge. *Journal of the American Psychoanalytic Association,* 54, 298–304.

Schmidt-Hellerau, C. (2002). Why aggression? *International Journal of Psychoanalysis,* 83, 1269–1289/

Slade, A. (2005). Parental reflective functioning: An introduction. *Attachment and Human Development, 7,* 269–281.

Sue, D. W. (2010). *Microaggressons in everyday life: Race, gender, and sexual orientation.* Hoboken, NJ: Wiley.

Chapter Six

Twenty-First-Century Medeas, Medusas, and Salomes

Violence Female Style

June F. Chisholm and Kristy Magee

Violence in our society committed by men, women, adolescents, and children is seemingly increasing and ubiquitous. Consider (1) the terrorist attacks in France in January and November of 2015: in January, the 17 individuals killed included the editor, cartoonists, and other staff of *Charlie Hebdo* (a satirical magazine), hostages taken at a Kosher grocery store, a police woman and a policeman, and three of the four terrorists; in November, gunmen and suicide bombers coordinated attacks on a concert hall, major stadium, restaurants, and bars killing more than 125 people and wounding hundreds; (2) the horrific criminal case in May 2014 of two 12-year-old girls who stabbed their 12-year-old girlfriend 19 times in a wooded area of Waukesha, Wisconsin, and left her for dead to impress "Slenderman," a fictitious person created in Florida circa 2009 by Eric Knudsen, who posted death and horror stories to websites—the victim survived her attack and the perpetrators are being charged as adults; (3) the news coverage of beheadings of journalists held hostage by terrorists of ISIS and a female jihadist prepared to behead hostages for the advancement of ISIS; (4) Aileen Wuornos, a convicted serial killer who was executed in 2002 for murdering seven men between 1989 and 1990 while working as a prostitute along the highways of Daytona Beach, Florida; and (5) hundreds of YouTube videos of girls physically fighting.

Why write a chapter on violent females at this time? The perception, if not the evidence, is that girls, adolescent females, and adult women may be changing, becoming more aggressive and violence prone than those of previous generations. The issues embedded in this question confound efforts to obtain information on the prevalence and nature of women's violent behavior: is the social concern about violent females more a reflection of the shifting nature of gendered social roles and boundaries in a patriarchal social structure or an indication of real changes in female offending? In this chapter we will discuss female-perpetrated violence. We will give an overview on gendered violence, discuss its characteristics, the demographics of female-perpetrated violence, and review different psychological perspectives that offer various explanations for why girls and women act violently. We will briefly discuss the impact of technology (e.g., cyberspace and information and communications technology, or ICTs), and racial/ethnic considerations on female-perpetrated violence. We present clinical material throughout to illustrate points raised and highlight the challenges that professionals face in the assessment, treatment, and prevention of violence.

The zeitgeist about violence, especially dating, domestic, and intimate partner violence, has generated a social climate supporting research and social science perspectives that frame males as "perpetrators" and females as "victims," despite research which shows that domestic violence and Intimate Partner Violence (IPV) occur in gay, lesbian, bisexual, and transgender (GLBT) relationships in which females are perpetrators and males are victims, respectively (Ahmed & Jindasurat, 2015; Baker et al., 2013). The power of social and political pressure which perpetuates this misconception was evident and illustrated on September 27, 2011, when Vice President Joe Biden appeared on the television show *The View* to discuss domestic violence against women and the Violence Against Women Act of 1994 (VAWA), a federal law that he helped formulate. As he was highlighting some of the provisions for prosecuting male offenders, co-host Whoopi Goldberg began to interject the comment that women should not hit. Vice President Biden cut her off before she could finish expressing her thought and returned to highlighting the main points of the legislation. His message seemed to be that men, not women, should be seen as the problem, i.e., men are the perpetrators of domestic violence; therefore legislation should rightly be directed toward providing services to women and children, the victims of violent men, who would now, under the law, be prosecuted for their crimes. Whoopi Goldberg's point of view was effectively silenced.

Indeed, women and girls worldwide are overwhelmingly the victims of violence in and outside of the home (e.g., the kidnapping of girls in Nigeria by the Boko Haram, sex trafficking, forced marriages, honor killings, female infanticides, etc.). Some argue that their victimization is due to gender inequality (i.e., lack of power relative to men). Others point to powerful resistance to the modifications in the socially constructed gendered behaviors, expectations, and roles for men and women witnessed in the second half of the twentieth century. That women are victims of violence is indisputable;

however, this truth has obscured efforts to understand them as potential perpetrators of violence also.

Tatum's (1997) comparison of cultural racism to smog is a useful analogy to understanding the impact of violence and those perpetrating violence in our daily lives. We live in a violent society, characterized by a cultural climate in which meanness and antisocial behaviors have seemingly become normative. The possibility and inevitability of exposure to some form of violence has intruded into aspects of everyone's public and private life, albeit, in varying degrees. Hence, all of us—children, adolescents, and adult men and women—deal with transgressions and mini microaggressions that inflict mini-traumas of everyday life on many. Others suffer profound trauma for which they may or may not receive professional help and/or from which they may or may not recover. The connection between trauma and violent behavior needs to be better understood as the research indicates its salience in female-perpetrated violence. Today, the sequence from the internal state of distress to the manifest violent outburst might be: rejection/ shunned/ hurt feelings, estrangement/social isolation/social withdrawal, retreat into fantasy, increased use of ICTs/computers into virtual fantasies with others who also have been rejected/shunned/ and/or are experiencing hurt feelings, release of anger/hate/rage, revenge in social media, blurred boundaries between fantasy/reality, physical aggression, infliction of emotional/psychological pain, stalking, and ultimately killing in real time. In short, hurt people hurt people.

It is noteworthy that Heidensohn (2010) argues that women's violent potential is real and not all violent acts by women stem directly from their involvement in abusive relationships. This idea of the violent female whose actions are not an outgrowth of her victimization by a male is threatening to the collective sense of why women become violent, given the socially constructed role females play as the "weaker sex," nurturers, and guardians of social mores. McHugh et al. (2005) posit a conceptualization of women's use of violence as a "complex, multifaceted, and dynamic aspect of human interaction that occurs in multiple forms and patterns. The experience and meaning of violence is viewed as being connected to both the relationship and the larger context in which the violence occurs" (p. 323).

UNDERSTANDING VIOLENT WOMEN: CONTEXT AND TRAJECTORY

Within the scientific community, a paradigm organizes the research and theory-building of its members. This paradigm defines the scope and breadth of a phenomenon, the methods of scientific inquiry, and what knowledge ensues from the replication of empirical studies. Aberrations and anomalies, if recognized as such at all, are initially seen as glitches in methodology rather than an indication that the theory is flawed. Knowledge acquired in this way is not linear but cyclical in nature. In other words, we don't know more about female-perpetrated violence than we did 100 years ago. What we know reflects the ebb and flow of our awareness and understanding, influenced not only by what occurs within scientific communities, but also what is occurring in society at large (Kuhn, 1962).

That said, our current scientific knowledge and consequent approaches to dealing with the phenomenon we call "violence" may not be indicative of and/or comprehensive enough to adequately address what is occurring now in our society. For example, current research methodologies may obscure and confound rather than elucidate the complexities of violent behavior and those who act violently; parsing out how variables such as ethnicity/race, class, gender, sexual orientation, and so on factor into violent behavior continues to be difficult.

This is apparent in the literature that has been examining for the past two decades the newer forms of violence involving electronic technologies. Cyberbullying, once associated with children, is now reported among college students, as well as young and older adults in the workplace (Aricak et al., 2008; Bhat, 2008; Finn, 2004; Liau et al., 2005; Muir, 2005; Pellegrini & Long, 2002; Smith & Williams, 2004). The intentional and repeated harm inflicted through the use of computers, cell phones, or other electronic devices (Hinduja & Patchin, 2009; Kowalski et al., 2007; Patchin & Hinduja, 2010) has expanded the mechanism by which harm can be exerted onto others and has necessitated attempts to clarify distinctions between "covert" and "overt" behaviors which often co-occur in online interactions. Research has found gender differences in the characteristics of perpetrators and victims of cyberbullying, suggesting in general that females engage in and are victimized more often by covert/relational aggression online. Aboujaoude (2011) suggests that the psychological functioning of users of these newer technologies changes as they develop a "virtual" personality or "virtual" identities characterized by anonymity and disinhibition that predispose them to act differently online than they do in face-to-face interactions. He writes,

> The result of all these online interactions is the unwitting creation of an e-identity, a virtual whole that is greater than its parts and that, despite not being real, is full of life and vitality. Unfettered by old rules of behaving, social exchange, etiquette, or even netiquette, this virtual personality is more assertive, less restrained, a little bit on the dark side, and decidedly sexier. (p. 20)

In light of the above examples of how changes in society impact scientific inquiry and knowledge about phenomena, the phenomenon of the "violent woman" also requires that we reexamine and reconceptualize the framework through which theories, research, and interventions/programs on violence have been based. McHugh, Livingston, and Ford (2005) make the important observation that as social scientists begin to recognize the varied contexts, types of relationships, and groups of people perpetrating violence, conceptions about the phenomenon change, and so do the terms used to describe it (e.g., from "wife abuse" to "intimate partner violence").

The idea of the "violent woman" does not fit neatly into an epistemology based on maleness and male behavior; our understanding of violence has been gendered in accordance with the culture, institutions, and systems that regulate social interactions, which in turn are gendered within a patriarchal society. Even when there is an apparent similarity in the actual violent behaviors committed by individual men and women, the meaning and context in which the behavior occurs may be lost when using a framework that cannot "see" a difference. For example, some research has found an apparent similarity in motivation (e.g., coercive control) for some males and females who perpetrate IPV (Robertson & Murachver, 2011); other research has found that there are gender differences in the meaning of "coercive control" (Hamby, McDonald, & Grych, 2014; McHugh et al., 2005).

Our understanding of the violent female has also been limited by the scientific community's continued struggle to incorporate diversity within concepts about groups that have heretofore been construed as homogeneous. Cole (1986) raised questions about research on the generic term "woman"; earlier research failed to examine the heterogeneity among women with respect to differences concerning ethnicity/race, socioeconomic status, sexual orientation, ableism, and ageism. Cole (1986) states, "that which women have in common must always be viewed in relation to the particularities of a group, for even when we narrow our focus to one particular group of women it is possible for differences within that group to challenge the primacy of what is shared in common" (p. 3).

MYTHICAL VIOLENT FEMALES: ALLEGORICAL IMAGES

Violent females have been seen in literature, Greek and Roman mythology, and sporadically over the years in scientific literature. However, the significance of their histories or "herstories" to our understanding of the vicissitudes of our human proclivity toward aggression and violence has neither been appreciated nor fully understood. Lord Astor, a British philanthropist, is credited with the following statement: "Everyone starts out totally dependent on a woman. The idea that she could turn out to be your enemy is terribly frightening" (Pearson, 1998, p. 1).

In Euripides' version of the Greek tragedy about Medea, she kills several people including two of the sons she had with Jason, her husband, who betrayed her by leaving her to marry King Creon's daughter, Glauce. The king, Glauce, and others were killed by Medea, who is portrayed as deadly aggressive in furthering her aims of ambition and revenge. The idea of a mother deliberately harming her children as a strategy to further another agenda is disturbing. Indeed, in Grimms' fairy tales this dangerous mother is not "mother" but "stepmother," lessening the threat by shifting attention away from aspects of the dynamics fraught with conflict, aggression, and rivalry between mother and child, especially the mother/daughter relationship.

Salome, a biblical figure, is depicted as an exemplar of dangerous female seductiveness because of her dance mentioned in the New Testament of the Bible. This dance supposedly had an erotic effect on Herod, who granted Salome's cold, callous request—egged on by her mother—to kill John the Baptist and serve his severed head on a platter. The violence committed by these mythical women—violence directed toward those close to them (children, partners, parents, relatives), violence tainted with sexuality, violence triggered by anger, jealousy, ambition, greed, shame, betrayal—shock and frighten us, particularly those among us who can recognize and resonate with our own capacity for destructiveness and/or that capacity for destructiveness in those close to us.

While few people can actually name infamous female serial killers, their nicknames (e.g., Giggling Grandma, Lonely Hearts Killer for women, vs. the Boston Strangler, Jack the Ripper, names given to male serial killers) convey the idea that the female serial killer goes against our views about the basic non-threatening nature of women and femininity; the statistics show that approximately one in every six serial killers in the United States is a woman; the total number of serial killers from 1800 to 1995 was approximately 400, with 16% of them female and whose total number is estimated to be between 400 to 600 (Vronsky, 2007).

WOMEN'S CONTRIBUTION TO VIOLENCE: DOMESTIC AND INTIMATE PARTNER VIOLENCE

Domestic violence involving criminal acts includes rape, sexual assault, robbery, and aggravated and simple assault committed by intimate partners (current or former spouses, boyfriends or girlfriends), immediate family members (parents, children, siblings) or other relatives. Children living in environments where there is domestic violence can be victimized in a number of ways. They can witness the violence among family members and/or they can be abused or neglected. It is noteworthy that in 2012, 45.3% of the perpetrators in child abuse cases were male and 53.5% were female (Safe Horizon, 2014). The majority of child homicides are committed by women (Pearson, 1998). For a more comprehensive discussion on the incidence of violence, see the introductory chapter and chapters 1 and 2 of this book. Below we will highlight some of this incidence only to emphasize women's contribution to these statistics.

According to the Bureau of Justice Statistics (2014), the majority of domestic violence between 2003 and 2012 was simple assault (64%); occurred at or close to the victim's home; was highest among the 18- to 24-year-old group and lowest for individuals 65 years or older. During that period: 48% of injuries were from IPV, 37% of injuries resulted from immediate family members, and 26% were perpetrated by other relatives. The percent of violence involving the use of a weapon was higher among other relatives (26%) and 19% for intimate partners and immediate family members. People of color had higher rates of IPV compared to non-Hispanic whites or Hispanics and non-Hispanic persons of other races (e.g., 16.5 victimizations per 1,000 persons compared to 3.9 per 1,000 persons, 2.8 per 1,000 persons, and 2.3 per 1,000 persons). The National Family Violence Resurvey found that crude rates of male-to-female partner violence perpetration (MFPV) and female-to-male partner violence perpetration (FMPV) among Hispanic couples were 1.5 times and 2.4 times higher, respectively, than the rates for White couples (Straus & Smith, 1990). From 2012 to 2013, the majority of victims of domestic violence was female (76%) compared to male (24%) and most of the perpetrators were current or former boyfriends or girlfriends; this was true for both females (39%) and males (30%).

IPV is a variant of domestic violence that happens between people who are dating, married, separated, divorced, and/or living together; it occurs in heterosexual as well as in GLBT relationships among adolescents and adults. In the past, the assumption that IPV was primarily perpetrated by men against women was supported by earlier research based on studies with seriously abused women (Jordan, 2009; Rhatigan, Moore, & Street, 2005). Indeed, women represent 95% of adult victims, with between 1 and 4 million women abused per year. Lifetime risk for women is about 20%. In terms of criminal behavior in IPV, between 8 and 14% of women of all ages reported physical assault in the previous year by a husband, boyfriend, or ex-partner; the lifetime prevalence was between 25 and 30%. While the majority of homicides recorded by the Federal Bureau of Investigation's Supplementary Homicide Report involved male victims, a larger percentage of females than males was murdered by an intimate partner when the offender relationship was known. In 2010, of the 3,032 homicide incidents involving females, 39% were committed by an intimate, 37% were committed by a non-intimate, and 24% by an unknown offender. During the same year, of the 10,878 homicide incidents involving males, 3% were committed by an intimate, 48% by a non-intimate, and 50% by an offender with an unknown relationship to the victim (Bureau of Justice Statistics, 2013).

Research has shown that women are as likely as men to perpetrate IPV (Anderson, 2002; Archer, 2000), but they are more likely to be physically harmed than their male partners (Hamberger, 1997; Vivian & Langhinrichsen-Rohling, 1994). This discrepancy between gender symmetry in perpetration and asymmetry in impact suggests women's violence is not equal to men's (Brush, 1990; Temple, Weston, & Marshall, 2005). Johnson (1996) suggests that unilateral violence in IPV (sole perpetrator) would be more severe than mutual violence (both males and females perpetrate violence). When considering male partners' behaviors, differences consistently indicate that IPV is more frequent when both the male and female are violent than when one partner is the sole perpetrator (Temple et al., 2005).

For women's behavior, the distinction between unidirectional aggression (e.g., only one partner perpetrates aggressive behavior) and bidirectional aggression (e.g., both partners perpetrate aggressive behaviors) is clear only for women who perpetrate severe violence. Research is now supporting the view that IPV is more complex and involves different patterns of perpetration: nonreciprocal IPV (one partner, either male or female is the perpetrator of physical and/or psychological coercion), reciprocal IPV, symmetrical violence, or mutual violence (both partners within a relationship perpetrate violence against their partners) (McHugh et al., 2005; Whitaker, Haileyesus, Swahn, & Saltzman, 2007).

The notorious domestic violence case involving Baltimore Ravens running back Ray Rice illustrates the points raised thus far about IPV. He is seen in a YouTube video that went viral, punching his fiancée in the face, knocking her unconscious, and then dragging her unconscious body from an elevator. Some commentators pointed out that it was the fiancée who hit first, as if that was justification for the action/inaction initially taken against Rice by the League and the initial reaction of some fans who expressed the sentiment that his private life and relationship with his fiancée should not influence his professional football career. She may have struck him first, but he retaliated with a punch to the head that knocked her unconscious!

Psychological perspectives on IPV have traditionally emphasized explanations involving personal traits, or deficits in communication/interpersonal skills. Early theories viewed partner violence as a function of individual pathology (Faulk, 1974; Jasinski, 2001). Early studies in this tradition examined those personal characteristics assumed to be biologically based and/or acquired through socialization to explain why certain individuals are perpetrators of violence (Gelles & Straus, 1979). See chapter 4 by Warburton and Anderson in this book for further discussion on this issue.

In both domestic and intimate partner violence, the perpetrator engages in one or more of the following types of aggression: (1) physical (e.g., arm twisting, attacking with or threatening with a weapon, beating, burning, choking, dragging, hair pulling, kicking, punching, pushing, shaking, slapping, throwing something), (2) sexual (e.g., forces the victim to have sexual intercourse and/or to perform sexual acts), (3) economic, (4) stalking (e.g., making unwanted phone calls, sending unsolicited or unwanted letters or emails, following or spying on the victim, showing up at places without a legitimate reason, waiting at places for the victim, leaving unwanted items, presents, or flowers, posting information or spreading rumors about the victim on the internet, in a public place or by word of mouth), and/or (5) psychological abuse in the form of threats, intimidation, emotional abuse, and isolating a person in an intimate relationship in order to establish and maintain *power and control* over that person—thus creating an atmosphere of fear, misery, loss, mistrust, humiliation, and despair (Breiding et al., 2015).

Theories on gender differences in motives for physical dating violence, supported by research, maintain that men's use of violence is indeed related to power and control, such as for instrumental reasons, or in retaliation for being hit first (but not necessarily to protect oneself from immediate harm), whereas women's use of violence is more commonly related to reactive or emotional expression (e.g., anger, jealousy, shame; Flynn & Graham, 2010; Follingstad, Wright, Lloyd, & Sebastian, 1991; Harned, 2001). The trend of current research focuses on the co-occurrence of multiple forms of violence victimization and/or perpetration and the intersection of different forms of violence (Grych & Kinsfogel, 2010; Hamby, Finkelhor, & Turner, 2012; Hamby & Grych, 2013). Different and competing concepts with similar meanings (e.g., poly victimization, complex trauma) generate confusion that complicates research efforts to better understand the scope of gender differences in motivation for violence (Hamby et al., 2014).

FEMALE-PERPETRATED VIOLENCE

It is very important to note that within the U.S. criminal justice system, women represent a consistently small proportion of those arrested (24%; Snyder, 2011) and sentenced (5%) for a violent offense (Guerino, Harrison, & Sabol, 2011). The likelihood of a woman being imprisoned at some point in her lifetime is 1 in 56. The likelihood varies by race: 1 in 19 for Black women, 1 in 45 for Hispanic women, and 1 in 118 for White women. In 2010, Black women were incarcerated at approximately three times the rate of White women (e.g., 133 compared to 47 per 100,000). Hispanic women were incarcerated at 1.6 times the rate of White women (e.g., 77 compared to 47 per 100,000). From 2000 to 2010, the rate of incarceration for Black women decreased 35% and increased 28% for Hispanic women and 38% for White women (The Sentencing Project, 2012). It is important to note the limitations of research methodologies that continue to group research participants into socially constructed racial groups which perpetuate stereotypic systemic cultural biases. Research methodologies that attempt to explore ethnic differences may provide more nuanced information about women and their experience with the criminal justice system (e.g., Italian/Irish Catholic vs. "White"; African American/Haitian American vs. "Black").

The motivation underlying the "violent" woman has revolved around essentially three different but not mutually exclusive constructs: "victim," "mad," and/or "bad." It is hypothesized that female aggression/violence is viewed more negatively by society than male aggression because it violates the socially constructed normative roles, identities, attitudes, and behaviors ascribed to females (Kruttschnitt, Gartner, & Hussemann, 2008; Paul & Baenninger,1991). Explanations for aggressive/violent females' behavior in the past were congruent with societal stereotypic expectations for appropriate and inappropriate gendered behavior: male aggression is seen as instrumental and rational while aggression by women is viewed as reactive, emotional, irrational, and pathological (Anderson, 1993; Campbell, 1993).

Interest in the type of behaviors reflective of women's violent potential has changed over the years. In the late 1980s and early 1990s, with the crack cocaine epidemic, there were efforts by some politicians and those in the criminal justice system to criminalize pregnant, drug-using women for their behavior and lifestyle that harmed unborn children, disrupted family life, and put their children at risk for a host of psychological and physical difficulties (Inciardi, Lockwood, & Pottieger, 1993). There has also been interest in female participation in gangs because of their more apparent active participation in violent activity (e.g., "gansta girls" considered to be as violent as their male counterparts; Taylor, 1993). The Battered Woman Syndrome, much researched in the 1980s and used as a defense in legal cases of women who kill their partners, reflected the view that female violence was related to mental state affected by being in abusive relationships (Walker, 1987). The contemporary consensus view is more nuanced in that the aggressive/violent females' behavior is considered complex, involving both instrumental and reactive features influenced by context.

The current profile of violent female perpetrators who inflict serious injury is that of an antisocial or borderline personality disorder with comorbid substance abuse and limited capacity to manage challenges in socially appropriate ways (Weizmann-Henelius, 2006).

Williams, Ghandour, and Kub (2008) reviewed 62 empirical studies and found that IPV is common among female adolescents, young college women, and adult women. In fact, some research shows that adolescent girls commit more acts of violence in intimate relationships than males (Lichter & McCloskey, 2004; Spencer & Bryant, 2000; Wolfe et al., 2001). Most of the violence perpetrated by women is emotional, as opposed to physical or sexual, and follows one of two developmental paths: (1) emerges in early adolescence, peaks in mid-adolescence, and decreases in late adolescence (adolescent limited) or (2) emerges early, escalates and persists (life course persistent; Williams et al., 2008). The most common behavior involved in sexual aggression reported by female perpetrators was forced kissing (West & Rose, 2000). Female perpetrators cited emotional abuse the most followed by physical and sexual IPV.

For some women, violence is a sign of: their attempt to thwart their partners' egregious actions, their actions to defend themselves or their children, their frustrations based on past abuse or current custody disagreements, and/or their underlying psychological disorder (Miller, 2005). These women have presumably experienced a history of trauma, have maladaptive survival skills, lack support systems, lack internal resources to examine their own behavior, and struggle with substance abuse-related issues; this is evident in those women who kill their newborns (Dobson & Sales 2000; Hamilton & Harberger, 1992).

As with other types of aggressive/violent behavior, more males are presumed to engage in stalking than females. However, despite limited research, there is evidence showing comparable rates of stalking among males and females (Meloy & Boyd, 2003; Thompson, Dennison, & Stewart, 2012). Stalking, as mentioned earlier, is a pattern of repeated and unwanted attention, contact, harassment, or any behavior toward a specific person which would cause a reasonable person to become fearful characterized by any of the following: following or waiting for the victim at various locations such as home, school, work, and so on; contacting the victim's friends, family, work, or neighbors; repeated frightening, intrusive and/or unwanted communications from the perpetrator via telephone, mail, email, and/or social media; posting information or spreading rumors about the victim online, in a public place, or by word of mouth; spying on the victim with a listening device, camera, or global positioning system (GPS) device; direct or indirect threats to harm the victim, the victim's children, relatives, friends, or pets; repeatedly leaving or sending the victim unwanted/unwelcomed items, presents, or flowers; damaging or threatening to damage the victim's property; and/or collecting personal information about the victim via public records, using internet search services, installing software without permission gaining access to computer files/programs, hiring private investigators, going through the victim's garbage.

Dutton and Winstead (2006) reported higher rates of moderate relational violence by female stalkers than male stalkers; several others have reported no gender differences in the perpetration of serious stalking violence, including studies conducted in Australia (e.g., Purcell, Pathe, & Mullen, 2001), the United States (e.g., Harmon et al., 1998; Rosenfeld and Harmon, 2002; Schwartz-Watts & Morgan, 1998; Thompson et al., 2012), and cross-national samples (Meloy & Boyd, 2003). One possible explanation for these results suggests that sociocultural beliefs are more accepting of violence perpetrated by females against males than violence perpetrated by males against females, which minimizes the significance of male victimization, especially with female perpetrators. As discussed earlier, it is important to understand the contexts in which violent behaviors occur and to examine the individual factors contributing to violence as well as elucidate, where possible, the broader social conditions that are age-based, gendered, class-based, and color-coded.

FEMALE JUVENILE OFFENDERS

According to the FBI's Uniform Crime Reporting (UCR), 29% of all juvenile arrests in 2003 were of females. This rate is due in part to changes in the juvenile arrest rates since the mid-1980s, which saw a sharp increase in violent crime arrests for both males and females. However, since the mid-1990s, arrest rates for violent crimes among juveniles fell; but because female arrest rates increased more sharply and then fell more gradually from 1980 to 2003, the rate of female juvenile arrests grew from 20% to 29% during that period (Office of Juvenile Justice Delinquency and Prevention, 2013).

Changes in self-reported offending and female juvenile arrest rates seem to indicate that girls are becoming more violent, not so much for murder and robbery but for aggravated assault. However, variations in policy and criminal justice practice, as well as the interpretation of arrest data, complicate analyses. This makes it more difficult to determine whether or not the increase in female arrests for violent offenses represents a true increase in violent behavior among female adolescents compared with males. What is clear is that a growing proportion of girls are involved with the juvenile justice system (Cauffman, 2008). Detained female juvenile offenders tend to be more aggressive than their male counterparts, and have higher rates of mental health problems (e.g., both internalizing and externalizing) than males (Espelage et al., 2003).

Research is inconclusive about gender differences in the age of onset of delinquent behavior and the trajectories for subsequent difficulties for female juvenile offenders. This is due, in part, because of the difficulty in determining when the offending begins. The evidence indicates that on average, the duration of offending seems to vary for females and for males, at 4.9 years and 7.4 years respectively (Cauffman, 2008). Some studies show that boys and girls begin their antisocial behavior around the age of 15 (Brown, 2006; Moffitt, Caspi, Rutter, & Silva, 2001); other research suggests that females start offending when they are younger. Early-onset-persistent-female offenders tend to engage in antisocial behavior well into their thirties including violent acts toward partners and children (Pulkkinen & Pitkanen, 1993); there is also evidence of higher crime and substance use in their marriages characterized by conflict and instability. This finding reflects gender differences about the influence of marriage on desistance; marriage seems to serve as a protective factor, reducing and/or eliminating violent behavior among males but not necessarily for females (Patton, 2012).

FEMALE GANGS

The research on female gangs suggests that adolescent girls who become active gang members are on a trajectory to starting or continuing involvement in antisocial and criminal behavior (De La Rue & Espelage, 2014; Fleisher & Krienerr, 2004). Within the gang population, female gang membership is estimated to range from a low of between 10% and 35% to a high of 20% to 46% (Esbensen & Huizinga, 1993; Snethen, 2010). The literature and research on gangs and the reasons for gang membership have, until recently, viewed gangs from a criminological perspective of being a homogeneous phenomenon (i.e., social groups that engage in crimes and violence). Current evidence from ethnographic studies of gangs recognize that gangs are more heterogeneous phenomena based on purpose, location, ethnicity, and gender (Chesney-Lind & Paramore, 2001; Hawkins et al., 1998; Sanchez-Jankowski, 2003). Hansen (2005) found differences between the characteristics of male gang networks and those of female gang networks (e.g., culture of violence, risk factors for becoming a gang member, relationships among gang members) but emphasized that the results of her ethnographic study of New York gang members may not necessarily generalize and/or be relevant to other gangs. For example, female gangs formed at a relatively early age for the purpose of self-preservation without violence have been called "crews" instead of gangs. Some "crew members," however, do exhibit a number of risk factors associated with gangs: violent or other deviant behavior, rejection of middle-class values, family disorganization and neglect, and fear of exclusion (Wiener, 1999).

The experience of victimization associated with the extent of sexual abuse, family conflict, parental drug and alcohol abuse, parental crime, and low parental monitoring seems to differentiate girls who join a gang from those girls who are recruited but resist (De La Rue & Espelage, 2014). The influence of the gang on a member's proclivity toward aggression and violence at an individual level or as part of the group is unclear; what is clear is that the domains of violence for girl gang members include: the street, their family, among members within their gang and between gangs, and their relationships with boyfriends who may or may not be gang members (Hunt & Joe-Laidler, 2001). IPV within gangs has not received much attention and needs to be better understood. Fleischer & Krienerr (2004) found that violence increases during the period between initial gang affiliation (e.g., girls' independence from parental household and increased street activity around age 14), and first pregnancy, and then decreases with pregnancy and childbirth.

The circumstances involved in the very recent arrest of a 16-year-old African American mother and gang member, who was one of several female teens seen in a YouTube video brutally beating another girl in a McDonald's in Brooklyn, New York, illustrates several points presented thus far. She has 10 prior arrests, including one for assault just 30 days before this current incident; her 64-year-old grandmother was granted an order of protection against her because she had physically attacked her. She stabbed her brother and hurt a police officer during an arrest for violating an order of protection (McCormack & Spargo, 2015).

LGBTQ COMMUNITY AND IPV

Lewis et al. (2017) concur with the consensus view that estimates of the prevalence of IPV within LGBTQ relationships, especially among lesbians, is difficult to determine. The findings of Todahl et al.'s (2009) exploratory study with focus groups within the LGBTQ community shed some light on the difficulty with accurate prevalence rates and this community's perceptions about the inadequate support services for a host of problems, including sexual assault. According to their findings, many in the LGBTQ community acknowledge that sexual violence is underreported by social conditions that force silence, contribute to denial, and hinder the establishment to LGBTQ-friendly services as well as access to them. That said, in general, the rates are equal to or higher than the rates among heterosexual women (e.g., prevalence estimates of lesbians' physical IPV victimization is 15% and prevalence estimates of perpetration is 12% [Messinger, 2011; Badenes-Ribera et al., 2015]).

The comparison between lesbian women and heterosexual women elucidates some of the presumed group differences between lesbians and heterosexual women associated with violent behavior. Among heterosexuals, psychological aggression predicts physical violence (Schumacher & Leonard, 2005; Testa, Hoffman, & Leonard, 2011). Lewis et al.'s (2017) conceptual model predicts psychological aggression and/or physical violence as the outcome variable for lesbian women. It is important to note that at the individual and couples level of analyses, lesbian women who are beset with sexual minority stress attempting to cope with perceived discrimination and internalized homophobia experience anger, partner/perpetrator alcohol use, perpetrator alcohol-related problems, and relationship dissatisfaction.

Brown and Pantalone (2011) point out that despite the proliferation of research in trauma studies and research on LGBT issues in which trauma is understood to be present, there are very few studies on the intersection of these two areas (e.g., trauma and LGBT psychology). Better research outcomes to describe and understand a range of problems such as violent behavior in LGBT relationships leading to more effective interventions are more likely to occur when empirical studies hone in on the intersection of these two areas.

INCARCERATED MOTHERS

Nationally, approximately two-thirds of incarcerated women and 55% of incarcerated men have children below the age of 18; most (72%) of the incarcerated mothers lived with their children before entering prison; approximately 25% of women are pregnant or have recently delivered when they enter prison (Glaze & Maruschak, 2008). Children of incarcerated parents are often uprooted from their homes and placed with relatives or in foster care. The living arrangements for children with incarcerated fathers and imprisoned mothers differ in several important ways. Most (90%) children of incarcerated fathers live with their mother. Only approximately 25% of children with incarcerated mothers live with their fathers. One half of children with incarcerated mothers live with their grandparents. An additional 2% of children with fathers in prison and 10% of children with mothers in prison live in a foster care home or an institution.

Ever since women first entered the U.S. prison system, social stereotypes about their fitness as mothers have dictated their housing, punishment, and ability to maintain family ties. At this point in history, when U.S. prisons house more women than ever before, it is especially important to revisit the underlying policies that determine a woman's punishment. A feminist analysis of current prison policies reveals that the modern treatment of incarcerated women continues to reflect the racist and sexist stereotypes of the past that denied—and actively destroyed—women of color's reproductive and parental rights. Today, the constitutional guarantees of the Fourteenth and Eighth Amendments, as well as effective public policy, mandate that prisons respect inmates' decisions to become mothers. Policies such as the creation of halfway houses and prison nurseries, the provision of prenatal care, and a prohibition against shackling are solutions that not only protect a mother's constitutional rights, but also increase her child's chances of living a healthy and productive life. In turn, the enhanced fitness of mother and child benefits society as a whole (Vainik, 2008).

PSYCHOLOGY OF WOMEN WHO ABUSE: THEORETICAL AND RESEARCH PERSPECTIVES ON VIOLENCE

Theories and research on violence have explored and attempted to understand violence from different perspectives ranging from the micro (e.g., the psychology of the offender), to the macro level (e.g., a focus on society itself examining sociopolitical, economic, institutional as well as cultural dynamics). Babcock, Miller, and Siard (2003) found differences between women who were violent toward others and those who were physically violent toward an intimate partner; specifically, women who were likely to use violence in a variety of situations also reported using more emotionally abusive tactics than women who use violence with their partners. Women who used violence in a variety of situations were also more likely to blame others for their actions or claim a lack of control than were women who abused their partners and reported more trauma symptoms; they were also more likely to have witnessed their mothers being aggressive toward their fathers. Factors most frequently discussed are multifaceted and no single pathway has been found to be sufficient to characterize females at risk of violent behaviors (Jimerson, Morrison, Pletcher, & Furlong, 2006; Reebye, 2005). Table 6.1 summarizes research findings of the psychology of the offender.

Reebye (2005) reviews eight pathways to aggression with origins in early childhood: (1) individual factors (e.g., teratogenicity in the intrauterine environment); (2) disturbed family dynamics, parental characteristics, and parenting practices; (3) exposure to violence and behavioral aggression, (4) living in violent neighborhoods; (5) attachment relationships, (6) aggression related to psychiatric/medical syndromes; (7) neurodevelopmental pathways influencing self-regulation and especially impulse control; and (8) psychodynamic models (e.g., maternal projections; Cramer, 1995) and mother's reflective capacity (Fonagy, Gergely, Jurist, & Target, 2002). His discussion supports a multifaceted view which attempts to incorporate and underscore the dynamic interplay between the individual's characteristics and the environmental interactions that ensue over different developmental time periods consistent with contextual framework models (Sameroff, 2009) and current research (Rodriguez et al., 2005; Rubin, Burgess, Dwyer, & Hastings, 2003).

Parents and family members in the home environment provide the first arena of social support for young children. A child's growth to healthy adulthood is more likely to be compromised by certain parental attitudes and child rearing practices that stifle the child's ability to learn how to manage anger, hurt, humiliation, frustration, and other negative emotions in life affirming ways. This is especially salient when considering the vast range of experiences in ordinary living which may elicit negative emotions in children. How parents respond as well as their role in generating these experiences determine the outcome and subsequent impact on the child's further development.

Miller (1991), refers to the child-rearing practices that suppress vitality, creativity, and feeling in the child as "poisonous pedagogy." She maintains that parents who, primarily through coercive methods, raise children to be obedient, compliant, "well behaved," and deferential to authority figures are replicating what was done to them; this is similar to Freud's concept of the compulsion to repeat. Confused by the insistence that one must understand a slap or some other form of physically inflicted pain by a parent as a sign of "love," they transmit this poisonous pedagogy on to future generations.

Parental hostility has also been characterized as a significant risk factor and strong predictor of childhood aggression (Campbell et al., 1996; Duman & Margolin, 2007). Children learn aggressive behavior via the modeling of aggressive social exchanges between their family members. Parenting style, coercive family environments, and communication patterns such as harsh discipline, authoritarian, hostile or punitive parent-child interactions, and maternal negative control as reflected in scolding prohibitions, shame and humiliation, non-responsive parenting, physical punishment, and restraint have been associated with the development of aggressive behavior patterns and externalizing difficulties (Bates, Pettit, & Dodge, 1995; Patterson, 2002; Pinderhughes, Dodge, Bates, Pettit, & Zelli, 2000; Rubin & Burgess, 2002; Shaw, Lacourse, & Nagin, 2005). The combination of a child's difficult temperament and parental negativity has been linked to aggressive behaviors (Rubin et al., 2003). Paternal depression has been reported to place girls at a higher risk for relational aggression (Park et al., 2005). Maternal age, alcohol/tobacco use during pregnancy, maternal antisocial history during school years, antisocial father, and inter-parental conflict have also been identified as risk factors for high aggression (Brennan et al., 1999; Hawkins et al., 1998; Kupersmidt et al., 1995; Tremblay et al., 2004).

On the other hand, consistent displays of parental positive regard have been associated with a decrease in externalizing problems (Collins, Maccoby, Steinberg, Hetherington, & Bornstein, 2000). Perceptions of parental support have been found to predict relatively low levels of relational aggression during adolescence (Zahn-Waxler, Park, Essex, Slattery &, Cole, 2005). Family systems theories and our understanding of unconscious motivations help to expand our knowledge about the transmission of family patterns across generations. Not only explicit family rules but also powerful implicit rules allow the expression of certain feelings and inhibit others (Staub, 1989). Within this framework, every family, every parent is implicated in the transmission of violence when it appears, not just dysfunctional families or parents known to have neglected and/or abused their children. Practices not sufficient to be classified as abuse and hence warrant legal sanction may nonetheless be precursors to maltreatment and/or detrimental to the development of the child. These qualitatively different disturbances in parent-child interaction are likely to be more subtle, more frequent, more continuous, and more detrimental in their long-term effects on the child and family (Lyons-Ruth, Connell, Zoll, & Stahl, 1987).

While our chapter has focused on externalizing female-perpetrated violence, it is noteworthy that research on internalizing self-destructive behaviors such as nonsuicidal self-injurious (NSSI) behaviors (e.g., deliberate, often impulsive, repetitive non-lethal harming of one's body to cope with and relieve painful feelings), which is prevalent among adolescents, especially adolescent females, and young adults, indicate the quality of disturbances in parent-child relationships discussed above. That is, the family atmosphere is characterized by invalidating family interactions associated with self-criticism and depressive symptoms, which in turn increase the risk of NSSI (Baetens et al., 2015; Blatt, 1974; Campos et al., 2010; Linehan, 1993).

The presence of siblings in the home may be a contributing factor to some types of aggression. Relational aggression has been reported to be used more often with siblings than friends in early childhood (Stauffacher & DeHart, 2005). The presence of delinquency among family members, siblings, and peers that provide negative social support has been identified as a risk factor for involvement in violent behavior (Demaray, Malecki, & DeLong, 2006). Neighborhood violence, residential crowding, and overall lower residential quality have also been related to self-regulating difficulties (Evans & English, 2002) which, as previously noted, are strong predictors of aggressive behavior patterns.

NEUROPSYCHOLOGICAL PERSPECTIVES ON EMOTIONAL AND BEHAVIORAL DYSREGULATION AS CORRELATES OF VIOLENCE

Harmon-Jones (2003) reviewed theoretical models on frontal cortical asymmetry and approach motivation with positive emotional valence, which posit that more left frontal activity is associated with more psychological/physical health than less left frontal cortical activity; greater right frontal cortical activity is associated with negative affect and/or withdrawal motivation. However, current theory and research indicate that approach motivations can be associated with negative subjective feelings and negative consequences. Negative affectivity (e.g., neuroticism) is important for understanding the underpinnings of violent behavior. More specifically, the emotional and cognitive processes of anger and hostility are two related but distinct constructs linked to aggression (Buss & Perry, 1992). Anger is conceptualized as an emotional state that ranges from irritation to rage with concomitant physiological arousal that prepares the body to act (e.g., fight or flight). Hostility is a cognitive construct associated with cynicism, mistrust, suspiciousness, and resentment of others characterized by negative feelings and a perception of ill will. Sadeh, Javdani, Finy, and Verona (2011) surmise that anger is directly linked to overt forms of aggression, and hostility is related to negative perceptions of others and possibly more covert forms of aggression.

Many of the individual characteristics of aggressive behavioral patterns reported in the literature can be traced to neurological impairment attributed to prenatal biological correlates and environmental factors. The neurological factors most associated with the regulation of aggressive behaviors are executive function and language-based verbal skills (Jimerson et al., 2006; Moffitt, 1990; Seguin & Zelazo, 2005). Executive function skills involve goal-directed problem solving and planning abilities—the identification of a problem, strategizing, execution, and evaluation of a plan (Seguin & Zelazo, 2005). To effectively accomplish the necessary steps of problem solving an individual must also incorporate inhibition and working memory skills (Zelazo & Mueller, 2002).

Self-regulation of thought, emotions, and action regarding frustration tolerance/delay of gratification, impulsivity, development of peer conflict, difficult temperament, and irritability balanced by resilient factors such as effortful control, compliance, internal locus of control, perception of self-control, personal control, and cooperation have been associated with aggression risk and violent behavior (Calkins, Gill, & Williford, 1999; Jessor, Van Den Bos, Vanderryn, Costa, & Turbin, 1995; Perry, 1997; Rodriguez et al., 2005; Shaw et al., 2005; White, Moffitt, Earls, Robins, & Silva 1990).

Self-regulation depends on the integrity of neural systems involving the prefrontal cortex (Seguin & Zelazo, 2005). Underdevelopment of cortical, subcortical, and limbic areas has been related to limited experiences across sensory, motor, emotional, cognitive, and social spheres (Perry, 1997). Infants' self-regulatory competence has been strongly related to sensitive and responsive caregiving, even when accounting for the role of infant characteristics (Raver, 2004). The attachment between infant and caregiver has been described as a biologically based regulatory system (Reebye, 2005). It is during the attachment process that infants learn development of self-regulatory capacity for affect and behavior (Weinfeld, Sroufe, Egeland, & Carlson, 1999).

Attachment patterns have been associated with childhood aggression (Reebye, 2005). Children who demonstrate high physical aggression have been reported to have diminished executive functioning (Seguin & Zelazo, 2005). Deficits in information processing have been associated with an antisocial behavioral style (Crick & Dodge, 1994). Victims of bullying tend to overattribute hostile intentions in ambiguous situations, while bullies have been reported to have superior theory of mind skills (Sutton et al.,1999). Negative emotions among preschoolers have been correlated with victimization. In particular, anger has been reported to predict victimization in early childhood (Hanish et al., 2004).

Lower language skills have been identified as having a critical role in aggression. They have been reported as a reliable predictor of physical aggression, particularly for boys (Adams, Snowling, Hennessy, & Kind, 1999). Preschool language abilities were found to predict the stability and pervasiveness of externalizing behaviors (Heller, Baker, Henker, & Hinshaw, 1996), although these results were mediated by socioeconomic status and maternal education.

Childhood attention deficit disorder, head injuries, or substance use are often cited as predisposing factors of violence (Warnken, Rosenbaum, Fletcher, Hoge, & Adelman, 1994). Additionally, biochemical factors, including abnormal glucose metabolism, the suppression of activity of serotonin and other neurotransmitters, as well as overactivity of dopamine systems in the brain, are cited as risk factors for perpetrating partner violence (Johnson, 1996).

PSYCHOSOCIAL THEORIES

Jimerson and colleagues (2006) reviewed theoretical models that may shed light on different aspects of aggressive behavior patterns: Social Learning Model (Patterson et al., 1992), Social Information Processing Model (Crick & Dodge, 1994), Life-course-persistent aggression, Adolescent-limited aggression (Moffitt, 1990), Social Development Model (Catalino & Hawkins, 1996), and the Transactional-Ecological Developmental Model (Sameroff, 2009) to name a few. Collectively, these models strive to identify and explore the impact of the characteristics and contexts associated with violence, with the aim of understanding how aggressive behavior patterns develop in particular individuals and are sustained in specific settings. There are different types and ways of classifying the relationship between aggression and violent acts. These include direct/indirect, relational, instrumental, and expressive forms of aggression. Until recently, criminologists, psychologists, and sociologists understood the violence of girls and women as indicative of "expressive" aggression. That is, females are emotional creatures who tend to bottle up their feelings that can, when triggered, erupt in aggressive/violent outbursts much like a volcano. Violence is viewed as impulsive.

What this view fails to consider is the considerable evidence that girls and women are just as capable as males of planning, strategizing, and engaging in other forms of aggressive and violent acts involved in instrumental aggression. They can be cold, calculating, mean, vindictive, vicious, and lacking empathy, in other words, displaying features of sociopathy. These females are becoming more familiar and known to us through popular literature, TV shows, and movies (e.g., the novels of Gillian Flynn, reality TV shows such as *Bridezilla* and *Jerry Springer*, the movie *Mean Girls*). Some individuals

Table 6.1. Gender-Specific and Gender-Invariant Risk Factors for Offending

MALES	MALES/FEMALES	FEMALES
Lower levels	ADHD Low cortisol levels Low resting heart rate Early pubertal maturation	Adversarial interpersonal relationships
Genotype	Neuropsychological impairments **Co-morbid mental health problems** **Lower levels of empathy** Heightened sensitivity to rewards/stimulation Dysfunctional families/antisocial socialization Harmful pre/post-natal biological experiences	EEG brain asymmetries
Fight or Flight	**Poor parental monitoring** **Early interpersonal victimization** Negative temperament Deviant peers Poverty Impulsivity Low IQ	R>L frontal activation

have had firsthand experiences with these females through postings on Facebook, Twitter, anonymous websites, and cell phone apps.

PROACTIVE (INSTRUMENTAL) AND REACTIVE (EXPRESSIVE) AGGRESSION

The distinction between proactive and reactive aggression has been studied by researchers who speculate how these subtypes of aggression correlate with a variety of behavioral outcomes (e.g., callous/unemotional traits and antisocial behavioral consequences vs. negative affects associated with depressive symptoms and suicidal behavior) (Bushman & Anderson, 2001;

Dodge, 1991; Fite, Stoppelbein, & Greening, 2009b). Proactive aggression is described as planful and goal-oriented aggression motivated by external reward; reactive aggression refers to aggressive responses to others' behavior that is perceived to be threatening and/or intentional (Card & Little, 2006; Dodge, 1991). The former is associated with social learning theory, which suggests that aggression serves as a means to obtain a desired goal or object whereas the theoretical underpinning for reactive aggression is based on the frustration aggression hypothesis, which speculates that aggression is an angry and/or hostile reaction to perceived threat (Fite, Raine, Stouthamer-Loeber, Loeber, & Pardini, 2009a). Social skills difficulties have been associated with externalizing/aggressive behaviors (Coie, Dodge, & Kupersmidt, 1990; Walker, Ramsey, & Gresham, 2004). Social–emotional deficits have also been linked to risk factors for victimization (Frey et al., 2005).

TRAIT AND STATE ANGER THEORY

Trait anger is defined as a disposition characteristic (e.g., predisposition) to experience frequent anger with varying intensity, ranging from mild irritability to intense rage, and generally accompanied by negative emotions like hate, envy, and resentment. One with this predisposition tends to respond to stressful and distressing situations with state anger (Shorey, Brasfield, Febres, & Stuart, 2011; Spielberger, 1988; Buss, 1961; Siegman, 1994). Martin, Watson, and Wan (2000), propose a three-factor model of trait anger that includes anger-related affect, behavior, and cognitions. Trait anger predisposes individuals to perceive situations to be frustrating or bothersome; they respond to these situations and experiences with elevations of state anger; women who score higher in trait anger are more likely to express their anger in a blaming or attacking way and typically have a more challenging time "letting it go" (Spielberger, 1988). Simply put, state anger captures angry feelings in a particular moment whereas trait anger is more enduring, experienced over time and may likely become repressed anger in response to abuse (Kubiak, Wiedig-Allison, Zgoriecki, & Weber, 2011).

GENDER ROLE STRAIN PARADIGM

Agnew (1992, 2001, 2006) suggests that some individuals may use maladaptive coping mechanisms resulting in violence, substance use, or property offending to alleviate negative emotions triggered by strain, a psychosocial construct defined as incidents or circumstances which are disliked by individuals or involve negative relations with others. A wide range of emotions have been linked to strain, the most researched is anger, especially anger as a stable characteristic of personality functioning (e.g., trait anger; Broidy,

2001). Slocum, Rengifo, and Carbone-Lopez (2012) researched the connections between strains, emotions, and violence among high rate female offenders and found support for the view that the experience of strain and emotional reactions are gendered. In their sample of female offenders, disputes over sexual jealousy were a common form of strain that resulted in a more nuanced interplay of anger, betrayal, depression, humiliation, and shame. The research findings suggest that anger may be the necessary component for violence to erupt, that it is a "master emotion" related to the progression from internalizing emotions like humiliation and shame to externalizing emotions such as rage; but not all strains are equally likely to elicit certain emotions.

RELATIONAL AGGRESSION THEORY

Society—through parents, peers, social institutions, and the mass media—encourages cooperation and emotional support among girls but competition, independence, and aggression among boys. This occurs in ways, according to the relational perspective within psychology, which foster disconnections for both males and females (Jordan et al., 1991; Miller, 1976; Robb, 2006). In the late 1980s, much of the research on youth aggression and violence focused on physical violence (e.g., fighting, gang violence, school violence, shootings, etc.) primarily among male youth. In the late 1990s, the discourse shifted from physical violence primarily among boys, to physical violence in real time to virtual violence in cyberspace, and to relational violence seen among girls.

Researchers have referred to female youth aggressive, bullying behavior as relational aggression (Mikel-Brown, 2003), social aggression (Underwood, 2003), or alternative aggression (Simmons, 2002) characterized by catty, vengeful, deceitful, manipulative, back-stabbing, or mean-spirited/vindictive behavior reflecting a hidden culture of aggression among girls (Simmons, 2002). This female phenomenon is seen as an outgrowth of, and reaction to, cultural expectations that distinguish between what are acceptable attitudes and behaviors for girls and boys based on gender, which impose structural/systemic inequitable distributions of power, creating dominant (male)/subordinate (female) groups (Miller, 1976). These cultural beliefs about gender and how they manifest in social contexts are the basis for contemporary gender stereotypes about girls and adolescent females as being more communal in their relationships and males as being more instrumental and more agentic (Eagly, Wood, & Diekman, 2000; Ridgeway & Correll, 2004).

Adolescents' ability to incorporate prosocial themes in their narratives predicted relatively low levels of relational aggression (Zahn-Waxler et al., 2005). Prosocial behaviors and peer acceptance (Asher & Coie, 1990) have also been positively correlated. Social competence reflects an individual's capacity to interact socially, take others' perspective, compromise, and engage in adaptive conflict resolution (Newman & Murray, 2005). These skills diminish the propensity to rely on aggressive behavior patterns and are closely tied to executive functioning, but are compromised by the dynamics involved in relational aggression.

From the relational perspective, the perpetrator and the victim are "in-a-relationship" characterized by disconnections (i.e., ways of engaging with the other that thwart emotional growth, healthy self-esteem, and reciprocal self-validation). The perpetrator's stance conceals aspects of the self, and his/her perceived vulnerabilities that then inflate a pseudo self-esteem. The inherent interactions associated with this stance, paradoxically serve to protect the perpetrator from experiencing the demands of a healthy, mutually satisfying relationship of sharing thoughts, feelings, hopes, and so on while enabling him/her to establish and maintain a disconnected and dysfunctional one. Relational theory refers to these disconnections as relational violations that cause "the relational paradox: trying to keep out of a relationship so that [one] can stay in it" (Robb, 2006, p. 304).

PSYCHOANALYTIC/PSYCHODYNAMIC PERSPECTIVES

McCarthy's (1978) review of psychoanalytic formulations on the relationship between narcissism and homicide committed by children and adolescents emphasizes that their violent behavior is the product of vengeful rage and the concurrent defensive response to lowered self-esteem to repair the self. The narcissistic disturbance is exacerbated by the unavailability of parents who themselves are damaged, neglectful, and/or rejecting. The requisite self-enhancing mirroring process (Kohut, 1971) for transforming the omnipotence and grandiosity of childhood narcissism to a cohesive integrated self with the capacity for realistic appraisals of self and others is compromised. Loss of control or episodic dyscontrol, the tendency to dehumanize victims, and violent sadistic fantasies are also related to violent behavior (Miller & Looney, 1974).

Lefer's (1984) psychoanalytic perspective discusses why some individuals can restrain themselves from acting out aggressively, while others cannot. Depending on the strength of repression, suppression, inhibition, reaction formation, rationalization, and conscience, a violence-prone individual (VPI) may be categorized as: (1) one who uses violence as a means to an end without a need for justification; (2) one who uses violence as a means to an end but must justify it to his/her conscience; (3) one who is violent only in a dissociated or drugged state; or (4) one who becomes symbiotic with another VPI and aids the other in committing violence. There were significant differences among the types of VPI in their dreams, which often reenacted the violence inflicted upon them and their intimates in childhood and youth.

CULTURAL/REGIONAL PERSPECTIVES

Some social scientists are investigating how subcultural and regional variations in socialization affect differences in the expression of violence. D'Antonio-del Rio, Doucet, and Chauvin (2010) found a relationship between Southern culture and female-perpetrated violence. They used the Southern Subculture Index (a measure combining the effects of the proportion of the county population born in the South, the proportion of the county adhering to Evangelical Protestant fundamentals, and the proportion of the county with Scots-Irish heritage) and hypothesized that dominant patriarchal cultural views modified by Scots-Irish traditions or adherence to Evangelical Protestantism, contribute to Southern culture displayed by men and also by women, allowing for more female-perpetrated crime.

The following case highlights some of the complexities associated with understanding female violence:

> At the time Dee began psychotherapy for what she described as depression, she was a 30-year-old married, working mother of 2 children, a daughter aged 10, and a 3-year-old son. She described herself as a Jamerican/African American; her father was from Jamaica in the West Indies and her mother was an African American woman born in Georgia and raised in New York. Dee was a teacher's aide at a special education school. Her husband of 10 years, an African American, was currently employed as an assistant manager at a department store in New York City. They had been high school sweethearts. Dee was concerned about her increasing difficulty with "getting things done" at work and at home (e.g., problems concentrating and attending to chores/work assignments); fatigue; sadness; irritability with her husband and children; and insomnia (i.e., difficulty falling asleep). What prompted her to seek treatment was a recent incident in which she overreacted to her daughter's misbehavior; she slapped her daughter in the face when her daughter yelled back at her. Her overreaction frightened her. She wanted help to be a "good mother" to her children; she did not want to do to her children what had been done to her. She was vague and evasive when queried about what had been done to her.
>
> Dee attributed her depression and overreaction to discovering that her husband had started abusing heroin again. He had been addicted during his teens but had successfully gone through rehab and was drug free when they married and had been drug free ever since (so she thought) until recently. She denied any other disturbance in mood or suicidal ideation. Her mother-in-law had recently been diagnosed with an aggressive pancreatic cancer. She had functioned as the benevolent, caring matriarch; her son, Dee's husband, was devastated by her declining health and impending death. She reported no other personal or familial medical/psychiatric history at this time.

She presented as an anxious, depressed, sincere, motivated young woman with some knowledge about psychologists, psychiatrists and psychotherapy which she attributed to her working in special education. There was something about her presentation that was a tad off; the image that came to mind was of a well-dressed young woman in clothing too mature for her and her slip was hanging. In other words, she probably was not as mature as she appeared to be and she was not as well put together as she seemed.

We agreed to meet for 5 sessions for psychodynamically oriented psychotherapy after which time we would evaluate the therapeutic relationship and progress to determine how best to continue helping her understand her current situation and working on her goal to be a good mother to her children. She was advised that she would need to have a psychiatric consultation as soon as possible to determine if medication was also indicated. She agreed, was seen, and placed on an antidepressant medication.

She brought her son to the fifth session stating that she couldn't get a babysitter. I observed the two of them. She focused on me as she talked about the increasing arguments and physical contact (e.g., shoving, hitting) with her husband about "his problem"; this euphemism seemed to be her way of acknowledging that she was aware her son was in the room, listening. Meanwhile her son explored the room looking around and glancing occasionally at me. At one point he stopped suddenly and went into what looked like a nod i.e., he stooped over, dropped his head to his chest, half shut his eyes and looked like he was going to fall to the floor but somehow maintained his balance despite the posture. I became alarmed but remained silent and attentive, wondering if someone had given this child drugs, when all of a sudden he straightened up and gave me the biggest smile. This was a very bright boy letting me know he knew what his mother was talking about and that he had witnessed his father on heroin. She made light of what he had done, stating, "Oh, he's just playing." It occurred to me at that time that he wasn't the only one pretending or play acting, that Dee was manifesting some character pathology in addition to a depression.

Dee was the youngest of three sisters who were raised by both parents. Dee's father was a functional alcoholic. He provided for his family working in the garment district during the week and drinking heavily on the weekends. Dee described her mother as a depressed, difficult woman who was an excellent cook and so-so housekeeper. Her parents argued often and her father, when he was very drunk, beat her mother and occasionally struck her older sisters; she indicated that he never hit her. She resisted exploring her thoughts, feelings, memories about this information recalled matter-of-factly, stating that her father was a "piece of work." He divorced her mother during Dee's teens and she had nothing to do with him afterwards; she saw him in and around the neighborhood, knew that he had a girlfriend who was a dead ringer for her mother (even had the same first name as her mother) but knew little else. Dee's relationship with her mother was strained; Dee felt that her mother blamed her for her father leaving. Dee called her mother by her first name—"Barbara only calls me when she wants something . . ."; "Barbara is only in my life now so that my kids have a grandmother."

What emerged in subsequent sessions over the next several months within the therapeutic relationship was an interaction in which from session to session and sometimes within a session there was a kind of struggle between us, within her, and within me that was . . . confusing, which is a gross simplification for what was happening. I was accused of not listening, not understanding her at one moment, to really "getting" her the next, which sometimes seemed to mean understanding her, at other times it seemed to mean capturing her/trapping her. There were sessions when she looked at me and rarely spoke saying only that either she was bad, or something was bad without being able to elaborate. Then there were other sessions when she sat with a deer-in-the-headlights expression, staring vigilantly then vacantly at me, particularly at my hands, as though she was in a dissociated state; in other sessions her hostility emanated from her silence, that is, she refused "to talk"; "talk is meaningless," she would say. These presentations of Dee were in stark contrast to the Dee who had entered therapy. During these presentations I felt like treading lightly, because it seemed like we were over dangerous terrain (there was one session several years into the treatment when I did feel threatened, that she could strike out at me). My working diagnosis at this time was Major Depressive Disorder, R/O PTSD and Borderline Personality.

Another pattern developed during this time involving Dee's attendance. She was punctual for sessions, arriving right on time. She indicated that she abhorred lateness and also couldn't tolerate sitting in the waiting area with people. She never missed an appointment, that is, she was never a "no show." Rather, there were times when she cancelled sessions, but never last minute. She gave sufficient notice for the cancellations and while plausible, her reasons seemed defensive but of what was unclear. At this point in treatment we were meeting twice a week, so when she cancelled it would be for a week to 10 days periodically. The significance of this pattern became evident quite serendipitously when I called her to reschedule an appointment because of an impending hurricane. She wanted to meet if at all possible (apparently it was okay for her to cancel, but not the other way round); She researched the path of the storm and determined when the eye of the storm would be over the city and how long the eye would be over the city before the winds picked up again. So it was possible to keep our regularly scheduled appointment date if we could meet early in the morning. I agreed and we met during the eye of the storm (it is noteworthy that she liked to listen to a music station on the radio, "Quiet Storm," that played smooth jazz which she said soothed her).

As I processed my experience of being outside in the eye of a hurricane—the sulfurous color of the sky, the static in the air, the eerie calmness, the ominous movement of the clouds overhead, the empty streets, combined with my experience of Dee in session—her elation that we didn't have to cancel the session, and her animated presentation, I realized that Dee was suffering from a bipolar condition, that she had been withholding information from me and her psychiatrist about her manic states because she felt alive, though out of control, during them and didn't want to lose them. I also realized that her mother was probably suffering from a bipolar condition as well and had probably fought her husband as well as struck Dee and her sisters when she flew into rages.

Dee was reevaluated and placed on Lithium; the antidepressant she was on actually potentiated hypomanic and/or manic episodes which she liked. During the course of treatment Dee was psychiatrically hospitalized two times for depressive episodes and suicide risk and a third time for depression and a homicide risk. She had called at 3AM one morning asking if she could be seen; what had happened earlier had frightened her. We met later that morning and she reported a dissociative episode where she "came to" standing over her sleeping husband in bed holding a butcher knife in her hand. She described the eerie atmosphere of the bedroom illuminated by the blue light from the television which was on with the sound muted.

The therapy continued to focus on feelings about mourning the loss of a part of herself she valued even though she got into trouble during her highs; working towards understanding how her earlier childhood experiences growing up contributed to what was happening now; figuring out how to shield her children from her husband's drug use while she figured out what to do about their relationship and working towards establishing a more stable relationship with them herself. Her husband went to a drug rehab program and was drug free for a short while but then relapsed. Therapy addressed how her experience of witnessing and being victim of her parents' emotional problems and violent behavior continued to affect her and her way of relating to her husband and her children. She "remembered" that she had been sent to live with her aunts in Georgia when she was approximately 9 or 10, the age her daughter was when Dee struck her.

Helping Dee become a good mother, given her diagnoses, history and her current circumstances was a challenge. She became aware of her narcissistic rages, violent outbursts and other inappropriate PTSD-like reactions when her daughter's behavior "wounded" her. For example, Dee came to understand why she became anxious at slapping her daughter which prompted her to enter psychotherapy. Her daughter, frustrated by her mother's hostility and lack of understanding about her poor performance on a test, talked back, defending herself by stating the obvious, "I'm not YOU, leave me ALONE." Dee's coercive parenting had been more of an attempt to maintain control over the function her daughter served in Dee's fragile mental state rather than a method of disciplining and/or guiding her daughter.

The therapy dealt with the vicissitudes of daily life for Dee in terms of her growing self- discovery, learning how to better regulate her emotions, developing a more realistic understanding of healthy parent/child interactions in which she learned to validate not only her children's experiences but also her own. She also anxiously broached the first time she remembered "losing it"; it was shortly after returning from Georgia where she said she had experienced real love and caring for the first time in her life. Her parents were physically fighting in the kitchen and her father was pummeling her mother badly. Dee grabbed a knife and stabbed him in the abdomen. The paramedics were called and he along with the family went to the hospital. Dee describes how she was scared, excited, but relieved because the "lie" they were living would be exposed. She was scared, but prepared to be arrested. Instead, her father lied about what happened. She remembered seeing him on the gurney all bloodied, answering questions about how he got his injury. She says that he looked directly at her as he said he tripped and fell, the knife slipped out of his hand and he fell on it. The idea that nothing was going to be done to stop the violence in their house, that the man she had tried to kill to stop the violence lied to protect her and with that lie, keep the family secret, was too much for her. She had a psychotic break which was misconstrued by the professional staff as a stress reaction to the accident.

Dee was determined to break the transmission of violence and its aftermath in her immediate family. She did not want her children to become part of the "system" as she and one of her sisters had been when they were temporarily removed from the home. We explored, monitored, and addressed her husband's interactions with the children (e.g., he couldn't pick them up from school and drive them home when he was using) and we also examined if and when it might be prudent to call protective services if what had been put in place wasn't sufficient to protect the children. She and her husband went for couples' therapy and agreed that it was best that he not stay with her and the children at night during this time so as to minimize their arguing and potential for violence. He instead slept at his parents' home which was a few blocks away and spent time with the children most days after school. In the marriage, he was emotionally abusive towards Dee whereas she was physically abusive towards him (e.g., hitting, shoving, slapping).

The first session after returning from summer vacation one year, Dee showed me the divorce papers. She had not talked about her decision to divorce her husband because she said, "It was just time to do it and get it done. Talking wasn't going to change what was happening with him." She had also legally changed her name back to her maiden name. It hadn't escaped her that she did to her husband what her father had done to her mother i.e., end the relationship, but she "didn't want to go there" and "talk about it."

Years later, as Dee was in Georgia burying her mother, her cellphone rang at the cemetery; she was told that her mother was hospitalized and in intensive care. She called me right after the call and asked if she could come in for a "tune up" when she got back to New York. We met; she was older, heavier, and more relaxed. She wanted to share her most unusual phone call ever. Obviously, the woman hospitalized was not her mother, but her father's girlfriend who, looked like her mother, had her mother's name. Apparently, her father had married this woman and she was now seriously ill. She died. Her father, with whom her sisters had kept in touch, had fallen on hard times. They gave the authorities Dee's information because she was "good with this stuff." When Dee went to see him, she saw an old, frail, frightened man. As she got him the help he needed from social services, she realized that he and her mother were flawed people who fell in love and made a mess of their lives and the lives of their children. She couldn't say that she'd forgiven him but she did say that as long as she was alive, nobody was going to take advantage of him or hurt him. Additionally, she talked about her children. She acknowledged that they have "issues" but being abusive/violent or being in abusive/violent relationships was not one of their difficulties.

Dee's treatment goal to be a "good mother" was overdetermined; in other words, had multiple meanings. Our work together enabled her to move beyond a dichotomous way of thinking—a characteristic of borderline personality—about "good mother" vs. "bad mother" to a broader schema—what Winnicott referred to as "good enough mother." For example, we explored her past experiences of good enough mothering (e.g., learning how to cook from her mother and many enjoyable and memorable social interactions in her mother's kitchen; the time spent with her maternal aunts when she went to live in Georgia; being mentored by a high school teacher who told her she had potential). She also began to be a "good enough mother" to herself by becoming more responsible in managing her medical treatment (e.g., following up on routine blood work to maintain appropriate Lithium levels), and taking appropriate action to protect herself and her children from her husband's substance abuse.

During therapy, Dee decided to resume her education; she obtained her masters' degree in special education and became a special education teacher. She resonated with her special ed students and was very good at her work. We explored what it was like for her and her own children to be students at the same time and how they helped and supported each other. Dee recognized that her children could benefit from psychotherapy; they were referred to separate therapists and seen as needed.

Dee's violent behavior toward others, circumscribed within her immediate family, particularly toward her husband, decreased overtime. However, her suicidal ideation and at-risk behaviors, that is, self-directed violence (e.g., internalized aggression), was supported for a time by her befriending and socializing with a group of co-workers who themselves were struggling with suicidal ideation and at-risk behaviors. It is beyond the scope of this chapter to discuss the therapeutic intervention enabling Dee to maintain a good working relationship with this group of co-workers while disengaging from participating in their group suicidal fantasies and at risk behaviors. It is important to reconsider the complex relationship between other-directed destructiveness and self-directed destructiveness especially in light of the contemporary influence of social media.

Ethnicity, religiosity, and socioeconomic status were a constant presence in the background of the treatment, occasionally coming to the foreground and explored in therapy from Dee's perspective. For example, she spoke of her parents' influence on her strong work ethic stating, "My father and my father's people (referring to her Jamaican heritage) are hard workers . . . he did provide for us . . . we weren't rich but we weren't poor either." Her mother was a homemaker who added to the family income by sewing; she was a seamstress who made clothing for people in the neighborhood. At times, Dee would refer to her mother as "a strong, independent b—." Her parents were not religious but Dee was immersed in a southern religious/spiritual household when she went to live in Georgia with her maternal aunts who were devout Methodists. The rituals and traditions of the South and the Black Church allowed for a comfortable intimacy for her among her extended family and their community that was free of the tension and conflict she had known at home.

In summary, this case illustrates several important findings in the literature on some violent females. Dee was diagnosed with Bipolar Disorder, Type I and Borderline personality; she also had PTSD symptoms. She was the initiator of hitting and slapping her husband and child, and at risk for suicide. As her past and present, conflict-laden relationships collided, she was thrust back emotionally into the drama of her family of origin, revisiting and reenacting the pain, and self-defeating ways of coping. Dee was also resilient, resourceful, highly motivated to change, sought psychological treatment, and responded well to psychotherapy.

ISSUES OF INTERVENTION AND PREVENTION

As with other public health concerns, reducing and hopefully eliminating the climate in which violence abounds requires comprehensive, multifaceted strategies—all of which recognize the scope of the problem and need to tackle it from the micro level (e.g., characteristics of the offender) to the macro level (e.g., cultural, economic, institutional, and sociopolitical domains).

The increasing number of women becoming involved with the criminal justice system and the research findings highlighting the differences between male and female offenders call attention to a range of correctional practices deemed "gender-neutral" (Bloom et al., 2003). Bauman, Van Voorhis, Wright, and Salisbury (2014) discuss salient issues regarding the implementation of the Women's Risk Needs Assessment (WRNA), an assessment measure developed in 2004 in a collaboration between the National Institute of Corrections and the University of Cincinnati. The WRNA incorporates both gender-neutral and gender-responsive scales to aid in effective intervention, rehabilitation, and lowering recidivism with this population. This measure reflects two paradigms: (1) that effective correctional treatment of the characteristics in offenders' lives which predict future criminal offending is necessary for changing the criminal behavior and reducing recidivism and (2) that it is vital to identify the unique set of needs incarcerated women have related to abuse/trauma, mental illness, dysfunctional relationships, and parenting stress. The assessment tool also taps into several strengths acting as resiliency factors keeping women from future criminal offending (e.g., educational assets, supportive relationships, parental involvement, and self-efficacy; Blanchette & Brown, 2006).

Implementing successful intervention and prevention programs for incarcerated women within the penal system designed to punish rather than rehabilitate the male offender is a real challenge. There are very few interventions designed specifically for women with violent offenses. Consequently, administrators in correctional settings often rely on treatment and rehabilitation programs designed for violent male offenders when working with violent female offenders, despite the evidence that women's trajectories into violent behavior—as well as their trajectory out—differ from their male counterparts (Kubiak et al., 2012). Research findings suggest that women who use violence, in contrast to men, have usually had a relationship with the victim (Pizarro, DeJong, & McGarell, 2010). Approximately three-quarters of women convicted of violent offenses were charged with simple assault and arrested perhaps because of mandatory arrest policies for domestic violence.

As discussed earlier, women's motivations for violence as well as the victims of their violent behaviors frequently differ from those of male-perpetrated violence with respect to differences in anger expression, experiences of victimization, exposure to traumatic events associated with posttraumatic stress disorder (PTSD), mental health, and substance use (Kubiak et al., 2010; Raj et al., 2008; Fazel et al., 2006; Pollock & Davis, 2005; Kruttschnitt, 2002). Given these differences, those working in correctional settings recognize the need for gender-specific and trauma informed services for incarcerated women (Kubiak et al., 2012; Bloom, Owen, & Covington, 2003). Developing interventions that effectively modify aggressive behavior as well as the underlying precursors of such aggression in female offenders will better serve this small but important subpopulation of women involved in the criminal justice system.

For those already in the mental health and/or penal systems, a variety of treatment modalities including cognitive behavioral therapy, relaxation training, social skills training, mindfulness, and systems approach including Multisystemic Therapy and Family therapy may be effective especially for an incarcerated female population. Contemporary psychotherapies and healing practices use imagination, ritual, and sharing of the unknown fragments of sensory experiences through the co-creative action of re-remembering haunted fragmented images, words, acts stored in the right hemisphere (van der Kolk, 2001) in implicit memories (Meekums, 1999; Williams, 2006).

Regardless of the approach, the quality of the "relationship" with the practitioner may be a crucial factor. What is challenging for the therapeutic relationship with violent female inmates is working together to build consistent, stable, and healthy channels of communication to facilitate whatever healing/recovery of innate healthy functioning is possible. If the capacity to aggress is inherent in human nature, teaching individuals (at any age) skills and encouraging a more cohesive sense of self to help them cope with, manage, and channel appropriately their aggression is key. *Beyond Violence*, a gender specific and trauma-informed intervention, has shown promise with this population in the reduction of symptoms associated with depression, anxiety, posttraumatic stress disorder, and serious mental illness (Kubiak et al., 2012).

IPV PREVENTION

Programs focused on decreasing positive attitudes toward men's and women's use of physical dating violence motivated by control and/or maintaining a tough guise would be beneficial for all young adults. Among women, programming on the minimization of attitudes toward women's use of physical dating violence especially for reasons pertaining to emotional expression (e.g., communication of anger or jealousy) should be the focus. For young men, dating violence programming should focus on deconstructing patriarchal values that legitimize controlling behavior toward women. Further, findings suggest that dating violence interventions could benefit from focusing on increasing adaptive coping strategies in response to relationship stress or conflict that includes aggressive or unwanted behaviors by a partner, as well as assertive communication skills for the expression of emotions (e.g., anger).

SCHOOL VIOLENCE INTERVENTIONS

School environments have also been recognized as contributing a contextual factor in the occurrence of violence in schools. Distinctions have been made between protective school environments that diminish the prevalence of school violence and disorderly school environments associated with high rates of school violence (Olweus, 1993). The latter have been characterized as having vague rules and expectations, and high suspension and expulsion rates (Morrison & Skiba, 2001). Teachers have been reported to intercede in only 15% to 18% of classroom bullying episodes (Craig, Pepler, & Atlas, 2000), reflecting an unsupportive school environment for the victims. Schools that have developed a clear statement of rules and expectations, consistently communicated and applied consequences, positive consequences for positive behavior, involvement of family/community/students, and early intervention services (Espelage & Swearer, 2004; Frey et al., 2005; Scott, Nelson, & Liaupsin, 2001; Sugai et al., 2000) have been typically associated with lower school violence. Future investigations are recommended in the area of assessment of students' perceptions of level of social support in schools (Demaray et al., 2006). The clear identification of specific types of social support from various sources is also suggested.

Research findings indicate that an increase in victimization and delinquency occurs between ages 11 and 12 for girls and between the ages of 13 and 14 for boys during latency, prepubertal, and early adolescent phases of psychological development. This strongly suggests that delinquency and victimization prevention efforts need to be in place around or before the fifth grade, and they need to include components that minimize sexual aggression and harassment.

The transition to high school may also be a crucial juncture, especially for boys. Further study may better determine how children at this juncture both are targeted as victims and initiators of delinquent activities. Better early-warning systems may identify students who need special guidance and education at the outset of their high school education (Cuevas et al., 2013).

A colleague and friend of mine (Chisholm) is a principal of a charter school for grades one through eight in an urban area. She shared a current situation she faces that illustrates the challenges involved in maintaining an educational climate in which ethnic minority boys and girls in crime-ridden, violent neighborhoods can learn, excel, pursue higher education, and prepare to fully participate in society as educated, skilled citizens (Skiba et al., 2011). She asked if I had any suggestions for how she could handle her "ankle bracelet problem." Students, both boys and girls, were coming to school with ankle bracelets. In ways characteristic for that age group, the bracelets had become a status item. She recounted how several years ago, thanks to an alert teacher/parent aide, she was able to quickly intervene and stop the emergence of a gang presence among the children who had begun to wear the colors of rival gangs. The intervention consisted of individual sessions with the student body in general assembly and separate meetings with all parents in addition to joint sessions with the student/parent bodies. Consultations with different professionals (e.g., psychologists, guidance counselors, the local police precinct, and community activists) helped this principal launch a successful campaign to restore her school environment to a setting for learning.

This time was different. The ankle bracelets worn were not jewelry; they were monitoring devices these children were mandated to wear by the criminal justice system. The "problem" for my colleague was that the monitors would begin beeping during class time because batteries needed to be recharged; the beeping noises were a distraction in the classroom; those wearing them attained enviable notoriety because they were able to disrupt class. My colleague was not notified by any city agency or parents, for that matter, of who among her student population was mandated to wear this device, or for what offenses and so forth. Her security personnel recommended that an ankle bracelet battery charging room be established so that children could recharge their batteries before classes and thus minimize the classroom disturbance. The bigger problem was the lack of communication between the criminal justice system and the charter school and the ways in which the mission of the charter school (i.e., to provide a quality education to underprivileged children who would then have access to opportunities and resources to lead better, enriching and productive lives) was compromised.

My colleague's efforts to resist a powerful trend in education poignantly illustrates what has been called the school-to-prison pipeline system in which the handling of students' disruptive behaviors has been transferred to the criminal justice and juvenile court system (Stucki, 2014). During the Obama administration, Attorney General Eric Holder and Education Secretary Arne Duncan questioned the usefulness of zero-tolerance policies or police officers assigned to schools for example, and the consequent procedures that ultimately disrupt the purpose of the educational system and increase the likelihood that some students will become more involved with the criminal justice system and prison system that is becoming increasingly privatized and run for a profit. This phenomenon was dramatically illustrated recently when an uploaded video on YouTube went viral showing a male police officer, called into a classroom by a teacher to discipline a female student, dragging and then throwing the student, who was seated in a chair, across the classroom while fellow students and the teacher watched.

CONCLUSION

In this chapter we have reviewed theories and research on gendered violence and the contexts in which it occurs. The percent of women incarcerated for committing violent acts is and has remained consistently small, however the perception and concern centers on whether or not females as a group are more prone now than ever before to act violently. Addressing how the criminal justice system and prisons need to be redesigned to adequately manage the needs of incarcerated females is an important endeavor. However, remedying these systems will not adequately address the broader issues of the apparent changes in our cultural/social mores about gender disparities and gendered violence. While anger and other powerfully felt negative emotions contribute to aggression which is part of human nature, the etiology of violent behavior is more complex and nuanced. While there is considerable evidence linking harsh and abusive child-rearing practices to later violent behavior, much more research is needed to comprehend the "misatunements" and "hidden cruelties" (Miller, 1990) of child-rearing more characteristic of a deprivation of caring rather than a deprivation of care. In other words, the misatunements of everyday life for children, adolescents, and adults within social contexts needs to be addressed from the top down (e.g., social institutions, compatible and incompatible cultural and subcultural values in our pluralistic society) regarding gendered behavior, and opportunities for men and women, boys and girls to realize their potential, fulfill their dreams, and participate fully in our society without limitations or restrictions based on prejudicial and discriminatory policies and practices reified in social structures/social systems against certain groups. At the beginning of this chapter, we quoted McHugh and colleagues' (2005) view on how to conceptualized women's use of violence. The solution or successful intervention/prevention of female perpetrated violence must also address the inherent complexities, dynamics, and meanings involved in the multiple forms and patterns of violence occurring in relationships in different contexts.

More research is needed to investigate and clarify the relationship among impulsivity, trait anger, and aggression in females, which can then lead to a clarification in the developmental pathways of aggression and violence. Additionally, it will be imperative to examine and account for the role and relationship of substance use, victimization, and witness to violence, and trauma and PTSD, in relation to impulsivity and other mental illness, trait and state anger, and the different types of aggression and violent acts. This information is important to determine pathways and trajectories which will inform intervention programs as well as preventative services and programs.

DISCUSSION QUESTIONS

1. What are the similarities and dissimilarities in the pattern of violence perpetrated by males and females? Is this pattern different among those with multiple gender identities, particularly among male-female transgender identity?
2. In what ways has the socially constructed gendered views of femininity and masculinity overshadowed or obscured an inquiry and understanding of violence perpetrated by women?
3. Compare and contrast two theoretical perspectives on violent females. Discuss the empirical evidence.
4. What is the evidence supporting the view that prevalence of female-perpetrated violence has remained stable and consistent over the years? What is the evidence supporting the claim that violence perpetrated by females is increasing?
5. Discuss the impact of gang membership on female-perpetrated violence.
6. What is the evidence supporting the view that prevalence of female-perpetrated violence has remained stable and consistent over the years? What is the evidence supporting the claim that violence perpetrated by females is increasing?
7. What are the experiences of incarcerated female offenders during incarceration and after?
8. What prevention programs show promise in addressing, reducing, remediating violence perpetrated by females?
9. Critique prison policies impacting female offenders from a feminist perspective.
10. What role does trauma play in women and male-female transgender who act violently?

11. What are the similarities and differences in female-perpetrated violence among women of different ethnic/racial backgrounds, among women in LGBTQ communities?

REFERENCES

Aboujaoude, E. (2011). *Virtually you: The dangerous powers of the e-personality*. New York: W.W. Norton.

Adams, J. W., Snowling, M. J., Hennessy, S. M., & Kind, P. (1999). Problems of behaviour, reading and arithmetic: Assessments of comorbidity using the Strengths and Difficulties Questionnaire. *British Journal of Educational Psychology, 69* (4), 571–585.

Agnew, R. (1992). Foundation for a general strain theory of crime and delinquency. *Criminology*, 30, 47–87.

Agnew, R. (2001). Building on the foundation of general strain theory: Specifying the types of strain most likely to lead to crime and delinquency. *Journal of Research in Crime and Delinquency, 38,* 319–361.

Agnew, R. (2006). *Pressured into crime: An overview of general strain theory.* Los Angeles, CA: Roxbury.

Ahmed, O., & Jindasurat, C. (2015). Lesbian, Gay, Bisexual, Transgender, Queer and HIV-Affected Hate Violence in 2014. National Coalition of Anti-Violence Programs. New York City Gay and Lesbian Anti-Violence Project, Inc.

Alexander, P. C. (2014). Dual trauma couples and intimate partner violence. *Psychological Trauma: Theory, Research, Practice, and Policy. 6,* (3), 224–231.

Anderson. K. L. (2002). Perpetrator or victim? Relationships between intimate partner violence and well-being. *Journal of Marriage and Family, 64,* 851–863.

Anderson, M. L. (1993). *Thinking about women: Sociological perspectives on sex and gender.* New York: Macmillan.

Archer, J. (2000). Sex differences in aggression between heterosexual partners: A meta-analytic review. *Psychological Bulletin, 126,* 651–680.

Aricak, T., Siyahhan, S., Uzunhasanoglu, A., Saribeyoglu, S., Ciplak, S., Yilmaz, N., & Memmedov, C. (2008). Cyberbullying among Turkish adolescents. *CyberPsychology & Behavior, 11*(3), 253–261.

Asher, S. R., & Coie, J. D. (1990). *Peer Rejection in Childhood.* New York: Cambridge University Press.

Babcock, J. C., Miller, S. A., & Siard, C. (2003). Toward a typology of abusive women: Differences between partner-only and generally violent women in the use of violence. *Psychology of Women Quarterly, 27,* 153–161.

Badenes-Ribera, L., Frias-Navarro, D., Bonilla-Campos, A., Pons-Salvador, G., & Monterde-i-Bort, H. (2015). Intimate partner violence in self-identified lesbians: A meta-analysis of its prevalence. *Sexuality Research & Social Policy, 12,* 47–59.

Baetens, I., Claes, L., Hasking, P., Smits, D., Grietens, H., Onghena, P., & Martin, G. (2015). The relationship between parental expressed emotions and nonsuicidal self-injury: The mediating roles of self-criticism and depression. *Journal of Child and Family Studies, 24,* 491–498.

Baker, N. L., Buick, J. D., Kim, S. R., Moniz, S., & Nava, K. L. (2013). Lessons from examining same-sex intimate partner violence. *Sex Roles*. 69, 182–192.

Barnett, O. W., & Fagan, R. W. (1993). Alcohol use in male spouse abusers and their female partners. *Journal of Family Violence, 8,* 1, 1–25.

Bates, J. E., Pettit, G. S., & Dodge, K. A. (1995). Family and child factors in stability and change in children's aggressiveness in elementary school. In J. McCord (Ed.), *Coercion and punishment in long-term perspectives*. New York: Cambridge University Press.

Bauman, A., Van Voorhis, P., Wright, E., & Salisbury, E. J. (2014). Assessing the risk and needs of women in jails. *American Jails, 27, 6,* 19–25.

Beckerman, L., & Nocero, J. (2003). You've got hate mail. *Principal Leadership, 3*(4), 38–41.

Berson, I., Berson, M., & Ferron, J. (2002). Emerging risks of violence in the digital age: Lessons for educators from an online study of adolescent girls in the United States. [electronic version]. *Meridian: A Middle School Computer Technologies Journal, 5*(2). Retrieved September 28, 2005 from http://www.ncsu.edu/meridian/sum2002/cyberviolence/index.html.

Bhat, C. S. (2008). Cyberbullying: Overview and strategies for school counselors, guidance officers, and all school personnel. *Australian Journal of Guidance and Counseling, 18*(1), 53–66.

Blanchette, K., & Brown, S. L. (2006). *The assessment and treatment of women offenders: An integrative perspective*. Chichester, UK: Wiley.

Blatt, S. J. (1974). Levels of object representation in anaclitic and introjective depression. *Psychoanalytic Study of the Child, 29,* 107–157.

Bloom, B., Owen, B., & Covington, S. (2003). *Gender-responsive strategies: Research, practice, and guiding principles for women offenders.* (NIC Publication No. 018017). Washington, DC: National Institute of Corrections.

Breiding, M. J., Basile, K. C., Smith, S. G., Black, M. C., & Mahendra, R. R. (2015). *Intimate partner violence: Uniform definitions and recommended data elements.* Version 2.0. Atlanta, GA: National Center for Injury Prevention and Control, Centers for Disease Control and Prevention.

Brennan, P. A., Grekin, E. R., & Mednick, S. (1999). Maternal cigarette smoking during pregnancy and adult male criminal outcomes. *Archives of General Psychiatry, 56,* 215–219.

Broidy, L. M. (2001). A test of general strain theory. *Criminology, 39,* 9–33.

Brown, L. S., & Pantalone, D. (2011). Lesbian, gay, bisexual, and transgender issues in trauma psychology: A topic comes out of the closet. *Traumatology, 17, 2,* 1–3.

Brown, M. (2006). Gender, ethnicity and offending over the life course: Women's pathways to prison in the Aloha State. *Critical Criminology, 14,* 2, 137–58.

Brush, L. D. (1990). Violent acts and injurious outcomes in married couples: Methodological issues in the National Survey of Families and Households. *Gender and Society, 4,* 56–67.

Bureau of Justice Statistics (2013). Intimate Partner Violence: Attributes of Victimization, 1993–2011. U.S. Department of Justice. November 2013, NCJ243300.

Bureau of Justice Statistics. (2014). Domestic violence accounted for about a fifth of all violent victimizations between 2003 and 2012. Retrieved on November 23, 2014, from: http://www.bjs.gov/content/pub/press/ndv0312pr.cfm.

Bushman, B. J., & Anderson, C. A. (2001). Is it time to pull the plug on hostile versus instrumental aggression dichotomy? *Psychological Review, 108,* 273–279.

Buss, A. H., & Perry, M. (1992). The Aggression Questionnaire. *Journal of Personality and Social Psychology, 63,* 452–459.

Calkins, S. D., Gill, K. A., & Williford, A. (1999). Externalizing problems in two-year-olds: Implications for patterns of social behavior and peers' responses to aggression. *Early Education and Development, 10,* 266–288.

Campbell, A. (1993). *Men, women, and aggression*. New York: Basic Books.

Campbell, S. B., Pierce, E. W., Moore, G., Markowitz, S., & Newby, K. (1996). Boys' externalizing problems at elementary school age: Pathways from early behavior problems, maternal control, and family stress. *Developmental and Psychopathology, 8,* 701–719.

Campos, R. C., Besser, A., & Blatt, S. J. (2010). The mediating role of self-criticism and dependency in the association between perceptions of maternal caring and depressive symptoms. *Depression and Anxiety, 27,* 1149–1157.

Card, N. A., & Little, T. D. (2006). Proactive and reactive aggression in childhood and adolescence: A meta-analysis of differential relations with psychosocial adjustment. *International Journal of Behavioral Development, 30,* 466–480.

Catalano, R. F., & Hawkins, J. D. (1996). The social development model: A theory of antisocial behavior. In J. D. Hawkins (Ed.), *Delinquency and crime: Current theories* (pp. 149–197). New York: Cambridge University Press.

Cauffman, E. (2008). Understanding the female offender. *The Future of Children, 18,* 2, 119–142.

Chesney-Lind, M. & Paramore, V. V. (2001). Are girls getting more violent? Exploring juvenile robbery trends. *Journal of Contemporary Criminal Justice, 17,* 2, 142–166.

Coie, J. D., Dodge, K. A., & Kupersmidt, J. B. (1990). Peer group behavior and social status. In: S. R. Asher & J. D. Coie (Eds.), *Peer rejection in childhood* (pp. 17–59). Cambridge, UK: Cambridge University Press.

Cole, J. (1986). *All american women: Lines that divide, ties that bind.* New York: Free Press.

Collins, W. A., Maccoby, E. E., Steinberg, L., Hetherington, E. M., & Bornstein, M. H. (2000). Contemporary research on parenting: The case for nature and nurture. *American Psychologist, 55* (2), 218–232.

Craig, W. M., Pepler, D., & Atlas, R. (2000). Observations of bullying in the playground and in the classroom. *School Psychology International, 21,* 1, 22–36.

Cramer, B. (1995). Short term dynamic psychotherapy for infants and their parents. In K. Minde (Ed.) *Child Adolescent Psychiatric Clinics of North America, 4,* 3, 649–660.

Crick, N. R., & Dodge, K. A. (1994). A review and reformulation of social information-processing mechanisms in children's social adjustment. *Psychological Bulletin, 115,* 74–101.

Cuevas, C., Finkelhor, D., Shattuck, A., Turner, H., & Hamby, S. (2013). Children's exposure to violence and the intersection between delinquency and victimization. National Survey of Children's Exposure to Violence, (NCJ Pub. No. 240555). Washington, DC: U.S. Department of Justice Office of Juvenile Justice and Delinquency Prevention, 1–9.

D'Antonio-del Rio, J. M., Doucet, J. M., & Chauvin, C. D. (2010). Violent and vindictive women: a re-analysis of the Southern subculture of violence. *Sociological Spectrum, 30,* 484–503.

De La Rue, L., & Espelage, D. L. (2014). Family and abuse characteristics of gang-involved, pressured-to-join, and non-gang-involved girls. *Psychology of Violence, 4,* 3, 253–265.

Demaray, M. K., Malecki, C. K., & DeLong, L. K. (2006). Support in the lives of aggressive students, their victims, and their peers. In S. R. Jimerson & M. J. Furlong (Eds.), *Handbook of school violence and school safety: From research to practice* (pp. 21–29). Mahwah, NJ: Lawrence Erlbaum Associates, Inc.

Dluzen, D. E., & Liu, B. (2008). Gender differences in methamphetamine use and responses: A review. *Gender Medicine, 5,* 24–35.

Dobson, V., & Sales, B. (2000). The science of infanticide and mental illness. *Psychiatry, Public Policy and Law, 6,* 1098–1112.

Dodge, K. A. (1991). The structure and function of reactive and reactive aggression. In D. J. Pepler & K. H. Rubin (Eds). *The development and treatment of childhood aggression* (pp. 201–218). Hillsdale, NJ: Erlbaum.

Duman, S., & Margolin, G. (2007). Parents' aggressive influences and children's aggressive problem solutions with peers. *Journal of Clinical Child & Adolescent Psychology, 36,* 1, 42–55.

Dutton, L. B., & Winstead, B. A. (2006). Predicting unwanted pursuit: Attachment, relationship satisfaction, relationship alternatives, and break-up distress. *Journal of Social and Personal Relationships, 23,* 565–586.

Eagly, A. H., Wood, W., & Diekman, A. (2000). Social role theory of sex differences and similarities: A current appraisal. In T. Eckes & H. M. Trautner (Eds.), *The Developmental Social Psychology of Gender,* pp. 123–174.

Esbensen, F., & Huizinga, D. (1993). Gangs, drugs, and delinquency in a survey of urban youth. *Criminology, 31,* 565–589.

Espelage, D. L., & Swearer, S. M. (2004). *Bullying in American schools: A social-ecological perspective on prevention and intervention.* Mahwah, NJ: Lawrence Erlbaum Associates.

Espelage, D. L., Cauffman, E., Broidy, L., Piquero, A. R., Mazerolle, P., Steiner, H. (2003). *Journal of the American Academy of Child & Adolescent Psychiatry, 42,* 7, 770–777.

Evans, G. W., & English, K. (2002). The environment of poverty: Multiple stressor exposure, psychophysiological stress, and socioemotional adjustment. *Child Development, 73,* 1238–1248.

Fagan, J. (1990). Social processes of delinquency and drug use among urban gangs. In C. R. Huff (Ed.), *Gangs in America* (pp. 183–219). Newbury Park, CA: Sage.

Faulk, M. (1974, July). Men who assault their wives. *Medicine, Science, and the Law.* 180–183.

Fazel, S., Bains, P., & Doll, H. (2006). Substance abuse and dependence in prisoners: A systematic review. *Addiction, 101*, 181–191.

Figley, C. (1995). *Compassion fatigue: Coping with secondary stress disorder in those who treat the traumatized.* New York: Brunner/Mazel.

Finn, J. (2004). A survey of online harassment at a university campus. *Journal of Interpersonal Violence, 19*(4), 468–483.

Fite, P. J., Raine, A., Stouthamer-Loeber, M., Loeber, R., & Pardini, D. A. (2009). Reactive and proactive aggression in adolescent males: Examining differential outcomes 10 years later in early adulthood. *Criminal Justice Behavior, 37,* 2, 141–157.

Fite, P. J., Stoppelbein, L., & Greening, L. (2009). Proactive and reactive aggression in a child psychiatric inpatient population. *Journal of Clinical Child Adolescent Psychology, 38,* 2, 199–205.

Flesisher, M. S., & Krienerr, J. L. (2004). Life-course events, social networks, and the emergence of violence among female gang members. *Journal of Community Psychology, 32, 5,* 607–622.

Flynn, A., & Graham, K. (2010). "Why did it happen?" A review and conceptual framework for research on perpetrators' and victims' explanations for intimate partner violence. *Aggression and Violent Behavior,15,* 239–251.

Follingstad, D. R., Wright, S., Lloyd, S., & Sebastian, J. A. (1991). Sex differences in motivations and effects in dating violence. *Family Relations, 40,* 51–57.

Fonagy, P., Gergely, G., Jurist, E., & Target, M. (2002). *Affect regulation, mentalization and the development of the self.* New York: Other Press.

Freud, S. (1962). *Sexuality and the Psychology of Love*. New York: Macmillan.

Frey, K. S., Snell, J. L., Hirschstein, M. K., Edstorm, L. V. S., MacKenzie, E. P., & Broderick, C. J. (2005). Reducing playground bullying and supporting beliefs: An experimental trial of the steps to respect program. *Developmental Psychology, 41,* 3, 479–491.

Gelles, R. J., & Straus, M. A. (1979). Determinants of violence in the family: Toward a theoretical integration. In W. R. Burr, R. Hill, F. I. Nye, & I. L. Reiss (Eds.), *Contemporary Theories About the Family (Vol. 1)* (pp. 549–581). New York: The Free Press.

Glaze, L. E., & Maruschak, L. M. (2008). Parents in prison and their minor children. *Bureau of Justice Statistics: Special Report.* U.S. Department of Justice.

Grych, J. H., & Kinsfogel, K. (2010). Exploring the role of attachment style in the relation between family aggression and abuse in adolescent dating relationships. *Journal of Aggression, Maltreatment & Trauma, 19,* 624–640.

Guerino, P., Harrison, P. M., & Sabol, W. J. (2011). *Prisoners in 2010* (NCJ Pub. No. 236096). Washington, DC: U.S. Department of Justice, Bureau of Justice Statistics. http://bjs.ojp.usdoj.gov/content/pub/pdf/p10.pdf.

Guerra, N. G., Huesmann, L. R., & Spindler, A. (2003). Community violence exposure, social cognition, and aggression among urban elementary school children. *Child Development, 74,* 1561–1576.

Hamberger. L. K. (1997). Female offenders in domestic violence: A look at actions in their contexts. *Journal of Aggression, Maltreatment & Trauma*, 117–129.

Hamby, S., Finkelhor, D., & Turner, H. (2012). Teen dating violence: Co-occurrence with other victimizations in the National Survey of Children's Exposure to Violence (NatSCEV). *Psychology of Violence, 2,*(2), 111–124.

Hamby, S., & Grych, J. (2013). *The web of violence: Exploring connections among different forms of interpersonal violence and abuse*. Dordrecht, Netherlands: Springer.

Hamby, S., McDonald, R., & Grych, J. (2014). Trends in violence research: An update through 2013. *Psychology of Violence, 4,* 1, 1–7.

Hamilton, J. A., & Harberger, P. N. (eds.) 1992. *Postpartum psychiatric illness: A picture puzzle*. Philadelphia: University of Pennsylvania Press.

Hanish, L. D., Eisenberg, N., Fabes, R. A., Spinrad, T. L., Ryan, P., & Schmidt, S. (2004). The expression and regulation of negative emotions: Risk factors for young children's peer victimization. *Development and Psychopathology , 16,* 335–353.

Hansen, L. L. (2005). Girl "crew" members doing gender, boy "crew" members doing violence: An ethnographic and network analysis of Maria Hinojosa's New York Gangs. *Western Criminology Review, 6,* 1, 134–144.

Harmon, R. B., Rosner, R., & Owens, H. (1998). Sex and violence in a forensic population of obsessional harassers. *Psychology, Public Policy and Law, 4,* 236–249.

Harmon-Jones, E. (2003). Clarifying the emotive functions of asymmetrical frontal cortical activity. *Psychophysiology, 40,* 838–848.

Harned, M. S. (2001). Abused women or abused men? An examination of the context and outcomes of dating violence. *Violence and Victims, 16,* 269–285.

Harris, S., Petrie, G., & Willoughby, W. (2002). Bullying among 9th graders: An exploratory study. *NASSP Bulletin, 86*(630), 3–14.

Hawkins, J. D., Herrenkohl, T., Farrington, D. P., Brewer, D., Catalano, R. F., & Harachi, T. W. (1998). A review of predictors of youth violence. In R. Loeber & D. P. Farrington (Eds.), *Serious and Violent Juvenile Offenders: Risk Factors and Successful Interventions* (pp. 106–146). Thousand Oaks, CA: Sage Publications, Inc..

Heidel, A. (1951). *The Babylonian Genesis: The Story of Creation.* Chicago: The University of Chicago Press.

Heidensohn, F. (2010). The deviance of women: a critique and an inquiry. *The British Journal of Sociology, 61,* 111–126.

Heller, T. L., Baker, B. L., Henker, B., & Hinshaw, S. P. (1996). Externalizing behavior and cognitive functioning from preschool to first grade: Stability and predictors. *Journal of Clinical Child Psychology, 25,* 376–387.

Herman, J. (1992). *Trauma and recovery.* New York: Basic Books.

Hinduja, S., & Patchin, J. (2009). *Bullying beyond the schoolyard: Preventing and responding to Cyberbullying.* Thousand Oaks, CA: Sage.

Hunt, G., & Joe-Laidler, K. (2001). Situations of violence in the lives of girl gang members. *Health Care for Women International, 22,* 363–384.

Inciardi, J., Lockwood, D., & Pottieger, A. (1993). *Women and crack-cocaine.* New York: Macmillan.

Jasinski, J. L. (2001). Pregnancy and violence against women: An analysis of longitudinal data. *Journal of Interpersonal Violence, 16*(7), 713–734.

Jessor, R., Van Den Bos, J., Vanderryn, J., Costa, F. M., & Turbin, M. S. (1995). Protective factors in adolescent problem behavior: Moderator effects and developmental change. *Developmental Psychology, 31,* 6, 923–933.

Jimerson, S. R., Morrison, G. M., Pletcher, S. W., & Furlong, M. J. (2006). Youth engaged in antisocial and aggressive behaviors: Who are they? In S. R. Jimerson & M. J. Furlong (Eds.), *The handbook of school violence and school safety: From research to practice* (pp. 3–20). New Jersey: Lawrence Erlbaum Associates.

Johnson, H. (1996). *Dangerous domains: Violence against women in Canada.* Toronto: Nelson Canada.

Jordan, C. E. (2009). Advancing the study of violence against women. *Violence Against Women, 15*(4), 393–419.

Jordan, J. V., Kaplan, A., Miller, J. B., Stiver, I., & Surrey, J. (1991). *Women's growth connection: Writings from the Stone Center.* New York: Guilford Press.

Kohut, H. (1971). *The analysis of the self.* New York: International Universities Press.

Kowalski, R. M., & Limber, S. P. (2007). Electronic bullying among middle school students. *Journal of Adolescent Health, 41(6 Suppl),* S22–S30.

Kruttschnitt, C. (2002). Women's involvement in serious interpersonal violence. *Aggression and Violent Behavior, 7,* 529–565.

Kruttschnitt, C., Gartner, R., & Hussemann, J. (2008). Female violent offenders: Moral panics or more serious offenders? *The Australian and New Zealand Journal of Criminology, 4,* 1, 9–35.

Kubiak, S. P., Beeble, M. L., & Bybee, D. (2010). Testing the validity of the K6 in detecting major depression and PTSD among jailed women. *Criminal Justice and Behavior, 37,* 64–80.

Kubiak, S., Kim, W. J., Fedock, G., & Bybee, D. (2012). Assessing short-term outcomes of an intervention for women convicted of violent crimes. *Journal of the Society for Social Work and Research, 3*(3),197–212.
Kubiak, T., Wiedig-Allison, M., Zgoriecki, S., & Weber, H. (2011). Habitual goals and strategies in anger regulation: The Anger-Related Reactions and Goals Inventory. *Journal of Individual Differences, 32*, 1–13.
Kuhn, T. (1962). The Structure of Scientific Revolutions. Chicago: University of Chicago Press
Kupersmidt, J. B., Burehinal, M., & Patterson, C. J. (1995). Developmental patterns of childhood peer relations as predictors of externalizing behavior problems. *Development and Psychopathology, 7,* 825–843.
Lefer, L.(1984). The fine edge of violence. *Journal of the Academy of Psychoanalysis*, 12, 253–68.
Lewis, R., Mason,T. B., Winstead, B. A., & Kelley, M. L. (2017). Empirical investigation of a model of sexual minority specific and general risk factors for intimate partner violence among lesbian women. *Psychology of Violence*, *7,* 1, 110–119.
Liau, A. K., Khoo, A., & Ang, P. H. (2005). Factors influencing adolescents' engagement in risky Internet behavior. *CyberPsychology and Behavior, 8*(6), 513–520.
Lichter, E. L., & McCloskey, L. A. (2004). The effects of childhood exposure to marital violence on adolescent gender-role beliefs and dating violence. *Psychology of Women Quarterly, 28*, 344–357.
Linehan, M. M. (1993). *Cognitive-behavioral treatment of borderline personality disorder.* New York: The Guilford Press.
Lyons-Ruth, K., Connell, D., Zoll, D., & Stahl, L. (1987). Infants at social risk: Relationships among infant maltreatment, maternal behavior, and infant attachment behavior, *Developmental Psychology, 23(2)*, 223–232.
Martin, R., Watson, D., & Wan, C. K. (2000). A three-factor model of trait anger: Dimensions of affect, behavior, and cognition. *Journal of Personality, 68,* 869–897.
May, R. (1972). *Power and innocence: A search for the sources of violence.* New York: W.W. Norton.
McCarthy, J. B. (1978). Narcissism and the self in homicidal adolescents. *The American Journal of Psychoanalysis, 38*, 19–29.
McCormack, D., & Spargo, C. (2015). Ringleader of McDonald's gang who brutally beat girl is arrested as it emerges she recently stabbed her own brother—but victim refuses to help cops while bragging about her "fame" on social media. *Daily Mail.* Retrieved from: http://www.dailymail.co.uk/news/article-2992632/Teenager-arrested-gang-girls-caught-vid.
McEwen, B. S. (1999). Allostasis and allostatic load: Implications for neuropsychopharmacology. *Neuropsychopharmacology, 22,* 2, 100–124.
McHugh, M. C., Livingston, N. A., & Ford, A. (2005). A postmodern approach to women's use of violence: Developing multiple and complex conceptualizations. *Psychology of Women Quarterly, 29*, 323–336.
Meekums, B. (1999). A creative model for recovery from child sexual abuse. *The Arts in Psychotherapy, 26*, 247–256.
Meloy, J. R., & Boyd, C. (2003). Female stalkers and their victims. *Journal of the American Academy of Psychiatry and Law, 31*, 211–219.
Messinger, A. M. (2011). Invisible victims: Same-sex IPV in the National Violence Against Women Survey. *Journal of Interpersonal Violence, 26,* 2228–2243.
Mikel-Brown, L. (2003). *Girlfighting: Betrayal and rejection among girls*. New York University Press: New York.
Miller, A. (1990). *For your own good. Hidden cruelty in child-rearing and the roots of violence*. New York: Noonday Press.
Miller, A. (1991). *Banished knowledge: Facing childhood injuries*. New York: First Anchor Books.
Miller, O., & Looney, J.(1974). The prediction of adolescent homicide: Episodic dyscontrol and dehumanization. *American Journal of Psychoanalyis, 34,* 187–198.
Miller, S. L. (2005). *Victims as offenders: The paradox of women's violence in relationships.* New Brunswick, NJ: Rutgers University Press.

Miller, J. B. (1976). *Toward a new psychology of women*. Boston: Beacon Press.

Mishna, F., Saini, M., & Solomon, S. (2009). Ongoing and online: Children and youth's perceptions of cyber bullying. *Children and Youth Services Review, 31*(12), 1222–1228.

Moffitt, T. E. (1990). Juvenile delinquency and attention deficit disorder: Boys' developmental trajectories from age 3 to age 15. *Child Development, 6*, 893–910.

Moffitt, T. E., Caspi, A., Rutter, M., Silva, P. A. (2001). *Sex differences in antisocial behaviour: Conduct disorder, delinquency, and violence in the Dunedin Longitudinal Study*. New York: Cambridge University Press.

Morrison, G. M., & Skiba, R. J. (2001). Predicting violence from school misbehavior: Promises and perils. *Psychology in the Schools, 38*, 173–184.

Muir, D. (2005). *Violence against children in cyberspace*. ECPAT International. Retrieved From www.ECPAT_cyberspace_2005_ENG.pdf.

Newman, R. S., & Murray, B. J. (2005). How students and teachers view the seriousness of peer harassment: When is it appropriate to seek help? *Journal of Educational Psychology, 97*(3), 347–365.

Office of Juvenile Justice Delinquency and Prevention. (2013). *Juvenile Justice Bulletin*. Washington, DC: U.S. Department of Justice, Office of Justice Programs.

Olweus, D. (1993). *Bullying at school: What we know and what we can do*. Oxford: Blackwells.

Park, J. H., Essex, M. J., Zahn-Waxler, C., Armstrong, J. M., Klein, M. H., & Goldsmith, H. H. (2005). Relational and overt aggression in middle childhood: Early child and family risk factors. *Early Education and Development, 16*(2), 233–257.

Patchin, J., & Hinduja, S. (2010). Cyberbullying and self-esteem. *Journal of School Health, 80*(12), 614–621.

Patterson, G. R. (2002). Etiology and treatment of child and adolescent antisocial behavior. *The Behavior Analyst Today, 3*, 133–144.

Patterson, G. R., Reid, J. B., & Dishion, T. J. (1992). *A social interactional approach: Vol. 4: Antisocial boys*. Eugene, OR: Castalia.

Patton, J. D. (2012). The moderating effects of risk, protection, and desistance on violence in female adolescents. *Child Adolescent Social Work Journal, 29*, 185–202.

Paul, L., & Baenninger, M. (1991). *Aggression by women: Mores, myths, & methods*. North Holland: Elsevier Science Publisher.

Pearson, P. (1998). *When she was bad: Violent women and the myth of innocence*. New York: Viking.

Pellegrini, A., & Long, J. (2002). A longitudinal study of bullying, dominance, and victimization during the transition from primary school through secondary school. *British Journal of Developmental Psychology, 20*(2), 259–288.

Perry, B. D. (1997). Incubated in terror: Neurodevelopmental factors in the "cycle of violence." In J. D. Osofsky (Ed.), *Children in a Violent Society*. New York: International Universities Press.

Pinderhughes, E. E., Dodge, K. A., Bates, J. E., Pettit, G. S., & Zelli, A. (2000). Discipline responses: Influences of parents' socioeconomic status, ethnicity, beliefs about parenting, stress, and cognitive-emotional processes. *Journal of Family Psychology, 14*, 380–400.

Pizarro, J. M., DeJong, C., & McGarell, E. F. (2010). An examination of the covariates of female homicide victimization and offending. *Feminist Criminology*, 51–72.

Pollock, J. M., & Davis, S. M. (2005). The continuing myth of the violent female offender. *Criminal Justice Review, 30*(5), 5–28.

Pulkkinen, L., & Pitkanen, T. (1993). Continuities in aggressive behavior from childhood to adulthood. *Aggressive Behavior, 19*, 4, 249–263.

Purcell, R., Pathe, M., & Mullen, P. E. (2001). A study of women who stalk. *American Journal of Psychiatry, 158*, 2056–2060.

Raj, A., Rose, J., Decker, M. R., Rosengard, C., Hebert, M. R., Stein, M., & Clarke, J. G. (2008). Prevalence and patterns of sexual assault across the life span among incarcerated women. *Violence Against Women, 14*, 528–541.

Raver, C. (2004). Placing emotional self-regulation in sociocultural and socioeconomic contexts. *Child Development, 75*, 2, 346–353.

Reebye, P. (2005). Aggression during early years: Infancy and preschool. *The Canadian Child and Adolescent Psychiatry Review, (14)*1, 16–20.

Rhatigan, D. L., Moore, T. M., & Street, A. E. (2005). Reflections on partner violence: 20 years of research and beyond. *Journal of Interpersonal Violence, 20*(1), 82–88.

Ridgeway, C. L., & Correll, S. J. (2004). Unpacking the gender system: A theoretical perspective on gender beliefs and social relations, *Gender & Society, 18,*4, 510–531.

Robb, C. (2006). *This changes everything: The relational revolution in psychology*. New York: Farrar, Straus and Giroux.

Robertson, K., & Murachver, T. (2011). Women and men's use of coercive control in intimate partner violence. *Violence and Victims, 26,2*, 208–217.

Rodriguez, M., Ayduk, O., Aber, L. J., Mischel, W., Sethi, A., & Shoda, Y. (2005). A contextual approach to the development of self-regulatory competencies: The role of maternal unresponsivity and toddlers' negative affect in stressful situations. *Social Development, 14,* 136–157.

Rosenfeld, B., & Harmon, R. B. (2002). Factors associated with violence in stalkers and obsessional harassment cases. *Criminal Justice and Behavior*, *29*, 671–691.

Rubin, K. H., & Burgess, K. B. (2002). Parents of aggressive and withdrawn children. In M. H. Bornstein (Ed.), *Handbook of parenting: Vol. 1 Children and parenting* (2nd ed., pp. 383–418). Mahwah, NJ: Lawrence Erlbaum Associates

Rubin, K. H., Burgess, K. B., Dwyer, K. M., & Hastings, P. D. (2003). Predicting preschoolers' externalizing behaviors from toddler temperament, conflict, and maternal negativity. *Developmental Psychology*, *39*, 164–176.

Sadeh, N., Javdani, S., Finy, M. S., & Verona, E. (2011). Gender differences in emotional risk for self- and other-directed violence among externalizing adults. *Journal of Consulting and Clinical Psychology*, *79,* 1, 106–117.

Safe Horizon. (2014). Child Abuse Facts, Retrieved on December 12, 2014 from: http://www.safehorizon.org/page/child-abuse-facts-56.html.

Sameroff, A. J. (Ed.) (2009). *The transactional model of development: How children and contexts shape each other.* Washington, DC: American Psychological Association.

Sanchez-Jankowski, M. (2003). Gangs and social change. *Theoretical Criminology*, *7,* 2, 191–216.

Schafer, J., Caetano, R., & Cunradi, C. B. (2004). A path model of risk factors for intimate partner violence among couples in the United States. *Journal of Interpersonal Violence, 19,* 2, 127–142.

Schumacher, J. A., & Leonard, K. E. (2005). Husbands' and wives' marital adjustment, verbal aggression, and physical aggression as longitudinal predictors of physical aggression in early marriage. *Journal of Consulting and Clinical Psychology, 73,* 28–37.

Schwartz-Watts, D., & Morgan, D. W. (1998). Violent versus nonviolent stalkers. *Journal of the American Academy of Psychiatry and Law*, *26*, 241–245.

Scott, T. M., Nelson, C. M., & Liaupsin, C. J. (2001). Effective instruction: The forgotten component in preventing school violence. *Education and Treatment of Children*, *24*, 309–322.

Seelig, B. J. (2002). The rape of Medusa in the Temple of Athena: Aspects of triangulation. *International Journal of Psycho-Analysis*, *83*, 895–911.

Seguin, J. R., & Zelazo, P. (2005). Executive function in early physical aggression. In R. W. Tremblay, W. H. Hartup, & J. Archer (Eds.), *Developmental Origins of Aggression* (pp. 307–329.) New York: The Guilford Press.

Shahinfar, A., Fox, N. A., & Leavitt, L. A. (2000). Preschool children's exposure to violence: Relation of behavior problems to parent and child reports. *American Journal of Orthopsychiatry*, *70*, 115–125.

Shaw, D. S., Lacourse, E., & Nagin, D. S. (2005). Developmental trajectories of conduct problems and hyperactivity from ages 2 to 10. *Journal of Child Psychology and Psychiatry*, *46*, 931–942.

Shorey, R. C., Brasfield, H., Febres, J., & Stuart, G. L. (2011). An examination of the association between difficulties with emotion regulation and dating violence perpetration. *Journal of Aggression, Maltreatment, and Trauma, 20*, 8, 870–885.

Siegman, A. W. (1994). From Type A to hostility to anger: Reflections on the history of coronary prone behavior. In A. W. Siegman & T. W. Smith , (Eds). *Anger, hostility and the heart* (pp. 1–22). NJ: Lawrence Erlbaum.

Simmons, R. (2002). *Odd girl out: The hidden culture of aggression in girls.* New York: Harcourt Brace.

Skiba, R. J., Horner, R. H., Chung, C-G., Rausch, M. K., May, S. L., & Tobin, T. (2011). Race isnot neutral: A national investigation of African American and Latino disproportionality in school discipline. *School Psychology Review, 40,* 1, 85–107.

Slocum, L. A., Rengifo, A., & Carbone–Lopez, K. (2012). Specifying the strain-violence link: The role of emotions in women's descriptions of violent incidents. *Victims and Offenders, 7,* 1–29.

Smith, A., & Williams, K. (2004) R U there? Ostracism by cell phone text messages. *Group Dynamics: Theory, Research and Practice, 8*(4), 291–301.

Snethen, G. (2010). Preventing female gang involvement: Development of the joint-interstate care and balance model of mother/daughter leisure functioning. *Aggression and Violent Behavior, 15,* 42–48.

Snyder, H. N. (2011). *Arrest in the United States,1980–2009.* (NCJ Pub. No. 234319). Washington, DC: U.S. Department of Justice, Bureau of Justice Statistics. http://bjs.ojp.usdoj.gov/content/pub/pdf/aus8009.pdf.

Spencer, G. A., & Bryant, S. A. (2000). Dating violence: A comparison of rural, suburban, and urban teens. *Journal of Adolescent Health, 27,* 302–305.

Spielberger, C. D. (1988). *Manual for the State-Trait Anger Expression Inventory.* Odessa, FL: Psychological Assessment Resources.

Staub, E. (1989). *The roots of evil: The origins of genocide and other group violence.* New York: Cambridge University Press.

Stauffacher, K., & DeHart, G. B. (2005). Preschoolers' relational aggression with siblings and with friends. *Early Education and Development, 16,* 185–206.

Straus, M. A., & Smith, C. (1990). Violence in Hispanic families in the United States: Incidence rates and structural interpretations. In M. A. Straus & R. J. Gelles (Eds.), *Physical violence in American families* (pp. 341–367). New Brunswick, NJ: Transaction.

Sugai, G., Sprague, J. R., Horner, R. H., & Walker, H. M. (2000). Preventing school violence: The use of office discipline referrals to assess and monitor school-wide discipline interventions. *Journal of Emotional and Behavioral Disorders, 8,* 2, 94–101.

Stucki, B.W.(2014). Rethinking zero tolerance: a new approach to discipline seeks to keep kids in school and, ultimately, out of prison. *The American Prospect,* 25(3), 7–11.

Sutton, J., Smith, P. K., & Swettenham, J. (1999). Bullying and "theory of mind": A critique of the "social skills deficit" view of anti-social behaviour. *Social Development, 8,* 1, 117–127.

Tatum, B. D. (1997). *Why are all the Black kids sitting together in the cafeteria and other conversations about race.* New York: Basic Books.

Taussig, H. N., & Litrownik, A. J. (1997). Methodological issues in classifying maltreatment: An examination of "protective issue" children. In G. Kaufman-Kantor (Ed.), *Out of the darkness: Contemporary perspectives on family violence.* Newbury Park, CA: Sage, pp. 136–147.

Taylor, C. (1993). *Girls, gangs, women, and drugs.* East Lansing: Michigan State University Press.

Temple, J. R., Weston, R., & Marshall, L. L. (2005). Physical and mental health outcomes of women in nonviolent, unilaterally violent and mutually violent relationships. *Violence and Victims, 20,* 3, 335–359.

Terr, L. (1991). Childhood trauma: An outline and overview. *American Journal of Orthopsychiatry, 148,* 1, 10–20.

Testa, M., Hoffman, J. H., & Leonard, K. E. (2011). Female intimate partner violence perpetration: Stability and predictors of mutual and nonmutual aggression across the first year of college. *Aggressive Behavior, 37,* 362–373.

The Sentencing Project (2012). *Incarcerated women.* Retrieved on Dec. 1, 2014 from: www.sentencingproject.org.

Thompson, C. M., Dennison, S. M., & Stewart, A. (2012). Are female stalkers more violent than male stalkers? Understanding gender differences in stalking violence using contemporary sociocultural beliefs *Sex Roles*, *66*, 351–365.
Todahl, J. L., Linville, D., Bustin, A., Wheeler, J., & Gau, J. (2009). Sexual assault support services and community systems: Understanding critical issues and needs in the LGBTQ community. *Violence Against Women*, *15*, 8, 952–976.
Tremblay, R. E., Nagin, D. S., Séguin, J. R., Zoccolillo, M., Zelazo, P. D., Boivin, M., Pérusse, D., & Japel, C. (2004). Physical aggression during early childhood: Trajectories and predictors. *Pediatrics*, *114*, 43–50.
Tyner, E. A., & Fremouw, W. J. (2008). The relation of methamphetamine use and violence: A critical review. *Aggression and Violent Behavior*, *13*, 285–297.
Underwood, M. (2003). *Social aggression among girls*. New York: The Guilford Press.
United States Department of Justice (2014). *Crime in the United States 2013*. Federal Bureau of Investigation.
Vainik, J. (2008). The reproductive and parental rights of incarcerated mothers. *Family Court Review*, *46*, 4, 670–694.
Van der Kolk, B. A. (2001). The assessment and treatment of complex PTSD. In R. Yehuda (Ed.), *Traumatic Stress*. Washington, DC: American Psychiatric Press.
Vivian, D., and Langhinricbsen-Rohling, J. (1994). Are bi-directionally violent couples mutually victimized? A gender-sensitive comparison. *Violence and Victims*, *9*, 107–124.
Vronsky, V. (2007). *Female serial killers: How and why women become monsters*. New York: Berkley Publishing Group.
Walker, H. M., Ramsey, E., & Gresham, F. M. (2004). *Antisocial behavior in school: Evidence-based practices* (2nd ed.). Belmont, CA: Wadsworth/Thomson Learning.
Walker, L. (1987). *Terrifying love: Why battered women kill and how society responds*. New York: Harper & Row.
Wallace, P. (1999). *The psychology of the Internet*. Cambridge: Cambridge University Press.
Warnken, W. J., Rosenbaum, A., Fletcher, K. E., Hoge, S. K., & Adelman, S. A. (1994). Head-injured males: A population at risk for relationship aggression? *Violence and Victims*, *9*, 153–166.
Weinfeld, N. S., Sroufe, L. A., Egeland, B., & Carlson, E. A. (1999). The nature of individual differences in infant-caregiver attachment. In: J. Cassidy & P. R. Shaver (Eds.), *Handbook of attachment: Theory, research and clinical applications*. New York: The Guilford Press.
Weizmann-Henelius, G. (2006). Violent female perpetrators in Finland: Personality and life events. *Nordic Psychology*, *58*, 4, 280–297.
West, C. M., & Rose, S. (2000). Dating aggression among low income African American youth: An examination of gender differences and antagonistic beliefs. *Violence Against Women*, *6*, 470–494.
Whitaker, D. J., Haileyesus, T., Swahn, M., & Saltzman, L. S. (2007). Differences in frequency of violence and reported injury between relationships with reciprocal and nonreciprocal intimate partner violence. *American Journal of Public Health*, *97*(5), 941–947.
White, J. L., Moffitt, T. E., Earls, F., Robins, L., & Silva, P. A. (1990). How early can we tell? Predictors of childhood conduct disorder and adolescent delinquency. *Criminology*, *28*, *4*, 507–533.
Wiener, V. (1999). *Winning the war against youth gangs: A guide for teens, families and communities*. Westport, CT: Greenwood Press.
Willard, N. (2003). Off-campus, harmful online student speech. *Journal of School Violence*, *1*(2), 65–93.
Williams, J. R., Ghandour, R. M., & Kub, J. E. (2008). Female perpetration of violence in heterosexual intimate relationships: Adolescence through adulthood. *Trauma, Violence, and Abuse*, *9*(4), 227–249.
Williams, W. I. (2006). Complex trauma: Approaches to theory and treatment. *Journal of Loss and Trauma*, *11*, 321–335.
Wolfe, D. A., Scott, K., Reitzel-Jaffe, D., Wekerle, C., Grasley, C., & Straatman, A. L. (2001). Development and validation of the conflict in adolescent dating relationships inventory. *Psychological Assessment*, *13*, 277–293.

Wright, S., & Klee, H. (2001). Violent crime, aggression and amphetamine: What are the implications for drug treatment services? *Drugs: Education, Prevention, and Policy, 8*, 73–90.

Ybarra, M., & Mitchell, K. (2004). Online Aggressor/targets, aggressors, and targets: A comparison of associated youth characteristics. *Journal of Child Psychology and Psychiatry. 45*(7), 1308–1316.

Zahn-Waxler, C., Park, J.-H., Essex, M., Slattery, M., & Cole, P. M. (2005). Relational and overt aggression in disruptive adolescents: Prediction from early social representations and links with concurrent problems. *Early Education and Development, 16*, 259–282.

Zelazo, P. D., & Mueller, U. (2002). Executive functions in typical and atypical development. In U. Goswami (Ed.). *Handbook of Childhood Cognitive Development* (pp. 445–469). Oxford: Blackwell.

II

Challenges and Interventions: Domestic Violence in Ethnic and Cultural Contexts

In the previous set of chapters we covered the major conceptual issues about domestic violence (DV). The reader may now be ready to venture into some specific manifestations of DV and how it relates to cultural and ethnic backgrounds. The chapters include a few examples of the various ways issues of culture and ethnicity can be involved in DV, while recognizing that DV is also an issue in groups not specifically covered here. The chapters included in this part are only meant to provide the reader with a glimpse of how cultural and ethnic issues can interact with other factors not only to affect the proliferation of DV but also to guide its intervention. With that in mind, the reader will be taken through a systematic discussion of DV among Arab Middle Easterner (chapter 7 by El-Jamil and Abi-Hashem), African American (chapter 8 by West), and Latino (chapter 9 by Clauss-Elhers, Millán, and Zhao) populations and the various sociocultural, religious, socioeconomic, legal, and ethno-political factors involved in DV in those populations, with the understanding that not all individuals within those cultural and ethnic groups are affected by these factors in the same way and degree. These chapters offer a wealth of information and analyses geared at providing a better understanding of the ways culture, ethnicity, race, class, and DV interact with one another; it also considers the psychology of individuals involved that makes the issue even more complex and difficult to address. Any intervention based on a failure to recognize these complexities is likely to become ineffective.

Making assumptions about homogeneity within different ethnic and cultural groups is one of the greatest obstacles to understanding the uniqueness of the experience of DV in these groups. Chapter 7 challenges the reader to consider the complex nature of how gender roles and relationships are determined in the context of cultural rules and expectations that appear mutually contradictory. Considering the sensitivity of the issues addressed in this chapter, El-Jamil and Abi-Hashem provide the reader sufficient and helpful insights to guide the proper intervention with this population at the end of the chapter.

Chapter 8 makes an important argument refuting the perception about Black Americans as being inherently more violent than other ethnic groups. It shows that intimate partner violence in the African American community can only be understood by broadening its definition to include the impact of risk factors that are unique to the African American experience, such as historical trauma, institutionalized violence, and coercive control. In this context, the author provides a comprehensive review of these and other risk factors as they interplay in the African American community, contributing to the development of the toxic environment likely to contribute to intimate partner violence.

Chapter 9 on DV within Latino cultures makes a similar point with regard to the risk factors involved in incidents of DV in this population. These authors found that once socioeconomic variables (such as education and income) are controlled for, intimate partner violence is not found more frequently in the Latino population than other groups, such as African Americans and White Americans. They highlight the importance of considering the issue of immigration when addressing DV in this population. Also highlighted in this chapter are the unique cultural ways this population attempts to navigate the tremendous stress associated with the immigration experience and its impact in their personal and family life.

At the end of each of these chapters, as in previous chapters, the reader will find a series of questions and tasks meant to encourage further exploration of the issues addressed in this section.

Chapter Seven

Family Maltreatment and Domestic Violence among Arab Middle Easterners

A Psychological, Cultural, Religious, and Legal Examination

Fatimah El-Jamil and Naji Abi-Hashem

The purpose of this chapter is to provide a detailed overview of the nature, dynamics, impact, phenomenology, and multi-layered aspects of domestic aggression and family violence among people of Arabic Middle Eastern background. It is also a guide for the healthcare providers, educators, social workers, clinicians, clergy, and professional caregivers to better understand and work more effectively with Arab Middle Eastern nationals or immigrants, who come from various geographic locations and nationalities.

People from the Middle East and Arabic-speaking countries are as varied and diverse as their national origin. They represent a rich ethnicity and multicultural tapestry. They are different in customs, educations, heritages, socioeconomic classes, mentalities, moral values, religious faiths, and verbal dialects. That is also true about their lifestyles, dress codes, and cuisines. Even within one particular region or country, there are a variety of societies, communities, and subcultures, which add to it a colorful social fabric and a mosaic texture.

What is normally referred to as the Middle East is a vast and complex region. It is composed of three main geographic areas: the East Mediterranean, the Arabic Gulf Peninsula, and the North Africa expanse. Besides the classical Arabic language (in written or highly spoken forms), some basic shared values, cultural habits, religious practices, and perhaps a collective memory about their rootedness in the land, there are actually a few things in common among these regions. Urban and cosmopolitan cities often share similarities, have an international atmosphere, and are multi-linguistic in nature. However, small towns, villages, and rural areas are often unique and different from each other. Each one displays some features of its own traditional customs, communal norms, tribal richness, and cultural heritage.

The term *Arab* or *Arabian* usually refers to someone or some group that is of Semitic background, who originally inhabited the *Arabia*, known as the Gulf Peninsula. Even before the rise of Islam, various tribes lived there for centuries in Jewish, Christian, or pagan communities. Later on, Arabic speaking people spread out and mixed with other ethnic-racial-linguistic groups across Asia, Europe, and Africa. Today, there are officially 22 nations that constitute the Arab League, or the League of Arabic Nations, which is a loose organization connecting these countries together, without any significant political or governing power.

Currently, there is some confusion, especially in the West, about who are the Arabs, the Muslims, and the Middle Easterners. What are the similarities and differences among these labels? Unfortunately, blank generalizations and misconceptions have been also encouraged by the mass media. Therefore it is very important to clarify our terms and labels, correct our misunderstandings, and distinguish what people we have in mind: (1) not all Middle Easterners are Arabs, for example, Iran, Turkey, Cyprus, and Israel; (2) not all Arabs are Muslims, for example, the significant presence of minorities like the Christians, Jews, Druze, Alawites, and so on, have been well established for centuries; (3) not all Arabic-speaking people are Middle Easterners, for example, the large North African countries; and (4) not all Muslims are Arabs or Middle Easterners either, for example, Indonesia, Pakistan, Malaysia, Afghanistan, including many Muslim communities, both Sunni and Shiite, widely spread around the world (Abi-Hashem, 2008a, 2011b, 2012a; Barakat, 1993; Jackson, 1997; Nydell, 2006; Patai, 2010; Zogby, 2010).

THE ROLE OF COMMUNITY

The concept of community is a rich and deep concept. Community is the glue that holds a group of people that share common ties, values and norms, and social space together. It is larger than the small family nuclear-unit and smaller than the society at large. It consists of the extended family members, relatives, neighbors, elders, teachers, spiritual leaders, mentors, and so on. Although the presence of community is a wonderful asset to human existence and relationship, it can be occasionally limiting and inflexible regarding the dysfunctional and unhealthy cycles present for generations. At times, the welfare of the group can work against the best interests of the individual. Maintaining the status quo and resistance to change are usual tendencies in all established societies and organizations.

Similarly, the concept of *culture* and the dynamic of tradition can enrich people's lives, give them roots and meaning, and help them celebrate their past and heritage. Yet, at the same time, some aspects of culture unfortunately limit people's progress and prevent them from correcting or improving the unfavorable ways. The challenge facing educators, clinicians, and caregivers is to know the difference between what is healthy and valuable in order to keep and encourage it, and what is unhealthy and damaging, in order to change and forsake it. In other words, we must acquire the skill of knowing what is cultural-reasonable and what is clinical-pathological. Therefore, the task is not to give up cultures and traditions, but to sort the healthy from the unhealthy and to remove the harmful practices and disturbing ways (cf. Hersh, 1998; Vannatter, 2017).

Naturally, there is a historic tension between the dual concepts of *individualism* and *collectivism*. Each polarity has its own set of advantages and disadvantages, but when carried to an extreme, both become troublesome, disruptive, and even diagnostic. For example, the "I, me, myself" can be lost in the "we, us, ourselves." And vice versa, the "us, we, togetherness" can be lost in the extreme individuality of persons by dismissing the family and community for the sake of glorifying self-reliance, personal autonomy, and private boundaries. Perhaps *interdependency* and *collective-individuality* are the best balance, where the person is accomplished and has a clear sense of self, identity, meaning, and frame as he or she exists through others and in relationship to the group and community—but not floating completely alone without any anchor point or mutually shared reference. In some industrialized societies, the concept of *community* is changing, disappearing, or nonexistent, while in others traditional regions and warm cultures around the world, the community is still alive, functioning in full a capacity and manifesting itself in powerful ways (cf. Abi-Hashem, 1997, 2011a, 2011b, 2013a, 2013b; 2014b, 2014c, 2015; Hutchison, 2016; Kim, Yang, & Hwang, 2006; Marsella, 1998; Nydell, 2006; Smart, 1999).

The benefits of an extended family and a tight community are indeed great: bonding, belonging, identity, support, meaning, values, reference, tradition, warmth, wisdom, resources, protection, and multiple-perspectives. However, as families, groups, or communities rally around a person to support, guide, and protect him or her, they can also rally around that person to pressure, silence, force, or totally deny his or her rights. There are repeated practices of such collective behaviors, obviously pressuring an adult, a child, or an elderly person to do something that is totally unreasonable, counterproductive, hurtful, or even destructive. Some extreme examples are: forced marriages and negotiating dowries (almost selling daughters—different from arranged or introduced marriages); child beating and cheap child labor; sexual mutilation and female circumcision; severe restrictions on household females' movements and other rights (by husbands, fathers, male relatives, brothers, and even grown up sons); forced intercourse and sexual submission; physical punishment of children and subordinates; secluding handicapped or mentally ill members of the family from society to avoid public shame (almost imprisoning them inside); gender-based discrimination; and so on (cf. Chantler, 2012; Passport to Dignity, 2011).

In addition, it seems that each time someone breaks the customs of tradition or cultural norms he or she gets punished, privately or publically, even if these customs and norms are quite unreasonable (e.g., marrying across ethnic, racial, or religious lines). At times, a person or a family is persecuted because they decided to lead a different lifestyle or convert to another faith and spirituality. Normally, offenders do not recognize the severity of their actions on the victim. If they do to some degree, they quickly justify their actions and subjections using reasons ranging from preserving ancient traditions to the necessary survival of the family or community—sacrificing one for the survival of the whole, to their given rights and authority, or to saving face, honor, and dignity.

FAMILY MALTREATMENT AND DOMESTIC VIOLENCE AMONG ARAB MIDDLE EASTERN PEOPLE

In the Middle East, like in other developing societies and countries, there are no clear records or statistics about family hostility, domestic violence, and sexual abuse. This is largely due to the absence of a confidential legal system or reliable social services. Besides, these matters are very sensitive and intimate issues, and as such are kept very private and often dismissed or reluctantly tolerated. The fear of causing public shame, dishonoring the relatives, and ruining one's reputation is a major deterrent for going public or pursuing legal action. Although general public education and social awareness are improving in the Middle East and North Africa, people continue to be hesitant or even resistant to disclose family secrets openly. That is also true for seeking serious help in form of consultation, counseling, pastoral care, or medical treatment for the obvious cases of repeated hostility or common violent behaviors.

The American Psychological Association's Task Force on Violence and the Family (APA, 1996) defined domestic violence as a pattern of abusive behaviors including a wide range of physical, mental-emotional, and sexual mistreatment used by one person in an intimate relationship against another. At the heart of this abuse is one person's quest to unfairly gain power or maintain tight control and authority over others. Furthermore, the dynamic of domestic violence increases the odds that more than one type of insult will occur and develop at home in the future. Increased efforts by governmental and non-governmental agencies, the World Health Organization (WHO), and the United Nations (UN) have identified domestic violence, in general, and aggression against women, in particular, as their top priorities. Such agencies have supported further research aimed at obtaining incidence- and prevalence-rates of domestic violence as well as devising laws and policies in an effort to limit it and prohibit it around the world. Yet globally, domestic violence remains a widespread problem. Some countries have been slower than others in identifying, condemning, and addressing family hostility due to particular sociocultural, religious, and legal reasons embedded in the civil structures, and local norms of those communities (Advocates for Youth, 2008; Colucci & Hassan, 2014; CSM Editorial, 2017; Sayed, 2003; Walker, 1999).

In developing countries, the rate of domestic violence is approximately equal to and, in some cases, higher than the rate of industrialized countries (Kishor & Johnson, 2004; Krug et al., 2002; Niaz & Tariq, 2017; Watts & Zimmerman, 2002). While reliable statistics in Middle Eastern and North African countries remain questionable due to a potentially large underreporting, several studies conducted throughout the Middle East have confirmed rates of domestic violence as slightly higher than those found in Western countries such as Canada, the USA, and the UK—where the incidences of intimate partner violence range from 25% to 29% of the population (UNICEF, 2000).

In numerous Arab countries, several studies have explored the prevalence rate of domestic violence. In Palestine, two studies conducted by Haj-Yahia (1998, 2000) found that approximately one-third of the married women surveyed reported being physically beaten by their husbands at least once during their marriage. In Morocco, 1,506 cases of violence against women were registered in the year 1993 alone, most of which were committed by a family member or a relative (Kadiri & Moussaoui, 2001). In Lebanon, an exploratory study of domestic abuse among women who were largely unemployed, from middle to low socioeconomic statuses with a high school education level or below, revealed that 35% of these women were subjected to insult and abuse within their families at least once. Psychological maltreatment and humiliation were reported as the most common type of mistreatment followed by physical aggression, threats of abandonment, and deprivation of income (Usta, Farver, & Pashayan, 2007).

In Syria, as in many places around the Middle East, male misbehavior can be dismissed easily or be blamed on the failure of the female or children. Beating and physical abuse are known to occur, especially in the suburbs and rural areas. But the conservative sociopolitical climate in Syria discourages public discussions of such matters, making it more difficult to estimate the extent of aggressive and abusive occurrences. Most findings are collected indirectly from physicians, lawyers, teachers, clergy, or caregivers. Like in other countries, Syrian women may have access to civil or religious courts, but they rarely press charges. At times, the abused family member flees the house and seeks shelter with a distant relative or religious institution (Abi-Hashem, 2003, 2008b; Ameela, 1995). Trying to find about women's level of awareness of abuse, Arabi (2006) conducted a survey-questionnaire in five provinces around the country of Syria targeting females 25 to 45 years of age to ask about their life experience or exposure to family violence and aggressive behavior. The higher the woman's education was, the higher her awareness of her rights and the less abusive incidents she experienced. Syrian husbands tend to impose their viewpoints and wills on their wives who are either full time homemakers or have little or no education. Almost half of the women interviewed said they would seek a trusted relative when mistreated and a quarter said they would not seek anyone at all. However, less than 1% said that they would seek a physician or police officer. Additionally, most Syrian women who were mistreated and abused reported they would not seek divorce for the sake of the children and for maintaining the family unit. Arabi (2006) also found that there are discrepancies between the actual Syrian Laws and the content of the Convention on the Elimination of all Forms of Violence against Women (UNWomen, 2008). There were numerous reservations on the application of the Convention Codes.

Presently, with the increased ethno-political turmoil, armed conflicts, and tragedies of war, in its fifth year and with no end in sight, millions of Syrians have been seriously traumatized, physically displaced, and emotionally scarred. Many families temporarily live in overcrowded camps or unplanned dense quarters. The extremely close proximity provides no breathing space or personal privacy, especially for girls and women. Along with severe depression, anxiety, and traumatic stress (and other mental disorders and social ills common to war-survivors—Abi-Hashem, 2006, 2012b), interpersonal friction and abusive aggression have become epidemic (Herman, 2015; Vannatter, 2017). In addition, child labor, street begging, gang-like behaviors, and sexual assaults have substantially increased (Finnerty & Shahmanesh, 2017). At times, young daughters are being forced to marry a wealthy man nearby or in far away land (even as his second or third wife) for a profitable financial trophy, or worse, black market rings have been recruiting children and women for trafficking and prostitution purposes (Anani, 2013; Johnson, 2013; Kullab, 2014; Lucas, 2014).

Additionally, cases of domestic abuse and violence have included migrant workers who are employed in the Middle East as live-in housemaids. Hundreds of thousands of female domestic workers are presently a significant part of the Arab Middle Eastern society and offer valuable contribution to employing families by keeping homes clean, cooking, and caring for young children (CNN World, 2013). Migrant workers come from various countries including Ethiopia, Bangladesh, Sri Lanka, Philippines, and Nepal and arrive in a random city in the Middle East on the hope of securing an income to send back home to their families. New to the culture, mentality, and Arabic language, they are expected to adapt almost immediately and begin functioning in the new home with completely different family values and ways of living from what they were previously accustomed to in their homeland. Recruiting agencies and business offices arrange for the importation of these workers and match them with local families and institutions on demand for a set fee (almost like a trade). While most migrant domestic workers are respected and treated well within the families they work for, many are subjected to high levels of mistreatment and abuse, which have ended at times in death or suicide. One recent case of an attempted suicide in Lebanon involved a maid who jumped from the seventh floor of the apartment building in Beirut (Naharnet, 2014). Abuse can take the forms of long working hours with minimal, delayed, withheld payment, forced confinement in the home with no time off, confiscation of passports to prevent fleeing, physical neglect (including poor living conditions, lack of personal privacy, and refusal to provide medical treatment), and verbal, physical, and sexual abuse including rape (CNN World, 2013). In a report by the Human Rights Watch in 2008, it was found that migrant domestic workers suffer an average of one death per week from unnatural causes in Lebanon while figures in other Middle Eastern countries remain unknown, especially in the Gulf area.

Domestic workers are excluded from the country's labor laws and thus there is often a culture of impunity when it comes to their mistreatment and abuse. Many activist groups blame the vulnerability of migrant workers on the *kefala* or sponsorship system, which ties each domestic worker to one employer through some type of a contract that exists outside of the country's labor laws (Slemrod, 2012). For the period of the contract, which is often two years, employees receive little protection and no way out of the contract for its entire duration. Currently eight non-governmental organizations in Lebanon alone, like KAFA (Enough Violence and Exploitation) and the Anti-Racism Movement, are working together to correct the recruitment process, abolish the sponsorship system, and include such foreign workers under the general labor laws, which would further allow them the right to report cases of maltreatment and abuse and receive better social protection.

Significantly less attention has been paid in the literature to the prevalence of domestic violence perpetrated against children, whether physical, emotional, or sexual abuse (Colucci & Hassan, 2014). Physical punishment under the larger umbrella of corporeal punishment is condoned in Arab Middle Eastern societies and thus researchers may be deterred from exploring potentially inflated rates of physical abuse. For example, Usta, Farver, and Danachi (2013) interviewed 1,028 Lebanese children (556 boys; 472 girls) to examine the prevalence, risk factors, and the consequences of maltreatment in their home. Thirty percent of the children reported witnessing at least *one* incidence of violence and 54% reported at least *one* incident of physical abuse during a year period, at the hands of their fathers, mothers, siblings, and/or other relatives. These accounts of aggression ranged from being pushed to being physically punished and beaten. Current measures of physical abuse, however, may prove culturally insensitive in their ability to differentiate between what is physical or corporeal punishment and what is actual abuse in the Arab world context.

THE TOPIC OF SEXUALITY IN THE MIDDLE EAST

Public discussion about sex in general and one's intimate sexual life or sensitive personal matters is uncommon and at times rare in Arab Middle Eastern society. Similar to the topics of death, HIV, or cancer, sexuality is not an open subject, especially among adults and the older generations. Even within one family unit, there is not much freedom to disclose one's sexual concerns, struggles, or experiences. In addition, sexuality is an area that has been largely avoided in psychosocial research in the Middle East, primarily because the subject remains taboo. People do not have the freedom, skill, or mechanism to talk about such an intimate function of their lives. Questions related to sexual experiences may be met with a felt sense of offensiveness, embarrassment, or shame. Extramarital sexual relations, although happening occasionally, are also considered harmful to the social norm and honor (*sharaf*) of the traditional family (An-na'm, 2003), and thus silence on topics related to sex ensues. When extramarital affairs, sexual molestations, or even rape are discovered, they are kept subtle and totally denied due to the lack of courage or knowledge on how to reveal, deal with, and confront such occurrences. In addition, the fear of public shame (*Ayeb; Aar*) and ruining the family's reputation (*fadeehah*) are major deterrents.

Nonetheless, domestic sexual abuse in particular has been examined in several research studies. One study succeeded in exposing the problem of sexual abuse in the Middle East and found that the general rates are somewhat similar to those found in other countries (Haj-Yahia & Tamish, 2001). Abu-Bakera (2013) aimed to identify the prevalence of domestic sexual abuse and the consequent reactions of the family members. The clinical records of 35 Palestinian-Israeli cases revealed that for 20 cases, the perpetrator was a family member. In all of these cases, the abuse was not reported to legal authorities in an effort to prevent further harm or humiliation to the family. Usta, Mahfoud, Abi-Chahine, and Anani (2008) conducted the first study in Lebanon to assess the prevalence and the risk-factors associated with child sexual abuse. This effort was supported by several NGOs following the encounter of many cases of child sexual abuse during and immediately after the July 2006 war. Usta et al. found that 16% of 1,035 children, between the ages of 8 and 17, reported at least one form of sexual abuse. About 56% of these cases took place at home with an uncle or a brother as the most common perpetrator. They mainly reported being touched, kissed, or fondled against their will. The abuse was most frequent among children whose parents were separated or deceased, and whose mothers were working outside the home. Almost half of these children said they disclosed what is happening to a family member, usually the mother; however, only 43% of those children felt that they were listened to or understood. The rest reported confused reactions, ranging from enforced silence to rebuke and scolding the child.

In Egypt most recently, sexual harassment and advancement toward women and girls have increased dramatically due to the popular uprising and social disorder that Egypt is experiencing today. Women and girls have been objecting to the sexual comments and misconduct they are experiencing, both in public and private, for more than 10 years. Women activists have held demonstrations pushing for new measures by the government (e.g., one group carried a sign stating, "Control your sons not your daughters"). In May 2014, the Egyptian cabinet approved a new, fresh, and detailed law that condemns and punishes sexual harassment in all its forms and means (verbal, non-verbal, electronic, suggestive, etc.) with major fines and imprisonment (Ahram Online, 2014). Currently, the Lebanese parliament is also considering an urgent draft of a law that would criminalize sexual harassment with clear penalties and prison punishment. The bill recommends a harsher penalty if the subject is a minor, an elderly, or a special-needs person (El-Hassan, 2014).

There remains a pressing need to understand the interplay of the cultural, religious, and legal factors associated with the prevalence of domestic violence and family mistreatment among Arab Middle Eastern people. These same factors also affect the varied societal and familial reactions and their coping strategies. The following sections will explore the numerous facets associated to the perpetuation and maintenance of these dynamics and phenomena.

THE LEVEL OF TOLERANCE FOR ABUSE AND DOMESTIC VIOLENCE

Societies differ in their perceptions and reactions toward family and marital violence. According to the World Health Organization, one of the most salient aspects of hostility against women is the tolerance of family aggression in certain cultures and societies (World Health Organization, 2000). In the Arab

Middle East, this tolerance is indeed striking. Many observers and investigators reported that many men and women find domestic violence normative and do not regard it as a serious problem that needs treatment or special attention (Arabi, 2006; Boy & Kulczycki, 2008; El-Youssef, 2010; Khawaja, 2004; Maziak & Asfar, 2003).

Moreover, such "indifferent tolerance" could have a number of reasons: (a) people's priority is set on surviving urgent challenges, financial hardships, or war-related stress and crises rather than dealing with domestic incidents; (b) people lack personal skills or someone knowledgeable to coach them in how to address violence and deal with abuses; (c) people focus on secrecy rather than broadcasting intimate affairs and on the sustainability of the family, maintaining a positive image (as a moral virtue) and trying to contain misbehaviors and mistakes; (d) people may consider the aggressive act as a single incident, insignificant by itself, and may dismiss sexual acting out as just an innocent interaction or an intimate play, with no intention for harm; and finally, (e) people from Middle Eastern backgrounds have a normally high degree of resiliency, coping, and rebounding in the face of adversity and misfortune. They can tolerate discomfort, pain, and hardship on the hope that life will improve, agonies will pass, and situations will get better (cf. Abi-Hashem, 2003, 2008a, 2011a, 2011b; Abu-Bakera, 2013; Douki, et al. 2003; El-Youssef, 2010; Sayed, 2003).

Most governments of the Middle East still consider domestic violence a private issue for the family and not a legal concern. For example, Haj-Yahia (1998) found that 80% of his sample of 625 Palestinian men and women did not consider that marital violence was a valid reason for women to consider reporting their husbands to available legal services. In a sample of 202 Arab Americans residing in a large Midwestern city in the United States, of whom only 20% completed a high school education, Kulwicki and Miller (1999) found that about 35% of women and about 33% of men approved of a man slapping his wife if she insults him while they are at home alone. Furthermore, 18% of women believed that a man has the right to kill his wife if she has been unfaithful to him.

Additionally, in several studies, both men and women tended to place the blame on the wives for the violence perpetrated against them, by means of agitating, challenging, or insulting their husbands, whom were already burdened by daily life struggles (Boy & Kulczycki 2008; Haj-Yahia, 1998). Seventy-six percent of a sample of Palestinian physicians who came face to face with victims of domestic violence tended to view the wives as the reason for the domestic violence, and their most often reported intervention was teaching the wife how to change her behavior with her husband (Haj-Yahia, 2013). Douki et al. (2003) similarly reported a systematic underrating of the health consequences and the traumatic injuries experienced by battered women.

Virtually, the attitudes of the younger generation are shifting in regards to marital violence (Middle East Program, 2016). Examining a group of 206 students in Lebanon, Obeid, Chang, and Ginges (2010) found more than half strongly opposed any justification for wife beating. They also found that both male and female students, who held more traditional gender role values, were more likely to endorse beliefs that overlook or condone wife beating. Such findings attest to the challenges being faced in Arab societies, where certain socio-cultural, religious-ideological, and civil-legal factors maintain traditional norms toward the family, where gender roles are still fostering inequality and ultimately compromise the stand against domestic maltreatment and brutality.

The following section will highlight the major socio-cultural considerations that can serve to explain the maintenance and perpetuation of such attitudes and perceptions.

SOCIO-CULTURAL FACTORS AFFECTING THE PREVALENCE OF DOMESTIC VIOLENCE AMONG ARAB MIDDLE EASTERN PEOPLE

The Middle Eastern society is mainly characterized by (a) a strong family cohesiveness and bond, (b) a strong social-national identity, (c) a strong rootedness in the land, and (d) a strong fondness of historical and traditional heritage (Abi-Hashem, 2006, 2008a, 2011b, 2013b; Barakat, 1993; Nydell, 2006). However, the unity and cohesiveness of the family remains the most important value of Middle Eastern society. The family unit is considered a highly important social and economic institution whereby each member of the family is usually considered responsible for the welfare of the other members. Each individual's reputation is reflected upon the family just as the family's status and honor is reflected upon the individual. While personal identity is mostly *achieved* in the West, it is mostly *ascribed* in the East.

The well-being of the family is traditionally defined by its reputation, and each member of the family is expected to exercise total commitment to the needs of the family in maintaining its solidarity and status in society. Thus, self-sacrifice is often encouraged in exchange for family cohesiveness. Likewise, any attempt by a family member to totally break away from the family unit is considered a betrayal and a turning away from their roots and heritage. Such an act is also considered as disowning, dishonoring, and disgraceful. Often it is met with harsh criticism, rejection, and societal and familial ostracization (Haj-Yahia, 1996).

When the Social Structure Favors the Male

The structure of a more traditional Arab Middle Eastern family is role-specific and male-oriented. The social system implies the preference or precedence of the husband/father over the wife/mother, coupled with a clear gender-role within the household. Men are the leaders and the public face of their families. Women however do have power, and influence the family, yet they remain subtle and behind the scenes. Historically, men and women enter the marriage bond or covenant mainly to build an institution, to fulfill expected duties, gain social status, and play a favorable role among the extended family (more than to primarily fulfill their personal desires and emotional needs, based on attraction and romance). This is why marriage in the Far and Near Eastern mentality is mainly a family affair and at times, a community and tribal affair as well. On the other hand, in less traditional families and in modern or cosmopolitan cities, where lifestyles are mostly complex and demanding, males and females lead a creative version of an egalitarian, balanced, and shared life.

Noticeably, a social framework that is built around the centrality of men has also been described in societies that embody the "culture of honor," where great concern is placed on the status and reputation of the male and on his family, as his kin (Vandello & Cohen, 2003). In line with this ideology, women are expected to embody characteristics such as warmth, high relatedness, concern, modesty, and shame, while men should uphold personalities characterized by agency, self-confidence, and leadership (Gerber, 1995). Thus the expectations of women include attending to the emotional and physical needs of the family while high importance is placed on femininity, motherhood, wifehood, and sexuality. Haj-Yahia (2003) found that "patriarchal" expectations of marriage were the most prominent predictors of the justification and tolerance of marital violence within an Arab community in Israel. However, while the patriarchal hierarchy may be the major contributor to violence against women, not every man in such societies beats his wife. Rather, when a man, who embodies male-biased values, perceives his wife as challenging his authority or control, he is more likely to resort to aggression and violence (Dobash & Dobash, 1977). Wife battering was tolerated when the wife disrespected her husband, insulted his family, challenged his masculinity, rejected sexual intercourse, committed adultery, and otherwise did not fulfill her household and family duties (El-Zanaty et al., 1996; Haj-Yahia, 2003). As such, if a man allows his partner to "stray" he may be perceived by society as weak, inattentive, or vulnerable (Schneider, 1971). In such cases, aggression becomes a means to redeem his status as the one in charge and in control of the functioning of the family unit (Dobash & Dobash, 1977; Dutton, 1988). Despite changes in Arab Middle Eastern mentalities over the past decades, which have strengthened women's status and their professional roles in society, the wife is still often expected to yield to the husband as head of the household (Haj-Yahia, 2000). Occasionally, when the woman yields to the man, especially in public, this could be considered as her way of subtle negotiation, compromise, or exchange for an internal gain, privilege, or power in running some aspects of the household.

It is important here to note as well that domination and maltreatment is not always a one-way street, from men as offenders toward women as victims. In many homes and communities, the status of women in the family can be very elevated, powerful, and at times intimidating. The wife, mother, grandmother, or mother-in-law can operate as the head or the manager of the whole extended family and as the reference point who supervises all affairs. Her blessing and approval are absolutely crucial to all activities and functions. She may keep the budget, make the final decisions, check on the behavior of members, and rule as an appointed queen. In such cases, males are usually the bosses "outside the home" but "inside the home" they do not challenge the authority, care, and role of the women (almost as matriarchs). Examples of this dynamic can also be found within some African American families in the deep South of the United Sates (Abi-Hashem, 2003).

The Place of the Extended Family

Social, economic, and political changes have forced the relocation of many families so they no longer live in close proximity to one another. Traditionally, extended family members reside close to one another and play an equally significant role in major decision-making within the family unit. Thus in instances of domestic abuse, extended family members at times play a protective role while at other times they increase the risk of intrusion and violence (Clark et al., 2010). Women experiencing marital violence may turn to their own families of origin and find that while support and shelter is initially offered, most often they are also encouraged to return to their homes in order to preserve the family's solidarity and privacy and refrain from tarnishing the family's reputation. Ultimate perceptions and reactions to the maltreatment and violence become highly affected by each partner's discourse with their families of origin, friends, or extended family members (Douki et al., 2003; Haj-Yahia, 1996). The pressure placed on the women to return to their homes then compromises their awareness of the seriousness and gravity of domestic hostility. Furthermore, the matter can be complicated by the reality that abuse of married women, especially the young ones, can occur at the hands of the husband's family members as well, including his mother, father, and even his siblings (Haj-Yahia, 2000). Usually, the elders of any traditional family hold a direct or an indirect influence over its members and have a say in their affairs. Clark et al. (2010) found that in Jordan the most common perpetrators of family mistreatment and domestic violence are generally the in-laws, particularly the mothers-in-law.

Honor Crimes and Honor Killings

The chief explanation of the homicide of girls and women in some countries is the *honor crime*. Personal and tribal honor, dignity, and integrity are among the highest virtues in the Arab-Muslim Middle East and North Africa, especially for older generations or traditional communities. Some people go to an extreme to protect or restore their actual or perceived lost honor. Violent punishments against female victims may range from restricting her movements, to denying of rights, to physically torturing or killing her.

The term *honor crime*, described also as *femicide* (Russel & Harmes, 2001) or as *honor killing* (Reimers, 2007; Terman, 2010), is defined as the willful torture or murder of a woman by one or more of her male kin (father, husband, brother, uncle, etc.), based on their judgment of her behavior; either sexual infidelity or adultery, in case of a married woman, or any premarital sexual relationship, in case of a virgin woman. Sexual misbehaviors, or marrying someone against the wish of the family, can also be perceived as grave mistakes that insult and shame the honor of the family and pollute the female's body, diminishing her value. Although honor crimes occur in some parts of the Arab Middle East and North Africa, they seem to be more prevalent in the Far Eastern countries. According to McCoy (2014), about 1,000 women die annually in honor killings in the country of Pakistan alone.

The belief behind such acts is the restoration of the family reputation and its recovery from severe humiliation. It is within these *patrilineal* communities that these honor crimes occur whereby any male relative is considered culturally, legally, and morally responsible for the attitudes and behaviors of any female relative and for her "sexual purity" in particular (Kulwicki, 2002; Van Baak et al., 2017). The vast majority of these victims have been either blood-relatives or actual spouses of the men who tortured, mutilated, or killed them.

Some national laws are often lenient toward *honor crimes* in that men who commit these crimes are either excused or met with less severe punishment. This leniency is due to a specific Islamic law, which states that acts of infidelity are subject to capital punishment. Yet according to the Koran (Quran or Qur'an), sexual infidelity is a crime whether committed by males or females. However, many religious leaders and lawmakers have conveniently overlooked their favoritism and clear lack of gender-distinctiveness.

Baydoun (2011) examined court proceedings of 66 trials involving family related cases of femicide that took place between 1978 and 2004 in six different regions of Lebanon. Those who admitted guilt reported that avenging one's dignity, restoring family honor, and cleansing one's shame were the primary reasons behind the violent act. All but four of the suspected perpetrators were found guilty and received jail sentences ranging from one and a half years to the death penalty, and in 47% of the cases, the judges referred to articles in the law that recognized mitigating circumstances.

Another sensitive matter is related to *rape*. While most countries consider public rape as a crime, there are still small pockets in rural areas of the Middle East and North Africa that force the female victim to marry her sex offender, thus inflicting double traumatization on the already victimized woman (Fakim, 2014). A man who rapes and yet agrees to marry his victim is viewed in these communities as redeeming himself and the situation. The sexual assault usually becomes a family-social affair and creates a moral-religious dilemma for all people involved.

RELIGIOUS AND LEGAL FACTORS AFFECTING DOMESTIC VIOLENCE

In the Middle East and North Africa, the religious identity of people is an integral part of their social identity. Because people are rooted in the land, culture and tradition are embedded in their mental-emotional history. Public discourses always include references to Deity, God, providence, faith, and spirituality. Separating the church-mosque-synagogue from the public life and civil state is not common or as clear and pronounced as in the segregated West (cf. Tillich, 1959). In the Middle East and North Africa, some countries have completely merged religious teachings, values, and regulations with the civil and legal laws in an effort to intimately integrate all aspects of life, referred to as the 3Ds: *Deen*—the religious faith, *Dunyah*—this present world, and *Dawlah*—the state government (Abi-Hashem, 2011b; Storey & Utter, 2002). Other countries, while highly respecting religious faith and tradition and their place in social life, have completely made a parallel distinction between church and state, but not a sharp division or total separation between them. Such interdependence has its benefits, yet has led to religious and legal endorsements of gender inequality and the dismissal of mistreatment. This fact has contributed to the vulnerability of women and children to domestic violence and abuse in the Arab-Muslim societies.

In most of these countries, faith institutions and religious courts handle family and marriage affairs first and then cooperate or transfer the cases to civil institutions and city halls. Even if there are clear laws in place to protect women and children and prohibit wife battering, the religious courts often fail to reinforce these laws and legal regulations. Instead, some religious figures and spiritual leaders may even coerce victimized women to return home to their family and to reconcile with their offending husbands (Usta, Farber, & Pashayan, 2007). Hajjar (2004) has examined the relationship between religious law and state power as it influences the permissibility of violence within the family. She looked closely at the interplay between intra-family violence, the struggle for women's rights, state power, and the *shari'aa*, with the objective of understanding the causes and means of social and legal impunity, which the perpetrators of domestic violence employ and often enjoy.

The *shari'aa* is a strict set of rules based upon specific interpretations of the Koran and from what is known about the Prophet's life, the *Sunna*. The *shari'aa* provides directives according to which one's personal, familial, social, economic, and political life must be led and conducted. Due to marked variations in the descriptions of the life of Mohammed, as well as in the interpretations of the *Koran*, believers should be careful not to equate the *shari'aa* with the *Koran* in general or with mainstream Islam as a whole (Dwairy & El-Jamil, 2015). Additionally, although many *Koranic* verses appear discriminatory toward women, other passages and sections do establish equality of men and women (Hajjar, 2004).

There are several countries in the broader Middle East that have declared themselves *Islamic* in nature and have adopted the text of *shari'aa* as their judiciary and civil laws. In other countries where Muslims are the majority, the states recognize Islam as their official religion and thus incorporate the guidance and principles of the *shari'aa* into their national law. Still in the other countries, religious authorities and institutions are semi-autonomous from the national-legal regime (cf. Hajjar, 2004). Thus, the *shari'aa* is observed in almost every Arab-Muslim country. In Saudi Arabia and Qatar for example, it is fully enforced; in countries such as Lebanon and Syria, it is partially enforced by religious courts and only upon citizens of Muslim faith (Dwairy & El-Jamil, 2015), and in Egypt, *shari'aa* courts were recently integrated into the national legal system. There is still a shared sentiment among various religious leaders, authorities, and regimes to preserve the hierarchical family system across many Judeo-Christian-Muslim tenets, which is naturally reinforced by both social and cultural expectations (Jefords, 1984; Zubaida, 2001). With the ongoing permissibility of domestic violence being directly related to the inequality of men and women, this feature becomes a question of harm, injustice, and violation of basic human rights (cf. Al-Hibri, 2001; Douki et al., 2003; Global Summit, 2014; Hajjar, 2004; Sidawi, 1998).

Interpretations of Koranic verses have been a controversial matter among many Islamic scholars, particularly on issues pertaining to gender roles and differences. Religious leaders upholding patriarchal ideologies have prevented a more progressive interpretation or application of the Koran and its universal moral values. However, some Islamic scholars have raised the concern that scriptures are often interpreted by religious authorities whose wish is to reinforce the dominance of men, which has ultimately resulted in tolerating a certain degree of family mistreatment and domestic violence (Douki et al., 2003, Hajjar, 2004). Such verses, which are selected from the Koran, refer to the headship of the man in the family, as in the following verse: "men have a degree of advantage over [women]" (Koran, Sura 2, verse 228) and "Men are the protectors and maintainers of women, because Allah has given one more than the other, and because men support them from their means. Therefore the righteous women are devoutly obedient . . . As for those women on whose part ye fear disloyalty and ill conduct, speak to them, then refuse to share their beds, then beat them. But if they return to obedience, seek not against them" (Koran, Sura 4, verse 34). The concluding statement of this verse remains one of the most controversial in the Koran. Islamic scholars refer to the social structure, culture, and normative practices of that early time to justify the occurrence of such verses, and as such, human behavior and gender roles are to be understood differently today with the development of our contemporary structure and personal realization, socio-cultural contexts, and mental-emotional relationships. It is important to apply the sacred teachings in a way consistent with our values and human accomplishments and relevant to the needs, challenges, potentials, and living standards of our times. Perhaps in the past, men felt they were fully responsible for the family and understood their authority to include serious correction and physical discipline of the wife and children (El-Youssef, 2010), and as such, Al-Hibri (2001) drew further meaning from controversial verses by arguing that such Koranic passages actually imposed limits on the earlier common practice of beating during that time, establishing it as a very last resort, yet best to be avoided altogether.

These examples, however, are also paralleled by verses in the Koran that promote equality between the man and woman, and describe marital relations as tranquil, merciful, and affectionate, such as, "O people, revere your Lord, who created you from a single soul" (Koran, Sura 4, verse 1), "He created for you mates from among yourselves, that ye may dwell in tranquility with them, and He has put love and mercy between you" (Koran, Sura 30, verse 21), and "Your wives, they are your garments and ye are their garments" (Koran, Sura 2, verse 187). Furthermore, in discussions on divorce, whether partners decide to reconcile or part ways, they must do so "on equitable terms" (Koran, Sura 65, verse 2). Al-Hibri (2001) referred to the prophet Mohammed, who is cited to have said to his followers: "The most perfect believers are the best in conduct and the best of you are those who are best to your wives," as reported in the *Sunna*. The *Sunna* also refers to one of his famous and widely repeated quotations: "Heaven lies beneath the feet of mothers."

Similarly, on the Christian side, the Bible is full of references and discussions on the nature, function, and dynamics of marriage and the family. The Old and New Testaments present several models of the family unit, dynamic, and structure as well as of human interactions and relationships, from Genesis to Revelation. Some principles are universal and global in nature, while others are specific and relevant to their socio-cultural contexts and historical times. Virtually, reading and interpreting any literary texts, scientific or scriptural, is a function of people's background, experiences, worldview, preferences, cultural lenses, personal tendencies, social customs, mental maps, and even biases. That has been true of many lay people, community leaders, professionals, theologians, social thinkers, and academics alike.

Taking scripture verses out of their context has always been a controversy and problematic. Also, some biblical themes like obedience, submission, respect, equality, dominance, can have various meanings and connotations and must be reconciled between their intentions at the time and applications in our contemporary situations. For example, the Ten Commandments include "Honor your father and your mother so your days may be long in the land" as if the honor is due equally to both parents because of their identical value. In the book of Genesis, God created Adam from the dust but created Eve directly from Adam himself (a better material than the raw dust), to crown the whole creation. In 1 Corinthians 11 we read, "But I want you to realize that the head of every man is Christ, and the head of the woman is the man" as an image and an emphasis on spiritual leadership and headship, but not dictatorship. Some men (practicing believers or just cultural Christians) may take only the second part of that verse, "the head of the woman is the man," to claim full control and dominion over their wives.

In Ephesians 5 we read, "Wives, submit yourselves to your own husbands as you do to the Lord. For the husband is the head of the wife as Christ is the head of the church, his body, and is himself its savior . . . Husbands, love your wives, as Christ loved the church and gave himself up for her . . . Even so husbands should love their wives as their own bodies . . . For this reason a man shall leave his father and mother and be joined to his wife, and the two shall become one flesh. This mystery is a profound one." Again, some Christian males dwell only on the opening first few words alone, demanding blind submission, not taking into account their serious duty to care for and sacrificially love their wives. At the time the apostle Paul wrote these words, social classes and cultural disorders prevailed. In addition, the verse that immediately preceded this paragraph reads, "Submit to one another" or "Be subject to one another out of reverence for Christ," but this is rarely quoted by those who prefer overall marital power and hierarchal status. Likewise, in 1 Peter 3 we read, "Husbands, likewise, dwell with *them* with understanding, giving honor to the wife, as to the weaker vessel, and as *being* heirs together of the grace of life." Galatians 3 also states, "There is neither Jew nor Greek, there is neither slave nor free, there is neither male nor female; for you are all one in Christ," and in chapter 6, "Carry each other's burdens, and in this way you will fulfill the law of Christ." Thus, sometimes, the spirits of the religious, legal, and political systems do not entirely coincide with the overall spirit of the sacred scriptures.

Many Muslims and Christians understand marriage as being part of a divine order. Some believe the marital relationship to be egalitarian with order and respect, but many others believe it to be hierarchical and privilege-based. Nevertheless, the maintenance of such a marriage becomes a mandate and a critical aspect of one's evolving spirituality (Hassouneh-Phillips, 2001). Additionally, both Islamic and Christian scriptures have many references on the distinction between the man and the woman and their separate functions and unique values. Often these are understood as implying the dominance and superiority of the male/husband/father over the female/wife/mother (Nason-Clark, 2004; Sherif, 1999). Thus, adherence to certain gender-role expectations has been perceived as being synonymous to being a faithful Christian or Muslim (Yick, 2008). This is yet another example of how culture and religion inform and influence each other reciprocally (Tillich, 1959).

Religious courts often decide who will also be granted divorce and on what basis, who will have the custody of the children, and ultimately who will inherit what portion of the joint assets. Divorce, which according to the Koran is a legal right granted to both husbands and wives alike, became restricted to male privilege. Following domestic violence, divorce can be granted to a woman only if she can provide proof of her physical harm, and only after some reconciliation efforts for the couple have failed (Tadross, 1995, as cited in Hajjar, 2004). Christian religious courts are usually more strenuous than Muslim courts in these matters, and therefore make it very difficult for couples to divorce and even prevent it. Religious laws often function alongside civil laws. Religious courts normally inform civil institutions of their decisions, in order to register and reinforce such actions and thus cooperate and reciprocate legal proceedings (cf. Center for Law and Religion, 2011; IRIN, 2009). Rigid divorce procedures, even after evidence of domestic violence, send direct and indirect messages to women suffering from domestic abuse, to tolerate, reconcile, and adapt to their circumstances.

OPPOSITION TO REFORM: SOCIO-ECONOMIC AND ETHNO-POLITICAL FACTORS AFFECTING DOMESTIC VIOLENCE

It has been argued that it is not simply gender, power, or social structures that perpetuate domestic aggression and family violence, but rather the intersections between these factors and other dimensions as well such as race, socioeconomic class, educational level, and political turmoil (Abi-Hashem, 2006; Bogard, 1999; Creshaw, 1994). For example, community strife or armed conflicts can contribute to a deteriorating socioeconomic status and mental health conditions of individuals and families alike, thus further increasing the rates of acting out behavior, domestic aggression, and family violence, as found with Palestinian youth (Al-Krenawi, Graham, & Sehwail, 2010) and with American inner-city youth (Sheidow, Gorman-Smith, Tolan, & Henry, 2001). Women, in the backdrop of political violence and military wars, are vulnerable to both the random cruelties perpetuated by the invading army as a perceived enemy and the various forms of domestic violence (Holt, 2013). Yet in a unique qualitative study conducted with Palestinian and Shi'a women in Lebanon, Holt found that there was a great unwillingness from women to acknowledge their experiences of domestic violence or to admit being abused, given the broader and more important cause of collective struggle and narrative of resistance against the outside aggression. Such a narrative increases women's feelings of empowerment and enhances their sense of communal identity and solidarity against the external dynamic forces. Men, in the context of political violence, also struggle with feelings of fear, vulnerability, humiliation, and an inability to feel in control. These feelings can linger long after the political violence has ended, leaving the entire family susceptible to the effects of various trauma, including aggression and abuse. As such, the trauma of political violence can be transmitted from one family member to another and from one generation to another (Weingarten, 2004).

Various national movements resisting maltreatment, abuse, and violence have taken place over the past few decades in the Arab Middle East (Sidawi, 1998). For example, the Palestinian Model Parliament set up a campaign for the equality and human rights of women under the initiative of the Woman's Center for Legal Aid and Counseling. The parliament provided a forum for proposing legislative amendments, new Palestinian laws, and recommendations concerning the legal status of women. Unfortunately, these valuable projects were hindered by the continuously escalating political unrest and turmoil in Israel/Palestine and the faltering negotiation toward peace and stability. Such an unstable and explosive political atmosphere results in the decline of the living conditions and economic standards of the Palestinian people and a redirection of efforts by the people and their government toward mere survival.

In Morocco, the beginning of an influential movement began in 1992 when the Women's Action Federation started the "one million signature campaign" aimed at addressing concerns related to divorce, polygamy, home, family possessions, custody, and guardianship. This campaign resulted in the successful amendments of governmental law and was viewed as a crucial step toward eliminating the sacred, yet discriminating, nature of family laws and statutes. However the amendments did not completely satisfy the aspirations of Moroccan women as the changes focused more specifically on divorce court proceedings and not more comprehensively on the status of women. In March of 2000, approximately 300,000 demonstrators took the streets, demanding better women's rights including a reform of the Code of Personal Status, which was established in 1958 and incorporated Sharia jurisprudence into national law (Hajjar, 2004). Opponents of these efforts claimed the defense of religion and family, and ultimately competing demonstrations led to the government's withdrawal of support to the activists. The main controversy focused on the proposal's demand to expand women's right to divorce. Today, the political upheaval that has taken place in Morocco sets back the work and agenda of the Women's Action Federation and other activists until the circumstances are more favorable and the political-economic stability can be regained.

In Yemen, at a time when the country had just signed the Convention for Children's Rights and the Convention for Eliminating Discrimination Against Women (CEDAW), in 1996, the Committee for Turning the Islamic Law into Legislature proposed modifying the regulations pertaining to marriage, polygamy, alimony, and inheritance in a way that further compromises the rights of women, making them more susceptible to abuse and discrimination. Yet various non-governmental groups, including the Center for Applied Research and Women's Studies, the Cultural Development Programs Planning Center, and the Office of Pioneering Lawyers, stood up to counter these initiatives and succeeded in blocking the decision. The women have continued to demand the application of CEDAW, despite ongoing contradiction between this convention and the laws practiced in Yemen.

In Lebanon, the League of Women's Rights drew up an Action Program in 1978 introducing a civil personal statutes code, guaranteeing equal rights between men and women in order to protect the family. It also specified the minimum age of women at 18 years, equal rights for the dissolving of the marriage contract, equal rights to inheritance and family possessions, and equal rights to children. The League met for its fourteenth conference in 1997 during which it drafted a Civil Code for Personal Statutes. Today the League continues to work alongside other NGOs in Lebanon including KAFA (Enough), in order to implement these changes for the protection of children and women against maltreatment and domestic abuse. On April 1, 2014, the Lebanese Parliament passed a law to protect women and the family from domestic violence. The law was officially established and made ready for implementation on May 15, 2014 (KAFA, 2014).

The Forum of Arab Women (Aisha) is composed of independent female activists across different countries in the Middle East who are engaged in the democratic struggle to achieve better rights and fight publically against domestic violence and abuse. Their aim is to urge Arab nations to apply international protective guidelines, such as CEDAW. Their aim is to change any discriminatory laws against women. Currently Saudi Arabia and Morocco are among the 11 countries that did not vote to incorporate CEDAW. However, many Arab Middle Eastern countries, such as Egypt, Libya, Iraq, and Jordan, did vote for CEDAW but established a few reservations clauses to preserve the application of *shari'aa* to specific matters pertaining to personal status and family laws (Hajjar, 2004).

A few years ago, a major international conference was held in London, United Kingdom, which has received significant publicity, titled Global Summit to End Sexual Violence in Conflict. It was the largest gathering of its kind, with 123 nations represented. Many community leaders and governmental dignitaries attended and participated in its extensive program. The summit created statements of action and youth consultation groups and agreed on practical steps to deal with impunity for the use of rape as a weapon of war (Global Summit, 2014). In some parts of the Arab Middle East, opposition to women's rights and equality movements are viewed as an act of defending traditional customs, religious beliefs, or societal heritages as well as resisting the importation of Western values and lifestyles into the local Middle Eastern communities (Hajjar, 2004). Unfortunately, these important activist movements continue to be met with many obstacles and challenges across many Arab-Islamic Middle Eastern nations.

MIDDLE EASTERN ARABS AND MUSLIMS LIVING IN THE WEST

People from Arabic and Middle Eastern backgrounds are found on all continents of the globe, and the waves of migration continue. Some travel for business or education, others to join family or friends, yet others to escape turmoil, persecution, and hardships in their homeland. Many are well integrated and function adequately in the respective hosting cultures, but others struggle to adapt, adjust, and assimilate. That process is often compounded with preexisting conditions and psycho-emotional scars, especially for the displaced, asylum-seeking, and refugees. Many carry with them traditional mentalities, strict religious values, and old social customs, and may show inflexibility and rigidity out of fear of losing their identity and heritage (and being tainted by Western lifestyles). These individuals, families, and groups will need mental health care, cultural coaching, and counseling. Special understanding and trainings are required of the general caregivers and therapeutic providers in order to effectively relate and serve such a population (Amer & Awad, 2015; St. George, 2017).

Arab American victims of domestic violence learn to accept and cope with abuse and derive strength and resilience from their beliefs in God (Alghoul, 2016; Hassouneh-Phillips, 2003; Khawaja, Linos, & El-Roueiheb, 2008), often because spirituality is an integral part of their mind-set and because they came from societies that did not provide legal protection and civic support. In Western countries, where resources including protections centers and shelters, psychological and legal services are often readily available, victims of violence or abuse can be unaware, unable, or unwilling to approach external care centers outside of the domains of their extended family and community of faith. The current social policies and healthcare procedures in the United States, for example, which clearly prohibit domestic violence and aim to protect victims, are considered inadequate, irrelevant, or insufficient to address the needs of most Arab Americans (Finigan, 2010; Kulwicki, Aswad, Carmona, & Ballout, 2010).

A study conducted with Muslim American women identified limited knowledge and awareness of the American legal system, language barriers, mistrust of the civic system, fear of intensifying already existing stereotypes (and of stigmatization particularly since 9/11), fear of immigration-related issues or deportation, apprehension of moving into a shelter upon reporting, and other socio-cultural and religious pressures as being the main reasons the victims of domestic abuse do not seek available help (Finigan, 2010). Many Arab American immigrants usually confirm these sentiments regarding the obstacles in the search for help and the utilization of local services. Virtually, their primary reason is the fear of disrupting the family status and ties with relatives and the fear of losing economic resources of their livelihood. Immigrants, who struggle with family disturbances, maltreatment, or aggression, often suggest that any intervention or breakthrough should take place first at the level of general family physicians, school teachers, and religious leaders, who probably are the first to notice any battering, violence, or mistreatment within their local neighborhood and community connections. Eventually, more resources and help-centers are needed to provide practical guidance, support, and treatment for potential and actual victims of family domestic abuse among Arab Middle Easterners (ACCESS, 2014; Advocates for Youth, 2008; Ahmed, 2017; APIAHF, 2009; Kulwicki, Aswad, Carmona, & Ballout, 2010; Kulwicki et al., 2015; NYSDOH, 2011; Runner, Yoshihama, & Novick, 2009).

GUIDELINES FOR INTERVENTION AND COUNSELING

An increase in public awareness campaigns, primarily among Arabic speaking communities, both in their homelands and abroad, remain one of the most important ways to penetrate some of the long held cultural and religious beliefs that prevent victims from seeking substantial help and better accessing external resources. Walker (1999) highlights the importance of taking a public health approach to building awareness and education among immigrant populations and isolated ethnic groups. Through this approach, practical information should be provided, linking family mistreatment and domestic violence with negative consequences, as health problems and other social ills, rather than presenting it from merely an ethical-moral or social justice perspective, which is likely to trigger defensive reactions toward change.

The compiled list below contains some major insights and guidelines for healthcare providers and professional caregivers on how to approach psychotherapy and counseling with people from Arab Middle Eastern descent living in Western countries, especially recent immigrants or first generation Arab Americans and those who may have been exposed to mistreatments, abuse, traumas, and violence or may be struggling with loss, grief, displacement, and stressful acculturation. Any intervention should incorporate the emotional, mental, social, spiritual, and cultural dimensions in order to be psychologically effective, cross-nationally relevant, and humanely respective for such a unique and diverse population (cf. Abi-Hashem, 2008a, 2008c, 2011a, 2011b, 2012b, 2012c, 2014a, 2014b; Abi-Hashem & Brown, 2013; Al-Krenawi & Graham, 2000; APIAHF, 2009; Chaleby & Racy, 1999; Dwairy, 2006; Dwairy & El-Jamil, 2015; El-Youssef, 2010; Erickson & Al-Timimi, 2001; Hakim-Larson & Nassar-McMillan, 2008; Kobeisy, 2004; Nassar-McMillan, Choudhuri, & Santiago-Rivera, 2010; NYSDOH, 2011; Pharaon, 2008; Sayed, 2003; Vannatter, 2017):

- Inquire gently and slowly, not in a fast questioning manner.
- Take time to build an inviting relationship and a warm environment, which may include a preliminary time to talk about general matters with no pressing agenda or technical specifics (and perhaps offering water or a refreshment, as Arab Americans value hospitality "diyaafa").
- Always try to be appropriate in your social manners and dress code, especially with the elderly, the opposite gender, and the traditional people.
- Learn about their background, values, heritage, customs, and religious faith as you go along. Investigate the demographic information and subcultures closely. Find out whether you are working with the elderly, young, educated, traditional, fresh immigrants, well acculturated, mixed marriages. Are they first, second, or third generation immigrants?
- Do not generalize, "All Arabs" or "all Muslims are . . ." "Is it true that women are suppressed and have no significant rights?" and so forth.
- Realize that not all Arabs, Muslims, Middle Easterners, or North Africans are the same; they may be quite different. You may meet the highly assimilated and Western type and the highly traditional and Eastern type of clientele.
- Be careful not to debate sensitive matters, polarized topics, or obvious differences in religious doctrines, foreign politics, or cultural hierarchies, especially early in the counseling or therapy process.
- Avoid using direct language, labeling questions, and heavy terminology, "Have you been abused? Since when have you suffered domestic violence? Are you a battered wife? Why didn't call and report your hus-

band?" They may not understand them in the same way that you, as a therapist, mean them.

- Do not immediately interpret silence or lack of eye contact and personal response as a psychological resistance. Rather there may be a cultural or linguistic barrier involved. At the same time, do not interpret their excessive politeness, repetition of accounts, or agreeability as appeasing or non-genuine.
- Realize that most of the people who end up in counseling or therapy are not there by choice; they might have been referred to your agency by the school or court or friends. Even most of those who seek counseling on their own may not be familiar with its many disciplines, procedures, and processes, and thus adequate introductions and psycho-educational hints at the start are essential.
- Avoid quick diagnosis and conceptualization (most of the time for insurance purposes). There are so many aspects and layers to consider, especially when working with cross-cultural cases compounded with various worldviews and multiple psycho-emotional factors.
- Be faithful to what you learn from them (names, places, histories, stories, etc.). They expect you to remember these details as a matter of honor and respect for them.
- Reemphasize the safety and confidentiality of your relationship with them, especially at the beginning.
- Use a more interactive style and movement. Distant and stoic therapists will not be effective with people from close knit and warm cultures and tight social backgrounds.
- Model some basic and general disclosures, so they can follow your example. Sharing some generic information about yourself will be beneficial, as they will be eager to learn some things about you and to trust you. That will bring you both closer together and greatly humanize the relationship (even though this may be discouraged in some theories or therapies).
- Ask for permission before taking any notes or voice/videotaping your interaction. Clearly explain the reason for that, that it is just for yourself (and maybe your supervisor) and not to be shared publically or legally with others. Remember that some Arab Americans may have a great mistrust in the whole psychological-psychiatric system.
- Be willing to speak slowly and simply with those with limited English or knowledge, even willing to work through an interpreter, which requires training and patience.
- Refrain from using bodily gestures, non-verbal communication, or popular jokes that are only understood in your local context or society.
- If hostility and violence are present, or if sexual abuse has somehow been disclosed, assure the person or family that they are not alone, and the risks

of disclosure are not as grave as they have thought, in order to calm their apprehensions and fears.

- When addressing aggressive behavior and domestic violence, carefully and sensitively weigh the pros and cons of seeking professional help, of reporting the abuse, of leaving the home, of legally separating from the offender, and so on. Do not assume that the client should or will obviously choose to report, separate, or divorce. Oftentimes the misunderstanding and cultural stigma, the social blame and alienation, and the financial repercussions associated with such a decision could have detrimental effects on the clients, and that must be delicately evaluated and worked through.
- If engaging the person in individual therapy, do not be resistant to involving other family members or friends who can serve as valuable support to the struggling client.
- Accept and respect the victim's version of the story and their evaluation of the situation as it will be expressed through their own cultural and religious lenses.
- Work toward empowering them before making major life changes or decisions. They must have the internal strength and external resources in place to manage some of the consequences of reporting abuse or separating from the perpetrator of violence. Agree with your clients on the objectives of empowerment and what changes they can appreciate and envision for their welfare.
- Let them know that you often deal with similar situations and you take each of these very seriously.
- Discover any residual grief, loss, and bereavement along with any traumatic stress, unresolved tragedy, or lingering critical crisis. Often these coexist and overlap. Apply therapies for grief resolution and trauma mastery simultaneously. Often, clinicians focus on one or the other, and mostly on the trauma at the expense of grief (since bereavement symptoms are less pronounced and pressing).
- Challenge some of them on any signs of isolation or rigidity that they may exhibit (at times, out of self-preservation or due to feeling intimidated). Assist them with skills for openness, flexibility, and interaction with locals, and for integration within the hosting society and/or general culture at large.
- Help them navigate the acculturation process if needed, and reconcile any inner tensions among the multiple layers of their identity and exposure—the struggles and rewards of being a trans-national person and a trans-cultural self.
- Develop a list of community resources, adequate for people from Arab, Muslim, and Middle Eastern background, which include physicians, social services, lawyers, volunteer centers, communities of faith, nurses and

psychiatrists, pastors and clergy, various hotlines and public libraries, as well as classes for English as a second language (when needed).

- Capitalize on their goodness, strengths, and resiliency. Many have a natural ability to tolerate pain and survive in the face of adversity.
- Finally, enhance your skills in cultural mediation and peace building, for these will allow you to make a larger contribution, perhaps on a global scale, and that can be a very rewarding investment indeed.

DISCUSSION QUESTIONS

1. As you learn about Arab Americans and Middle Easterners, in what way do you find them similar to other minorities or ethnic groups and in what do you find them different and unique?
2. How would migration and immigration-dynamics affect the occurrences of domestic violence? And what mental-social adjustments (regarding treatment of other family members) do immigrants need to make as they transition into a new society?
3. In what ways do the socio-political climate and civil-legal context in the Middle East and North Africa affect the rate of domestic violence among families of these origins living elsewhere, especially in the West?
4. How can you make your conceptualizations and interventions more socially appropriate and culturally sensitive, so to enhance your counseling relationship and therapy outcome?
5. What do you think is the role of the mass media and news agencies in help creating a negative view, impression, or generalization of all Arabs and Middle Easterners?
6. In dealing with victims of domestic violence and relational traumas (including their families and relatives), how can you begin to differentiate between what is merely diagnostic-clinical and what is social-cultural? In addressing that question, please, discuss the differentiating characteristics in cases of individuals with multiple identities.
7. Considering that the rate of domestic violence in families of Middle Eastern and North African origin are similar to that of Western families, how can we further comprehend the influence and impact of the specific cultural, religious, and ethno-political factors on domestic violence? Encouraging or deterrent factors (or both)?
8. How can Western and North American therapists increase their socio-cultural and religio-spiritual competencies to be able to better help, understand, and guide people from Middle Eastern descent?

ACKNOWLEDGMENT

Fatimah El-Jamil would like to acknowledge the work of two graduate students, Shereen Eid and Fahed Hassan, on helping with the literature review for some parts of this manuscript.

REFERENCES

Abi-Hashem, N. (1997). Reflections on "International Perspectives in Psychology." *American Psychologist, 52*(5), 569–570.

Abi-Hashem, N. (2003). Syria. In B. Sherif-Trask (Ed.), *The Greenwood encyclopedia of women's issues worldwide: The Middle East and North Africa* (pp. 355–380). Westport, CT: Greenwood.

Abi-Hashem, N. (2006). The agony, silent grief, and deep frustration of many communities in the Middle East: Challenges for coping and survival. In P. T. P. Wong & L. C. J. Wong (Eds.), *Handbook of multicultural perspectives on stress and coping* (pp. 457–486). New York: Springer.

Abi-Hashem, N. (2008a). Arab Americans: Understanding their challenges, needs, and struggles. In A. Marsella, P. Watson, F. Norris, J. Johnson, & J. Gryczynski (Eds.), *Ethnocultural perspectives on disasters and trauma: Foundations, issues, and applications* (pp. 115–173). New York: Springer.

Abi-Hashem, N. (2008b). Syria. In I. Epstein & G. H. Talhami (Eds.), *The Greenwood encyclopedia of children's issues worldwide: North Africa and the Middle East* (pp. 269–292). Westport, CT: Greenwood.

Abi-Hashem, N. (2008c). Working with Arab Americans. *APA Psychotherapy Training Videos [DVD]: Multicultural Counseling Series*. Washington, DC: American Psychological Association.

Abi-Hashem, N. (2011a). On cultural resiliency. *The Australian Community Psychologist, 23*(2), 23–31. Retrieved from https://groups.psychology.org.au/Assets/Files/Abi-Hashem-ACP-2-11.pdf.

Abi-Hashem, N. (2011b). Working with Middle Eastern immigrant families. In A. Zagelbaum & J. Carlson (Eds.), *Working with immigrant families: A practical guide for counselors* (pp. 151–180). New York: Routledge.

Abi-Hashem, N. (2012a). Understanding Middle Easterners and Arab Americans. *APA's International Psychology Bulletin, 16* (2), 41–43. Retrieved from http://internationalpsychology.files.wordpress.com/2013/01/ipb_spring_2012-04-16-1_final.pdf

Abi-Hashem, N. (2012b). Clinical trauma psychology. In C. R. Figley (Ed.), *Encyclopedia of trauma: An interdisciplinary guide* (pp. 98–100). Thousand Oaks, CA: Sage.

Abi-Hashem, N. (2012c). Religious and pastoral responses to trauma. In C. R. Figley (Ed.), *Encyclopedia of trauma: An interdisciplinary guide* (pp. 542–544). Thousand Oaks, CA: Sage.

Abi-Hashem, N. (2013a). Religion and spirituality. In K. D. Keith (Ed.), *Encyclopedia of cross-cultural psychology* (pp. 1091–1094). Malden, MA: Wiley-Blackwell.

Abi-Hashem, N. (2013b). Self-esteem. In K. D. Keith (Ed.), *Encyclopedia of cross-cultural psychology* (pp. 1146–1148). Malden, MA: Wiley-Blackwell.

Abi-Hashem, N. (2014a). Counseling Middle Eastern Arab Americans. In D. A. Leeming (Ed.), *Encyclopedia of psychology and religion* (2nd ed., pp. 402–407). New York: Springer.

Abi-Hashem, N. (2014b). Cross-cultural psychology and counseling: A Middle Eastern perspective. *Journal of Psychology and Christianity, 33*(2), 156–163.

Abi-Hashem, N. (2014c Spring/Summer). Social support: A psychological and cultural perspective. *APA's International Psychology Bulletin 18*(2–3), 74–77. Retrieved from https://internationalpsychology.files.wordpress.com/2014/07/ipb_spring-summer_2014_7-19_final.pdf.

Abi-Hashem, N. (2015) Revisiting Cultural Awareness and cultural relevancy. *American Psychologist, 70*(7), 660–661.

Abi-Hashem, N., & Brown, J. R. (2013). Intercultural adjustment. In K. D. Keith (Ed.), *Encyclopedia of cross-cultural psychology* (pp. 744–746). Malden, MA: Wiley-Blackwell.

Abu-Bakera, K. (2013). Arab parents' reactions to child sexual abuse: A review of clinical records. *Journal of Child Sexual Abuse, 22*(1), 52–71.

ACCESS. (2014). Community Health & Research Center: Domestic Violence Prevention Program. Retrieved from https://www.accesscommunity.org/node/320.

Advocates for Youth. (2008). Dealing with sexual abuse and family violence. Retrieved from http://www.advocatesforyouth.org/for-professionals/lesson-plans-professionals/1258?task=view.

Ahmed, M. B. (2017). Domestic violence: Empowering families. *The Muslim Community Center for Human Services*. Retrieved from http://mcc-hs.org/?page_id=61.

Ahram online. (2014, May 7). Egypt's cabinet approves new anti-sexual harassment law. Retrieved from http://english.ahram.org.eg/News/100741.aspx.

Al-Hibri, A. (2001). Muslim women's rights in the global village: Opportunities and challenges. *Journal of Law and Religion, 15*, 29–81.

Al-Krenawi, A., & Graham, J. R. (2000). Culturally sensitive social work practice with Arab clients in mental health settings. *Health and Social Work, 25* (1), 9–22.

Al-Krenawi, A., Graham, J. R., & Sehwail, M. A. (2010). Tomorrow's players under occupation: An analysis of the association of political violence with psychological functioning and domestic violence among Palestinian youth. *American Journal of Orthopsychiatry, 77*(3), 427–433.

Alghoul, N. (2016, March 9). Domestic violence in the Arab-American community. Retrieved from http://www.chicagotalks.org/?p=57849.

Ameela, S. (1995). *Women and social transformation* (in Arabic). Damascus, Syria: Dar al-Tibaah.

Amer, M. M., & Awad, G. H. (Eds.). (2015). *Handbook of Arab American psychology*. New York: Routledge.

American Psychological Association. (1996). APA presidential task force on violence and the family report. Washington, DC: Author.

An-na'm, A. A. (2003). The role of community discourse in combating "crimes of honor": Preliminary assessment and prospects. In L. Welchman & S. Hossain (Eds.), *"Honor" crimes, paradigms and violence against women* (pp. 64–77). London: Zed Press.

Anani, G. (2013). Syria crisis: Dimensions of gender-based violence against Syrian refugees in Lebanon. *Forced Migration Review*. Retrieved from http://www.fmreview.org/detention/anani.

APIAHF (2009). Domestic violence programs for Muslim communities: Services, advocacy, and training directory. Retrieved from http://www.peacefulfamilies.org/pdf/APIIDVDirectory.pdf.

Arabi, B. (2006). The women's rights and family violence in Syria. Woman in Syria Today. Retrieved from http://www.fafo.no/ais/middeast/syria/syrianwomen/SW-Arabi.pdf.

Barakat, H. (1993). *The Arab world: Society, culture, and states.* Los Angeles: University of California Press.

Baydoun, A. C. (2011). Cases of femicide before Lebanese courts. Beirut, Lebanon: KAFA Violence & Exploitation.

Bogard, M. (1999). Strengthening domestic violence theories: Intersections of race, class, sexual orientation, and gender. *Journal of Marital and Family Therapy, 25*(3), 275–289.

Boy, A., & Kulczycki, A. (2008). What we know about intimate partner violence in the Middle East and North Africa. *Violence Against Women, 14*(1), 53–70.

Center for Law and Religion (2011). Social cohesion and civil law: Marriage, divorce and religious courts. Retrieved from http://www.law.cf.ac.uk/clr/research/cohesion.html.

Chaleby, K. S., & Racy, J. (Eds.). (1999). *Psychotherapy with the Arab patient*. Sierra Vista, AR: QSOV.

Chantler, K. (2012). Recognition of and intervention in forced marriage as a form of violence and abuse. *Trauma, Violence, & Abuse, 13*(3), 176–183. doi: 10.1177/1524838012448121.

Christian Science Monitor Editorial Board. (2017, August 1). An Arab model for curbing domestic violence. *The Christian Science Monitor*. Retrieved from https://www.csmonitor.com/Commentary/the-monitors-view/2017/0801/An-Arab-model-for-curbing-domestic-violence.

Clark, C. J., Silverman, J. G., Shahrouri, M., Everson-Rose, S., & Groce, N. (2010). The role of the extended family in women's risk of intimate partner violence in Jordan. *Social Science and Medicine, 70*(1), 144–151.

CNN World (2013, April, 27). Lebanon's "uncomfortable" maid culture. Retrieved from http://cnnphotos.blogs.cnn.com/2013/04/27/lebanons-uncomfortable-maid-culture/.

Colucci, E., & Hassan, G. (2014). Prevention of domestic violence against women and children in low-income and middle-income countries. *Current Opinion in Psychiatry, 27*(5), 350–357.

Creshaw, K. (1994). Mapping the margins: Intersectionality, identity politics and violence against women of color. In M. Fineman & R. Mykitiuk (Eds.), *The public nature of private violence* (pp. 93–118). New York: New Press.

Dobash, R. E., & Dobash, R. P. (1977). Wives: The "appropriate" victims of marital violence. *Victimology, 2*, 426–442.

Douki, S., Nacef, F., Belhadj, A., Bouasker, A., & Ghachem, R. (2003). Violence against women in Arab and Islamic countries. *Archives of Women's Mental Health, 6*(3), 165–171.

Dutton, D. G. (1988). *The domestic assault of women: Psychological and criminal justice perspectives*. Needham Heights, MA: Allyn & Bacon.

Dwairy, M. (2006). *Counseling and psychotherapy with Arabs and Muslims: A culturally sensitive approach*. New York: Teachers College Press.

Dwairy, M., & El-Jamil, F. (2015). Counseling Muslims and Arabs. In P. Pederson, J. G. Draguns, W. J. Lonner, J. G. Draguns, J. E. Trimble, & M. Scharron-del Rio (Eds.), *Counseling across cultures (7th ed.)*. Thousand, Oaks, CA: Sage.

El-Hassan, J. (2014, May 14). MP fast-tracks law criminalizing sexual harassment. *The Daily Star*, p. 4.

El-Youssef, A. A. (2010). *El-ounf el-ousary* (in Arabic), "The familial violence: An exploration of causes, consequences, and solutions." Beirut, Lebanon: Dar Almahajja.

El-Zanaty, F., Hussein, E. M., Shawky, G. A., Way, A. A., & Kishor, S. (1996). *Egypt demographic and health survey—1995*. Calverton, MD: National Population Council and Macro International.

Erickson, C. D., & Al-Timimi, N. R. (2001, November). Providing mental health services to Arab Americans: Recommendations and considerations. *Cultural Diversity & Ethnic Minority Psychology, 7*(4), 308–327.

Fakim, N. (2014, January 23). Morocco amends controversial rape marriage law. Retrieved from http://www.bbc.com/news/world-africa-25855025.

Finigan, M. K. (2010). Intimate violence, foreign solutions: Domestic violence policy and Muslim-American Women. *Duke Forum for Law & Social Change, 2*, 141–154.

Finnerty, F., & Shahmanesh, M. (2017). Sexual and reproductive health in the European refugee crisis. *British Medical Journal, 92*(7), 485–486.

Gerber, G. L. (1995). Gender stereotypes and the problem of marital violence. In L. L. Adler & F. L. Denmark (Eds.), *Violence and the prevention of violence* (pp. 145–155). Westport, CT: Praeger.

Global Summit. (2014). Global summit to end sexual violence in conflict. Retrieved from https://www.gov.uk/government/topical-events/sexual-violence-in-conflict.

Haboush, K. L., & Alyan, H. (2013). "Who can you tell?" Features of Arab culture that influence conceptualization and treatment of childhood sexual abuse. *Journal of Child Sexual Abuse, 22*(5), 499–518.

Haj-Yahia, M. M. (2001). The incidence of witnessing interparental violence and some of its psychological consequences among Arab adolescents. *Child Abuse Neglect, 25*, 885–907.

Haj-Yahia, M. M. (1996). Wife abuse in the Arab society in Israel: Some challenges for future change. In J. L. Edleson & Z. L. Eisikovits (Eds.), *The future of intervention with battered women and their families* (pp. 87–101). Thousand Oaks, CA: Sage.

Haj-Yahia, M. M. (1998). Beliefs about wife beating among Palestinian women: The influence of their patriarchal ideology. *Violence Against Women, 4*(5), 533–558.
Haj-Yahia, M. M. (2000). Wife abuse and battering in the sociocultural context of Arab society. *Family Process, 39*(2), 237–255.
Haj-Yahia, M. M. (2003). Beliefs about wife beating among Arab men from Israel: The influence of their patriarchal ideology. *Journal of Family Violence, 18*(4), 193–206.
Haj-Yahia, M. M. (2013). Attitudes of Palestinian physicians toward wife abuse: Their definitions, perceptions of causes, and perceptions of appropriate interventions. *Violence against Women, 19*(3), 376–399.
Haj-Yahia, M. M., & Tamish, S. (2001). The rates of child sexual abuse and the psychological consequences as revealed by a study among Palestinian university students. *Child Abuse and Neglect, 25*(10), 1303–1327.
Hajjar, L. (2004). Religion, state power, and domestic violence in Muslim societies: A framework for comparative analysis. *Law and Social Inquiry, 29*(1), 1–38.
Hakim-Larson, J., & Nassar-McMillan, S. (2008). Middle Eastern Americans. In *Culturally alert counseling: A comprehensive introduction* (pp. 293–322). Thousand Oaks, CA: Sage.
Hassouneh-Phillipps, D. S. (2001). Marriage is half of faith and the rest is fear of Allah: Marriage and spousal abuse among American Muslims. *Violence Against Women, 7*(8), 927–946.
Hassouneh-Phillipps, D. S. (2003). Strength and vulnerability: Spirituality in abused American Muslim women's lives. *Issues in Mental Health Nursing, 24*(6–7), 681–694.
Herman, J. L. (2015). *Trauma and recovery: The aftermath of violence—from domestic abuse to political terror*. United Kingdom: Hachette.
Hersh, L. (1998). Giving up harmful practices, not culture. *Advocates for Youth.* Retrieved from http://www.advocatesforyouth.org/publications/publications-a-z/521-giving-up-harmful-practices-not-culture.
Holt, M. (2013). Violence against women in the context of war: Experiences of Shi'i women and Palestinian refugees women in Lebanon. *Violence Against Women, 19*(3), 316–337.
Hutchison, E. D. (2016). *Essentials of human behavior: Integrating person, environment, and the life course*. Thousand Oaks, CA: Sage.
IRIN humanitarian news and analysis. (2009). Lebanon: Move to take domestic violence cases from religious courts to civil courts. Retrieved from http://www.irinnews.org/report/86247/lebanon-move-to-take-domestic-violence-cases-out-of-religious-courts.
Jackson, M. L. (1997). Counseling Arab Americans. In C. Lee (Ed.), *Multicultural issues in counseling: New approaches to diversity* (2nd ed., pp. 333–349). Alexandria, VA: American Counseling Association.
Jeffords, C. R. (1984). The impact of sex-role and religious attitudes upon forced marital intercourse norms. *Sex Roles, 11,* 543–552.
Johnson, J. (2013, January 29). Syrian refugees describe horrors left behind. Retrieved from http://www.washingtonpost.com/world/middle_east/syrian-refugees-describe-horrors-left-behind/2013/01/28/1d838d8a-6571-11e2-9e1b-07db1d2ccd5b_story.html.
Kadiri, N., & Moussaoui, D. (2001). Women's mental health in the Arab World. In A. Okasha & M. Maj (Eds.), *Images in psychiatry: An Arab perspective* (pp. 189–206). World Psychiatric Association Series. Cairo, Egypt: Scientific Book House.
KAFA (2014, May 15). Bill for the protection of women and family members against domestic violence. *KAFA: Enough violence and exploitation.* Retrieved from http://www.kafa.org.lb/FOAPDF/FAO-PDF-11-635120756422654393.pdf.
Khawaja, M. (2004). Domestic violence in refugee camps in Jordan. *International Journal of Gynecology and Obstetrics, 86*(1), 76–69.
Khawaja, M., Linos, N., & El-Roueiheb, Z. (2008). Attitudes of men and women towards wife beating: Findings from Palestinian refugee camps in Jordan. *Journal of Family Violence, 23*(3), 211–218.
Kim, U., Yang, K-S., & Hwang, K-K. (Eds.). (2006). *Indigenous and cultural psychology: Understanding people in context*. New York: Springer.
Kishor, S., & Johnson, K. (2004). *Profiling domestic violence—A multi-country study.* Calverton, MD: ORC Macro.

Kobeisy, A. N. (2004). *Counseling American Muslims: Understanding the faith and helping the people.* Westport, CT: Praeger.

Krug, E., Dahlberg, L., Mercy, J., Zwi, A., & Lozano, R. (2002). *World report on violence and health.* Geneva, Switzerland: World Health Organization.

Kullab, S. (2014, March 11). Syria sparks surge in human trafficking. Retrieved from http://dailystar.com.lb/News/Lebanon-News/2014/Mar-11/249855-syria-sparks-surge-in-human-trafficking.ashx#axzz2vdDsPPOC.

Kulwicki, A. D. (2002). The practice of honor crimes: A glimpse of domestic violence in the Arab world. *Issues in Mental Health Nursing, 23*(1), 77–87.

Kulwicki, A., & Miller, J. (1999). Domestic violence in the Arab American population: Transforming environmental conditions through community education. *Mental Health Nursing, 20*(3), 199–216.

Kulwicki, A., Aswad, B., Carmona, T., & Ballout, S. (2010). Barriers in the utilization of domestic violence services among Arab immigrant women: Perceptions of professionals, service providers and community leaders. *Journal of Family Violence, 25*(8), 727–735.

Kulwicki, A., Ballout, S., Kilgore, C., Hammad, A., & Dervartanian, H. (2015). Intimate partner violence, depression, and barriers to service utilization in Arab American women. *Journal of Transcultural Nursing, 26*(1), 24–30.

Lucas, R. (2014, March 11). UN: 5.5 million Syrian children affected by war. Retrieved from http://bigstory.ap.org/article/un-syrian-children-hardest-hit-civil-war.

Marsella, A. J. (1998). Toward a global-community psychology: Meeting the needs of a changing world. *American Psychologist, 53*(12), 1282–1291.

Maziak, W., & Asfar, T. (2003). Physical abuse in low-income women in Aleppo, Syria. *Health Care for Women International, 24*(4), 313–326.

McCoy, T. (2014, May 28). In Pakistan, 1,000 women die in "honor killing" annually. Retrieved from http://www.washingtonpost.com/news/morning-mix/wp/2014/05/28/in-pakistan-honor-killings-claim-1000-womens-lives-annually-why-is-this-still-happening/.

Middle East Program. (2016). Five years after the Arab Spring: What's next for women in the MENA region? *Wilson Center.* Retrieved from https://www.wilsoncenter.org/publication/five-years-after-the-arab-spring-whats-next-for-women-the-mena-region.

Naharnet (2014, May 11). Foreign maid jumps off seventh floor in Dahyieh. Retreived from http://naharnet.com/stories/en/130089.

Nason-Clark, N. (2004). When terror strikes home: The interface of religion and domestic violence. *Journal for the Scientific Study of Religion, 43*(3), 303–310.

Nassar-McMillan, S., Choudhuri, D. D., & Santiago-Rivera, A. (2010). *Counseling & diversity: Counseling Arab Americans.* Florence, KY: Cengage Learning/Wadsworth.

Niaz, U., & Tariq, Q. (2017). Situational analysis of intimate partner violence interventions in South Asian and Middle Eastern countries. *Partner Abuse, 8*(1), 47–88.

Nydell, M. K. (2006). *Understanding Arabs: A guide for modern times* (4th ed.). Yarmouth, ME: Intercultural Press.

NYSDOH. (2011). Special considerations for caring for diverse populations domestic violence intervention: A guide for health care professionals. *New York State Department of Health.* Retrieved from https://www.health.ny.gov/professionals/protocols_and_guidelines/sexual_assault/docs/protocol_appendix_o.pdf.

Obeid, N., Chang, D. F., & Ginges, J. (2010). Beliefs about wife beating: An exploratory study with Lebanese students. *Violence Against Women, 16*(6), 691–712.

Passport to dignity. (2011). Critical area of concern: Violence against women. Retrieved from http://www.pdhre.org/passport-ch8.html.

Patai, R. (2010). *The Arab mind.* Tucson, AZ: Recovery Resources.

Pharaon, N. A. (2008). The interface of psychic trauma and cultural identity within Arab American groups post-9/11. *Group, 32*(3), 223–234.

Reimers, E. (2007). Representations of an honor killing: Intersections of discourses on culture, gender, equality, social class, and nationality. *Feminist Media Studies, 7* (3), 239–255.

Runner, M., Yoshihama, M., & Novick, S. (2009). Intimate partner violence in immigrant and refugee communities: Challenges, promising practices, and recommendations. *Family Vio-*

lence Prevention Fund. Retrieved from https://www.futureswithoutviolence.org/userfiles/file/ImmigrantWomen/IPV_Report_March_2009.pdf.

Russel, D. E. H., & Harmes, R. A. (2001). *Femicide in the global perspective*. New York: Teachers College Press.

Sayed, M. (2003). Conceptualisation of mental illness within Arab cultures: Meeting challenges in cross-cultural settings. *Social Behaviour and Personality, 31,* 333–342.

Schneider, J. (1971). Of vigilance and virgins. *Ethnology, 9,* 1–24.

Sheidow, A. J., Gorman-Smith, D., Tolan, P. H., & Henry, D. B. (2001). Family and community characteristics: Risk factors for violence exposure in inner-city youth. *Journal of Community Psychology, 29,* 345–360.

Sherif, B. (1999). The prayer of a married man is equal to seventy prayers of a single man: The central role of marriage among upper-middle-class Muslim Egyptians. *Journal of Family Issues, 20*(5), 617–632.

Sidawi, R. R. (1998). *Arab public hearing on legal violence and equality in the family.* Beirut, Lebanon: Arab Court.

Slemrod, A. (2012, April 30). Rally calls for migrant workers' rights. *The Daily Star Lebanon.* Retrieved from http://www.dailystar.com.lb/News/Local-News/2012/Apr-30/171878-rally-calls-for-migrant-workers-rights.ashx#axzz37e4fD64h.

Smart, N. (1999). *Worldviews: Crosscultural explorations of human beliefs* (3rd ed.). Cambridge, UK: Pearson.

St. George, M. (2017, May 5). ASU faculty, students work to combat misunderstandings between Arab, American cultures. Retrieved from https://asunow.asu.edu/20170505-asu-faculty-students-work-combat-misunderstandings-between-arab-american-cultures.

Storey, J. W., & Utter, G. H. (2002). *Religion and politics: A reference handbook.* Santa Barbara, CA: ABC Clio.

Terman, R. L. (2010). To specify or single out: Should we use the term "honor killing"? *Muslim World Journal of Human Rights, 7*(1), 1554–4419.

Tillich, P. (1959). *Theology of culture.* New York: Oxford University Press.

UNICEF (2000). Domestic violence against women and children. *Innocenti Digest,* 6, 1–21.

UNICEF UK (2014). Global summit marks a watershed in the fight against sexual violence in conflict. Retrieved from http://www.unicef.org.uk/UNICEFs-Work/What-we-do/Our-campaigns/End-sexual-violence/.

UNWomen (2008). United Nations for gender equality and the empowerment of women. Retrieved from http://www.un.org/womenwatch/daw/cedaw/.

Usta, J. A., Farver, J. M., & Danachi, D. (2013). Child Maltreatment: The Lebanese children's experiences. *Child: Care Health and Development, 39*(2), 228–236.

Usta, J. A., Farver, J. M., & Pashayan, N. (2007). Domestic violence: The Lebanese experience. *Public Health, 121*(3), 208–219.

Usta, J. A., Mahfoud, Z. R., Abi-Chahine, G., & Anani, G. A. (2008). Child sexual abuse: The Lebanese situation. Retrieved from http://resourcecentre.savethechildren.se/sites/default/files/documents/2659.pdf.

Van Baak, C., Hayes, B. E., Freilich, J. D., & Chermak, S. M. (2017). Honor crimes in the United States and offenders' neutralization techniques. *Deviant Behavior*, 1–16. Retrieved from http://www.tandfonline.com/doi/full/10.1080/01639625.2016.1266870?scroll=top&needAccess=true.

Vandello, J. A., & Cohen, D. (2003). Male honor and female fidelity: Implicit cultural scripts that perpetuate domestic violence. *Journal of Personality and Social Psychology, 84*(5), 997–1010.

Vannatter, T. (2017). Intimate Partner Violence and humanitarian action: Considering cultural context and gender dynamics. Retrieved from https://www.cerahgeneve.ch/files/5914/9303/4131/WP43-Intimate-Partner-Violence.pdf.

Walker, L. E. (1999). Psychology and domestic violence around the world. *American Psychologist, 54*(1), 21–29.

Watts, C., & Zimmerman, C. (2002). Violence against women: Global scope and magnitude. *The Lancet, 359,* 1232–1237.

Weingarten, K. (2004). Witnessing the effects of political violence in families: Mechanisms of intergenerational transmission of trauma and clinical interventions. *Journal of Marital and Family Therapy, 30*(1), 45–59.

World Health Organization. (2000). Women's mental health: An evidence-based review. Geneva, Switzerland: WHO.

Yick, A. G. (2008). A metasynthesis of qualitative findings on the role of spirituality and religiosity among culturally diverse domestic violence survivors. *Qualitative Health Research, 18*(9), 1289–1306.

Yount, K. M. (2005). Resources, family organization, and domestic violence against married women in Minya, Egypt. *Journal of Marriage and Family, 67*(3), 579–596.

Zogby, J. (2010). *Arab voices: What they are saying to us, and why it matters*. New York: Palgrave Macmillan.

Zubaida, S. (2001). Islam and the politics of community and citizenship. *Middle East Report, 31*(4), 20–27.

Chapter Eight

Crucial Considerations in the Understanding and Treatment of Intimate Partner Violence in African American Couples

Carolyn M. West

When compared to their White and Latino/a counterparts, African Americans, whether as individuals or couples, consistently reported higher rates of overall, severe, mutual, and recurrent past year and lifetime physical IPV victimization and perpetration in general population, community, and university samples (for a review, see West, 2012). To illustrate, in a national survey, 45.1% of Black[1] women and 40.1% of Black men had been victims of sexual violence, physical aggression, and/or stalking that was committed by an intimate partner during their lifetime (Smith, Chen, Basile, Gilbert, Merrick, Patel, Walling, & Jain, 2017). Based on these prevalence rates, it is estimated that more than 6 million African American women and nearly 5 million African American men are survivors of some form of intimate partner violence (IPV) (Black, Basile, Breiding, Smith, Walters, Merrick, Chen, & Stevens, 2011).

The purpose of this chapter is to provide a brief overview of prevalence rates of IPV among African Americans, describe an ecological model, which is a more comprehensive theoretical approach to understanding the risk factors that elevate the probability that African American couples will experience intimate abuse, describe some of the challenges to understanding IPV in this population, and offer some suggestions for areas to explore when conducting a culturally sensitive assessment.

INTIMATE PARTNER VIOLENCE AMONG AFRICAN AMERICANS: AN OVERVIEW

In this section, I will define IPV, briefly discuss the prevalence rates of IPV among African Americans, highlight the patterns of relationship violence in these couples, and explain the gendered nature of partner violence. First, defining what constitutes intimate partner violence is challenging and complex; however, a comprehensive definition includes *physical aggression*, ranging from less injurious violence, such as slapping and shoving, to more lethal forms of violence, including beatings and assaults with weapons. *Rape* can take the form of completed or attempted alcohol- or drug-facilitated forced anal, oral, or digital penetration. Other forms of sexual violence include *reproductive coercion* (e.g., pressuring a woman to become pregnant against her wishes, preventing her from using birth control), *sexual coercion* (e.g., unwanted penetration obtained through nonphysical pressure), and *unwanted sexual contact* (e.g., kissing, fondling). Examples of *psychological aggression* include name-calling, insulting, or humiliating, and *coercive control* includes behaviors that are intended to monitor, control, or threaten an intimate partner. Finally, *stalking* encompasses being the recipient of unwanted communication via email or through social media; or being watched or followed at home, work, or school. These forms of violence can occur in any intimate partnership and can be perpetrated by legal or common-law spouses, boyfriends/girlfriends, cohabitating, dating, or casual sexual partners (Smith et al., 2017).

The National Intimate Partner and Sexual Violence Survey (NISVS) is an ongoing, nationally representative random digit dial telephone survey that collects information about experiences of sexual violence, intimate partner violence, and stalking among non-institutionalized English and Spanish speaking adults (9,086 women and 7,421 men) in the United States. Based on the NISVS, Black women reported a broad range of IPV victimization: 41% had been physically assaulted, 14.6% had been stalked, and 12.2% had been raped by an intimate partner during their lifetime. Too few Black men reported rape and stalking by an intimate partner to produce reliable prevalence estimates; however, 36.8% of Black men reported physical aggression that was perpetrated by an intimate partner during their lifetime (Breiding, Chen, & Black, 2014).

Ideally, both IPV victimization and perpetration should be measured in couples over time. This was accomplished in the National Longitudinal Couples Survey (NCLS) by interviewing both members of the couple in 1995 and 2000. In the 12 months before the 1995 survey, 23% of Black couples reported some form of male-to-female perpetrated partner violence (MFPV) and 30% reported some form of female-to-male perpetrated partner violence (FMPV). Most of the violence was categorized as minor or moderate (e.g., throwing items; pushing, shoving, grabbing; slapping) (Caetano, Cunradi, Clark, & Schafer, 2000). However, when Black couples were resurveyed in 2000, MFPV and FMPV minor physical assault (15% vs. 16%) and minor psychological aggression (53% vs. 51%) appeared to be comparable. In addition, Black couples reported similar rates of male-perpetrated and female-perpetrated severe physical assault (4% vs. 6%) and psychological aggression (28% vs. 30%) (Caetano, Field, Ramisetty-Mikler, & Lipsky, 2009).

Nevertheless, it is important to identify two patterns in relationship violence among African American couples. First, Black women were more likely to identify themselves as perpetrators than Black men were to identify themselves as victims (Caetano, Schafer, Field, & Nelson, 2002). For example, in the 1995 NCLS, Black couples more frequently reported female-perpetrated IPV than male-perpetrated IPV (30% vs. 23%, respectively). Although it was unclear if these gender differences were statistically significant, more Black women than men engaged in the following aggressive acts: threw something (22.1% vs. 5.4%); pushed, shoved, or grabbed (21.3% vs. 19.7%); slapped (9.7% vs. 7.8%); kicked, bit, hit (9.9% vs. 4.1%); and hit with something (15.8% vs. 5.1%) (Caetano et al., 2000).

Another important violent relationship pattern was the high frequency of mutual or bidirectional IPV. Specifically, 61% of Black couples reported that both partners had used physical aggression. One-third of Black couples who reported bidirectional partner violence described it as severe, defined as beat up, choked, raped, or threaten with a weapon. Five years later, 17% of Black couples continued to engage in mutual violence and 11% of those couples progressed into severe IPV. Moreover, bidirectional partner violence was reported independent of education, income, employment status, drinking, alcohol problems, and history of violence in the family of origin (Caetano, Ramisetty-Mikler, & Field, 2005).

Although not to minimize Black women's use of violence, it is important to pause here and put these findings into context. First, Black women's use of physical violence often occurs in the context of their victimization; therefore, it should not be concluded that they are the primary aggressors. Furthermore, these relationships may be better characterized as bidirectional asymmetric violence (Temple, Weston, & Marshall, 2005).[2] Alternatively stated, although the violence may appear to be mutual it does not mean that women's and men's violent acts or equivalent. When motives, frequency, and severity of violence are considered, the physical and mental health consequences associated with IPV are often greater for women (West, 2007).

To further illustrate the gendered nature of IPV, when compared to Black men and women of other ethnic groups, African American women were overrepresented among victims of certain severe forms of violence. For example, 40% of Black women have reported nonfatal strangulation (Glass, Laughon, Campbell, Block, Hanson, Sharps, & Taliaferro, 2008). Between

2003 and 2014, the rate of intimate partner homicide among Black women was 4.4 per 100,000, which was primarily committed by former or current intimate partners (Petrosky, Blair, Betz, Fowler, Jack, & Lyons, 2017). Finally, among Black couples, the overall rate of male-to-female sexual assault (MFSA) was 23.2%, which most commonly involved pressuring the partner (without the use of physical force) to engage in sexual intercourse, often without a condom. Although categorized as "minor," sexual coercion frequently occurred in conjunction with psychological abuse and physical violence (Ramisetty-Mikler, Caetano, & McGrath, 2007).

ECOLOGICAL MODEL: A COMPREHENSIVE THEORETICAL APPROACH

No single factor can explain why some people or groups are at higher risk for interpersonal violence; rather, violence is an outcome of a complex interaction among many factors. Therefore, in order to understand what accounts for the higher rates of IPV among Black Americans we need to utilize a theory that considers multiple risk factors (West, 2016c).

An ecological model, which considers risk factors at four levels, can be beneficial to help us understand IPV in the lives of African Americans (Centers for Disease Control and Prevention [CDC], 2009). At the *individual level* we should consider how a person's sociodemographic characteristics, such as social class or gender, and formative history, such as exposure to child abuse and substance use increase their risk of IPV. The *relationship level* considers the interactions between the survivor and her partner, family members, and peers. Whereas the *community level* considers the environment in which the person lives; for example, exposure to neighborhood crime. Finally, the ecological model includes larger *societal-level* factors, such as norms, policies, and structural inequalities, including racism and sexism (for a more detailed application of the ecological model to African American intimate partner violence see West, 2016c).

Below I will discuss individual-level (age, gender, income, alcohol use/abuse, and childhood victimization); relationship-level (relationship conflict); community-level (neighborhood poverty and community violence); and societal-level risk factors (experiences with racial discrimination) (see table 8.1). Although each level will be discussed separately, it is difficult to detangle the individual-, relationship-, community-, and societal-level correlates and risk factors associated with violence among African Americans because they are interrelated. For example, the combination of attitudes supporting IPV (individual-level), inadequate conflict resolution skills (relationship-level), and exposure to neighborhood violence (community-level) converge to increase the risk that low-income, urban Black men will assault their intimate partners (Raiford, Seth, Braxton, & DiClemente, 2013).

INDIVIDUAL LEVEL

Age

Victimization occurs most frequently among younger individuals and couples. When compared to Black couples who were 40 years or older, the rates of severe IPV were more than three times greater among Black couples who were under age 30 (Hampton & Gelles, 1994).

Gender

Although Black couples reported a pattern of female-perpetrated (Caetano et al., 2000) and mutual IPV (Caetano et al., 2005), African American women also experienced high rates of severe gender-based violence. More specifically, when compared to Black men or women of ethnic groups, African American women reported higher rates of nonfatal strangulation (Glass et al., 2008), domestic violence homicide (femicide) (Violence Policy Center, 2016), rape/sexual assault, and stalking (Black et al., 2011).

Income

Annual household income had the greatest relative influence on the probability of partner violence, with lower income being associated with higher rates of IPV. Specifically, Black couples who reported either MFPV or FMPV had significantly lower mean annual incomes than nonviolent couples (Cunradi, Caetano, & Schafer, 2002).

Alcohol Use and Abuse

When faced with extreme, persistent, economic and social inequalities, individuals are more likely to use and abuse alcohol or drugs. There is substantial evidence that alcohol-related dependence indicators (e.g., withdrawal symptoms and alcohol tolerance), alcohol-related social problems (e.g., job loss, legal problems), and greater mean male and female alcohol consumption were especially strong predictors of IPV among African American couples, independent of who in the couple reported a drinking problem (Cunradi, Caetano, Clark, & Schafer, 1999).

Table 8.1. Summary of risk factors associated with violence among African Americans by ecological level

Risk Factors	Research Findings
Individual Level	
Age	• Rates of severe IPV were more than three times greater among Black couples under age 30 (Hampton & Gelles, 1994)
Gender	• Black couples reported a pattern of bidirectional violence (Caetano et al., 2005) • Black women reported higher rates of intimate partner homicide (Violence Policy Center, 2014) • Black women reported higher rates of rape and stalking (Black et al., 2011)
Income	• Black couples who reported MFPV ($22,838) had lower mean annual incomes than those couples who did not report MFPV ($32,685) (Cunradi, Caetano, & Schafer, 2002) • Black couples who reported FMPV ($23,238) had lower mean annual incomes than those couples who did not report FMPV ($33,541) (Cunradi, Caetano, & Schafer, 2002)
Alcohol use/ abuse	• Black couples with male alcohol problems were at a sevenfold risk for MFPV compared to those without male alcohol problems (Cunradi, Caetano, Clark, & Schafer, 1999) • Black couples reporting female alcohol problems had a fivefold risk for MFPV compared to those without female alcohol problems (Cunradi, Caetano, Clark, & Schafer, 1999) • Black women in the heaviest drinking category were twice as likely to report FMPV than abstainers and infrequent drinkers (Caetano, Cunradi, Clark, & Schafer, 2000)
Childhood victimization	• Black couples in which the female reported childhood violence victimization were more likely to report MFPV than couples in which the female did not report victimization (Cunradi, Caetano, Clark, & Schafer, 1999) • Blacks who were hit as a teenager by their mother or observed parental violence had higher rates of husband-to-wife violence (Hampton & Gelles, 1994) • Blacks who were hit as a teenager by either parent were twice as likely to be in households with severe intimate partner violence (Hampton & Gelles, 1994)
Relationship Level	
Relationship Conflict	• Nearly two-thirds of non-felony related homicides (168 out of 268) involved arguments between the Black female victim and male offender (Violence Policy Center, 2016) • The rates of IPV perpetration increased as attitudes supporting IPV increased among Black men who reported high ineffective couple conflict resolution skills (Raiford, Seth, Braxton, & DiClemente, 2013)

Community Level	
Neighborhood poverty	• The risk for MFPV was threefold higher among Black couples who lived in impoverished neighborhoods compared to those not living in poor areas (Cunradi, Caetano, Clark, & Schafer, 2000) • The risk for FMPV was twofold higher among Black couples who lived in impoverished neighborhoods compared to those not living in poor areas (Cunradi, Caetano, Clark, & Schafer, 2000)
Neighborhood violence	• Community violence was correlated with emotional dating victimization among young black urban women (Stueve & O'Donnell, 2008) • Perception that neighborhood violence was frequent, personal involvement in street violence, and gang violence were associated with IPV perpetration among urban Black men (Reed et al., 2009)
Societal Level	
Racial Discrimination	• Experiencing racial discrimination was a predictor of physical and emotional IPV victimization and perpetration among young, low-income, urban African American women (Stueve & O'Donnell, 2008) • Black men who reported high rates of racial discrimination perpetrated IPV in their current relationship when compared to those who reported less discrimination (28% vs. 16%) (Reed, Silverman, Ickovics, Gupta, Welles, Santana, & Raj, 2010)

Exposure to Family Violence During Childhood

Black children who experienced serious childhood or adolescent victimization in their homes, such as beatings and threats with weapons, were more likely to engage in both male- and female-perpetrated intimate partner violence in adulthood (Caetano et al., 2000). In addition, African Americans who witnessed violence between their parents or who were hit by either parent during their teenage years reported higher rates of husband-to-wife IPV in adulthood (Hampton & Gelles, 1994).

RELATIONSHIP LEVEL

Relationship Conflict

Relationship conflict has been associated with IPV and femicide. To illustrate, in a sample of low-income African American men, perceptions of how well they and their partners resolved conflict were measured by such items as: "By the end of an argument, you and your partner have really listened to each other," "You and your partner's arguments are left hanging and unsettled," and "You and your partner go for days being mad at each other."

Among Black men who reported high ineffective couple conflict resolution skills, the rates of IPV perpetration increased as attitudes supporting IPV increased (Raiford et al., 2013). Lack of conflict resolution skills, coupled with easy access to guns, can facilitate, escalate, and amplify anger, conflicts, and arguments. According to the Violence Policy Center (2016), nearly two-thirds (168 out of 268) of Black women were murdered by a male offender, most frequently a current or former boyfriend or husband, often during the course of an argument. Fifty-two percent (88 victims) were shot with a handgun.

COMMUNITY-LEVEL

Neighborhood Poverty

Approximately one-half of the Black couples in the NCLS resided in impoverished neighborhoods. Compared to Black couples who lived in more middle-class communities, those who lived in economically distressed areas were at a threefold risk for MFPV and a twofold increase for FMPV (Cunradi, Caetano, Clark, & Schafer, 2000). Thus, it appears that individual economic distress, in the form of low household income (Cunradi et al., 2002), and residing in poor neighborhoods worked in tandem to increase the risk of inflicting and sustaining IPV.

Neighborhood Violence

Exposure to community violence in any role (witness, victim, or perpetrator) has been associated with higher rates of intimate partner abuse. For example, community violence was correlated with emotional dating victimization among young Black urban women (Stueve & O'Donnell, 2008). Black men were more likely to batter their girlfriends if they had been involved in street violence, had a history of gang involvement, or perceived that there was a "great deal" of violence in their neighborhood (Reed, Silverman, Welles, Santana, Missmer, & Raj, 2009).

Discrimination

Among young, low-income, urban African Americans, IPV perpetration and victimization have been linked to microaggressions in the form of perceived racial discrimination in their community (e.g., being unfairly stopped and frisked by police or followed by store clerks, called insulting names, or physically attacked because of skin color/race). For example, experiencing the aforementioned forms of discrimination was a predictor of physical and emotional IPV victimization and perpetration among African American women (Stueve & O'Donnell, 2008). Black men who reported high rates of such discrimination perpetrated IPV in their current relationship when compared to those who reported less discrimination (28% vs. 16%) (Reed, Silverman, Ickovics, Gupta, Welles, Santana, & Raj, 2010).

There are several benefits of using an ecological model. Researchers have persuasively argued that when individuals live with multiple community disadvantages, which have their foundations in historical and structural racism, their frustration and anger can spill over into intimate relationships and culminate in interpersonal violence, including homicide (Cheng & Lo, 2015). Thus, an ecological model moves us beyond viewing victimization as an abnormality or personal defect that resides within the individual survivor or within the relationship. Instead, an ecological model compels us to consider the structural inequalities and the context in which the survivor and the couple exist. Thereby, the web of trauma and the barriers to help-seeking in the lives of Black victim-survivors become more visible (West, 2016c).

CHALLENGES IN UNDERSTANDING INTIMATE PARTNER VIOLENCE AMONG AFRICAN AMERICANS

Our biggest challenges to understanding the pervasive nature of IPV among African American couples has been our failure to situate contemporary Black couple's experience with relationship violence in a historical context, our reluctance to recognize the similarities and parallels between the violence that is perpetrated by intimate partners and service providers who are tasked with helping survivors, and the erasure of the intersecting and multiple identities of survivors and perpetrators.

Historical Trauma

During 250 years of slavery, followed by 90 years of de facto and de jure segregation in the form of Jim Crow laws, and the shameful incompletion of the modern civil rights movement, one thing remained constant in the lives of African-Americans: high levels of interpersonal and institutional violence in the forms of beatings, rapes, lynchings (Williams-Washington, 2010, p. 32). This is not to suggest that every destructive act, including the perpetration of interpersonal violence, is the direct result of slavery. Exposure to racism, quality of their social support system, and knowledge of these historical events can determine how contemporary African Americans experience historical trauma. Still, slavery and its aftermath have left an indelible mark on the Black psyche and consciousnesses have hindered the ability of some African Americans to develop healthy interpersonal relationships (Dixon, 2017; Williams-Washington, 2010).

As previously discussed in the ecological model, exposure to racial discrimination is a societal-level risk factor that has been associated with IPV victimization and perpetration among low-income, urban African Americans (Reed et al., 2010; Stueve & O'Donnell, 2008). Empirical research is limited in this area. Furthermore, cross-sectional research is unable to establish the temporal sequence of discrimination and IPV; therefore, we cannot conclude that experiences with racial discrimination cause IPV perpetration or victimization. Still, it is important to investigate how Black male-female relationships are negatively impacted by this form of racial trauma.

Structural Violence

Beyond the psychological consequences of historical trauma, racial discrimination has created structural inequalities, in the form of higher rates of poverty, unemployment, and residential segregation that have increased the probability that Black Americans will experience all forms of violence in their families and communities. This is a reflection of *institutional racism*, which are unfair policies and discriminatory practices of particular institutions that have a disparate impact on people of color. Relatedly, *structural racism* is the cumulative and compounding effects of an array of societal factors including the history, cultural, ideology, and interactions of institutions and policies that systematically privilege White people and disadvantage people of color (West, 2016b, 2016c).

Too often, there are similarities and parallels between various forms of coercive control utilized by the abusive intimate partner as identified by the Power and Control Wheel (Chavis & Hill, 2009) and that are utilized by agents of the state and service providers who are tasked with assisting African American victims (for a detailed discussion, see West, 2016b). For example, after they are physically abused by their intimate partner, Black women sometimes face excessive force from police officers when they report the abuse. Black women are frequently psychologically, verbally, and emotionally abused by partners and then face a similar type of psychological maltreatment when they seek services from domestic violence shelters (Nnawulezi & Sullivan, 2014). Therefore, it is crucial that we acknowledge and understand how African Americans who have experienced IPV are sometimes mistreated by the institutions that should be assisting them.

Intersectionality and Multiple Identities

Intersectionality is a term coined by Kimberle Crenshaw (1994) to describe overlapping or intersecting social identities and related systems of oppression, domination, or discrimination as well as privilege and power. The premise is simple: "It is fallacious to suppose that one experiences abuse first as a human being, then as a woman, then as a black person, then as a lesbian, and so forth. A woman's responses cannot be correlated to aspects of her social identity on a neat flowchart" (West, 1999, p. 56).

Alternatively stated, there is rich demographic diversity among Black Americans. In order to make these subpopulations more visible, it is important to use an intersectional analyses that considers the victims' social location in terms of age, socioeconomic class, ethnicity, and sexual orientation (for a visual representation of an intersectionality of cultural diversity among IPV survivors, see Lockhart & Mitchell, 2010). To illustrate, by understanding the social location in which low-income Black women reside, intersectionality can help us to understand how and why they experience IPV in the context of high rates of poverty, mass incarceration, housing instability, and community violence, which in turn, elevates their risk for a host of physical and mental health problems—HIV, substance abuse, and anxiety (O'Leary & Frew, 2017). Intersectionality can also help us to understand how current batterer intervention programs that focus on patriarchy as a cause of IPV perpetration are ineffective when they fail to consider ways in which Black men are disempowered by social, political, and economic inequalities (Waller, 2016).

CULTURALLY SENSITIVE ASSESSMENT

Even for the most seasoned professional, assessing for possible interpersonal violence can be intimidating. However, knowing what questions to ask and when can make the difference in providing the best care for victim-survivors (for a review of assessment tools see Carney, 2015; Mortiere, 2015). In this section I will discuss how to consider intersecting identities of African American couples in our assessments, recommend a range of violence (IPV, community, and structural) to explore with our clients, and discuss respectful ways to explore mental and physical health problems (see table 8.2).

INTERSECTIONALITY AND MULTIPLE IDENTITIES

It is imperative that we recognize and acknowledge the multiple identities of our clients. An intersectional analyses is crucial because "continuing to offer fragment services, wherein issues are individually treated and not considered within the context of their intersections, is an inefficient, and ultimately *ineffective*, means of providing services" (Bent-Goodley, Chase, Circo, & Rodgers, 2010, p. 74). For example, Sarita, an impoverished, urban dwelling, battered Black lesbian with mental health problems explained the challenges of accessing services:

Table 8.2. Areas of assessment to conduct with African American victims and perpetrators of intimate partner violence

Assessment of African American Victims and Perpetrators of Intimate Partner Violence	
Areas to Assess	**Possible Themes to Explore**
Intersectionality of identities and multiple identities	• Age • Educational Level • Ethnicity (African American, Caribbean, African immigrant) • Geographic Location (urban, rural, suburban) • Religious affiliation • Sexual identity (cisgender, transgender) • Sexual orientation (gay, lesbian, bisexual) • Socioeconomic class
Range of IPV, community, and structural violence	Intimate partner violence • Women's use of violence • Reproductive coercion • Strangulation • Domestic homicide Historical trauma Structural violence Community violence
Mental Health Disorders	• Mood disorders (dysthymia, major depression disorder, and bipolar disorder) • Anxiety disorders (panic disorder, agoraphobia, generalized anxiety disorder, obsessive-compulsive disorder, and posttraumatic stress disorder) • Substance disorders (alcohol abuse/dependence, drug use/dependence) • Eating disorders • Suicidal ideation and attempts
Physical Health Disorders	• Injuries/Hospitalizations • Central nervous system (headaches, fainting, back pain, seizures) • Gynecological/reproductive health problems (abnormal vaginal bleeding, vaginal infection, pelvic pain, painful intercourse, fibroids, urinary tract infection, and sexually transmitted infections, including HIV/AIDS) • Gastrointestinal problems (loss of appetite, digestive problems, abdominal problems)

> You offer me this place over here for mental illness. Then I go to this domestic violence shelter . . . that's not helping me with my mental illness . . . So, I go back over here [mental health agency] so at least they can monitor my meds. (Simpson & Helfrich, 2014, p. 455)

We should avoid asking our clients to fragment themselves and to present one identity when they seek help, while neglecting other important parts of themselves. Instead, a social justice–based, culturally responsive comprehensive service would welcome her to bring all aspects of her identity into treatment. What Sarita and most of our clients want is simple: "the opportunity to define for themselves who they are and what aspects of their identities are most important or relevant to their situations at a particular point in time" (Simpson & Helfrich, 2014, p. 459).

Therefore, we should consider asking how some of the following identities influence the victim's or perpetrator's experiences with violence and help-seeking efforts (for a more detailed discussion, see West, in press).

Age

Special attention should be paid to unique forms of violence and challenges that victims and perpetrators experience across the age-spectrum. Black adolescents, particularly those who are poor, are at risk for dating violence in their intimate relationships, family violence in their homes, and sexual harassment in their neighborhoods and schools (Miller, 2008). At the other end of the age continuum, older African American women may be financially abused by their adult children and physically and emotionally abused by their spouses. In addition, older victims often lack resources for independent living, including stable housing, personal income, and good physical health (Lichtenstein & Johnson, 2009).

Ethnicity

The abuse experience can vary based on ethnicity of the couple. For example, African immigrant couples may face unique challenges around language barriers, immigration status, and gender roles (West, 2016a). Likewise, the demographic risk factors and mental health consequences that are associated with IPV between African American and Caribbean battered women may vary (Lacey, Sears, Matusko, & Jackson, 2015). Consequently, mental health providers should consider ethnicity and immigration status and avoid the assumption that every phenotypically Black person identifies as African American and traces his or her roots to the transatlantic slave trade.

Geographic Location

Although the research is limited, it appears that the types of abuse, location of the assault, and response to intimate partner violence varies between urban and rural African American couples. For example, rural woman were more likely to be attacked by kitchen knives and pieces of furniture; whereas urban women were assaulted with guns. Urban women reported that their abuse occurred in public places, such as shopping malls and gas station and, in contrast, rural women were beaten in private settings, including houses and apartments. Furthermore, the way the abusers controlled the lives of women in the two settings differed. Urban abusers told the victim how to wear her hair and/or how to dress, while rural abusers battered their partners for failing to perform domestic duties, such as cooking and cleaning (Bhandari, Bullock, Richardson, Kimeto, Campbell, & Sharps, 2015).

Social Class

Much of the research in this area has focus on impoverished African Americans (O'Leary & Frew, 2017); yet their middle-class peers also face challenges. Revealing that they were victims of IPV could jeopardize the status and reputation of professional Black women and their partners. Moreover, their disclosure of abuse or request for services may be met with skepticism because they appear to be financially secure (West, 2016b).

Sexual Orientation/Gender Identity

Transgender Black women and Black lesbians face barriers that prevent them from freely and safely accessing services, such as heterosexism, discrimination, and stigma. They also encounter institutional and agency-specific barriers, homophobia, and transphobia in the Black community, and racism in the LGBTQ community (Simpson & Helfrich, 2014).

Mental health providers can use the Multicultural Power and Control Wheel as a visual representation to help themselves and their clients, both victims and perpetrators, to grasp how various systems of oppression (e.g., ageism, heterosexism, ableism, racism, classism) shape their experiences with IPV (Chavis & Hill, 2009). As we put intersectionality into practice, it is important that we remember that many diverse factors correlate with privilege (such as sex, race, and socioeconomic status) are based on visible traits or observable characteristics. However, numerous identity factors, including gender identity, immigration status, dis/ability challenges, religion, sexual orientation, and education are sometimes ambiguous or invisible. Therefore, we have to listen to the victims and perpetrators tell their stories and describe their identities.

RANGE OF VIOLENCE

To strive for social justice and cultural sensitivity, we should make all forms of violence more visible, both to ourselves as mental health professionals and our clients. Again, the Multicultural Power and Control Wheel can be used to illustrate how perpetrators' coercive control tactics are shaped by intersecting identities and varying systems of oppression. These forms of abuse include isolation, emotional abuse, sexual abuse, using children to control and harass the victim, intimidation, and physical violence (Chavis & Hill, 2009). However, service professionals need to be aware of several neglected forms of violence that disproportionately impact Black victims. They are specific types of IPV (women's use of aggression, reproductive coercion, nonfatal strangulation, intimate partner homicide) as well as historical trauma, structural violence and inequalities, and community violence.

Women's Use of Aggression

African American women sometimes use aggression as a form of self-defense, in retaliation for past abuse, or to preempt future abuse. However, the use of aggression may not serve them well. Direct confrontation may not stop the primary aggressor over the long term; in fact, the violence may escalate. Black women who used this strategy seldom felt a sense of control, independence, or power within their relationships; rather, they reported symptoms of depression, anxiety, and PTSD (West, 2007; West, 2016b). Moreover, when they are arrested, the social and legal consequences can be devastating and include the problems that are associated with a felony conviction: unemployment or possible eviction from public housing. Although they are not the primary perpetrator, Black women victim-defendants also may be court mandated to participate in batterer's treatment programs (West, 2007).

Mental health providers can discuss the advantages and disadvantages of using aggression and strategize about more appropriate tactics to end the violence. They may also educate clients about arrest policies and the legal consequences associated with their use of violence. Remembering that their use of aggression often occurs in the context of their victimization can help us to avoid the unconscious bias and stereotype of the inherently angry and hyper-violent Black woman (West, 2007).

Reproductive Coercion

A frequently overlooked form of sexual violence that impacts Black victims is reproductive coercion, such as birth control sabotage (removing the condom during intercourse, destroying a woman's contraceptive device or birth control pills) or pregnancy pressure (verbal or emotional pressure to get pregnant or to terminate a pregnancy). This form of victimization has often resulted in high rates of unintended pregnancies among African American women (Nikolajski, Miller, McCauley, Akers, Schwarz, Freedman, et al., 2015). Accordingly, mental health providers should become familiar with all forms reproductive coercion and be prepare to conduct a culturally sensitive assessment with their clients (for a toolkit on reproductive coercion see Cappelletti, Gatimu, & Shaw, 2014).

Strangulation

When compared to battered women of other ethnic backgrounds, African American women are at elevated risk for strangulation. It is important to ask our clients about strangulation, a unique form of physical aggression, which can be used, sometimes just once, to immobilize and terrorize the victim. It is a potentially lethal, but invisible form of violence, in that there is seldom immediate external evidence. Bruising and swelling may not appear until days later, especially on darker complexions. Immediate and lasting fear are the primary post-event reactions to strangulation (Glass et al., 2008).

Domestic Homicide

When compared to victims of other ethnic backgrounds, Black women are murdered at higher rates by their intimate partners, often with a handgun during the course of an argument (Violence Policy Center, 2016). Therefore, it is imperative that mental health providers use a lethality screening tool, such as the Danger Assessment, which considers nonfatal strangulation, to determine a client's risk for intimate partner homicide (Campbell, Webster, Koziol-McLain, Block, Campbell, Curry, et al., 2003).

Historical Trauma

Williams-Washington (2010) has defined *historical trauma*, as "the collective spiritual, psychological, emotional and cognitive distress perpetuated intergenerationally deriving from multiple denigrating experiences originating with slavery and continuing with patterns forms of racism and discrimination to the present day" (p. 32). Marriage and family therapists and other mental health professionals should strive to educate themselves about the impact that historical trauma of slavery has had on African Americans and the clinical implications of this trauma (Danzer, Rieger, Schubmehl, & Cort, 2016; Dixon, 2017; Wilkins, Whiting, Watson, Russon, & Moncrief, 2013).

Structural Violence and Inequalities

In order to capture the full range of violence that is experienced by African Americans, we need to have a discussion about institutional racism and structural violence. Although they seem to be invisible, these forms of inequalities are very real in the lives of our clients. A comprehensive medical and mental health assessment could include a measure of "structural vulnerability" to help providers to think more clearly, critically, and practically about the ways in which social structures and inequalities result in health disparities (Bourgois, Holmes, Sue, & Quesada, 2017).

Community Violence

A form of trauma that disproportionately impacts African Americans is community violence. It may involve experiencing or witnessing homicide, gun violence, assaults, robberies, or exposure to drug markets. The combination of interpersonal violence within the home and violence in the neighborhood means that safety is illusive for many Blacks, which further compromises their physical and emotional health and elevate their risk for IPV. Therefore, our assessments should ask survivors about the communities that they call home (Stueve & O'Donnell, 2008; Violence Policy Center, 2017).

ASSESS FOR PHYSICAL AND MENTAL HEALTH PROBLEMS

In a national sample of Black battered women, severe physical IPV was associated with an increased risk of suicide attempts and ideation as well as lifetime mental health problems, including mood disorders (dysthymia, major depression disorder, and bipolar disorder); anxiety disorders (panic disorder, agoraphobia, generalized disorder, obsessive disorder, and posttraumatic stress disorder [PTSD]); substance disorders (alcohol or drug use, abuse/dependence); and eating disorders (bulimia, binge eating) (Lacey et al., 2015). In addition, when compared to survivors who had experienced one or two forms of victimization, Black women who sustained cumulative violence (physical, sexual, and emotional abuse) reported higher rates of clinically significant depressive symptoms, PTSD, self-mutilation, suicidal thoughts/attempts, drug problems, and eating disorders in the past year (Sabri, Holliday, Alexander, Huerta, Cimino, Callwood, et al., 2016).

The physical health of African American battered women also is compromised by IPV. When compared to their nonvictimized counterparts, survivors of recent assaults sustained bruises and facial, dental, and head injuries, which often required stitches and surgeries; broken bones and dislocated jaws, and a loss of consciousness. Furthermore, in the year prior to the study, recent victims were hospitalized or sought treatment in the emergency room more frequently (Anderson, Stockman, Sabri, Campbell, & Campbell, 2015). In addition to their immediate medical trauma, Black victims reported a range of health concerns in the past year, including problems with their central nervous system (headaches, fainting, back pain, seizures); gynecological/reproductive health problems (abnormal vaginal bleeding, vaginal infection, pelvic pain, painful intercourse, fibroids, urinary tract infection, and sexually transmitted infections, including HIV/AIDS); and gastrointestinal problems (loss of appetite, digestive problems, abdominal problems) (Schollenberger, Campbell, Sharps, O'Campo, Gielen, Dinemann, et al., 2003). African American women who reported more frequent partner violence, particularly if it was accompanied by PTSD symptoms (Iverson, Bauer, Shipherd, Pineles, Harrington, & Resick, 2013), cumulative violence exposure (Sabri et al., 2016), and recent violence exposure (past year compared to lifetime exposure to IPV) (Schollenberger et al., 2003), were more likely to self-rate their overall physical health as "fair," "poor," or "very poor."

We can assess for mental health problems without seeing our clients as personifying a diagnosis. Instead, we can ask them how they cope with symptoms of depression or PTSD (e.g., intrusive recollections, distressing dreams, flashbacks, emotional numbing). While keeping in mind that they may have experienced IPV in conjunction with multiple types of violence (structural inequalities, historical trauma, community violence), have they adopted healthy or unhealthy coping strategies? (Sullivan, Weiss, Price, Pugh, & Hansen, 2017).

To conclude, in order to practice cultural competency, mental health providers should strive to become more culturally sensitive and aware, which "is more than being politically correct or tolerating diversity, it is a sincere commitment, active engagement in, and dedication to a lifelong learning process to enrich the delivery of services to domestic violence survivors and other persons seeking the services of helping professionals" (Lockhart & Mitchell, 2010, p. 6). Although it is challenging, considering intersecting identities of African Americans, exploring a range of violence in their lives, and gathering information about mental health and physical health problems that are related to IPV is an important step in the process of cultural awareness.

CONCLUSION

In this chapter, I provided a brief overview of the prevalence rates of IPV among African Americans, described an ecological model, which is a more comprehensive theoretical approach to understanding the risk factors that elevate the probability that African American couples will experience intimate abuse, described some of the challenges to understanding IPV in this population, and offered some suggestions for areas to explore when conducting a culturally sensitive assessment. Mental health professionals, in collaboration with those impacted by abuse, should strive to commit to activism at the local, state, and national levels. It is imperative that a greater awareness of racism and other forms of oppression in the lives of African Americans is reinforced by deliberate engagement in efforts to reduce the impact of these forms of oppression within society. This will not only result in successful and culturally sensitive treatment of survivors, it will address prevention in violence in all forms.

DISCUSSION QUESTIONS

1. What historical and cultural factors do you think account for higher rates of female-perpetrated and mutual violence among African American couples?
2. In what ways can individual-, relationship-, community-, and societal-level correlates and risk factors converge to elevate the risk of intimate partner violence among African American couples?
3. In what ways has historical trauma contributed to the elevated rates of intimate partner violence in contemporary African American couples?
4. Can you identify similarities and parallels between various forms of coercive control utilized by abusive intimate partners and by agents of the state (e.g., police officers, judges) and service providers (e.g., shelter workers, mental health professionals) who are tasked with assisting African American victims?
5. How can we use the concept of intersectionality and multiple identities of clients to improve service provision?
6. Can you identify some sources of resilience among African American victims and perpetrators of intimate partner violence?

NOTES

1. The term *Black* and *African American* are used interchangeably in this chapter.

2. To illustrate, Janay Palmer and her fiancé, now husband, Ray Rice, a former running back for the NFL's Baltimore Ravens, was described as having "little more than a very minor physical altercation." However, in later video footage he could be seen dragging her limp body from an Atlantic City casino elevator after he had allegedly knocked her unconscious. Although both partners use violence, at least in this case, the woman sustained more serious injuries (Christensen, Gill, & Perez, 2016).

REFERENCES

Anderson, J. C., Stockman, J. K., Sabri, B., Campbell, D. W., & Campbell, J. C. (2015). Injury outcomes in African American and African Caribbean women: The role of intimate partner violence. *Journal of Emergency Nursing, 41,* 36–42.

Bent-Goodley, T. B., Chase, L., Circo, E. A., & Rodgers, S. T. (2010). Our survival, our strengths: Understanding the experiences of African American women in abusive relationships. In L. L. Lockhart & Fran S. Danis (Eds.), *Domestic violence: Intersectionality and cultural competent practice* (pp. 67–99). New York: Columbia University Press.

Bhandari, S., Bullock, L. F., Richardson, J. W., Kimeto, P., Campbell, J. C., & Sharps, P. W. (2015). Comparison of abuse experiences of rural and urban African American women during perinatal period. *Journal of Interpersonal Violence, 30,* 2087–2108.

Black, M. C., Basile, K. C., Breiding, M. J., Smith, S. G., Walters, M. L., Merrick, M. T., Chen, J., & Stevens, M. R. (2011). *The National Intimate Partner and Sexual Violence Survey (NISVS): 2010 Summary Report*. Retrieved from https://www.cdc.gov/violenceprevention/pdf/nisvs_report2010-a.pdf (access September 10, 2011).

Bourgois, P., Holmes, S. M., Sue, K., & Quesada, J. (2017). Structural vulnerability: Operationalizing the concept to address health disparities in clinical care. *Academic Medicine, 92,* 299–307.

Breiding, M. J., Chen, J., & Black, M. C. (2014) *Intimate partner violence in the United States—2010*. Atlanta, GA: National Center for Injury Prevention and Control, Centers for Disease Control and Prevention. Retrieved on July 26, 2017 from https://www.cdc.gov/violenceprevention/pdf/cdc_nisvs_ipv_report_2013_v17_single_a.pdf.

Caetano, R., Cunradi, C. B., Clark, C. L., & Schafer, J. (2000). Intimate partner violence and drinking patterns among White, Black, and Hispanic couples in the U.S. *Journal of Substance Abuse, 11*, 123–138.

Caetano, R., Field, C., Ramisetty-Mikler, S., & Lipsky, S. (2009). Agreement on reporting of physical, psychological, and sexual violence among White, Black, and Hispanic couples in the United States. *Journal of Interpersonal Violence, 24*, 1318–1337.

Caetano, R., Ramisetty-Mikler, S., & Field, C. A. (2005). Unidirectional and bidirectional intimate partner violence among White, Black, and Hispanic couples in the United States. *Violence and Victims, 20*, 393–404.

Caetano, R., Schafer, J., Field, C., Nelson, S. M. (2002). Agreement on reports of intimate partner violence among White, Black, and Hispanic couples in the United States. *Journal of Interpersonal Violence, 17*, 1308–1322.

Campbell, J. C., Webster, D., Koziol-McLain, J., Block, C., Campbell, D., Curry, M. A., et al. (2003). Risk factors for femicide in abusive relationships: Results from a multisite case control study. *American Journal of Public Health, 93*, 1089–1097.

Cappelletti, M. M., Gatimu, J. K., & Shaw, G. (2014). *Exposing reproductive coercion: A toolkit for awareness raising, assessment, and intervention*. The Feminist Women's Health Center (FWHC) and The National Coalition Against Domestic Violence (NCADV). Retrieved on July 26, 2017 from https://www.ncadv.org/files/RCtoolkit.pdf.

Carney, A. (2015). Assessing for intimate partner violence. In P. T. Clements, J. Pierce-Weeks, K. E. Holt, A. P. Giardino, S. Seedat, & C. M. Mortiere (Eds.), *Violence against women: Contemporary examination of intimate partner violence* (pp. 17–31). Saint Louis, MO: STM Learning, Inc.

Centers for Disease Control and Prevention (2009). *The socialecological model: A framework for prevention*. Retrieved on July 26, 2017 from https://www.cdc.gov/violenceprevention/overview/social-ecologicalmodel.html.

Chavis A. Z., & Hill, M. S. (2009). Integrating multiple intersecting identities: A multicultural conceptualization of the Power and Control Wheel. *Women & Therapy, 32*, 121–149.

Cheng, T. C., & Lo, C. C. (2015). Racial disparities in intimate partner violence examine through the multiple disadvantage model. *Journal of Interpersonal Violence, 31*, 2026–2051.

Christensen, M. C., Gill, E., & Perez, A. (2016). The Ray Rice domestic violence case: Constructing Black masculinity through newspaper reports. *Journal of Sport and Social Issues, 40,* 363–386.

Crenshaw, K. W. (1994). Mapping the margins: Intersectionality, identity politics, and violence against Women of Color. In M. A. Fineman & R. Mykitiuk (Eds.), *The public nature of private violence: The discovery of domestic abuse* (93–117). New York: Routledge.

Cunradi, C. B., Caetano, R., Clark, C. L., & Schafer, J. (1999). Alcohol-related problems and intimate partner violence among White, Black, and Hispanic couples in the US. *Alcoholism: Clinical and Experimental Research, 23*, 1492–1501.

Cunradi, C. B., Caetano, R., Clark, C. L., & Schafer, J. (2000). Neighborhood poverty as a predictor of intimate partner violence among White, Black, and Hispanic couples in the United States: A multilevel analysis. *Annals of Epidemiology, 10,* 297–308.

Cunradi, C. B., Caetano, R., & Schafer, J. (2002). Socioeconomic predictors of intimate partnerviolence among White, Black, and Hispanic couples in the United States. *Journal of Family Violence, 17*, 377–389.

Danzer, G., Rieger, S. M., Schubmehl, S., & Cort, D. (2016). White psychologists and African Americans' historical trauma: Implications for practice. *Journal of Aggression, Maltreatment, and Trauma, 25*, 351–370.

Dixon, P. (2017). *African American relationships, marriages, and families: An introduction.* New York: Routledge.

Glass, N., Laughon, K., Campbell, J., Block, C. R., Hanson, G., Sharps, P. W., & Taliaferro, E. (2008). Non-fatal strangulation is an important risk factor for homicide of women. *The Journal of Emergency Medicine, 35*, 329–335.

Hampton, R. L., & Gelles, R. J. (1994). Violence toward Black women in a nationally representative sample of Black families. *Journal of Comparative Family Studies, 25*, 105–119.

Iverson, K. M., Bauer, M. R., Shipherd, J. C., Pineles, S. L., Harrington, E. F., & Resick, P. A. (2013). Differential associations between partner violence and physical health symptoms among Caucasian and African American help-seeking women. *Psychological Trauma: Theory, Research, Practice, and Policy, 5*(2), 158–166.

Lacey, K. K., Sears, K. P., Matusko, N., & Jackson, J. S. (2015). Severe physical violence and Black women's health and well-being. *American Journal of Public Health, 105*, 719–724.

Lichtenstein, B., & Johnson, I. M. (2009). Older African American women and barriers to reporting domestic violence to law enforcement in the rural deep South. *Women & Criminal* Justice, 19, 286–305.

Lockhart, L. L., & Mitchell, J. (2010). Cultural competence and intersectionality: Emerging frameworks and practical approaches. In L. L. Lockhart & Fran S. Danis (Eds.), *Domestic Violence: Intersectionality and cultural competent practice* (pp. 1–28). New York: Columbia University Press.

Miller, J. (2008). *Getting played: African American girls, urban inequality, and gendered violence*. New York: New York University Press.

Mortiere, C. (2015). Risk assessment in intimate partner violence. In P. T. Clements, J. Pierce-Weeks, K. E. Holt, A. P. Giardino, S. Seedat, & C. M. Mortiere (Eds.), *Violence against women: Contemporary examination of intimate partner violence* (pp. 33–47). Saint Louis, MO: STM Learning, Inc.

Nikolajski, C., Miller, E., McCauley, H. L., Akers, A., Schwarz, E. B., & Freedman, L. et al., (2015). Race and reproductive coercion: A qualitative assessment. *Women's Health Issues, 25*, 216–223.

Nnawulezi, N. A., & Sullivan, C. M. (2014). Oppression within safe spaces: Exploring racial microaggressions within domestic violence shelters. *Journal of Black Psychology, 40*, 563–591.

O'Leary, A., & Frew, P. M. (2017). *Poverty in the United States: Women's voices.* New York: Springer.

Petrosky, E., Blair, J. M., Betz, C. J., Fowler, K. A., Jack, S., & Lyons, B. H. (2017). Racial and ethnic differences in homicides of adult women and the role of intimate partner violence—United States, 2003–2004. *Morbidity Mortality Weekly Report, 66*, 741–746.

Raiford, J. L., Seth, P., Braxton, N. D., & DiClemente, R. J. (2013). Interpersonal and community-level predictors of intimate partner violence perpetration among African-American men. *Journal of Urban Health, 90*, 784–795.

Ramisetty-Mikler, S., Caetano, R., & McGrath, C. (2007). Sexual aggression among White, Black, and Hispanic couples in the U.S.: Alcohol use, physical assault, and psychological aggression as its correlates. *The American Journal of Drug and Alcohol Abuse, 33*, 31–43.

Reed, E., Silverman, J. G., Ickovics, J. R., Gupta, J., Welles, S. L., Santana, M. C., & Raj, A. 2010). Experiences of racial discrimination and relation to violence perpetration and gang involvement among a sample of urban African-American men. *Journal of Immigrant Minority Health, 12*, 319–326.

Reed, E., Silverman, J. G., Welles, S. L., Santana, M. C., Missmer, S. A., & Raj, A. (2009). Associations between perceptions and involvement in neighborhood violence and intimate partner violence perpetration among urban, African-American men. *Journal of Community Health, 34*, 328–335.

Sabri, B., Holliday, C. N., Alexander, K. A., Huerta, J., Cimino, A., Callwood, G. B., et al. (2016). Cumulative violence exposures: Black women's responses and sources of strength. *Social Work in Public Health, 31*, 127–139.

Sabri, B., Huerta, J., Alexander, K. A., St. Vil, N. M., Campbell, J. C., & Callwood, G. B. (2015). Multiple intimate partner violence experiences: Knowledge, access, utilization and barriers to utilization of resources by women of the African Diaspora. *Journal of Health for the Poor and Underserved, 26*, 1286–1303.

Schollenberger, J., Campbell, J., Sharps, P. W., O'Campo, P., Gielen, A. C., Dinemann, J., et al. (2003). African American HMO enrollees: Their experiences with partner abuse and its effects on their health and use of medical services. *Violence Against Women, 9*, 599–618.

Simpson, E. K., & Helfrich, C. A. (2014). Oppression and barriers to service for Black, lesbian survivors of intimate partner violence. *Journal of Gay & Lesbian Social Services, 26*, 441–464.

Smith, S. G., Chen, J., Basile, K. C., Gilbert, L. K., Merrick, M. T., Patel, N., Walling, M., & Jain, A. (2017). *The National Intimate Partner and Sexual Violence Survey (NISVS): 2010–2012 State Report.* Atlanta, GA: National Center for Injury Prevention and Control Centers for Disease Control and Prevention. Retrieved on July 26, 2017 from https://www.cdc.gov/violenceprevention/pdf/NISVS-StateReportBook.pdf.

Stueve, A., & O'Donnell, L. (2008). Urban young women's experiences of discrimination and community violence and intimate partner violence. *Journal of Urban Health, 85*, 386–401.

Sullivan, T. P., Weiss, N. H., Price, C., Pugh, N., & Hansen, N. B. (2017). Strategies for coping with individual PTSD symptoms: Experiences of African American victims of intimate partner violence. *Psychological Trauma: Theory, Research, Practice, and Policy.*

Temple, J. R., Weston, R., & Marshall, L. L. (2005). Physical and mental health outcomes of women in nonviolent, unilaterally violent relationships. *Violence and Victims, 20*, 335–359.

Violence Policy Center (2016). When men murder women: An analysis of 2014 homicide data. Washington, DC. http://www.vpc.org/studies/wmmw2016.pdf (accessed September 10, 2017).

Violence Policy Center (2017). *The relationship between community violence and trauma: How violence affects learning, health, and behavior*. Retrieved on July 26, 2017 from http://www.vpc.org/studies/trauma17.pdf.

Waller, B. (2016). Broken fixes: A systematic analysis of the effectiveness of modern and postmodern interventions utilized to decrease IPV perpetration among Black males remanded to treatment. *Aggression and Violent Behavior, 27*, 42–49.

West, C. M. (2007). "Sorry, we have to take you in": Black battered women arrested for intimate partner violence. *Journal of Aggression, Maltreatment and Trauma, 15*, 95–121.

West, C. M. (2012). Partner abuse in ethnic minority and gay, lesbian, bisexual, and transgender populations. *Partner Abuse, 3*(3), 336–357.

West, C. M. (2016a). African immigrant women and intimate partner violence: A systematic review. *Journal of Aggression Maltreatment and Trauma, 25*, 4–17.

West, C. M. (2016b). Hidden in plain sight: Structural inequalities and (in)visible violence in the lives of African American women. In L. Wilton & E. Short (Eds.), *Talking about structural inequalities in everyday life: New politics of race in groups, organizations, and social systems* (pp. 85–102). Charlotte, NC: Information Age Publishing.

West, C. M. (2016c). Living in a web of trauma: An ecological examination of violence among African Americans. In C. C. Cuevas & C. M. Rennison (Eds.), *The Wiley-Blackwell handbook on the psychology of violence* (pp. 649–665). John Wiley & Sons.

West, C. M. (in press). Treatment interventions for intimate partner violence in the lives of African American women: A social justice approach. In S. Gelberg, M. Poteet, D. Moore, & D. Coyhis (Eds.), *Radical psychology: Multicultural and social justice decolonization initiatives*. Lanham, Maryland: Lexington Books.

West, T. C. (1999). *Wounds of the spirit: Black women, violence, and resistance ethics.* New York: University of New York University Press.

Wilkins, E. J., Whiting, J. B., Watson, M. F., Russon, J. M., & Moncrief A. M. (2013). Residual effects of slavery: What clinicians need to know. *Contemporary Family Therapy, 35*, 14–28.

Williams-Washington, K. N. (2010). Historical trauma. In R. L. Hampton, T. P. Gullotta, & R. L. Crowel (Eds.), *Handbook of African American health* (p. 31–49). New York: The Guilford Press.

Chapter Nine

Understanding Domestic Violence within a Latino/Hispanic/Latinx Context

Environmental, Cultural, and Ecological Mapping as a Culturally Relevant Assessment Tool

Caroline S. Clauss-Ehlers, Fred Millán, and Clare Jinzhao Zhao

INTRODUCTION

Latinos/Hispanics/Latinx[1] currently comprise the largest minority in the United States (U.S.), estimated at 57.5 million (data reflects July 1, 2015, to July 1, 2016; U.S. Census Bureau, 2017). In addition, the report *Fulfilling America's Future: Latinas in the U.S.*, 2015 (Gándara & The White House Initiative on Educational Excellence for Hispanics, 2015) states that "One in five women in the U.S. is a Latina" (p. 7). Latino/Hispanic/Latinx communities residing in the U.S. include people originating from twenty-two countries. Often connected through a love of the Spanish language, although not all Spanish speakers in the U.S. are Latino/Hispanic/Latinx, 35.8 million persons ages five years and older speak Spanish at home (Krogstad, Stepler, & Lopez, 2015). As such, Latinos have a significant impact on the United States' increasingly heterogeneous society.

It is also important to note the heterogeneity within Latino/Hispanic/Latinx communities. Write Javier and Camacho-Gingerich (2004): "In the United States 'Latino' and 'Hispanic' are terms frequently used to identify an individual whose place of origin, either by birth or inherited culture, is a Latin American country or Spain. Many have attempted to group such a diverse people under a single term or 'ethnic' category. Until recently many government agencies, educational and business institutions were using the term 'Hispanic' as a racial category. Some still do. They do not take into consideration the historical, geographical, racial, socio-economic, educational, linguistic, religious and other cultural factors that differentiate these groups of individuals not only from one country of origin to another but within the same country" (pp. 66–67).

DOMESTIC VIOLENCE

Domestic violence is prevalent across demographic variables that include race, ethnicity, social class, and sexual orientation (American Psychological Association, 2017). Data at the end of the twentieth century, reported in population reports, found that approximately one-third of women worldwide suffer from intimate partner violence (IPV) or are physically/sexually abused by a family member (Heise, Ellsberg, & Gottemoeller, 1999a, 1999b). In the United States, at the recent turn of the twenty-first century, a national sample showed that approximately one quarter of women reported experiencing an act of violence by an intimate partner during their lifetime that included rape, physical assault, and stalking (Tjaden & Thoennes, 2000a). Among women, 1.8 million reported being physically or sexually assaulted by current or former partners, and more than a million reported being stalked each year (Rennison & Planty, 2003; Tjaden & Thoennes, 2000b). These startling figures call for both professional attention and that of society as a whole.

With regard to the nature of the violent acts that women reported and the length of time over which they occurred, Murdaugh, Hunt, Sowel, and Santana (2004) reported that violent acts included pushing, grabbing, beating, punching, and marital rape. These authors found that three-quarters of women reported victimization during the past 12 months. Forty-three percent of respondents reported having experienced physical violence often during the past year and shared that they were harmed, on average, six times per year (Murdaugh et al., 2004). Almost one-fifth (17%) of the women in the Murdaugh et al. (2004) study reported having been abused for 10 years or more. Similarly, Carcedo and Sagot (2002) found that between 60 and 78% of all female homicides were committed by a partner, ex-partner, or male relative.

In more recent findings, the *National Intimate Partner and Sexual Violence Survey: 2010–2012 State Report*, published by the Division of Violence Prevention of the National Center for Injury and Prevention and Control, Centers for Disease Control and Prevention (Smith et al., 2017), outlined "key findings for combined years 2010–2012 (average annual estimates)" in its executive summary (p. 1). With regard to prevalence data related to violence reported by Latina/Hispanic women the report indicated that in the U.S.: "26.9% of Hispanic women . . . experienced some form of contact SV [e.g., sexual violence] during their lifetime"; "1 in 7 Hispanic (14.5%) women . . . experienced stalking at some point in their lives"; and "nationally, . . . 34.4% of Hispanic women . . . experienced contact SV, physical violence, and/or stalking by an intimate partner in their lifetime" (p. 3).

The purpose of this chapter is to explore domestic violence in Latino/Hispanic/Latinx communities within the context of reference group identities such as culture, ethnicity, social class, gender, and sexual orientation (American Psychological Association, 2017). Guzman (2001) reported that Latinos living in the United States suffer disproportionately from poverty and have lower levels of educational attainment in comparison to non-Latinos. While a lack of financial support is commonly identified as a domestic violence risk factor, after controlling socioeconomic variables such as education and income, studies have often found that IPV does not occur more frequently among Latinos than among non-Latino Whites or African Americans (Aldarondo, Kantor, & Jasinski, 1994; McFarlane, Parker, Soeken, Silva, & Reed, 1999; Sorenson & Telles, 1991; Straus, Gelles, & Smith, 1990; Tjaden & Thoennes, 2000b; Torres, 1991; Moracco, Hilton, Hodges, & Frasier, 2005). However, reports indicate that domestic violence tends to be reported more frequently in Latino/Hispanic/Latinx communities than others (Moracco, Hilton, Hodges, & Frasier, 2005). Further, Sorenson and Telles (1991) indicated that U.S.-born Latinos reported higher rates of IPV than Latinos who immigrated to the United States. Despite existing research that demonstrates the negative impact that domestic violence has among Latino/Hispanic/Latinx communities, as with other groups, we were surprised by the dearth of existing studies that address this critical topic. Our review of the status of research on domestic violence in Latino/Hispanic/Latinx communities from 2004–2017, conducted on September 17, 2017, using an advanced PsychINFO search of PsychARTICLESJournals using the focus option with mapping terms "Latinos/Latinas" and "domestic violence" identified a mere 47 scholarly works focused on this topic. Of these, four works were authored or edited books, 29 were journal articles, and 14 were dissertations. This chapter discusses existing research and implications for diverse models of practice and intervention. It concludes with a framework that presents a culturally relevant way to assess domestic violence situations in Latino/Hispanic/Latinx communities as well as a call to the profession to engage in research, teaching, and practice in this area.

CULTURAL CONCEPTIONS OF DOMESTIC VIOLENCE

As researchers examine how socioeconomic factors, cultural norms, immigration status, sexual orientation, and acculturation influence domestic violence, it appears that the very definition of the term varies among communities. For instance, many Latino/Hispanic/Latinx communities tend to include both partner and intergenerational violence in their definition, whereas non-Hispanic American couples often limit their definition to intimate partners only (Aldarondo, Kantor, & Jasinski, 2002; Bauer, Rodriguez, Quiroga, & Flores-Ortiz, 2000; Caetano, Cunradi, Clark, & Schafer, 2000; Gabler, Stern, & Miserandino, 1998; Kantor, Jasinski, & Aldarondo, 1994; McFarlane et al., 1999; Pan, Daley, Rivera, Williams, Lingle, & Reznik, 2006; Perilla, Bakeman, & Rorris, 1994; Rodriguez, 1999; West, Kandor, & Jasinski, 1998). The broader definition of domestic violence among Latino/Hispanic/Latinx communities may reflect a cultural approach that is more collectively focused as opposed to one that is individualistic in nature (Clauss-Ehlers, 2008; Vazquez & Clauss-Ehlers, 2005). Further, while mainstream American culture may view domestic violence in terms of physical, verbal, emotional, sexual, and spiritual abuse, Latino/Hispanic/Latinx communities may generally focus on physical violence (Pan et al., 2006).

Across communities, an avoidance of involving law enforcement results in a decreased prevalence rate. Bograd (1999) suggests that domestic violence is not a monolithic phenomenon, stating that "intersectionalities color the meaning and nature of domestic violence, how it is experienced by self and responded to by others, how personal and social consequences are represented, and how and whether escape and safety can be obtained" (p. 276). The idea here is that patterns of violence may vary from the more widely recognized physical abuse to its less visible forms. An understanding of the seriousness of violence can also differ based on personal perceptions as well as the influence of family and community members. Understanding domestic violence from a cultural framework proposes that sociocultural variables and structural inequalities (i.e., inequalities across race, gender, and social class) be understood in the context of the individual's experience.

Gender Roles

In Latino/Hispanic/Latinx communities, as in others, there may be differing cultural scripts for men and women. Among Latinos, understanding the cultural concept of machismo is vital to understanding distinctive traditional gender role expectations. Villereal and Cavazos (2005) note that machismo can be positive in the form of taking care of the family, showing valor among peers, working hard to support one's family, and taking pride in raising one's children. On the other side of the equation, negative aspects of machismo may be associated with violence toward women and other men, alcoholism, and having sexual partners other than one's wife. Related beliefs include a focus on male dominance, the value of family privacy, and the centrality of family unity. Such values may collectively contribute to Latinas' victimization or prevent them from leaving abusive partners (Bauer et al., 2000; Jasinski, 1998; Perilla et al., 1994).

Vandello and Cohen's (2003) research supports this contention. Their research explores the notion of "honor as a cultural syndrome" (Triandis, 1994, p. 997) or the extent to which cultures value honor in terms of loyalty and generosity, as well as in terms of the man's reputation as being tough and a provider. Vandello and Cohen (2003) describe how the role for women in cultures of honor focuses on their not engaging in behaviors that might decrease the family's honor (e.g., adultery). Culture of honor refers to those cultures where interpersonal relationships are organized around status, precedence, and reputation. Cultures of honor tend to value generosity, hospitality, and loyalty, with different honor norms applied for males and females. In many Latino/Hispanic/Latinx cultures, for instance, traditional gender roles and strong familism (i.e., focus and commitment to family) characterize interpersonal and familial relationships. Males may play a dominant role and be expected to be tough and work hard to support their families. For females, behaviors may be seen as vital to determining the family's reputation. Women in cultures of honor may be socialized to be nurturing and submissive with the thought that they are required to keep their virginity before marriage and maintain silence about violence that occurs within the household (Vandello & Cohen, 2003, p. 998).

Vandello and Cohen (2003) explore three hypotheses: "(a) female infidelity will cause greater damage to a male's reputation, (b) this reputation can be partially restored through the use of violence, and (c) women are more often expected to remain loyal in the face of such violence" (p. 997). Their study included a sample of Brazilian and U.S. students who completed questionnaires that presented scenarios involving married couples. In the first scenario, the wife was depicted either as being unfaithful by having an affair that neighbors were aware of or as being faithful. In the second scenario, the husband's response to his wife having an affair was to either yell at her, yell and hit her, do nothing, or ask for a divorce. Study participants rated the husband based on two dimensions of honor: "trustworthiness or good character (trustworthy/untrustworthy, reliable/unreliable, selfish/unselfish, reasonable/unreasonable, good person/bad person, smart/dumb) and strength or manliness (masculine/feminine, strong/weak, cowardly/courageous, manly/not manly, timid/self-confident, macho/not macho, tough/wimpy, competent/incompetent, submissive/not submissive)" (Vandello & Cohen, 2003, pp. 1000–1001). Study findings supported the culture of honor interpretation in that culture influenced perceptions about the man who hit his wife upon learning about her affair. The authors conclude: "A man was seen as less honorable (trustworthy, manly) if his wife had an affair. . . . However, this was particularly the case for the culture of honor, where the woman's infidelity seemed to reflect more negatively upon the man" (Vandello & Cohen, 2003, p. 1002).

Within this belief system, Latinas may be generally socialized to be nurturing and submissive, while men may be encouraged to play a dominant role. Thus men and women have distinct ways to maintain honor. *Marianismo* is the cultural counterpart to machismo for Latinas that refers to women's cultural and gender roles whereby they sacrifice their own needs and desires, putting those of family before their own (Gil & Vazquez, 1996; Kessler, McGonagle, & Zhao, 1994; Vazquez & Clauss-Ehlers, 2005). As described by Gil and Vazquez (1996), key components of *marianismo* include self-sacrifice, submissiveness to men, and being passive. While *marianismo* provides women with a valued role within their cultural context, this position is devalued through a domestic violence experience where the woman suffers partner abuse.

Cultural scripts of *machismo* and *marianismo* can be further understood in the context of research findings about views of domestic violence among Latinos and Latinas (Goddard & Wierzbicka, 2004). For instance, in their study with primarily immigrant participants, Moracco et al. (2005) found that both men and women believed it was wrong for a man to hit his partner even if he was angry; yet when it came to women hitting men when they were angry, men had a stronger objection than the women. This finding is consistent with the Pan et al. (2006) study conducted by staff involved with the Ahimsa for Safe Families Project. This project provided support for immigrant and refugee families affected by domestic violence in San Diego. Much of their work included outreach with Latino, Somali, and Vietnamese communities. Key issues identified by Pan et al. (2006) focused on gender equity issues (e.g., men could have more than one woman and women should accept this); economic stress; and immigration status (e.g., immigration status and threat of deportation being used as a way to control the women). Taken together, these studies have implications for rigid sex role differentiation.

On the other hand, acculturation processes also allow us to consider how traditional gender roles might support greater gender equity (Hancock & Siu, 2009). For instance, Hancock and Siu (2009) found an increased awareness among Latinos that women's contribution to the family in the domestic realm (e.g., cooking and cleaning) is vital and respectful. Other research indicates that acculturation and a bicultural experience have led to women's increased employment outside the home as their families adjust to life in the United States (Vazquez & Gil, 2006; Vazquez & Clauss-Ehlers, 2005).

Issues of intimate partner violence (IPV) are further complicated for diverse and multifaceted Latina LGBTQ+ communities because of stressors created by homophobia and heterosexism. Sexual minority stress (SMS) includes distal experiences of violence, harassment, and discrimination, and proximal stressors related to concealment of sexual identity and negative feelings about one's self as a sexual minority individual (Meyer, 2003).

CAUSES

Cultural Scripts

An understanding of how cultural scripts can influence domestic violence provides a base from which to examine causative factors (Goddard & Wierzbicka, 2004). The literature indicates that Latino men and women hold different perceptions about the causes of IPV (Moracco et al., 2005). Latino men rated a lack of understanding or communication between couples as the primary reason for IPV, followed by jealousy, substance use, and male control (i.e., the male partner controlling the female partner; Moracco et al., 2005). In contrast, Latinas identified alcohol and drugs as the primary cause of domestic violence, followed by a lack of understanding or communication, male control, and jealousy (Moracco et al., 2005).

In another study, Murdaugh et al. (2004) found that Latinas reported jealousy and possessiveness, alcohol and drug use, as well as worrying about money and employment as top causes for abuse. Jealousy arising from infidelity or suspected adultery was a factor in IPV within Latino/Hispanic/Latinx communities. Male control or possessiveness, as expected in traditional gender roles, was another contributing factor to domestic violence among Latino/Hispanic/Latinx communities (Moracco et al., 2005; Sokoloff & Dupont, 2005). Heise and Ellsberg (2001) noted that in many cultures, violence against women is often justified when women do not follow traditional gender roles or norms.

Vandello and Cohen (2003) regard "honor" as having a meaning other than virtue and being connected to status, precedence, and reputation. As described above, these authors contend that several cultures are recognized as "cultures of honor," Latino/Hispanic/Latinx cultures being among them. Infidelity in many cultures is stigmatized and discouraged around the world. However, in a culture of honor, such as in Latino communities, even the suspected adultery of the woman is believed to harm her male partner. The potential damage to reputation that can come from the woman's infidelity may provide an eventual rationale for the husband's choice to use physical violence (Vandello & Cohen, 2003).

Immigration Status

Immigration status is another significant stressor that puts Latinas at risk for domestic violence (Perilla et al., 1994). Here the research contends that cultural factors are intertwined with structural inequities. For instance, among immigrant families, substantial stress combined with unemployment and economic hardship have been found to contribute to domestic violence situations within Latino/Hispanic/Latinx communities (Cunradi, Caetano, & Schafer, 2002). Immigrant women without the family support and social networks they had in their countries of origin may largely depend upon their abusive partners for economic support (Gorton & Van Hightower, 1999). Although aware of it being illegal for their partners to beat them, fear of deportation may prevent Latinas from seeking out support from law enforcement and human service agencies. Research has also indicated that many undocumented immigrant women fear involving authorities such as the police due to experiences in their home countries (e.g., if they were subject to or feared political reprisal) or racism experienced in the United States (Bauer et al., 2000; Clauss-Ehlers, Acosta, & Weist, 2004; McFarlane et al., 1999).

Perceptions of Seriousness

Research indicates that Latino men and women differ in whether they perceived domestic violence as a problem. Moracco et al. (2005) interviewed 100 recent Latino immigrants in a rural North Carolina county, investigating knowledge and attitudes about intimate partner violence. This study found that men and women agreed that domestic violence had a long-term detrimental impact on children (Moracco et al., 2005). However, results suggested that male participants tended to believe that the children were often unaware the violent incidents had occurred, while the women in the study confirmed that their children knew what was going on in the household. These researchers concluded that this distinction was partially due to differing parental roles where mothers serve as primary caregivers, and fathers have respectively less direct contact with their children. In addition, children who witness a parent or close relative experience domestic violence receive a confusing message about relationships and intimacy. Exposure to domestic violence may remain with children with regard to their own gender-role expectations as well as their approach to relationships during childhood and later in life (Moracco et al., 2005).

Stressors Created by Homophobia and Heterosexism

Issues of IPV are further complicated for diverse and multifaceted Latina LGBTQ+ communities because of stressors created by homophobia and heterosexism. Sexual minority stress (SMS) includes distal experiences of violence, harassment, and discrimination, and proximal stressors related to concealment of sexual identity and negative feelings about one's self as a sexual minority individual (Meyer, 2003). LGBTQ+ people may face barriers to seeking help that are unique to their sexual orientation and gender identity. These include:

- "Legal definitions of domestic violence that exclude same-sex couples
- Dangers of 'outing' oneself when seeking help and the risk of rejection and isolation from family, friends, and society
- The lack of, or survivors not knowing about, LGBT-specific or LGBT-friendly assistance resources
- Potential homophobia from staff of service providers or from non-LGBT survivors of IPV and IPSA with whom they may interact
- Low levels of confidence in the sensitivity and effectiveness of law enforcement officials and courts for LGBT people" (Brown & Herman, 2015, p. 3)

Lesbians of color also face two types of pressure that may be serious stressors in their lives. The first is from their cultural and ethnic norms, for example, if the internalized cultural norm for "happiness" is marriage to a man then a Latina lesbian must negotiate what it means not to meet that ideal. The second is the batterers' use of cultural/racial identity as a means of manipulation. If a Latina lesbian is experiencing IPV, her partner may use her past experiences of racism, internalized homophobia, and societal stereotypes to control her and maintain her fear. For example, if the abusive partner uses the societal stereotype that all Latino/Hispanic/Latinx are undocumented, the Latina may believe she has no rights—even if she is in the United States legally (Casa de Esperanza, 2008). Latinas may also experience discriminatory treatment from their Latino/Hispanic/Latinx communities and families, particularly when they are trying to "come out" and be open about their sexuality, or when engaging in forms of social and political organizing.

Application of a Cross-Cultural Perspective

An examination and application of a cross-cultural perspective to domestic violence provides a foundation from which to compare and contrast existing models in the domestic violence treatment literature. To this end, the following paragraphs discuss Duluth/feminist, and environmental/cultural/ecological models. This discussion is followed by a clinical case that illustrates relevant cultural and treatment approaches when working with a Latino/Hispanic/Latinx family experiencing domestic violence. We conclude with a professional call to action that proposes a comprehensive research, training, and practice agenda to increase responsiveness to domestic violence within Latino/Hispanic/Latinx communities.

DULUTH MODEL/FEMINIST MODELS

Historically, much of the domestic violence treatment literature has been grounded in a Western middle-class perspective that has been universally applied to all populations (Perrilla, Lavizzo, & Ibañez, 2007). A common theoretical foundation for these treatment programs has been the Duluth model that is based upon feminist theory and posits domestic violence as a function of patriarchal structure where men exert control over women (Pence & Paymar, 1993; Wray, Hoyt, & Gerstle, 2013). More specifically, programs based on the Duluth model view battering "as a pattern of actions used to intentionally control or dominate an intimate partner" and will actively work to "change societal conditions that support men's use of tactics of power and control over women" (Domestic Abuse Prevention Programs, n.d.).

Perilla et al. (2007) argue that the conceptualizations of domestic violence proposed by models like the Duluth model are not only ineffectual because they do not account for the norms and values of everyone involved, but also that they may actually contribute to stress and potentially create a re-victimization situation for Latinas experiencing domestic violence as well as for their children. The goal of dividing the family and making the woman equal to the man may not necessarily be therapeutic or productive to Latino/Hispanic/Latinx families who may see this as contrary to their own values. This has generated reluctance among some Latinas to seek help from mainstream domestic violence organizations because of the programmatic emphasis on separating women from their husbands and promoting living independently (Lown & Vega, 2003; Menjivar & Salcedo, 2002; Murdaugh, Rivera, Williams, Lingle, & Reznik, 2004; Yoshioka & Choi, 2005).

Such strong cultural and familial values can potentially be pathologized within these models if the entire context is not considered and there is an overinvestment in individualism. The *National Intimate Partner and Sexual Violence Survey: 2010–2012 State Report* (Smith et al., 2017) addresses the need for culturally adaptive domestic violence prevention efforts among diverse groups. The report states: "Sexual and intimate partner violence prevention programming may differ for different audiences, and should be culturally relevant and tailored to specific groups and evaluated within those groups. For example, there may need to be specific, culturally informed prevention program development and implementation for historically marginalized groups, such as racial/ethnic minorities, individuals who are lesbian, gay, bisexual, transgender, or questioning (LGBTQ), individuals with disabilities, and other marginalized groups" (Smith et al., 2017, p. 204).

COMMUNITY-BASED INTERVENTION MODELS IN WORK WITH DOMESTIC VIOLENCE

More recent literature looks to contextualize domestic violence within a social-emotional-political context to understand the many variables that have an impact on the behaviors of those involved. This has been described as a social structural (Hancock & Ames, 2008; Sokoloff & Dupont, 2005) and ecological approach to domestic violence (Ramirez Hernandez, 2002). Stressors associated with domestic violence that reside in the social, political, and economic environments of low-income, newly arrived immigrants suggest the utility of environmental interventions (Hancock & Ames, 2008). Sokoloff and Dupont (2005) argue that factors such as age, employment status, residence, poverty, social embeddedness, and isolation combine to explain rates of abuse more than race or culture. They also describe the importance of not confusing patriarchy with culture but emphasize looking at how patriarchy operates differently in different cultures.

Perilla et al. (2007) view domestic violence as a violation of fundamental human rights that needs to be approached from a societal perspective. There is support that culturally relevant practice with immigrant populations requires both community-based and individually oriented interventions (Budde & Schene, 2004; Yoshioka, Gilbert, El-Bassel, & Baig-Amin, 2003).

The following presents several community-based intervention models for working with domestic violence within a Latino/Hispanic/Latinx context, including the role of the church, and opportunities for partnerships. This section is followed by a presentation of a clinical case composite (i.e., details reflect a combination of case experiences and also hypothetical information) that presents key issues highlighted throughout the chapter.

Many authors emphasize the need for ongoing community dialogue to engage, understand, and empower Latinos receiving services (Bonilla, Morrison, Norsigian, & Rosero, 2012; Cervantes & Cervantes, 1993; Pan, Daley, Rivera, Williams, Lingle, & Reznik, 2006; Perilla et al., 2007). Hancock and Ames aim to "build on Latino cultural and familial strengths to protect Latinas from abuse and help their partners stop the abuse" (2008, p. 625). This may present particular challenges for Latinos in rural areas that might have difficulty navigating the distance from service locations and who may experience an overall sense of isolation.

Models that Help the Victims

Caminar Latino (Perilla et al., 2007; Perilla et al., 2012) offers group treatments in separate programs for Latinos/Latinas and children whose home lives are affected by domestic violence. The model is "an integration of an ecological human rights framework, U.S. feminist therapy, theory from Latino scholars and the voices of participants" (Perilla et al., 2012, p. 102). Authors reference the work of liberation psychology's Martín-Baró (1994) and Freire (1997, 1978) as the foundational theorists of their perspectives.

The *Caminar Latino* perspective challenges the service provider to engage in an ongoing dialogue with the community being served so that members can develop a critical awareness of their situation and learn how to write their own histories. There is a reciprocal learning process between community members and service providers that enriches both parties and meaningfully informs the treatment model that evolves from the interaction. Groups for women who have been victims are facilitated by women advocates who are considered participants and share equally as do other group members. The sharing of experiences and mutual support create the intervention. Additionally, *Caminar Latino* has a *Men's Program* (see below) and a number of group programs for the children of different ages from homes affected by domestic violence.

Bonilla et al. (2012) described another program where they conduct health education workshops with Latina immigrants based on participatory education and critical consciousness. Participants share their experiences, discuss the social and political structures that have an impact on the information they receive, and develop a body of knowledge that is directly relevant and useful for their lives.

Models that Treat the Batterers

Saez-Betancourt, Lam, and Nguyen (2008) affirm the benefits of participation in a batterers' program for Latino immigrant batterers. They also emphasize the need for community education about existing domestic violence services available to the Latino/Hispanic/Latinx community. Throughout, they discuss the importance of considering cultural norms and gender role expectations when developing treatment programs geared toward working with perpetrators of domestic violence.

In the *Caminar Latino Men's Program*, intervention is specifically geared to work with men who have battered their partners. The *Caminar Latino Men's Program* is a 24-week, state-licensed group that uses a two-level format. The first level is a 10-week curriculum that provides basic information about domestic violence in a structured format. Men can move to the next level if they have not been violent during this time and pass an oral test on the material. The second level allows men to explore the material in more depth (Perilla et al., 2007).

Hancock and Siu (2009) propose a program for immigrant men who have engaged in domestic violence behaviors that aims to "stop the abuse, preserve partner relationships and strengthen family life" (p. 209). Their program specifically does not intend to equalize power between male and female partners but seeks to help the men change their attitudes and attain skills for respectful relationships. They found that a treatment model that directly challenged the newly arrived immigrant man's view of masculinity (that is, did not incorporate a view of self as family leader and authority figure) interfered with the development of a therapeutic alliance. Rather, their view was to help the men gain the attitudes and relationship skills needed for respectful and compassionate family leadership.

The *Centro de Capacitación para Erradicar la Violencia Intrafamiliar Masculina* (CECEVIM—*Training Center to Eradicate Masculine Intrafamily Violence*; See http://www.cecevim.org) is a program that is theoretically based on feminist gender analysis, ecology, and ancient native spiritual concepts (Ramírez Hernandez, 2002). CECEVIM is divided into four phases that consist of 17 two-hour sessions each. Program objectives are for Latino men who have been perpetrators of domestic violence to: (1) learn how and why they are violent in the home and develop strategies to stop being abusive; and (2) learn how to create "intimate, cooperative, supportive, equal, democratic, and nonviolent relationships" (Ramírez Hernandez, 2002, pp. 12–17). CECEVIM attempts to facilitate participants' in-depth discussion about the roots of violence against women and provides strategies to change both the patriarchal culture and patriarchal masculine identities.

Considerations for Interventions with Latina LGBTQ+ Communities

Lewis, Mason, Winstead, and Kelley (2017) suggest that addressing external and internal minority stressors and relationship issues in lesbians' individual and couple's counseling may be useful. As with heterosexual couples, identification and treatment of alcohol use and related problems should play a significant role in addressing problems of relationship violence among lesbian women. Also, helping lesbian women appreciate the connections between stressors, anger, and IPV may assist them in breaking these links and/or developing mechanisms to cope with stressors in less destructive ways.

Service providers are encouraged to implement cultural competency trainings that actively confront and educate providers around not only the unique life experiences of Latina LGBTQ+ women, but also on the pervasive attitudes of racism, sexism, biphobia, transphobia, and homophobia/heterosexism. Service providers can develop programs that both take seriously and sustain a sense of wellness among Latina LGBTQ+ women (*Amigas Latinas*).

Based on their review of the IPV literature related to the experiences of self-identified lesbians in same-sex couples, Badenes-Ribera, Bonilla-Campos, Frias-Navarro, Pons-Salvador, and Moterde-i-Bort (2016) suggest developing programs that: (1) account for the specific characteristics of abuse in sexual minority couples; (2) teach strategies for coping with discrimination and stress experienced in a heterosexist society; (3) train providers not serving LGBTQ+ populations about same-sex and sexual minority IPV; and (4) increase knowledge about same-sex couple abuse aimed at the LGBTQ+ community itself.

Mixed Interventions

Wray et al. (2013) describe a pilot intervention for IPV among mutually violent couples that offers a dyadic curriculum in equivalent but separate forms for each partner. Participants attended 12 closed, psycho-educational men's and women's groups based on cognitive behavioral principles with dyadic intervention components. Participant self-reports of their own and their partner's behavior at the end of treatment indicated decreased IPV incidents.

Working with Church Leaders

Involving community organizations to address domestic violence in Latino/Hispanic/Latinx communities is critical. The church is one such organization. The church can be a particularly relevant resource to address domestic violence in rural areas where a lack of Spanish-speaking services may result in Latino clergy serving multiple functions such as addressing mental health, financial, and career needs (Behnke, Ames, & Hancock, 2012). Evidence suggests abuse rates for immigrant Latinas in rural areas may be significantly higher than national prevalence rates, even though much of the research has involved urban populations (Murdaugh, Hunt, Sowell, & Santana, 2004).

Hancock and Ames (2008) propose a three-part model that utilizes lay ministers to "build on Latino cultural and familial strengths to protect Latinas from abuse and help their partners stop the abuse" (p. 625). The Hancock and Ames (2008) model is more appropriate for mild and moderate abusers. Mild and moderate abuse is defined as "a pattern of failed interactional, recursive sequences driven by thoughts and feelings translated into conflict tactics (behaviors) that may be initiated by either partner simultaneously or at different points in time to resolve differences" (Horwitz, Santiago, Pearson, & LaRussa-Trott, 2009, p. 254). The model assumes that: (a) church leaders have a professional and ethical obligation not to sacrifice the health and emotional well-being of abused women to preserve family units; (b) wives have the right to be protected from physical and emotional abuse; and (c) male perpetrators of abuse are responsible for stopping the violence.

The first part of the model helps church leaders identify material (e.g., food banks, emergency financial assistance, clothing), social (e.g., assistance to family members, linkages to domestic violence services), and educational (via sermons, family life, parenting programs) supports to aid Latino couples at risk of/or experiencing domestic violence. The second part of the model assesses the severity of the abuse, evaluating the abuser's potential for change and making appropriate referrals. In the third part of the program, church leaders offer constructive counseling or advice to help deal with domestic violence situations.

THALIA: DOMESTIC ISOLATION AS A FORM OF DOMESTIC VIOLENCE

The following case study explores the experience of a Latina who immigrated to the United States and was confronted with a domestic violence situation. It illustrates several of the cultural/community issues presented throughout the chapter. The case is a composite and hypothetical, integrating the lived experiences of several individuals while also adding hypothetical information into the case presentation. Identifying information has been changed or omitted to protect confidentiality. An analysis of the case follows that provides an integration of key concepts and theoretical approaches, as well as the first author's development of a new model to address domestic violence issues within a Latino/Hispanic/Latinx context. The case presentation and theoretical application utilizes the terms clinician, service provider, and professional interchangeably given the range of professionals that might implement the proposed model in clinical work.

Thalia* was a 26-year-old Guatemalan woman who attended a parenting workshop given by the first author. The workshop, delivered in Spanish and English, was held at a community center. Its focus was positive discipline, presenting ways that parents could set age-appropriate limits with their children, promote personal growth, and engage in positive modeling. Participants learned of the program through local postings.

Participants spent an hour talking about ways to engage in authoritative rather than authoritarian discipline styles with their children (Darling & Steinberg, 1993). They were interested in taking a supportive rather than a punitive approach to child rearing. Many of the participants, men and women who ranged in age from their 20s through their 60s, shared how their own parents had been physically abusive with them, and how they often witnessed their mothers being abused by their fathers. Participants talked about how they wanted something different for their children and grandchildren.

As the group came to a close, participants began to leave, and organizers started to clean up the meeting space. It was at this time that Thalia approached the presenter. Initially hesitant to talk, the presenter was struck by the fact that Thalia continued to look behind her as she spoke. She talked quietly, sharing that her boyfriend and the father of her 4-year-old daughter, was just outside the building. Thalia explained how her boyfriend followed her everywhere and didn't like her leaving the house. At times he monitored her activities so intensely that she didn't leave her home for weeks.

Thalia heard about the workshop through a friend and was desperate to learn more about potential options. She was not in the United States legally, so deportation was a constant fear. She shared that her boyfriend was a U.S. citizen and often threatened to contact immigration if she tried to leave the household or disobey him. Even more frightening than potential deportation was the fear of a long-term separation from her daughter, who was born in the United States, should her partner report her to the authorities. After hastily but quietly sharing this information, Thalia said she needed to go. She asked how to contact the presenter in the future, but was adamant about leaving before her partner came to find her, and possibly learn about her participation and conversation.

AN INTRODUCTION AND APPLICATION OF ENVIRONMENTAL, CULTURAL, AND ECOLOGICAL MAPPING

An application of environmental, cultural, and ecological approaches helps us understand Thalia's experience. Figure 9.1 illustrates what the first author calls *environmental, cultural, and ecological mapping* (ECEM) to understand Thalia's experience of domestic violence within a cultural framework. The main tenet of this approach is to examine domestic violence within a social-political context to fully understand the many factors that have an impact on the individual. The first author identifies 6 ECEM components that capture individual and/or familial experience: *ecological factors embedded in program implementation*; *social/emotional stressors*; *political stressors*; *personal strength/resilience*; *point of contact with the human service provider*; and *ecological factors in the provision of future support*. While this is an initial conceptualization of the ECEM approach and no empirical evidence of the model has been conducted as of yet, it is thought that the model's application can be effectively used with Latino/Hispanic/Latinx communities as it incorporates cultural values (e.g., language of service delivery), political histories, immigration experiences, and resilience, while also examining the interplay of these factors in the relationship with human service providers and their organizations. Future investigations that explore the application of the ECEM approach with Latino/Hispanic/Latinx communities are encouraged.

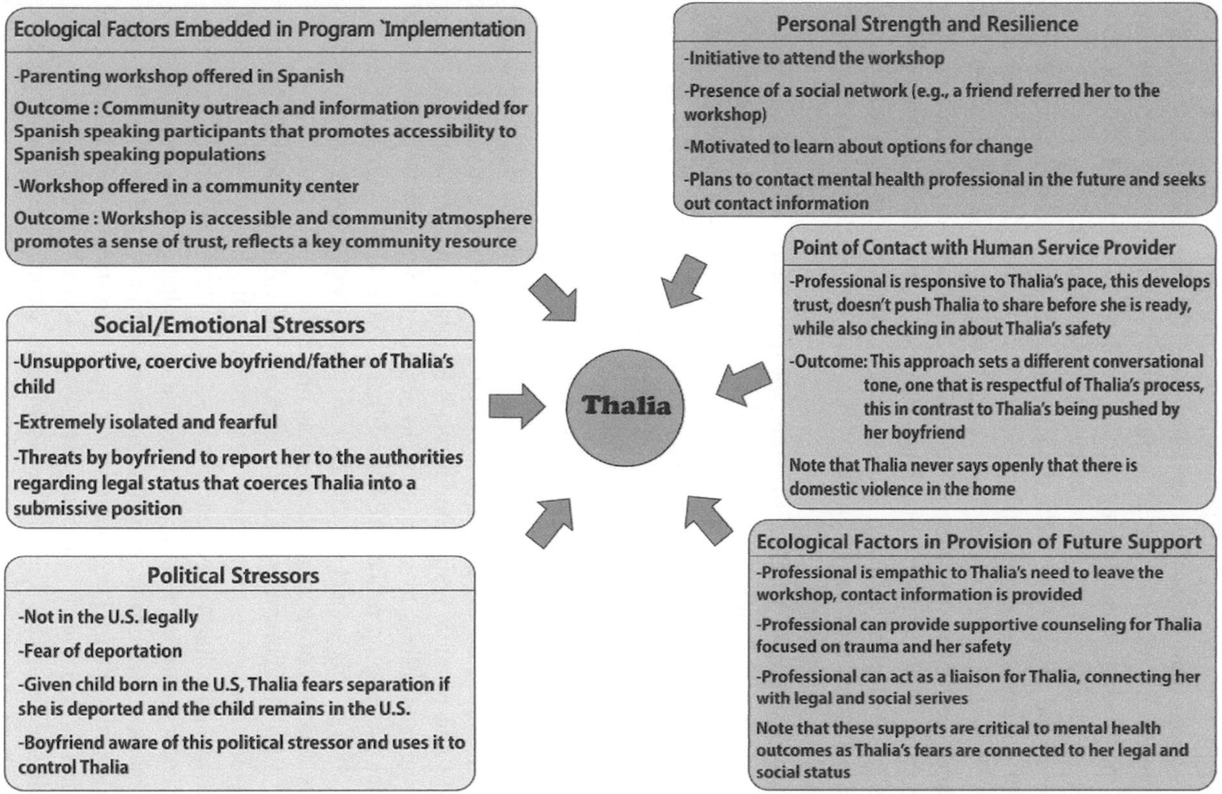

Figure 9.1. Environmental, Cultural, and Ecological Mapping to Understand the Experience of Domestic Violence within a Latino/Hispanic/Latinx Context. Created by the authors

In the first domain, *ecological factors embedded in program implementation*, the clinician identifies how services are responsive to the cultural needs of the individual/family and/or community being served. At the same time, mapping ecological program factors helps clinicians identify the ways in which services can be adapted to better meet the needs of the community being served. Examples of the ecological factors embedded in the workshop Thalia attended included it being offered in Spanish, delivered in a community setting, and involving participants across generations.

The second component of the model examines *social/emotional stressors* from an environmental/cultural/ecological perspective. Thalia's experience of domestic violence is understood in the context of a situation where her boyfriend threatens to reveal her illegal status to authorities, thus keeping her in a position of being coerced by him. The social/emotional stressors center on Thalia's fear of deportation should her boyfriend report her illegal status and the potential separation from her child. This fear keeps Thalia trapped in an abusive relationship.

An examination of *political stressors*, the third factor, allows clinicians to consider how legal factors and political situations influence domestic violence and help seeking behaviors. For instance, Thalia's experience of domestic violence is fueled by the understandable fear that if she is deported, she will be separated from her daughter who was born in the United States. Again, this reality enhances her partner's ability to control and manipulate the situation (Clauss-Ehlers & Akinsulure-Smith, 2013).

Identifying social and political stressors is followed by an examination of *personal strength and resilience*, the fourth factor in the model. A strength-based perspective allows the clinician to consider interventions that build on strengths and promote resilience. Thalia's insight about her situation, desire to change, and efforts to seek out help are all strengths that can positively influence the helping process (Clauss-Ehlers, 2008; Clauss-Ehlers, Yang, & Chen, 2006). This aspect of the ECEM encourages clinicians to identify client resources that facilitate the helping process.

The fifth component considers the extent to which the *point of contact with the human service provider* is responsive to the client's environmental, ecological, and cultural experience. In work with Thalia and others in domestic violence situations, it is imperative that the helping professional engages the client in a supportive, empathic manner that promotes rapport between counselor and client. The reader will note, for instance, that Thalia never fully reveals a domestic violence experience. Rather, it is implied by the dynamic she describes. The professional in this situation must be responsive to Thalia's pace, not pushing her to disclose too soon (thus creating a respectful, collaborative relationship dynamic in contrast to the one she has with her partner), while also letting Thalia know that the clinician is committed to her safety.

It is from this empathic base, along with an acknowledgment of social and political stressors, and individual and familial strengths, that the sixth component of the model emerges: consideration of *ecological factors in the provision of future support*. Future support does not simply involve individual counseling; it also addresses social and political stressors, and seeks connections with social and legal services. Determinations about the nature of these supports can be made in part by examining dynamics within the relationship affected by domestic violence and whether they are exacerbated by political and social factors. Understanding domestic violence within an ecological context can help the service provider connect Thalia with relevant services.

CONCLUSION: A CALL TO THE PROFESSION

It warrants repeating that our review of the literature identified 47 publications through an advanced PsychINFO, PsychARTICLESJournals focused search using terms "Latino/Latina" and "domestic violence" for years 2004–2017 (Please note that these were the mapping terms that the search listed through the advanced search mechanism). That only 47 works were identified over a 13-year span indicates a lack of research in this area and presents an important call to the profession to fill this gap. We urge the helping professions to take a comprehensive approach in response to the experience of domestic violence in Latino/Hispanic/Latinx communities that incorporates research, training, and practice. Figure 9.2 provides a visual depiction of what this approach looks like across the helping professions.

Our comprehensive approach addresses the fact that there can be many points of access to support services for individuals who experience domestic violence. For Thalia, access to support occurred in a community setting with a mental health professional. For others, access to support may occur through interactions with nurses in hospital settings, doctors in emergency rooms, clergy in religious institutions, school personnel, social service providers, and community outreach workers, to name a few.

Our call to the human service professions involves a tripartite model that includes research, training, and practice. As spelled out in figure 9.2, our research agenda encourages researchers to conduct empirical studies that examine the impact of domestic violence within Latino/Hispanic/Latinx communities through an exploration of the following variables: correlates of domestic violence, helping seeking behaviors, barriers to support, gender roles, impact of immigration, efficacy of domestic violence intervention programs, and efficacy of community supports to address domestic violence. It is our hope that exploration in these areas can facilitate the beginnings of a comprehensive national research agenda that fills the current gap in knowledge.

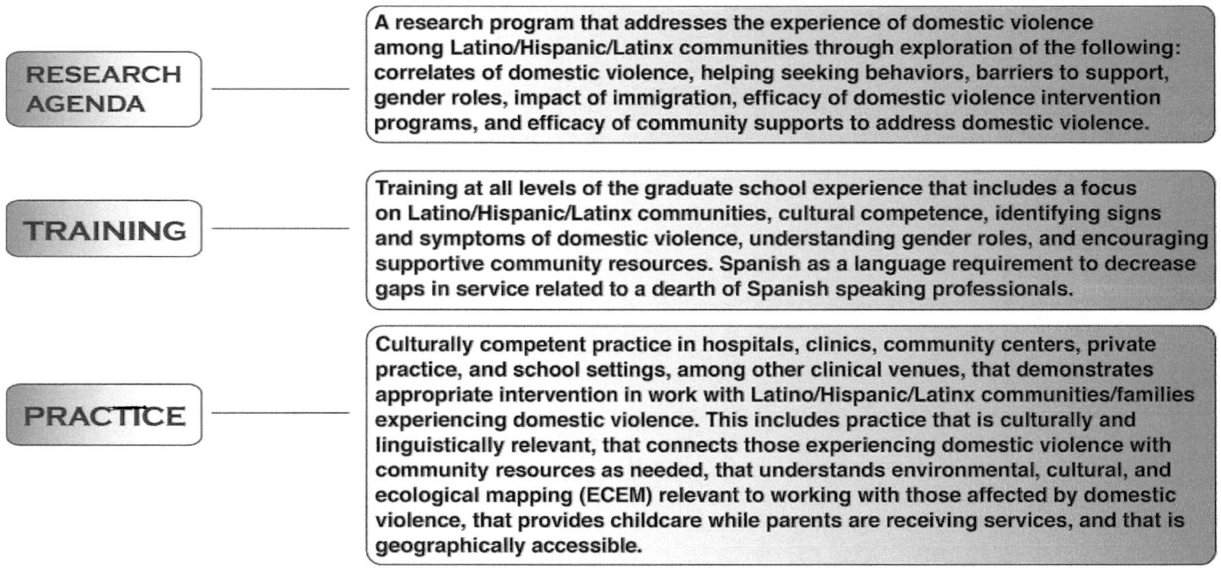

Figure 9.2. A Call to the Profession: Addressing the Need for Research, Training, and Practice in Domestic Violence Awareness and Intervention among Latino/Hispanic/Latinx Communities. Created by the authors

The importance of a comprehensive research agenda is further underscored by the fact that having an empirical base provides insight into effective training and practice. Without process and outcome research that explores the efficacy of specific interventions geared to address domestic violence in Latino/Hispanic/Latinx communities, the provision of evidence-based services is limited.

Like the call for research, the training component of the agenda is presented broadly—referring to training across human service programs. As mentioned in figure 9.2, training can occur at all levels of the graduate school experience (e.g., master's and doctoral levels) and includes a focus on Latino/Hispanic/Latinx communities, cultural competence, identifying signs and symptoms of domestic violence, understanding gender roles, and integrating supportive community resources. Making Spanish as a second language a graduate school requirement is one strategy that will promote the training of bilingual clinicians and promote an increase in Spanish-speaking human service professionals.

Practice is the final component of the agenda. Clinical practice builds on training and seeks to incorporate the development of an evidence base. Figure 9.2 highlights how practice aims to be culturally and linguistically relevant, to connect those experiencing domestic violence with community resources as needed, to incorporate ECEM in work with those affected by domestic violence, to provide childcare while parents receive services, and to promote geographic accessibility.

In sum, given the experience of domestic violence among Latino/Hispanic/Latinx communities, along with the need for linguistically and culturally relevant intervention, we encourage the human services professions to explore a tripartite research, teaching, and training agenda that builds on ECEM.

DISCUSSION QUESTIONS

1. What implication does the culture of honor concept have for gender roles in Latino/Hispanic/Latinx communities? How do these implications influence the potential for domestic violence?
2. What are the major causes of domestic violence in Latino/Hispanic/Latinx communities?
3. What are some of the stressors that Latinas who identify as LGBTQ+ may confront as they seek support to help them deal with domestic violence?
4. Discuss gender role–based challenges that treatment programs need to confront as they address domestic violence among Latinos/Latinas. How can these challenges have an impact on treatment?

5. What are the advantages of contextualizing domestic violence among Latino/Hispanic/Latinx individuals within a broader cultural and societal context?
6. How can the application of Environmental, Cultural, and Ecological Mapping inform one's approach to case conceptualization, intervention, and treatment?
7. How would you incorporate notions of personal strength and resilience in clinical work with Latinas who have experienced domestic violence?

*Name has been changed to protect confidentiality.

Note: Correspondence regarding this article should be sent to Caroline S. Clauss-Ehlers, PhD, Graduate School of Education, Rutgers, The State University of New Jersey, 10 Seminary Place, New Brunswick, NJ 08901, caroline.clauss-ehlers@gse.rutgers.edu.

NOTE

1. The term Latinos/Hispanics/Latinx is used to capture the range of geographical, sociohistorical, political, and intersectionality variables that span the group and is used to describe the community. However, we have also attempted to use the original terms of choice by authors of cited works.

REFERENCES

Aldarondo, E., Kantor, G. K., & Jasinski, J. L. (2002). A risk marker analysis of wife assault in Latino families. *Violence Against Women, 8*, 429–454.

American Psychological Association (2017). *Multicultural guidelines: An ecological approach to context, identity, and intersectionality, 2017.* Retrieved from: http://www.apa.org/about/policy/multicultural-guidelines.pdf.

Amigas Latinas (2006). *Latina portrait: Latina queer women in Chicago.* www.amigaslatinas.org.

Badenes-Ribera, L., Bonilla-Campos, A., Frias-Navarro, D., Pons-Salvador, G., & Monterde-i-Bort, H. (2016). Intimate partner violence in self-identified lesbians: A systematic review of its prevalence and correlates. *Trauma, Violence, & Abuse, 17*(3) 284–297.

Bauer, H. M., Rodriguez, M. A., Quiroga, S. S., & Flores-Ortiz, Y. G. (2000). Barriers to health care for abused Latina and Asian immigrant women. *Journal of Health Care for the Poor and Underserved, 11*, 33–44.

Behnke, A. O., Ames, N., & Hancock, T. U. (2012). What would they do? Latino church leaders and domestic violence. *Journal of Interpersonal Violence*, *27*(7), 1259–1275.

Bograd, M. (1999). Strengthening domestic violence theories: Intersections of race, class, sexual orientation, and gender. *Journal of Marital and Family Therapy, 25*, 275–289.

Bonilla, Z. E., Morrison, S. D., Norsigian, J., & Rosero, E. (2012). Reaching Latinas with Our Bodies, Ourselves and the Guía de Capacitación para Promotoras de Salud: Health education for social change. *Journal of Midwifery Women's Health, 57*, 178–183.

Brown, N. T., & Herman, J. L. (2015). *Intimate partner violence and sexual abuse among LGBT people: A review of existing literature*. Report of the Williams Institute.

Budde, S., & Schene, P. (2004). Informal social support interventions and their role in violence prevention. *Journal of Interpersonal Violence, 19*, 341–355.

Caetano, R., Cunradi, C. B., Clark, C. L., & Schafer, J. (2000). Intimate partner violence and drinking patterns among White, Black, and Hispanic couples in the U.S. *Journal of Substance Abuse, 11*, 123–138.

Carcedo, A., & Sagot, M. (2002). Medicina Legal de Costa Rica. *Femicidio in Costa Rica: balance mortal, 19*(1), 5–16.

Casa de Esperanza (2008). *A tool for reflection: The realities and internalized oppression faced by lesbians of color*. www.casadeesperanza.org

Cervantes, N. N., & Cervantes, J. M. (1993). *Battering and family therapy: A feminist perspective*. Newbury Park, CA: Sage Publications.

Clauss-Ehlers, C. S. (2008). Sociocultural factors, resilience, and coping: Support for a culturally sensitive measure of resilience. *Journal of Applied Developmental Psychology, 29*, 197–212.

Clauss-Ehlers, C. S., Acosta, O., & Weist, M. D. (2004). Responses to terrorism: The voices of two communities speak out. In C. S. Clauss-Ehlers & M. D. Weist (Eds.), *Community planning to foster resilience in children* (pp. 143–159). New York: Kluwer Academic Publishers.

Clauss-Ehlers, C. S., & Akinsulure-Smith, A. M. (2013). Working with forced migrant children and their families: Mental health, developmental, legal, and linguistic considerations in the context of school-based mental health services. In C. S. Clauss-Ehlers, Z. Serpell, & M. D. Weist (Eds.), *Handbook of culturally responsive school mental health: Advancing research, training, practice, and policy* (pp. 135–146). New York: Springer.

Clauss-Ehlers, C. S., Yang, Y. T., & Chen, W. J. (2006). Resilience from childhood stressors: The role of cultural resilience, ethnic identity, and gender identity. *Journal of Infant, Child, and Adolescent Psychotherapy, 5*, 124–138.

Cunradi, C. B., Caetano, R., & Schafer, J. (2002). Socioeconomic predictors of intimate partner violence among White, Black, and Hispanic couples in the United States. *Journal of Family Violence, 17*, 377–338.

Daly, M., & Wilson, M. (1988a, October). Evolutionary social psychology and family homicide. *Science, 242*, 519–524.

Daly, M., & Wilson, M. (1988b). *Homicide.* Hawthorne, NY: Aldine de Gruyter.

Darling, N., & Steinberg, L. (1993). Parenting style as context: An integrative model. *Psychological Bulletin, 113*(3), 487–496. doi: 10.1037/0033-2909.113.3.487.

Domestic Abuse Prevention Programs (n.d.). *What is the Duluth model?* Retrieved from http://www.theduluthmodel.org/about/index.html.

Ellsberg, M., & Heise, L. (2005). *Researching violence against women: A practical guide for researchers and activists*. Geneva, Switzerland: World Health Organization, Washington, DC: Program for Appropriate Technology in Health (PATH).

Freire, P. (1978). *Education for a critical consciousness.* New York: Seabury Press.

Freire, P. (1997). *Pedagogy of the oppressed.* New York: Continuum.

Gabler, M., Stern, S. E., & Miserandino, M. (1998). Latin American, Asian, and American cultural differences in perceptions of spousal abuse. *Psychological Reports, 83*, 587–592.

Gándara, P., & The White House Initiative on Educational Excellence for Hispanics (2015). *Fulfilling America's future: Latinas in the U.S., 2015.* Retrieved from https://sites.ed.gov/hispanic-initiative/files/2015/09/Fulfilling-Americas-Future-Latinas-in-the-U.S.-2015-Final-Report.pdf.

Gil, R. M., & Vazquez, C. I. (1996). *The Maria paradox: How Latinas can merge old world traditions with new world self-esteem*. New York: G. P. Putnam's Sons.

Goddard, C., & Wierzbicka, A. (2004). Cultural scripts: What are they and what are they good for? *Intercultural Pragmatics, 1–2*, 153–166.

Gorton, J., & Van Hightower, N. R. (1999). Intimate victimization of Latina farm workers: A research summary. *Hispanic Journal of Behavioral Sciences, 21*(4), 502–507.

Grant, J. M., Mottet, L. A., Tanis, J., Harrison, J., Herman, J. L., & Keisling, M. (2011). *Injustice at every turn: A Report of the National Transgender Discrimination Survey*. Washington, DC: National Center for Transgender Equality & National Gay and Lesbian Task Force.

Guzman, B. (2001). *The Hispanic population* (No. C2KBR/01–3). Washington, DC: U.S. Department of Labor, Bureau of the Census.

Hancock, T., & Ames, N. (2008). Toward a model for engaging Latino lay ministers in domestic violence intervention. *Families in Society, 89*(4), 623–630.

Hancock, T. U., & Siu K. (2009). A culturally sensitive intervention with domestically violent Latino immigrant men. *Journal of Family Violence, 24*, 123–132.

Heise, L., Ellsberg, M., & Gottemoeller, M. (1999a). *Ending violence against women*. Baltimore, MD: Johns Hopkins University School of Public Health, Population Information Program.

Heise, L., Ellsberg, M., & Gottemoeller, M. (1999b). Population reports: Ending violence against women. *Issues in World Health, L*(11), 1–44.

Horwitz, S. H., Santiago, L., Pearson, J., & LaRussa-Trott, M. (2009). Relational tools for working with mild to moderate couple violence: Patterns of unresolved conflict and pathways to resolution. *Professional Psychology: Research and Practice, 40*, 249–256.

Jasinski, J. L. (1998). The role of acculturation in wife assault. *Hispanic Journal of Behavioral Sciences, 20*, 175–192.

Javier, R. Art., & Camacho-Gingerich, A. (2004). Risk and resilience in Latino youth. In C. S. Clauss-Ehlers & M. D. Weist (Eds.), *Community planning to foster resilience in children* (pp. 65–81). New York: Kluwer Academic Publishers.

Kantor, G. K., Jasinski, J. L., & Aldarondo, E. (1994). Sociocultural status and incidence of marital violence in Hispanic families. *Violence and Victims, 9*, 207–222.

Kessler, R. C., McGonagle, K. A., & Zhao, S. (1994). Lifetime and 12-month prevalence of DSM-III-R psychiatric disorders in the United States: Results from the National Comorbidity Survey. *Archives of General Psychiatry, 51*, 8–19.

Krogstad, J. M., Stepler, R., & Lopez, M. H. (2015, May 12). *English proficiency on the rise among Latinos*. Retrieved from http://www.pewhispanic.org/2015/05/12/english-proficiency-on-the-rise-among-latinos/.

Lewis, R. L., Mason, T. L., Winstead, B. A., & Kelley, M. L. (2017). Empirical investigation of a model of sexual minority specific and general risk factors for intimate partner violence among lesbian women. *Psychology of Violence, 7*(1), 110–119.

Lown, A. E., & Vega, W. A. (2003). Prevalence and predictors of physical partner abuse among Mexican American women. In M. Aguirre-Molina & C. W. Molina (Eds.), *Latina health in the United States: A public health reader* (pp. 572–584). San Francisco, CA: Jossey-Bass.

Martín-Baró, I. (1994). *Writings for a liberation psychology*. Cambridge, MA: Harvard University Press.

McFarlane, J., Parker, B., Soeken, K., Silva, C., & Reed, S. (1999). Severity of abuse before and during pregnancy for African American, Hispanic, and Anglo women. *Journal of Nurse Midwifery, 44*, 139–144.

Menjivar, C., & Salcedo, O. (2002). Immigrant women and domestic violence: Common experiences in different countries. *Gender & Society, 16*, 898–920.

Meyer, I. H. (2003). Prejudice, social stress, and mental health in lesbian, gay, and bisexual populations: Conceptual issues and research evidence. *Psychological Bulletin, 129*, 674–697. http://dx.doi.org/10.1037/0033-2909.129.5.674.

Miranda, A. O., Frevert, V. S., & Kern, R. M. (1998). Lifestyle differences between bicultural and low-and high-acculturation-level Latino adults. *Journal of Individual Psychology, 54*, 119–134.

Moracco, K. E., Hilton, A., Hodges, K. G., & Frasier, P. Y. (2005). Knowledge and attitudes about intimate partner violence among immigrant Latinos in rural North Carolina. *Violence Against Women, 11*(3), 337–352.

Murdaugh, C., Hunt, S., Sowell, R., & Santana, I. (2004). Domestic violence in Hispanics in the Southeastern United States: A survey and needs analysis. *Journal of Family Violence, 19*(2), 107–115.

Nisbett, R. E., & Cohen, D. (1996). *Culture of honor: The psychology of violence in the South.* Boulder, CO: Westview Press.

Pan, A., Daley, S., Rivera, L. M., Williams, K., Lingle, D., & Reznik, V. (2006). Understanding the role of culture in domestic violence: The Ahimsa Project for Safe Families. *Journal of Immigrant and Minority Health, 8*(1), 35–43.

Pence, E., & Paymar, M. (1993). *Education groups for men who batter: The Duluth model.* New York: Springer.

Perilla, J. L., Bakeman, R., & Rorris, F. H. (1994). Culture and domestic violence: The ecology of abused Latinas. *Violence and Victims, 9*, 325–339.

Perilla, J. L., Lavizzo, E., & Ibañez, G. (2007). Toward a community of psychology of liberation: A domestic violence intervention as a tool for social change. In E. Aldarondo (Ed.), *Advancing social justice through clinical practice* (pp. 291–311). Mahwah, NJ: Lawrence Erlbaum Associates.

Perilla, J. L., Vasquez Serrata, J., Weinberg, J., & Lippy, C. A. (2012). Integrating women's voices and theory: A comprehensive domestic violence intervention for Latinas. *Women & Therapy, 35*(1/2), 93–105. DOI: 10.1080/02703149.2012.634731.

Ramirez Hernandez, A. (2002). CECEVIM—Stopping male violence in the Latino home. In E. Aldarondo & F. Mederos (Eds.), *Programs for men who batter: Intervention and prevention strategies in a diverse society* (pp. 12-1–12-30). Kingston, NJ: Civic Research Institute.

Rennison, C., & Planty, M. (2003). Non-lethal intimate partner violence: Examining race, gender and income patterns. *Violence and Victims, 18*(4), 433–443.

Rodriguez, R. (1999). The power of the collective: Battered migrant farmworker women creating safe spaces. *Health Care for Women International, 20*, 417–426.

Saez-Betancourt, A., Lam, B. T., & Nguyen, T. (2008). The meaning of being incarcerated on a domestic violence charge and its impact on self and family among Latino immigrant batterers. *Journal of Ethnic and Cultural Diversity in Social Work, 17*(2), 130–156.

Smith, S. G., Chen, J., Basile, K. C., Gilbert, L. K., Merrick, M. T., Patel, N., Walling, M., & Jain, A. (2017). *The National Intimate Partner and Sexual Violence Survey (NISVS): 2010–2012 State Report.* Atlanta, GA: National Center for Injury Prevention and Control, Centers for Disease Control and Prevention. Retrieved from: https://www.cdc.gov/violenceprevention/pdf/NISVS-StateReportBook.pdf.

Sokoloff, N., & Dupont, I. (2005). Domestic violence at the intersections of race, class, and gender. *Violence Against Women, 11*(1), 38–64

Sorenson, S. B., & Telles, C. A. (1991). Self-reports of spousal violence in a Mexican-American and non-Hispanic White population. *Violence and Victims, 6*, 3–15.

Straus, M. A., Gelles, R. J., & Smith, C. (1990). *Physical violence in American families: Risk factors and adaptations to violence in 8,145 families*. New Brunswick, NJ: Transaction Publishers.

Tjaden, P., & Thoennes, N. (2000a). *Extent, nature, and consequences of intimate partner violence*. Washington, DC: U.S. Department of Justice, National Institute of Justice.

Tjaden, P., & Thoennes, N. (2000b). *Full report of the prevalence, incidence and consequences of violence against women: Findings from the National Violence Against Women Survey.* Washington, DC: U.S. Department of Justice, National Institute of Justice.

Torres, S. (1991). A comparison of wife abuse between two cultures: Perceptions, attitudes, nature, and extent. *Issues in Mental Health Nursing, 12*, 113–131.

Triandis, H. C. (1994). *Culture and social behavior.* New York: McGraw-Hill.

U.S. Census Bureau (2017). The nation's population is becoming more diverse. https://www.census.gov/newsroom/press-releases/2017/cb17-100.html.

Vandello, J. A., & Cohen, D. (2003). Male honor and female fidelity: Implicit cultural scripts that perpetuate domestic violence. *Journal of Personality and Social Psychology, 84*(5), 997–1010.

Vazquez, C. I., & Clauss-Ehlers, C. S. (2005). Group psychotherapy with Latinas: A cross-cultural and interactional approach. *New York State Psychologist, 17*, 10–13.

Villereal, G. L., & Cavazos, A. (2005). Shifting identity: Process and change in identity of aging Mexican-American males. *Journal of Sociology and Social Welfare, 32*, 33–41.

Wray, A. M., Hoyt, T., & Gerstle, M. (2013). Preliminary examination of a mutual partner violence intervention among treatment-mandated couples. *Journal of Family Psychology, 27* (4), 664–670.

West, C. M., Kantor, G. K., & Jasinski, J. L. (1998). Sociodemographic predictors and cultural barriers to help-seeking behavior by Latina and Anglo American battered women. *Violence and Victims, 13*, 361–375.

Wyatt-Brown, B. (1982). *Southern honor: Ethics and behavior in the Old South*. New York: Oxford University Press.

Yoshioka, M., & Choi, D. Y. (2005). Culture and interpersonal violence research: Paradigm shift to create a full continuum of domestic violence services. *Journal of Interpersonal Violence, 20*(4), *513–519.*

Yoshioka, M., Gilbert, L., El-Bassel, N., & Baig-Amin, M. (2003). Social support and disclosure of abuse: Comparing South Asian, African American, and Hispanic battered women. *Journal of Family Violence, 18*, 171–181.

III

Treatment Intervention Issues

We have structured this book to include clinical examples and treatment recommendations throughout the different chapters in our attempt to make the material discussed in the book more clinically relevant for the reader. In this section, we decided to include more specific discussions on treatment and intervention approaches not frequently mentioned in the literature on DV. In this context, we dedicate three chapters that examine the traumatic effects left on the victims of DV. Chapter 10 provides, in this regard, an important discussion of the subtle neuropsychological effects on the victims of violence that are often left undetected by unsuspecting professionals. In chapter 11 the reader will find a discussion on the debilitating impact of stigma on the survivors of IPV, a condition that tends to result in furthering victimizing and making even worse for the victim an already devastating condition. Finally, chapter 12 focuses on essential elements for an effective treatment model of DV in a complex world and provides insightful and important recommendations by experts, who over the years, have been leaders in addressing treatment issues with this population. There are specific treatment recommendations that the reader may find helpful in many DV cases.

Again, as is the case with previous sections presented in the book, you will find a series of questions and activities meant to encourage further exploration of the issues addressed in these chapters.

Chapter Ten

Victimized and Disabled

Neuropsychological Issues at the Intersection of Gender and Ethnicity

Martha E. Banks

OPENING SCENARIO

> News Headline: "Injured Woman Found Barely Alive"
> Late last evening, after a 2-day search, Ms. Blank was found in an open field 10 miles from where she lives. A personal assistant reported that Ms. Blank, who has a disability, was not at home when he arrived for work 4 days earlier. Police said they were notified after Ms. Blank had been absent for 2 days. There is no suspicion of foul play.

There are many problems with this scenario. The news story ended with "There is no suspicion of foul play." That conclusion is inconsistent with the reporting of the number of days Ms. Blank had been missing, the fact that she had a personal assistant, and the indication that she has a disability. Unfortunately, the fictitious scenario reflects the reality that, in US society, the experiences of Women with Disabilities are ignored or minimized (Banks, 2010b). This chapter provides an overview of the risks faced by Women with Disabilities, types of disability-related abuse, types of injuries sustained during abuse with a focus on traumatic brain injury (TBI), and considerations in responding to the needs of Women with Disabilities who have been abused.

Here is a glimpse into details of Ms. Blank's situation:

> When asked about how often Ms. Blank, who uses a wheelchair and does not speak English, leaves home, the personal assistant said she was always at home. He was surprised when he arrived at her home and she was not there.

His agency sent him to assist her with bathing and dressing. He said it was useless to talk to her because she was "dumb"; he did not know what was "wrong" with her.

Ms. Blank's ex-husband had called her mother when he visited and she was absent. Her mother called the police. Ms. Blank was taken to an emergency room where she was treated for cuts and bruises on her arms and head.

She was released to her ex-husband who returned her to her home. Her wheelchair is still missing; she will be eligible for a replacement in 8 months.

One month after Ms. Blank returned home, her mother called an ambulance because there was blood on her clothes. Emergency room staff determined that Ms. Blank had aborted a 7-week fetus. She had also been a victim of sexual assault.

SOCIAL SITUATIONS OF WOMEN WITH DISABILITIES

Women with Disabilities experience the same broad range of social situations and relationships as women who are temporarily abled.[1] Yet participation in the larger society is often limited for Women with Disabilities, especially for those of color. Thirty-one percent of the women living with disabilities, ages 21 to 64 years, are employed and 28.4% live in poverty (Erickson, Lee, & von Schrader, 2014; Nazarov & Lee, 2012). In addition, nearly seven million women with severe disabilities require personal assistance (Steinmetz, 2006).

Banks (2003) examined the impact of disability on families across the lifespan. Women with Disabilities are spouses, daughters, mothers, sisters, aunts, nieces, and so on, fulfilling many roles within their families. Some function as caregivers for other members of the family (Nabors & Pettee, 2003). Women's ability to manage education, employment, and family roles are constantly and repeatedly challenged (Banks, 2015). The impact of a woman's disability is based in large part on the cultural interpretation of disability (Marshall, Kendall, Banks, & Gover, 2009), with particular attention to gender (Banks, 2010b, 2013b). When disability is of a nature or severity that a woman needs personal assistance, responsibility and provision of that assistance generally falls on family members, particularly women (Johnson et al., 2010). Some mothers who provide caregiving for adult children have difficulty passing along that responsibility to subsequent generations, whereas some children become caregivers for mothers with disabilities at early ages (Banks, 2003).

RISKS AND TYPES OF ABUSE FACED BY WOMEN WITH DISABILITIES

Women with Disabilities are at higher risk for physical abuse and psychological abuse than women without disabilities. . . . In some cases it is not clear

> which came first: the abuse or the disability. There is a cycle of abuse and disability in which it is possible for abuse to result in disability . . . and for a disability to be exacerbated by abuse. (Banks, 2010b, p. 439)

Thirty-three percent of women in the United States experience physical violence inflicted by an intimate partner (Breiding, Chen, & Black, 2014). There are ethnic disparities as 31.7% of White Women, 35.2% of Hispanic[2] Women, 41% of Black women, 45.9% of American Indian or Alaska Native women, and 50.4% of Multiracial women experience physical intimate partner violence at some time during their lives (Breiding et al., 2014). Rennison, DeKeseredy, and Dragiewicz (2013) found disparate rates in intimate partner violence among geographic locations with impact on 19.2% of urban women, 21% of suburban women, and 25.2% of rural women. In a 2012 survey of People with Disabilities, "70% of people with disabilities who took the survey reported they had been victims of abuse" (Baladerian, Coleman, & Stream, 2013, p. 3). Personal assistance by people untrained and unprepared for providing assistance can result in serious degradation of interpersonal, including family, relationships, sometimes leading to a level of abuse that creates or exacerbates health problems (Banks, 2010b; Robles, Slatcher, Trombello, & McGinn, 2014).

DISABILITY-RELATED ABUSE

Women with Disabilities are at risk for the same kinds of abuse as temporarily abled women. In addition, however, they are vulnerable to disability-related abuse (Banks, 2007). This includes disability-related emotional abuse, disability-related physical abuse, disability-related sexual abuse, and abuse related to helping relationships.[3]

Disability-related emotional abuse includes actual or threatened abandonment, isolation, denial of relationship, difficulty leaving an identified abusive relationship due to reliance on an abusive spouse for financial and/or emotional needs as well as most basic needs of mobility and physical access, power imbalance due to socialization of Women with Disabilities to be passively compliant and pleasant, intolerance and rejection, threats to neglect children or pets, refusal to acknowledge disability, and threats of losing custody of or access to children (Corbett, 2003; Crawford & Ostrove, 2003; Nosek, Foley, Hughes, & Howland, 2001). Nabors and Pettee (2003) wrote about putting unrealistic demands on Women with Disabilities to carry out prescribed family roles and ways in which families prioritize men's disabilities over women's disabilities, causing women to put their needs, acquired disabilities, and much-needed rehabilitation on hold so that they can take care of men in their families. Baladerian et al. (2013) found that 87.2% of surveyed People with Disabilities experienced verbal-emotional abuse and 37.3% were neglected.

Physical abuse specific to disability includes withholding or otherwise preventing the use of assistive devices or medication (Curry, Hassouneh-Phillips, & Johnston-Silverberg, 2001; Nosek et al., 2001; Saxton et al., 2001). Such abuse was experienced by 50.6% of People with Disabilities surveyed in 2012; of those experiencing physical abuse women (34%) were more likely to be victims than men (27%) (Baladerian et al., 2013). While physical abuse is generally considered in the context of family and other face-to-face interpersonal relationships, it is important to recognize that private and public insurance policies also render Women with Disabilities helpless if they do not have access to the types of devices or medications that remove barriers to their health, general well-being, and participation in society. Other forms of disability-related physical abuse include families' allowing access of known abusive relatives to Women with Disabilities, families' refusal to permit or arrange for personal assistance, and supplying alcohol or drugs contraindicated by the women's health conditions (Bergeron, 2005; Zweig, Schlichter, & Burt, 2002).

A third type of disability-related abuse is sexual abuse; 41.6% of People with Disabilities experience sexual abuse (Baladerian et al., 2013). This can include threats of physical violence to coerce sexual activity, unwanted fondling, or demanding sexual activity as "payment" for assistance (Nosek et al., 2001). In situations in which assistance is provided for sexual activity, there can be confusion between "helping an individual with sexual activity and participating in sexual activity" (Mona, 2003, p. 220). "The line between appropriate touching as an essential part of the job of providers and inappropriate touching, which could lead to unwanted or ambiguous sexual contact, was not always clearly definable . . . Bathing and dressing are such intimate activities that it is not surprising that blurry boundaries can create confusion" (Saxton et al., 2001, p. 401).

Abuse related to helping relationships overlaps with the other types of abuse, but with a specific focus on personal assistants. Personal assistants can be hired professionals or unpaid family members, friends, or other volunteers. Some of the problems are rough handling, infantilization, and delays in responding to requests for assistance (Mona, Cameron, & Crawford, 2005; Nosek et al., 2001; Saxton et al., 2001). These problems are seldom taken seriously due to a combination of lack of understanding of the nature of personal assistance relationships and stereotypes that Women with Disabilities are incompetent (Mona et al., 2005). There is particular danger for women who receive care from the same people who have inflicted violence on them: "Family members, particularly intimate partners, are more apt than strangers to inflict violence that causes disabilities" (Banks, 2010b, p. 439). Family members are seldom provided with personal assistance training. They are infrequently included in rehabilitation to observe ways in which health professionals address problems or assist the women. Furthermore, family members are not prepared for changes in function that result from traumatic brain injury, complicated by the fact that many of those changes are subtle and involve invisible disability (Banks, 2013a).

> More than 90% of people with disabilities who were victims of abuse said they had experienced such abuse on multiple occasions. Some 57% of these victims said they had been victims of abuse on more than 20 occasions, with 46% saying it had happened too many times for them to even count. (Baladerian et al., 2013, p. 3)

Baladerian and colleagues (2013) noted that Women with Disabilities are particularly at risk for abuse due to dependence on other people for care, perpetrators' perception of ability to abuse with impunity, high risk of not being believed, social isolation, and vulnerability due to disability; this is particularly problematic for Women of Color (Lightfoot & Williams, 2009). Abuse experienced by Women with Disabilities is witnessed by children, leading to intergenerational repetition of such abuse with the children at risk for becoming victims and/or perpetrators (Brent & Silverstein, 2013), as well as experiencing chronic health problems (Shalev et al., 2013). Such abuse has economic impact on both the victims and society at large as victims have limited access to gainful employment (Helfrich, Badiani, & Simpson, 2006; Lindhorst, Oxford, & Gillmore, 2007; Logan, Walker, & Hoyt, 2012; Warrener, Koivunen, & Postmus, 2013; Waters, Hyder, Rajkoti, Basu, & Butchart, 2012) and experience serious health problems that require health care (David & Messer, 2011).

INTIMATE PARTNER ABUSE WITH NEUROPSYCHOLOGICAL CONSEQUENCES

Head injuries have been identified as red flags indicating that women are victims of intimate partner violence; unintentional, accidental injuries tend to involve other parts of the body (Kyriacou et al., 1999; Nicolaidis & Liebschutz, 2009; Sheridan & Nash, 2007; Trojan & Krull, 2012; Wu, Huff, & Bhandari, 2010). Dentists and eye doctors have identified victims of intimate partner violence who have had teeth knocked out and sustained ruptured eyeballs (Wilson, Dodson, & Halpern, 2009). "It is difficult to seriously injure the head or face without simultaneously injuring the brain" (Ackerman and Banks, 2009, p. 108).

Victims of intimate partner violence sustain traumatic brain injury (TBI), an injury caused by external physical force (e.g., penetrating injuries, closed head injuries, and oxygen deprivation) (Ackerman & Banks, 2009; Antai,

2011; Jackson, Philip, Nuttall, & Diller, 2004). Kwako and colleagues (2011) also documented TBI as a consequence of attempted strangulation. Petridou and colleagues (2002) found that 17.9% of women and 7.7% of men sustained brain injury through intimate partner violence, as compared to 5.5% who sustained brain injuries in unintentional circumstances. Vanderploeg (2013) described TBI impairment as ranging from mild to severe, with impact on cognition, emotions, behavior, and physical functioning.

> Cognitive difficulties might include decreased ability to concentrate, pay attention and solve problems, and communicate. Difficulties with executive functioning, such as difficulty with making decisions, considering long-term consequences, taking initiative, feeling motivated, starting and finishing actions, and disinhibition and impulsiveness are often evident. Changes in behavior, personality or temperament, such as irritability, difficulty tolerating frustration, and emotional expression that does not fit the situation are also common consequences of TBI secondary to IPV [intimate partner violence]. The physical effects may include headaches, vision problems, insomnia, loss of coordination, and seizures. (Banks, 2016, p. 485)

TBI interferes with several aspects of women's lives. Some women can benefit from neuropsychological rehabilitation. In order to develop treatment plans, neuropsychological evaluation should be conducted to assess victims' strengths and weaknesses, with attention to safety (Banks, 2013a).

IDENTIFYING PROBLEMS AND SOLUTIONS FOR MS. BLANK

There are difficulties with the attitude of the personal assistant. Given that he was working through an agency, one might assume that he had some training. It is not clear whether he determined that Ms. Blank was not at home by observing her physical absence or whether he simply received no response to ringing a doorbell, knocking on a door, or calling her on a telephone or through an apartment house callbox. It is a serious concern that he perceived Ms. Blank as "dumb"; his use of that word (unable to speak and/or not smart) is not only unclear but also pejorative and unethical for a care provider. This is an example of abuse related to helping relationships (Banks, 2007). Coble (2001) observed that Women with Disabilities often lack the skills to select, negotiate with, and successfully hire effective or trustworthy personal assistants; she provided detailed recommendations for interviewing and evaluation, including development of a hiring process and being specific about tasks to be handled and the preferred manner in which they should be accomplished. In order to facilitate cooperation of personal assistants, Coble emphasized the importance of clear communication, assertiveness, empathy, careful listening, and focusing on "only the immediate issues of concern" (p. 8). In addition, Coble noted that relationships between Women with Disabilities and personal assistants could be enhanced with psychotherapy using "a combination of education, conflict resolution and enhancing communication skills" (p. 8).

An ideal response to Ms. Blank's situation would have included earlier contacting of the police. The personal assistant did not appear to understand that Ms. Blank's absence was a problem that needed to be addressed immediately. His expression of "surprise" at her absence was an inadequate response. He should have called the family or his agency to determine if someone else was aware of Ms. Blank's location and, in absence of knowledge of her whereabouts, to collaborate with family to find out if she was in distress within her home. If the personal assistant, the family, and other people in Ms. Blank's social circle did not know where she was, the police should have been contacted without delay.

EMERGENCY ROOM RESPONSES

The initial visit to the emergency room (ER) after Ms. Blank was found included treatment for cuts and bruises on her arms and head. This is consistent with concerns expressed by Banks (2013a) that after head injury, "victims either receive no health care at all or are discharged after being medically stabilized and receive no rehabilitation thereafter" (p. 153). The health evaluation during the first visit to the ER did not include a gynecologic/obstetric examination. Lack of such evaluation is, unfortunately, not unusual for Women with Disabilities, who are stereotyped to be asexual (Crawford & Ostrove, 2003; Dotson, Stinson, & Christian, 2003; Drew & Short, 2010; Mona et al., 2005), despite increasing resources for health professionals to address reproductive health of Women with Disabilities (Huff, 2010; Iezzoni, Yu, Wint, Smeltzer, & Ecker, 2014; Kaplan, 2006; Peterson, 2005; Sheppard-Jones, Kleinert, Paulding, & Espinosa, 2008; Smeltzer, 2007). The delay in appropriate health assessment is another example of abuse related to helping relationships (Mona et al., 2005).

Attention also needs to be given to cultural gaps in assessment of Women with Disabilities. The emergency room staff did not deal directly with Ms. Blank's language. While it was understood that she did not speak English, there was no assessment of her mastery of her native tongue or ability to speak or otherwise communicate in second and additional languages (Cosentino, Manly, & Mungas, 2007). An additional consideration is that, for multilingual women, the abuse might not be remembered in a language to which the women have conscious recall, but might be buried in a language to which they do not have immediate access when speaking or writing.

Ideally, the first ER visit would have included a professional interpreter, preferably one with health care experience and knowledge, as Ms. Blank does not speak English. Examination should have included Ms. Blank's entire body, including gynecologic/obstetric status for determination of sexual assault and pregnancy. Withholding of such examination is disabilities-related physical abuse and interferes with determining the existence of disability-related sexual abuse. Rather than being treated only for cuts and bruises on her arms and head, consideration should have been given to TBI as a consequence of the outward injuries to her head. Culturally adapted neuropsychological assessment should have been automatically included in the evaluation (Banks, 2010a, 2013a). The adaptations should have included language (and consideration of regional linguistic differences), ethnic definitions or connotations of test items, formal and informal education attainment, both the quantity and quality of education, as well as comparison with appropriate ethnic, age, and gender norms. In addition, Petridou and colleagues (2002) documented that the presence of multiple injuries, particularly to the face, rest of head, and the trunk, are red flags for domestic violence.

After the first visit to the emergency room, Ms. Blank was released to her ex-husband. At that time, there had been no investigation about how she had gotten to a field 10 miles from where she lived. The fact that Ms. Blank was found outdoors, so far away from her home, without her wheelchair, is an extreme example of disability-related physical and emotional abuse. Without assessment of domestic violence and determination of the reason for the termination of her marriage, it was inappropriate to release Ms. Blank to her ex-husband. It is not clear why her ex-husband was visiting her, what the nature of their current relationship is, and why he contacted her mother rather than the police. Assessment in the emergency room should have included private questioning about a history of abuse or anyone with whom Ms. Blank did not feel safe (Basile, Hertz, & Back, 2007; de Boinville, 2013). If such an assessment were not possible in the emergency room, Ms. Blank should have been referred for protective placement, preferably in an accessible shelter, while the safety of her home setting and relationships were evaluated (Banks, 2013a). At the same time, the police should have been in pursuit of (a) suspect(s) in the assault and removal of Ms. Blank from her home, including questioning of her ex-husband and the personal assistant (Mona et al., 2005; Saxton et al., 2001).

The second emergency room visit should have included a thorough physical examination. Ms. Blank should have been given the opportunity to discuss the circumstances of the pregnancy. Women with Disabilities are often deprived of the opportunity to have and raise children, despite resources available to them and health care providers (e.g., American Congress of Obstetricians and Gynecologists, 2014). It is important to learn the circumstances of the pregnancy (consensual sex or sexual assault), whether or not Ms. Blank was aware of the pregnancy, whether or not Ms. Blank had wanted or would have wanted to continue or terminate the pregnancy, and whether the abortion was spontaneous or induced. Given that Ms. Blank's whereabouts were unknown for at least four days and that she was found in an open field to which she had been transported, every effort should have been made to determine all of the abuse she had suffered during that time, before her disappearance, and since her return. The second emergency room visit should have included detailed assessment of how Ms. Blank was managing in her home, especially without her wheelchair, and whether or not she was safe in that home. If her ex-husband was the father of the fetus and the pregnancy was the result of sexual assault, that would be an example of spousal rape. Paternity by the personal assistant would involve disability-related sexual abuse and abuse related to helping relationships (Banks, 2007).

NEUROPSYCHOLOGICAL ASSESSMENT AND TREATMENT

As soon as there is a suspicion of traumatic brain injury, a person should be referred for neuropsychological assessment to determine if there are injuries that can interfere with victims' lives. Some of the neuropsychological problems can be successfully addressed through rehabilitation. The goal of neuropsychological assessment for victims of intimate partner violence should be safety and rehabilitation (Banks, 2013a).

The framework of the Ackerman-Banks Neuropsychological Rehabilitation Battery (Ackerman & Banks, 2006) will be used to address how neuropsychological function impacts safety. That battery specifies weaknesses and interpersonal difficulties that a victim is experiencing, strengths that can be used in treatment, and recommendations for referral to targeted treatment. Table 10.1 provides an overview of the battery domains; how problems might impact work, education, and/or social relationships; and health care disciplines that provide treatment within each of the domains.

Problems with alertness keep victims trapped in abusive relationships (Frieze & Chen, 2010; Green & Brownell, 2007) and interfere with parenting. Parenting requires not only the ability to shift attention and stay on task, but also simultaneous handling of multiple tasks.

Emotional expression and understanding of other people's emotions are key factors in interpersonal relationships. From a safety standpoint, if a person is unable to gauge another person's emotions, there is high risk for staying in dangerous situations. If emotional expression is a problem, family and friends describe women who have acquired TBI as having "changed" personalities; they are perceived as insensitive or having minimal empathy. This same impediment can result in problems obtaining help. For parents, it is critical to perceive and appropriately respond to the emotions of their children, especially when the children are too young to verbally express themselves.

Table 10.1. Brain Injury, Social Functions, and Treatment Options

Neuropsychological Functions	Impact on Work and/or Education	Impact on Social Relationships	Treatment Disciplines
Alertness	Difficulty shifting attention Unable to stay on task	Trouble doing more than one thing at a time	Cognitive therapy Neuropsychology Rehabilitation Psychology
Emotional Processing	Difficulty recognizing and appreciating other people's emotions Difficulty expressing emotion Speaks in a monotone	Difficulty relating to other people Family and friends describe "changed personality" (insensitive, minimal empathy) Unable to recognize abusive emotions in time to pursue safety Unable to respond to emotions of children	Cognitive therapy Music therapy Neuropsychology
Memory	Problems recalling old information (own name, address, general information learned in elementary and secondary school)	Inability to remember instructions Easily distracted	Cognitive therapy Neuropsychology Nursing Rehabilitation Psychology
Sensorimotor	Inability to see visual stimuli Inability to hear auditory stimuli Unable to discriminate among similar sounds Unable to recognize objects by feel Difficulty writing or drawing, because of problems handling pens or pencils Unable to identify and/or duplicate	Difficulty picking up items Problems walking Inability to determine where one is in space Problems with balance, walking, and posture Stumbling Misjudging distances	Cognitive therapy Kinesiotherapy Neuropsychology Nursing Occupational therapy Physiatry Physical therapy Rehabilitation Psychology Speech therapy

	printed words, pictures, and three-dimensional objects Inability to identify similarities and differences among items Recognition of color, shape, and placement of objects Organizational qualities involved in drawing, writing, and arrangement of three-dimensional items		
Speech	Stuttering Confabulation Lisping Breathiness	Slurring of words Poor voice inflection Lack of fluency	Cognitive therapy Neuropsychology Occupational therapy Rehabilitation Psychology Speech therapy
Academic Abilities	Problems with word recognition, pronunciation, and comprehension of printed material Difficulty with or inability to print or write	Unable to manage arithmetic skills necessary for the management of finances	Cognitive therapy Educational therapy Neuropsychology Occupational therapy Rehabilitation psychology Social work Speech therapy
Cognitive Problem Solving	Inability to use abstractions or make generalizations Inability to remember and organize components of problems in order to solve them Unable to understand instructions Inaccurate analysis of problems Difficulty with integration of	Inability to approach everyday problems, determine that something needs to be managed, identify what needs to be done, develop ways to address the problems, and create and implement solutions Unable to make socially acceptable decisions	Cognitive therapy Educational therapy Neuropsychology Nursing Occupational therapy Psychology Rehabilitation Psychology Social work

	previous knowledge and new information for the purpose of recognizing and solving new problems Slow processing		
Organic Emotions	Depression Anxiety Impulsivity	Depression Anxiety Impulsivity	Neuropsychology Nursing Psychiatry Rehabilitation Psychology
Asymmetry	Left-right confusion Getting lost easily and repeatedly Difficulty following maps and directions from one location to another Lacking symmetry in facial features Difficulty with sensation on one side of the body	Difficulty walking Balance problems Poor coordination	Neurology Neuropsychology Nursing Physiatry Occupational therapy Physical therapy Rehabilitation Psychology
Treatment Problems	Peripheral nerve damage on one or both sides of the body Unaware of deficits (laissez-faire, unconcerned attitude when making mistakes) Socially inappropriate behaviors (refusing to follow directions, getting undressed in public)	Low frustration tolerance (crying out, exhibiting high anxiety and avoidant behavior, unable to moderate disappointment or expressions of frustration)	Cognitive therapy Neurology Neuropsychology Nursing Occupational therapy Orthopedics Physiatry Physical therapy Rehabilitation Psychology

Memory is crucial to safety planning (Banks, 2013a, 2013b). TBI can lead to inability to remember instructions and easy distraction, which interferes with safety.

People use sensorimotor skills (visual-spatial, auditory, and tactile processing) to assess their immediate environments. If people cannot interpret what they see, hear, or feel, they are at risk for injury. "In order to maintain safety, victims need to use their senses and, as much as possible, organize motor skills to escape or fight back in an effort to minimize injury and save their own and their families' lives" (Banks, 2016, p. 487).

Speech problems make it difficult for victims to let people know what they need, especially during emergencies. Neuropsychological assessment should differentiate between neuropsychological speech problems and assessment limitations when tests are conducted in languages other than those with which victims are fully fluent (Buré-Reyes et al., 2013).

Basic academic skills are necessary for most employment, as well as household management. Assessment of these skills, especially when working with victims who are members of marginalized ethnic groups, must include attention to quality, as well as quantity of formal education (Jefferson et al., 2011). Some victims might benefit from new training rather than traditional rehabilitation.

Safety planning is particularly complicated when cognitive function is compromised (National Clearinghouse on Abuse in Later Life & The Wisconsin Coalition Against Domestic Violence, 2003). It is important for victims to be able to quickly recognize problems, pull together information, and develop practical solutions to the problems.

Some women with acquired TBI experience severe depression (Hicks & Li, 2003; Homaifar, Brenner, Forster, & Nagamoto, 2012), anxiety (Ponsford et al., 2012), and impulsivity. Depression and anxiety are often experienced by victims of intimate partner violence, but impulsivity is not. However, impulsivity can be a symptom of TBI.

Neuropsychologists assess physical and behavioral problems that interfere with overall functioning. Left-right confusion or inability to move parts of one's body are difficulties that can be caused or exacerbated by physical abuse. Victims who have poor awareness of deficits (e.g., *laissez-faire*, unconcerned attitude when making mistakes), socially inappropriate behaviors (e.g., refusing to follow directions, getting undressed in public), and low frustration tolerance (e.g., crying out, exhibiting high anxiety and avoidant behavior, inability to moderate expressions of disappointment or frustration) are likely to have difficulty in employment settings, in rehabilitation, in shelters, or at home.

Culturally relevant services are needed for Girls and Women with Disabilities who have been victimized (Banks, 2013a, 2016). Considerations include ethnic, gender, and other cultural traditions and understanding of the victimization. The combination of a woman's ability for socialization and health concerns specific to her disability determine the baseline for appropriate health care. Social class can be expected to impact the expectations and attitudes of service providers and their relationships with Women with Disabilities. Culturally relevant preparation for caregiving and personal assistance is needed for both formal and informal service providers.

Ideally, services will be based on an Integrative Model (Seelman, 2004) that "addresses medical concerns, while removing social barriers, emphasizing the right to health care that allows women to pursue independence from abusive situations, and addressing programs that discriminate against them because of the acquired disabilities" (Banks, 2013a, p. 155). The educative component of support systems must include training for formal (e.g., health professionals, attorneys, judges, and advocates) and informal (e.g., family members, friends) service providers.

BEYOND MS. BLANK: MEETING THE NEEDS OF VICTIMIZED WOMEN WITH DISABILITIES

> Identity development models typically describe how individuals move from internalized oppression or privilege to (a) heightened sensitivity, personal upheaval, and anger in response to knowledge and experience of oppression or privilege; and (b) subsequent efforts to gain knowledge and explore positive and new aspects of a social identity that culminate in a flexible and positive organization of attitudes toward oneself and others. (Enns, 2010, p. 337)

Disability identity is a critical factor in the achievement of ideal recovery. This is a complex issue, further complicated when disability acquired or exacerbated by abuse results in a change in a woman's ability to function in one or more areas (Banks, 2013a). For women with invisible disabilities, there is a struggle to have their symptoms taken seriously. If the disabilities are visible, other people react to disability before responding to other characteristics of the women (Rohmer & Louvet, 2009). Victimization itself involves appraisal of the abusive situation, including uncertainty about a victim's responsibility for the abuse, and the development of a victim identity, which can lead to a survivor identity. Part of the development of a victim identity is an understanding that *the behavior of a perpetrator of abuse is* ***never*** *the fault of the victim* and that the victim is deserving of treatment leading to recovery. The interaction between the disability and victim/survivor identities can interfere with a woman's ability to advocate for herself in order to pursue services that support recovery. That advocacy is further compromised by sexism, racism, homophobia, ageism, classism, and/or other marginalization (Banks, 2012, 2013b).

When women sustain traumatic brain injuries through interpersonal violence, they need safe shelter, legal support, appropriate health care, immediate attention to physical injuries, and rehabilitation (Banks, 2013a). Safety involves separation from the abuser in a place that is as accessible as possible and prepared to meet a wide variety of needs. It is important to note that, in some jurisdictions, reports of intimate partner violence lead to the arrest of both the perpetrator and the victim. This is particularly problematic for Women with Disabilities who, during even brief incarceration, are treated as perpetrators rather than victims and unlikely to receive needed health care.

Victimized Women with Disabilities need assistance with planning for safe residence, accommodation for disability, and personal assistance. In a hospital setting, the assistance is provided by health care professionals. While in shelters, Women with Disabilities need access to human personal assistants and/or appropriately matched service animals (Banks, 2013a).

There are higher costs of health care for women victims of intimate partner violence than for those who have not sustained such violence (Jones et al., 2006; Rivara et al., 2007). This health disparity is seldom discussed. When assessment and rehabilitation for TBI are standards of care for victims of intimate partner violence who have sustained head injuries, costs can be expected to increase. Prior to the Patient Protection and Affordable Care Act (ACA), disability and domestic violence were both considered "preexisting conditions" that insurance companies used to exclude people from policies (Chin, Yee, & Banks, 2014), making health care particularly inaccessible to abused Women with Disabilities. Section 2705 of the ACA (Prohibiting Discrimination Against Individual Participants and Beneficiaries Based on Health Status) provides support for access to health care insurance for victims of domestic violence, including Women with Disabilities (U.S. Congress, 2010). In combination with the Violence Against Women Reauthorization Act of 2013 and the 1990 Americans with Disabilities Act (amended in 2008), the ACA makes it possible for victimized Women with Disabilities to receive the comprehensive health care needed for recovery from abuse and safety from perpetrators. The real needs of victimized Women with Disabilities should be revealed through health disparities research, which is mandated in ACA Section 4302 (Understanding Health Disparities: Data Collection and Analysis).

CLOSING STATEMENT

In the best of all worlds, peace would reign between nations, in communities, and within families. Until that time, however, it will be necessary to provide treatment and support for the injured victims of mass and local terrorism. Women who receive traumatic brain injury from intimate partner violence are among the invisible victims who can benefit from a variety of services that exist but have, heretofore, been seldom available and accessible to them. Let's have peace!

DISCUSSION QUESTIONS

1. What are some risks faced by Women with Disabilities?
2. What are examples of disability-related abuse?
3. What are some safety considerations for Women with Disabilities?
4. How does TBI compromise safety?
5. What are some cultural factors that must be considered during neuro-psychological evaluation?
6. What are the benefits of the Affordable Care Act for Women with Disabilities who are victims of intimate partner violence?
7. What are the additional factors to consider when assessing disabilities in those with multiple gender identities?

NOTES

1. The term "temporarily abled" is used to indicate that people who are not currently disabled are at risk for disability as a consequence of illness or accident.

2. Ethnic groups reported with names used in cited references.

3. Due to the intimate nature of personal assistance, abuse by personal assistants, whether otherwise related or not, is considered under the umbrella of domestic violence. Similar to domestic violence perpetrated by intimate partners, the dynamic involves power and control. See, e.g., Banks, M. E. (2007). Women with Disabilities, domestic violence against. In N. A. Jackson (Ed.), *Encyclopedia of domestic violence* (pp. 723–728). New York: Taylor & Francis.

Mona, L. R., Cameron, R. P., and Crawford, D. (2005). Stress and trauma in the lives of Women with Disabilities. In K. A. Kendall-Tackett (Ed.), *Handbook of women, stress, and trauma* (pp. 229–244). New York: Brunner-Routledge.

Saxton, M., Curry, M. A., Powers, L. E., Maley, S., Eckels, K., and Gross, J. (2001). "Bring my scooter so I can leave you": A study of disabled women handling abuse by personal assistance providers. *Violence Against Women, 7*, 393–417.

REFERENCES

Ackerman, R. J., & Banks, M. E. (2006). *Ackerman-Banks Neuropsychological Rehabilitation Battery© Professional Manual, Fourth Edition*. Akron, OH: ABackans Diversified Computer Processing, Inc.

Ackerman, R. J., & Banks, M. E. (2009). Traumatic brain injury and disability as a consequence of assault: Focus on intimate partner violence assault. In C. A. Marshall, E. Kendall, M. E. Banks, & R. M. S. Gover (Eds.), *Disabilities: Insights from across fields and around the world. Volume 1: The experience of disability: Definitions, causes and consequences* (pp. 107–122). Westport, CT: Praeger Press.

American Congress of Obstetricians and Gynecologists (2014). Interactive site for clinicians serving women with disabilities. Retrieved March 15, 2014 from http://www.acog.org/About_ACOG/ACOG_Departments/Women_with_Disabilities/Interactive_site_for_clinicians_serving_women_with_disabilities.

Americans with Disabilities Act of 1990, as Amended, 42 U.S.C. 12101 et seq (2008).

Antai, D. (2011). Traumatic physical health consequences of intimate partner violence against women: What is the role of community-level factors? *BioMed Central Women's Health, 11*, 1–13. doi: 10.1186/1472-6874-11-56.

Baladerian, N. J., Coleman, T. F., & Stream, J. (2013). Abuse of People with Disabilities: Victims and their families speak out: A report on the 2012 National Survey on Abuse of People with Disabilities. Los Angeles, CA: Spectrum Institute, Disability and Abuse Project.

Banks, M. E. (2003). Disability in the family: A life span perspective. *Cultural Diversity and Ethnic Minority Psychology, 9(4)*, 367–384. doi:10.1037/1099-9809.9.4.367.

Banks, M. E. (2007). Women with Disabilities, domestic violence against. In N. A. Jackson (Ed.), *Encyclopedia of domestic violence* (pp. 723–728). New York: Taylor & Francis.

Banks, M. E. (2010a). Special issues for Women with Disabilities. In M. A. Paludi (Ed.), *Feminism and women's rights worldwide* (pp. 149–160). Santa Barbara, CA: ABC-CLIO.

Banks, M. E. (2010b). 2009 Division 35 presidential address: Feminist psychology and Women with Disabilities: An emerging alliance. *Psychology of Women Quarterly, 34*(4), 431–442.

Banks, M. E. (2012). Multiple minority identities and mental health: Social and research implications of diversity within and between groups. In R. Nettles & R. Balter (Eds.), *Multiple minority identities: Applications for practice, research, and training* (pp. 35–58). New York: Springer.

Banks, M. E. (2013a). Ideal recovery for women who receive traumatic brain injury from intimate partner violence. In H. Muenchberger, E. Kendall, & S. Prout (Eds.), *Traumatic brain injury: Systems of support for healing and health* (pp. 153–167). Santa Barbara, CA: Praeger.

Banks, M. E. (2013b). Women of color with disabilities. In L. Comas-Díaz & B. Greene (Eds.), *Psychological health of women of color: Intersections, challenges, and opportunities.* (pp. 219–231). Westport, CT: Praeger.

Banks, M. E. (2015). Whiteness and disability: Double marginalization. *Women and Therapy, 38*(3–4), 220–231. doi:10.1080/02703149.2015.1059191.

Banks, M. E. (2016). Neuropsychological consequences of intimate partner violence among ethnic minority and cross-cultural populations. In F. R. Ferraro (Ed.). *Minority and cross-cultural aspects of neuropsychological assessment: Enduring and emerging trends.* New York: Taylor & Francis.

Basile, K. C., Hertz, M. F., & Back, S. E. (2007). *Intimate partner violence and sexual violence victimization assessment instruments for use in healthcare settings: Version 1*. Atlanta, GA: Centers for Disease Control and Prevention, National Center for Injury Prevention and Control. Retrieved March 15, 2014 from http://www.cdc.gov/ncipc/pub-res/images/ipvandsvscreening.pdf.

Bergeron, L. R. (2005). Abuse of elderly women in family relationships: Another form of violence against women. In K. A. Kendall-Tackett (Ed.), *Handbook of women, stress, and trauma* (pp. 141–157). New York: Brunner-Routledge.

Breiding, M. J., Chen, J., & Black, M. C. (2014). *Intimate Partner Violence in the United States—2010.* Atlanta, GA: National Center for Injury Prevention and Control, Centers for Disease Control and Prevention.

Brent, D. A., & Silverstein, M. (2013). Shedding light on the long shadow of childhood adversity. *JAMA: Journal of the American Medical Association, 309*(17), 1777–1778. http://dx.doi.org/10.1001/jama.2013.4220.

Buré-Reyes, A., Hidalgo-Ruzzante, N., Vilar-López, R., Gontier, J., Sánchez, L., Pérez-García, M., & Puente, A. E. (2013). Neuropsychological test performance of Spanish speakers: Is performance different across different Spanish-speaking subgroups? *Journal of Clinical and Experimental Neuropsychology, 35*(4), 404–412. doi:10.1080/13803395.2013.778232.

Chin, J. L., Yee, B. W. K., & Banks, M. E. (2014). Women health and behavior health issues in health care reform. *Journal of Social Work in Disability and Rehabilitation, 13*. doi:10.1080/1536710X.2013.870509. Retrieved March 15, 2014 from http://www.tandfonline.com/doi/full/10.1080/1536710X.2013.870509#.UxKnjnm-938.

Coble, A. C. (2001, Winter). When the challenge of maintaining personal care attendants becomes the focus of treatment. *Rehabilitation Psychology News*, 7–9.

Corbett, C. A. (2003). Special issues in psychotherapy for minority deaf women. In M. E. Banks & E. Kaschak (Eds.), *Women with visible and invisible disabilities: Multiple intersections, multiple issues, multiple therapies* (pp. 311–329). New York: Haworth Press.

Cosentino, S., Manly, J., & Mungas, D. (2007). Do reading tests measure the same construct in multiethnic and multilingual older persons? *Journal of the International Neuropsychological Society, 13*(2), 228–236.

Crawford, D., & Ostrove, J. M. (2003). Representations of disability and the interpersonal relationships of Women with Disabilities. In M. E. Banks & E. Kaschak (Eds.), *Women with visible and invisible disabilities: Multiple intersections, multiple issues, multiple therapies* (pp. 179–194). New York: Haworth.

Curry, M. A., Hassouneh-Phillips, D., & Johnston-Silverberg, A. (2001). Abuse of women with disabilities: An ecological model and review. *Violence Against Women, 7*, 60–79.

David, R., & Messer, L. (2011). Reducing disparities: Race, class and the social determinants of health. *Maternal and Child Health Journal, 15*(Suppl. 1), S1–S3. http://dx.doi.org/10.1007/s10995-011-0878-6.

de Boinville, M. (2013). *Screening for domestic violence in health care settings*. Washington, DC: U.S. Department of Health and Human Services, Office of Human Services Policy.

Dotson, L. A., Stinson, J., & Christian, L. (2003). "People tell me I can't have sex": Women with Disabilities share their personal perspectives on health care, sexuality, and reproductive rights. In M. E. Banks & E. Kaschak (Eds.), *Women with visible and invisible disabilities: Multiple intersections, multiple issues, multiple therapies* (pp. 195–209). New York: Haworth.

Drew, J. A. R., & Short, S. E. (2010). Disability and Pap smear receipt among U.S. women, 2000 and 2005. *Perspectives on Sexual and Reproductive Health, 42*(4), 258–266. doi:10.1363/4225810.

Enns, C. Z. (2010). Locational feminisms and feminist social identity analysis. *Professional Psychology: Research and Practice, 41*(4), 333–339. doi:10.1037/a0020260.

Erickson, W., Lee, C., & von Schrader, S. (2014). Disability statistics from the 2012 American Community Survey (ACS). Ithaca, NY: Cornell University Employment and Disability Institute (EDI). Retrieved July 5, 2014 from www.disabilitystatistics.org.

Frieze, I. H., & Chen, K. Y. (2010). Intimate partner violence: Perspectives from racial/ethnic groups in the United States. In H. Landrine & N. F. Russo (Eds.), *Handbook of diversity in feminist psychology* (pp. 427–447). New York: Springer.

Green, D. L., & Brownell, P. (2007). Poverty, women, welfare, work, and domestic violence. In A. R. Roberts (Ed.), *Springer series on family violence. Battered women and their families: Intervention strategies and treatment programs* (3rd Ed.) (pp. 423–450). New York: Springer.

Helfrich, C. A., Badiani, C., & Simpson, E. K. (2006). Worker role identity development of women with disabilities who experience domestic violence. *Work: Journal of Prevention, Assessment & Rehabilitation, 27*(3), 319–328.

Hicks, M. H.-R., & Li, Z. (2003). Partner violence and major depression in women: A community study of Chinese Americans. *Journal of Nervous and Mental Disease, 191*(11), 722–729. doi:10.1097/01.nmd.0000095124.05023.e1.

Homaifar, B. Y., Brenner, L. A., Forster, J. E., & Nagamoto, H. (2012). Traumatic brain injury, executive functioning, and suicidal behavior: A brief report. *Rehabilitation Psychology, 57*(4), 337–341. doi:10.1037/a0030480.

Huff, M. B. (2010). Disabled women and reproductive healthcare in the United States. *International Journal on Disability and Human Development, 9*(2–3), 225–229. doi:10.1515/IJDHD.2010.024.

Iezzoni, L. I., Yu, J., Wint, A. J., Smeltzer, S. C., & Ecker, J. L. (2014). General health, health conditions, and current pregnancy among U.S. Women with and without chronic physical disabilities. *Disability and Health Journal, 7*(2), 181–188. doi:10.1016/j.dhjo.2013.12.002 .

Jackson, H., Philip, E., Nuttall, R. L., & Diller, L. (2004). Battered women and traumatic brain injury. In K. A. Kendall-Tackett (Ed.), *Health consequences of abuse in the family: A clinical guide for evidence-based practice* (pp. 233–246). Washington, DC: American Psychological Association.

Jefferson, A. L., Gibbons, L. E., Rentz, D. M., Carvalho, J. O., Manly, J., Bennett, D. A., & Jones, R. N. (2011). A life course model of cognitive activities, socioeconomic status, education, reading ability, and cognition. *Journal of the American Geriatrics Society, 59*(8), 1403–1411. doi:10.1111/j.1532-5415.2011.03499.x.

Johnson, C. L., Resch, J. A., Elliott, T. R., Villarreal, V., Kwok, O.-M., Berry, J. W., & Underhill, A. T. (2010). Family satisfaction predicts life satisfaction trajectories over the first 5 years after traumatic brain injury. *Rehabilitation Psychology, 55*(2), 180–187. http://dx.doi.org/10.1037/a0019480.

Jones, A. S., Dienemann, J., Schollenberger, J., Kub, J., O'Campo, P., Gielen, A. C., & Campbell, J. C. (2006). Long-term costs of intimate partner violence in a sample of female HMO enrollees. *Women's Health Issues, 16*(5), 252–261.

Kaplan, C. (2006). Special issues in contraception: Caring for women with disabilities. *Journal of Midwifery & Women's Health, 51*(6), 450–456. doi:10.1016/j.jmwh.2006.07.009.

Kwako, L. E., Glass, N., Campbell, J., Melvin, K. C., Barr, T., & Gill, J. M. (2011). Traumatic brain injury in intimate partner violence: A critical review of outcomes and mechanisms. *Trauma, Violence, & Abuse, 12*(3), 115–126. doi:10.1177/1524838011404251.

Kyriacou, D. N., Angelin, D., Taliaferro, E., Stone, S., Tubb, T., Linden, J. A., et al. (1999). Risk factors for injury to women from domestic violence. *New England Journal of Medicine, 341*, 1892–1898. doi:10.1056/NEJM199912163412505.

Lightfoot, E., & Williams, O. (2009). The intersection of disability, diversity, and domestic violence: Results of national focus groups. *Journal of Aggression, Maltreatment & Trauma, 18*(2), 133–152. http://dx.doi.org/10.1080/10926770802675551.

Lindhorst, T., Oxford, M., & Gillmore, M. R. (2007). Longitudinal effects of domestic violence on employment and welfare outcomes. *Journal of Interpersonal Violence, 22*(7), 812–828. http://dx.doi.org/10.1177/0886260507301477.

Logan, T. K., Walker, R., & Hoyt, W. (2012). The economic costs of partner violence and the cost-benefit of civil protective orders. *Journal of Interpersonal Violence, 27*(6), 1137–1154. http://dx.doi.org/10.1177/0886260511424500.

Marshall, C. A., Kendall, E., Banks, M. E., & Gover, R. M. S. (Eds.) (2009). *Disability: Insights from across fields and around the world, Volumes I, II, and III*. Westport, CT: Praeger.

Mona, L. R. (2003). Sexual options for people with disabilities: Using personal assistance services for sexual expression. In M. E. Banks & E. Kaschak (Eds.), *Women with visible and invisible disabilities: Multiple intersections, multiple issues, multiple therapies* (pp. 211–221). New York: Haworth Press.

Mona, L. R., Cameron, R. P., & Crawford, D. (2005). Stress and trauma in the lives of Women with Disabilities. In K. A. Kendall-Tackett (Ed.), *Handbook of women, stress, and trauma* (pp. 229–244). New York: Brunner-Routledge.

Nabors, N. A., & Pettee, M. F. (2003). Womanist therapy with African American women with disabilities. In M. E. Banks & E. Kaschak (Eds.), *Women with visible and invisible disabilities: Multiple intersections, multiple issues, multiple therapies* (pp. 331–341). New York: Haworth.

National Clearinghouse on Abuse in Later Life and the Wisconsin Coalition Against Domestic Violence. (2003). *Safety planning: How you can help*. Retrieved November 14, 2014 from http://wcadv.org/safety-planning-guide-individuals-cognitive-disabilities.

Nazarov, Z, & Lee, C. G. (2012). *Disability statistics from the current population survey (CPS)*. Ithaca, NY: Cornell University Rehabilitation Research and Training Center on Disability Demographics and Statistics (StatsRRTC). Retrieved June 2, 2014 from www.disabilitystatistics.org.

Nicolaidis, C., & Liebschutz, J. (2009). Chronic physical symptoms in survivors of intimate partner violence. In C. Mitchell & D. Anglin (Eds.), *Intimate partner violence: A health-based perspective* (pp. 133–145). New York: Oxford University Press.

Nosek, M. A., Foley, C. C., Hughes, R. B., & Howland, C. A. (2001). Vulnerabilities for abuse among Women with Disabilities. *Sexuality and Disability, 19*, 177–189.

Peterson, M. M. (2005). Assisted reproductive technologies and equity of access issues. *Journal of Medical Ethics: Journal of the Institute of Medical Ethics, 31*(5), 280–285. doi:10.1136/jme.2003.007542.

Petridou, E., Browne, A., Lichter, E., Dedoukou, X., Alexe, D., & Dessypris, N. (2002). What distinguishes unintentional injuries from injuries due to intimate partner violence: A study in Greek ambulatory care settings. *Injury Prevention, 8*(3), 197–201.

Ponsford, J., Cameron, P., Fitzgerald, M., Grant, M., Mikocka-Walus, A., & Schönberger, M. (2012). Predictors of postconcussive symptoms 3 months after mild traumatic brain injury. *Neuropsychology, 26*(3), 304–313. doi:10.1037/a0027888.

Rennison, C. M., DeKeseredy, W. S., & Dragiewicz, M. (2013). Intimate relationship status variations in violence against women: Urban, suburban, and rural differences. *Violence Against Women, 19*(11), 1312–1330. doi: 10.1177/1077801213514487.

Rivara, F. P., Anderson, M. L., Fishman, P., Bonomi, A. E., Reid, R. J., Carrell, D., & Thompson, R. S. (2007). Healthcare utilization and costs for women with a history of intimate partner violence. *American Journal of Preventive Medicine, 32*(2), 89–96.

Robles, T. F., Slatcher, R. B., Trombello, J. M., & McGinn, M. M. (2014). Marital quality and health: A meta-analytic review. *Psychological Bulletin, 140*(1), 140–187. http://dx.doi.org/10.1037/a0031859.

Rohmer, O., & Louvet, E. (2009). Describing Persons with Disability: Salience of disability, gender, and ethnicity. *Rehabilitation Psychology, 54*(1), 76–82. doi:10.1037/a0014445 .

Saxton, M., Curry, M. A., Powers, L. E., Maley, S., Eckels, K., & Gross, J. (2001). "Bring my scooter so I can leave you": A study of disabled women handling abuse by personal assistance providers. *Violence Against Women, 7*, 393–417.

Seelman, K. (2004). *Trends in rehabilitation and disability: Transition from a medical model to an integrative model* (part 3). Disability World, Issue 22; January–March. Retrieved March 15, 2014 from: http://www.disabilityworld.org/01-03_04/access/rehabtrends3.shtml.

Shalev, I., Moffitt, T. E., Sugden, K., Williams, B., Houts, R. M., Danese, A., & Caspi, A. (2013). Exposure to violence during childhood is associated with telomere erosion from 5 to 10 years of age: A longitudinal study. *Molecular Psychiatry, 18*(5), 576–581. http://dx.doi.org/10.1038/mp.2012.32.

Sheppard-Jones, K., Kleinert, H., Paulding, C., & Espinosa, C. (2008). Family planning for adolescents and young women with disabilities: A primer for practitioners. *International Journal on Disability and Human Development, 7*(3), 343–348. doi:10.1515/IJDHD.2008.7.3.343.

Sheridan, D. J., & Nash, K. R. (2007). Acute injury patterns of intimate partner violence victims. *Trauma, Violence, & Abuse, 8*(3), 281–289. doi:10.1177/1524838007303504.

Smeltzer, S. C. (2007). Pregnancy in women with physical disabilities. *Journal of Obstetric, Gynecologic, & Neonatal Nursing: Clinical Scholarship for the Care of Women, Childbearing Families, & Newborns, 36*(1), 88–96. doi:10.1111/j.1552-6909.2006.00121.x.

Steinmetz, E. (2006, May). Americans with Disabilities: 2002, *Current Population Reports*, 70–107. Washington, DC: U.S. Census Bureau.

Trojan, C., & Krull, A. C. (2012). Variations in wounding by relationship intimacy in homicide cases. *Journal of Interpersonal Violence, 27*(14), 2869–2888. doi:10.1177/0886260512438285

U.S. Congress. *Patient Protection and Affordable Care Act*, H.R. 3590. Public Law 111–148. 111th Cong., March 23, 2010.

Vanderploeg, R. D. (2013). Neuropsychological assessment. In D. B. Arciniegas, N. D. Zasler, R. D. Vanderploeg, & M. S. Jaffee (Eds.), *Management of adults with traumatic brain injury* (pp. 73–97). Washington, DC: American Psychiatric Publishing.

Violence Against Women Reauthorization Act of 2013. 42 USC 13701.

Warrener, C., Koivunen, J. M., & Postmus, J. L. (2013). Economic self-sufficiency among divorced women: Impact of depression, abuse, and efficacy. *Journal of Divorce & Remarriage, 54*(2), 163–175. http://dx.doi.org/10.1080/10502556.2012.755066.

Waters, H. R., Hyder, A. A. H., Rajkoti, Y., Basu, S., & Butchart, A. (2012). The costs of interpersonal violence—An international review. In D. M. Patel & R. M. Taylor (Eds.) and Institute of Medicine, National Research Council of the National Academies, *Social and economic costs of violence: Workshop summary* (pp. 34–51). Washington, DC: National Academies Press.

Wilson, S. R., Dodson, T. B., & Halpern, L. R. (2009). Maxillofacial injuries in intimate partner violence. In C. Mitchell & D. Anglin (Eds.), *Intimate partner violence: A health-based perspective* (pp. 201–221). New York: Oxford University Press.

Wu, V., Huff, H., & Bhandari, M. (2010). Pattern of physical injury associated with intimate partner violence in women presenting to the emergency department: A systematic review and meta-analysis. *Trauma, Violence, & Abuse, 11*(2), 71–82. doi:10.1177/1524838010367503.

Zweig, J. M., Schlichter, K. A., & Burt, M. R. (2002). Assisting women victims of violence who experience multiple barriers to services. *Violence Against Women, 8*, 162–180.

Chapter Eleven

The Impact of Stigma on Survivors of Intimate Partner Violence

Implications for Counseling

Christine E. Murray and Allison Crowe

Intimate partner violence (IPV) has long been a significant public health and social issue that affects far too many people in our country and world. Intimate partner violence—defined as any form of physical, sexual, emotional, and/or verbal abuse between current or former relationship partners (Murray & Graves, 2012)—is an all-too-common phenomenon. About one-half of all people report experiencing any form of violence—approximately half of both women and men report psychological abuse, and about one-third of women and one-fourth of men report physical and/or sexual abuse (Black et al., 2011).

However, even today, many people do not recognize the significant toll that IPV has on society. Stereotypes abound that suggest that survivors are somehow to blame for their abuse, or there must be something wrong with them for being subject to such violence. Through our research, we have studied the significant impact of the stigma that surrounds IPV, and we believe that this stigma contributes to many barriers and challenges for survivors and society as a whole. These include making it more difficult for survivors to seek and access help, compounding the traumatic effects that abuse has upon survivors, making it more difficult for domestic violence agencies to receive the resources they need to provide sufficient services to survivors, and keeping the issue hidden and under-recognized in our society.

In this chapter, we aim to familiarize readers with the nature of the stigma surrounding IPV so that they are better prepared to provide support to survivors with whom they work in counseling. We begin by reviewing the concept of stigma in general, based on previous theoretical and research work. We cover mental illness stigma, since this has been heavily studied across a variety of social science disciplines. Then, we explore specifically stigma as it relates to IPV, including some of the highlights from our own series of research studies on the topic. Finally, we provide a set of recommendations for counselors to consider when working with clients impacted by IPV. For the most part, our focus in this chapter is on victims (i.e., those facing current abuse) and survivors (i.e., those who have experienced abuse in the past but no longer are experiencing abuse). However, the stigma surrounding this issue also affects other groups, including child witnesses to parental IPV and even perpetrators.

UNDERSTANDING STIGMA

Theoretical Foundations

The stigma construct has long been studied by researchers across social science disciplines (Link & Phelan, 2001) dating back to Goffman's early writings (1963) on social stigma. In his seminal book, *Stigma: Notes on the Management of Spoiled Identity* Goffman interviewed members of marginalized groups including those with physical disabilities, mental illness, substance use disorders, among others, using autobiographies and case studies to explore the lives of those who felt stigmatized to reach a deeper understanding of the stigma experience. Three types of stigmas were discussed—*character traits, physical stigmas*, and *stigmas from group identities*. Character traits are those parts of individual character that are perceived negatively such as having weak will (e.g., substance use disorders) or unnatural passions, inferred from knowing one's history of mental illness or addiction. Physical stigma referred to visible disabilities or imperfections on the body stigma related to group identity referred to association with a racial, ethnic, or religious group membership that evokes negative assumptions from others outside of the group.

One of the most heavily researched stigmas is the stigma associated with having a mental illness. Building on early writings, scholars have identified various factors that combine to form mental illness stigma, including stereotype, prejudice, and discrimination (Corrigan, 2004). Stereotype is a knowledge structure one has about a group of people, with an example of a negative stereotype being "persons with mental illness are dangerous." Prejudice is agreement with said stereotype resulting in an emotional reaction (e.g., agreeing that persons with mental illness are indeed dangerous, resulting in the emotional reaction fear). Discrimination describes the behavioral response based on prejudice, such as avoiding the person with a mental illness because of fear from the prejudice and belief of dangerousness.

An additional theoretical foundation related to stigma is labeling and its impact on those who are the target of such labels (Scheff, 1974; Socall & Holtgraves, 1992). According to this notion, persons internalize a label, resulting in a snowball effect in which the experience of the stigma itself increases upset and negative emotional reactions, subsequently strengthening the symptoms the person might have experienced initially (e.g., depression, anxiety). A modification of labeling theory posits that even if labeling does not directly exacerbate mental illness, the negative label engenders self-devaluation, strengthening the belief that others are devaluing so that the negative attitudes increase one's vulnerability to mental illness (Link, 1987; Link, Cullen, Struening, Shrout, & Dohrenwend, 1989).

Previous Research on Stigma's Impact on Other Populations

It is well documented that negative attitudes are damaging and result in internal and external consequences for clients who experience them. Internal consequences include decreases in self-esteem and increases in shame, fear, and avoidance (Byrne, 2001; Corrigan, 2004; Link, Struening, Neese-Todd, Asmussen, & Phelan, 2001; Perlick et al., 2001). For example, a person with a mental illness might anticipate rejection from society and develop unhealthy coping strategies such as withdrawing from interaction with others to avoid discrimination and rejection. External consequences of stigma include exclusion, discrimination, prejudice, stereotyping from others, and social distance (Byrne, 2001; Corrigan, 2004; Link, Yang, Phelan, & Collins, 2004). Those who experience stigma are more inclined to be noncompliant with recommended mental health care and prescribed medications and have discontinued medication when they fear being stigmatized by others (Sirey et al., 2001). Authors have found that persons diagnosed with a mental illness are more likely to adhere to a medication regimen when they perceived lower levels of stigma associated with their mental illness and discontinue medication when they feared stigmatization from others (Sirey et al., 2001).

Previous Research on How Stigma is Addressed in Counseling

In the last decade, the counseling literature has begun to address the topic of mental illness stigma (Bathje & Pryor, 2011; Brown & Bradley, 2002; Crowe, 2013; Smith & Cashwell, 2010, 2011). Scholars have explored negative attitudes from professionals toward clients with mental illness in order to see if professional identity, among other factors, might contribute to attitudes toward mental illness (Smith & Cashwell, 2010). Since mental health professionals are important figures in the lives of those diagnosed with mental illness, it is of paramount importance that research related to attitudes continue in order to assess what helps, hurts, or simply contributes to negative attitudes toward mental illness.

Smith and Cashwell (2010) explored attitudes of counselors, social workers, psychologists, and non-mental health professionals, as well as trainees. Results suggested that mental health trainees and professionals had less stigmatizing attitudes than did non-mental health trainees and professionals. There were no differences in attitudes between mental health trainees and professionals based on professional orientation, and those mental health professionals who were in supervision had more positive attitudes than those who were not in supervision, suggesting the efficacy of ongoing supervision on attitudes toward mental illness. In a similar study (Smith & Cashwell, 2011) on social distance, or the proximity one desires in various social situations, mental health professionals and trainees desired less social distance than did non-mental health professionals and trainees from adults with mental illness, and women desired less social distance than men. There was a main effect found for professional orientation—counselors and psychologists desired less social distance than social workers and non-mental health professionals, suggesting professional orientation might make a difference in desired social distance toward those with a mental illness.

Aside from exploring how mental health professionals can reduce their own biases, larger efforts with the general population have been made to combat stigma by national programs sponsored by NAMI, SAMSHA, and similar advocacy groups. Examples include *StigmaBusters*, a group of the National Alliance on Mental Illness (NAMI) that searches popular media for stigmatizing portrayals of people with mental illness so that these can be excluded from the media. *In Our Own Voice* was established by the NAMI and was developed by consumers to educate the general population on mental illness through a contact program where adults with mental illness interact with audiences on the topic of mental illness. The *Elimination of Barriers Initiative*, a campaign developed by the Center for Mental Health Services, was used in eight pilot states to educate the public on stigma and mental illness. From this initiative, public service announcements to educate the public on mental illness were provided using radio, television, and print media (Corrigan & Gelb, 2006).

THE STIGMA SURROUNDING INTIMATE PARTNER VIOLENCE

Only recently, scholars have begun to apply the substantial body of literature on stigma to the phenomenon of IPV. Previously, researchers addressed components of this stigma, especially victim-blaming and the myths and stereotypes that surround IPV (e.g., Bryant & Spencer, 2003; Wuest & Merritt-Gray, 2001). However, a more in-depth analysis of the stigma surrounding

IPV has emerged, and we review those developments in this section. Following a more general overview of this stigma, we discuss the stigma that survivors may experience directly from counselors, especially when counselors lack the training and understanding to properly address IPV in their clinical work.

The Intimate Partner Violence Stigmatization Model

In 2013, Overstreet and Quinn published the first theoretical conceptualization of IPV-related stigma, which they called the Intimate Partner Violence Stigmatization Model. According to this model, there are three major sources of stigma that occur at three different levels: the individual level, the relational level, and the cultural level. First, *internalized stigma* refers to survivors internalizing and coming to believe negative views of themselves in relation to the IPV they experienced. Second, *anticipated stigma* refers to survivors' beliefs that others will treat them in stigmatizing ways when they reach out to them for help. This includes friends, family members, and more formal sources of potential support, such as counselors or law enforcement officials. Third, *cultural stigma* refers to stigmatizing beliefs that are perpetuated by larger social forces, such as organizational policies or traditions and the media.

According to Overstreet and Quinn (2013), each of these components of stigma impacts the extent to which survivors are willing and able to reach out for and receive the help and support they need. At the internalized level, they may feel that they are responsible for the abuse they experienced and therefore not believe they are worthy of help. With regard to anticipated stigma, survivors may believe that others will judge or discriminate against them, and therefore they may be less willing to reach out for help out of fear of these reactions. At the cultural level, survivors may encounter barriers to reaching out for help within social systems, such as if their experiences are minimized or denied when they seek help from their workplaces or religious communities. Overstreet and Quinn suggested that the degree to which survivors are impacted by stigma is influenced by the extent to which they view their experiences of IPV as being central and salient to their identities.

Types of Stigma

In our own research (Crowe & Murray, in press; Murray, Crowe, & Akers, manuscript under review; Murray, Crowe, & Brinkley, manuscript in preparation), we built upon previous research on stigma in general to identify the specific types of stigma that survivors may encounter. This focus is complementary to the work of Overstreet and Quinn (2013), in that their Intimate Partner Violence Stigmatization Model focused primarily on sources of stigma (i.e., internalized, relational, and cultural), and our framework focuses on types of stigma that may occur from any of these sources. Building primarily on conceptualizations of stigma presented by Byrne (2000) and Link and Phelan (2001), we have focused primarily on the following five categories of stigma:

1. **Blame:** Survivors may be blamed or viewed as somehow responsible for the abuse they experienced.
2. **Discrimination:** Survivors may be treated differently from others or encountered judgment and stereotypes as a result of their abuse.
3. **Loss of status:** Survivors may lose standing and/or power within social networks and systems as a result of having experienced abuse.
4. **Isolation:** Survivors may be isolated and separated from others due to having been abused.
5. **Shame:** Survivors may experience negative, painful emotions—such as guilt, embarrassment, and secrecy—as a result of their abuse experiences.

Taken together, we view these five stigma categories as intersecting to present a significant set of internal and external barriers that can have detrimental effects for survivors. In integrating these categories with the Intimate Partner Violence Stigmatization Model (Overstreet & Quinn, 2013), we contend that survivors may experience any of these components at any level of the model. Consider loss of status, for example. Survivors may come to believe that they are unworthy or less valuable than others because they have been abused (i.e., internalized stigma), they may anticipate that others will treat them with less respect or view them as less worthy if they find out about their abuse experiences (i.e., anticipated stigma), and they may perceive that survivors of abuse are not valued in society based on the messages they receive from the media (i.e., cultural stigma). At the present time, we are working with Overstreet to develop an integrated model of IPV-related stigma that will account for these various levels and types of abuse, and we anticipate that these advancements will provide an even more in-depth understanding of how IPV survivors experience stigma related to their abuse.

Additional insights from our previous research help to further explain the stigma surrounding abuse. First, we conducted a hierarchical cluster analysis study to examine whether certain types of stigma appear more likely to co-occur (Murray, Crowe, & Brinkley, manuscript in preparation). The results demonstrated four identifiable patterns of stigma experiences among a sample of 343 participants, who were all survivors of past abuse who had been out of any abusive relationships for at least two years. One group of participants (about one-quarter of the sample) demonstrated generally low experiences of stigma overall. Two groups experienced moderate levels of stigma.

One of these groups (14% of participants) noted higher levels of being blamed and treated as a "black sheep of the family," and the others' (19% of the sample) stigma-related experiences centered around the themes of secrecy, separation, shame, social exclusion, and stereotyping. The fourth group, representing about 43% of the participants, experienced generally high levels of stigma overall. In examining differences between these groups based on the types of abuse they'd experienced, we found only one statistically significant difference. Participants in the group that reported the highest levels of stigma also reported the highest rates of verbal abuse. Therefore, it appears that experiences of verbal abuse within an intimate relationship may be linked to higher experiences of abuse, although this finding is in need of further examination in future research.

In addition to our research with survivors, we sought input from an expert panel of 16 leaders of national advocacy organizations that work to address domestic and sexual violence (Murray, Crowe, & Akers, manuscript under review). Using Delphi methodology (i.e., a multi-phase, mixed-methodology approach that aims to achieve consensus among a group of recognized experts on a topic), the expert panel members participated in three rounds of questionnaires in order to move toward consensus views regarding the social context of the stigma surrounding domestic and sexual violence, how this stigma impacts resources available for victims and survivors, and strategies that can be taken at multiple levels to end the stigma. Several themes identified in this study are particularly relevant to the work of counselors. First, expert panel members affirmed that the stigma is fueled by such dynamics as victim-blaming, stereotypes, separation and isolation, and institutional barriers and obstacles that survivors encounter. Second, panel members noted that multiple levels of stigma may be compounded for survivors who have overlapping marginalized identities (e.g., immigration, disability, or socioeconomic status). Third, survivors may be reluctant to seek help due to the stigma, and they may encounter stigmatizing responses from potential sources of support when they do reach out for help. Finally, professional practices that can help to eliminate the stigma include creating non-stigmatizing environments, working to educate the community about the dynamics of IPV, collaborating with other organizations to ensure that they are not perpetuating the stigma, connecting survivors to sources of support and empowerment, and addressing the unique cultural dynamics that influence the nature of the stigma that individual survivors may encounter.

Sources of Stigma

Another major focus of our work has been on understanding the nature of the stigma that survivors encounter from specific sources of help (Crowe & Murray, in press). Since earlier research (Smith & Cashwell, 2010, 2011) had revealed stigma from professionals toward those with mental illness, we were curious to determine whether this occurred for survivors of IPV. In addition to the five types of stigma noted above, this research also identified two additional types of stigma that survivors may encounter from professionals. First, their experiences may be *dismissed or denied*, such as when they reach out for help but are either not believed or are told that their experiences are not important. Even worse, the professional may encourage the survivor to accept the abuse or even may side with the abuse perpetrator. Second, survivors may encounter *blatantly unprofessional behaviors*, including those that are unethical, disregard professional boundaries, and/or violate survivors' rights to competent, professional, and respectful services.

We should note that, overall, we believe that most professionals, and even informal helpers, who have roles that put them in the position to provide potential support to survivors of IPV are well-intentioned and typically provide responsive and supportive services. In our research, which has included both qualitative interviews and Internet-based surveys with survivors of past abusive relationships, we have specifically asked participants to describe stigmatizing responses they encountered. Given that we have drawn from convenience samples in our research, we cannot generalize these findings to populations outside of our studies, and we are not able to provide any definitive rates of stigma-related experiences among certain professional groups. That is, we can make no such claims at this point at some designated percentage of law enforcement officers, for example, perpetuate stigma.

We will note that some of the stories and details we heard about stigma-related experiences are, at first glance, hard to believe, as they run counter to general assumptions that professionals will use sound judgment and be compassionate and caring toward people who have experienced traumas like IPV. However, we have no reason to doubt the truthfulness of the stories shared with us by the participants in our research. First, the bulk of our research data has been drawn from anonymous surveys of survivors, collected via the Internet. As anonymous research, the participants' responses would not in any way provide identifiable information that would allow us to track down the people whose reactions and behaviors they described. Participants never identified these people by name, and their responses were private and secure. Therefore, we do not believe anyone would have made up stories as a result of "having an axe to grind" against any of the people they described. Second, we heard many times from survivors in our research that they were sharing their stories because they hoped their stories would help others. Although survey participants could have completed the survey in about 20 minutes, a good number of them took hours to provide detailed information about their experiences, thereby making a personal commitment and investment in this research. The level of detail provided, along with statements indicating their intention to help others, suggest to us that participants were truthful and forthcoming about their experiences. Finally, although survivors can find many sources of positive, supportive help in relation to their abuse, we have heard anecdotally from many survivors and professionals who work with them that experiences of stigma are common. So, while some of the experiences of survivors may be difficult to believe or comprehend at first, we believe they are accurate representations of the potentially stigmatizing responses that survivors may encounter when they reach out for help, especially by professionals who are inadequately trained to address IPV.

The professionals that survivors in our research (Crowe & Murray, in press) noted as providing stigmatizing responses included law enforcement officials, the court system, medical professionals, domestic violence agencies, parenting-related resources, religious organizations, employment and educational organizations, and mental health professionals. As the focus of the current chapter is on counselors, we will provide a brief overview of the most frequently encountered types of stigma from other professional groups before we address mental health professionals in a separate section below. All quotes are taken from participants in our research, as cited in Crowe and Murray (in press).

> Law enforcement. Survivors noted the most frequent stigma experience from law enforcement officials was being dismissed or denied. For example, one participant said, "I was told since I had no visible injuries they couldn't make him leave."
>
> The court system. The most common stigma-related experience in the court system was blame. One participant said, "(The judge) often asked why I hadn't done anything earlier."
>
> Medical professionals. Blame and discrimination were noted among participants as experiences they encountered with medical professionals. A participant said, "The people at the hospital . . . act like your [*sic*] making things up for attention."
>
> Domestic violence agencies. Some survivors encountered professionals who dismissed or denied their experiences, such as is reflected in the following quote: "I'd begin to explain and she would interrupt."
>
> Parenting-related resources. Survivors may feel blamed as parents when seeking help for their children. One participant said, "I was told that it was my fault for being depressed and anxious."
>
> Religious organizations. Survivors also may encounter blaming when seeking help from their religious organizations. For example, a participant was told, "You need to submit yourself to God and become a better wife."

> Employment and education. Survivors may be discriminated against in their workplaces or while pursuing education. For example, they may be fired or less likely to be hired because they are viewed as "a high risk for calling in."

It is important to note that most survivors do not experience stigma from all potential professional sources of support, but rather they may encounter different responses from different professionals. This also almost certainly varies from community to community.

IPV-related Stigma from Counselors and Other Mental Health Professionals

Unfortunately, many mental health professionals lack substantial training to understand and address IPV (Gauthier & Levendosky, 1996; Murray & Graves, 2012; Wingfield & Blocker, 1998). As such, it should not be surprising that our research provided examples of IPV survivors encountering stigmatizing responses when seeking help from mental health professionals. In our research on the stigma that survivors encounter from professionals, 34 statements made by participants reflected stigma from mental health professionals. These statements included 15 representing dismiss/denied, 5 for blame, 4 for discrimination, 3 for blatant unprofessionalism, and 7 for shame. Below are just some of the quotes from survivors that illustrate how some survivors experienced stigma from counselors, drawing from our research (Crowe & Murray, in press, and more recent data we have collected in our ongoing studies):

- "My marital counselor said, 'make a list of all the sins you committed against him, and ask him for forgiveness.'"
- "He told me I was 'triggering' my ex's controlling behavior and sexual assaults, and encouraged me to focus on my own 'contributions' to the problem rather than find[ing] ways to stay safe."
- "The counselor actually said during our first session that she did not like to, or want to work with past victims of IPV."
- "One time I went to a counselor because I was having a hard time with my libido (go figure, who wouldn't after experienced such horrors) and the therapist told me to give my ex more blow jobs."
- "The first counselor I went to completely ignored it when I told him I was raped in my relationship—only wanted to focus on depression symptoms."
- "My counselor did not believe me in the most recent rape/sexual assault so that was very shaming. Because she 'latched' onto this, instead of helping me with my presenting issues, I did not return. Instead I suffered in fear that he [abuser] would find out I went to a counselor. The other counselor

I saw was more accepting, but never really addressed it with me. I wanted to hide from it, and she let me."

- "One of the mental health counselors treated me like I was 'untrustworthy' and I felt imprisoned (yes, I went back to the abuser)."
- "In multiple attempts to seek therapy and counseling, I experienced a counselor who blamed me for not 'talking to him' enough, for not 'trying to open dialogue' about the way I felt. I also experienced a counselor who stated, 'I'm not going to candy-coat this, this is abuse' and admonished me for not leaving immediately with my two toddler children. I experienced a counselor who told me I had 'boundary issues'; one who tried to provide couples' counseling and admonished me to 'just do the little things he asks you to do. Is that so hard?'"

These quotes from survivors of abuse are alarming, although again we do not believe that they are representative of the responses that counselors and other mental health professionals overall offer to survivors when they seek help. Nonetheless, in our view, the fact that *any* survivor *ever* has had to encounter such responses from counselors who were in prime positions to help and support them is a call to action for all counselors to work proactively to ensure that they and other counselors with whom they work are better prepared to provide supportive, responsive help to survivors seeking help.

RECOMMENDATIONS FOR COUNSELORS

In light of the potential for counselors to perpetuate stigma, we believe it is critical for counselors to take steps to provide competent, supportive, nonstigmatizing services when survivors of IPV reach out to them for help. Therefore, we conclude this chapter with recommendations for counselors to guide them in their work with clients impacted by IPV.

Ensure Competence to Address IPV in Clinical Work

Coverage of IPV is often limited in mental health professional training programs (Gauthier & Levendosky, 1996; Murray & Graves, 2012; Wingfield & Blocker, 1998). Therefore, counselors working in settings in which they may work with clients impacted by IPV—which, given the high rates of IPV among the general population, includes virtually any clinical practice setting—should seek out additional training to ensure that they are competent to understand, assess, and provide counseling related to IPV. This may come in the form of continuing education workshops, self-directed reading, and participation in trainings offered by domestic violence advocacy agencies. Recently, we developed a checklist for clients to use to help them find a counselor competent to work with survivors of IPV (See http://www.seethetriumph.

org/blog/finding-a-counselor-who-is-competent-to-serve-survivors), and the following self-reflection questions are derived from that checklist:

- What level of training have I received related to IPV? Do I understand the safety and relational dynamics involved in IPV to a sufficient level?
- What have I learned from my past experiences working with clients impacted by IPV? What do I still need to know?
- Am I prepared to help clients with safety planning and otherwise addressing the safety concerns that may arise in light of IPV?
- Am I familiar with best practice guideline for treating IPV (e.g., not providing couples counseling when IPV is present)?
- Do I know how to account for trauma symptoms in making mental health disorder diagnoses?
- Am I familiar with resources in my community to help clients impacted by IPV?

Counselors can review their responses to these questions to help them identify areas for building increased competence to work with this population.

Avoid Stigmatizing Practices

It should be clear that the types of counselor responses and behaviors that survivors described in the quotes in the above section should be avoided. More broadly, counselors should continuously monitor their interactions with clients to ensure that they do not perpetuate any of the types of stigma— such as blame, discrimination, loss of status, isolation, shame, dismissal/denial, and blatant unprofessionalism— that survivors have reported experiencing from professionals. Of course, blatant or extreme examples of these types of stigma, such as those illustrated in the survivors' quotes above, are more readily identified. However, these forms of stigma also may be conveyed in more subtle or indirect ways. For example, a counselor who asks a victim, "What did you say or do to him/her before he/she was violent toward you?" may subtly imply that the victim is responsible for the abuse. Even if this question is asked in a supportive, nonjudgmental manner, the client may perceive judgment and blame in this statement, especially if s/he has a high degree of anticipated stigma (Overstreet & Quinn, 2013). Therefore, working with this client population requires a high degree of self-reflection, self-monitoring, and attunement to clients' nonverbal reactions to ensure that any infractions are addressed and corrected as soon as possible so as not to hinder the therapeutic relationship.

Work Proactively to Create a Safe, Non-Stigmatizing Climate

Beyond merely avoiding stigmatizing actions, counselors can actively work to ensure that they deliver services in a supportive, emotionally safe, and empowering climate. One step toward doing this is to ensure that the impact of trauma is considered the assessment and diagnosis process. According to Helfrich, Fujiura, and Rutkowski-Kmitta (2008), "It is imperative that IPV not be equated with mental illness but rather considered as a risk factor that, when identified, serves to initiate a series of informed responses and further exploration of each individual woman's presentation and service needs" (p. 450).

Diagnoses should only be applied when they are clearly appropriate, and the implication of labeling survivors with a mental health disorder through diagnosis should be considered carefully, as these diagnoses could add a compounding layer of stigma to survivors. Overall, it is important to account for trauma symptoms in the diagnosis process (Murray & Graves, 2012).

In addition, counselors can create non-stigmatizing therapeutic climates for their clients by making IPV a visible issue in various aspects of their work. For example, they can display empowering and informational materials about IPV in their office space, such as posters with empowering messages (e.g., "It's not your fault") and brochures for local domestic violence service agencies. Also, counselors can universally screen clients for IPV experiences (Murray & Graves, 2012). By asking this question of all clients, they avoid falling into stereotypes that only certain client populations are susceptible to IPV. Further, when asking about IPV experiences, counselors can use open-ended questions and normalizing language, such as by saying, "Many people have experienced unhealthy or abusive relationship dynamics in their lives. How would you say this applies to you, if at all?" Therefore, by opening up the dialogue with a sense of acceptance and support, counselors can convey to their clients that they are comfortable with talking openly about IPV, and that they view this as a relatively normal experience for clients in counseling that the client need not feel ashamed to disclose.

Help Clients Address and Overcome Stigma from Other Sources

Although some clients may not view stigma as part of their experiences related to IPV, such as the 25% of participants in our study (Murray, Crowe, & Brinkley, manuscript in preparation), other clients may present for counseling having experienced moderate to high levels of stigma, often from internal, relational, and/or cultural sources (Overstreet & Quinn, 2013). Counselors can help clients address this stigma, both as they experience it currently and as a result of past experiences. Clients currently in the process of seeking help from other sources (e.g., law enforcement or the court system) may encounter stigma from people within these systems and/or as a result of institutional policies or barriers. If this type of stigma arises, counselors can work collaboratively with their clients to help buffer them from its impact, such as by developing strategies for counteracting the stigma or coping with its consequences.

In addition, counselors can support clients in overcoming past stigma-related experiences that they encountered with others, which may even include past counselors from whom they sought help. To this end, counselors can ask clients about their experiences and how they were impacted by those experiences. Cognitive interventions may be useful for challenging internalized stigma-related beliefs, such as self-blame or feelings of being less worthy as a result of the abuse. Keeping in mind the stigma conceptualizations reviewed in this chapter, counselors can address stigma from a multidimensional framework, including different sources of stigma (Overstreet & Quinn, 2013) and different types of stigma (Crowe & Murray, in press).

Connect Survivors to Supportive, "Stigma-Free" Environments

Finally, counselors can help clients who are survivors of IPV with various resources that provide a stigma-free environment for connecting with others and receiving support. One valuable source for this may be a local support group run through a women's center or domestic violence agency. In addition, we encourage counselors to visit our See the Triumph campaign (www.seethetriumph.org) as an additional resource for the clients with whom they work. Based on the research that we have conducted on how survivors overcome the stigma surrounding abuse, we co-founded the See the Triumph campaign. The campaign has two main goals. First, we aim to end the stigma surrounding IPV. Second, we work to create resources to provide support and motivation for survivors. Our initiatives include a blog, various social media platforms through with survivors and others can connect with us (e.g., Pinterest, Twitter, Facebook, and Causes), Collections that bring together resources we've created around specific topics, and the creation of specific tools, such as the Counselor Checklist noted above and workbooks for groups of survivors to use for support groups (the latter of which are currently in development).

CONCLUSION

In sum, we believe that the stigma surrounding IPV presents a host of significant challenges for survivors, as well as for professionals and organizations that support them. Although IPV-related stigma has only recently garnered substantial research and theoretical attention, preliminary findings support the need for greater attention to this issue, both in future research and practice developments. Counselors are called upon to help provide non-stigmatizing support to survivors, as well as to provide assistance to clients in helping them overcome the stigma they may have faced from other sources. Counselors have a valuable opportunity to assist victims and survivors of IPV in knowing that they are not to blame for their abuse, that they are worthy of support and healing, and that they can feel proud of their strength in overcoming their abuse and the stigma that surrounds it.

DISCUSSION QUESTIONS

1. What were your reactions to the survivor quotes presented throughout the chapter?
2. In what ways do you think the stigma that survivors of IPV face impacts their willingness to seek help?
3. What stereotypes or biases do you think you hold toward IPV, perpetrators, victims, and survivors? What steps do you need to take in order to examine and re-evaluate these biases?
4. What are the unique biases faced by individuals with the multiple gender identities in this regard? What steps do you need to take to address these biases?
5. Think about the way that IPV is depicted in the media, including news reports, magazines, movies, television shows, advertising, and so on. In what ways do you think that the media perpetuates the stigma surrounding IPV?
6. What are some proactive steps you could take in your counseling practice to create a stigma-free environment for clients seeking help related to experiences with IPV?

REFERENCES

Bathje, G. J., & Pryor, J. B. (2011). The relationship of public and self-stigma to seeking mental health services. *Journal of Mental Health Counseling, 33,* 161–177.

Black, M. C., Basile, K. C., Breiding, M. J., Smith, S. G., Walters, M. L., Merrick, M. T., Chen, J., & Stevens, M. R. (2011). *The national intimate partner and sexual violence survey (NISVS): 2010 summary report.* Atlanta, GA: National Center for Injury Prevention and Control, Centers for Disease Control and Prevention. Retrieved from www.cdc.gov/ViolencePrevention/pdf/NISVS_Report2010-a.pdf.

Brown, K., & Bradley, L. J. (2002). Reducing the stigma of mental illness. *Journal of Mental Health Counseling, 24,* 081–087.

Bryant, S. A., & Spencer, G. A. (2003). University students' attitudes about attributing blame in domestic violence. *Journal of Family Violence, 18,* 369–376.

Byrne, P. (2000). Stigma of mental illness and ways of diminishing it. *Advances in Psychiatric Treatment, 6,* 65–72.

Corrigan, P. W. (2004). Target-specific stigma change: A strategy for impacting mental illness stigma. *Psychiatric Rehabilitation Journal, 28,* 113–121.

Corrigan, P. W., & Gelb, B. (2006). Three programs that use mass approaches to challenge the stigma of mental illness. *Psychiatric Services, 57,* 393–398.

Crowe, A. (2013). Mental illness stigma: Early lessons. *Counseling Today, 56,* 24–25.

Crowe, A., & Murray, C. E. (2015). Stigma from professional helpers toward survivors of intimate partner violence. *Partner Abuse, 6* (2), p. 157–179.

Gauthier, L. M., & Levendosky, A. A. (1996). Assessment and treatment of couples with abusive male partners: Guidelines for therapists. *Psychotherapy, 33,* 403–417.

Goffman, E. (1963). *Stigma: Notes on the management of spoiled identity.* New York: Simon & Schuster.

Helfrich, C. A., Fujiura, G. T., & Rutkowski-Kmitta, V. (2008). Mental health disorders and functioning of women in domestic violence shelters. *Journal of Interpersonal Violence, 23,* 437–453.

Link, B. G. (1987). Understanding labeling effects in the area of mental disorders: An assessment of the effects of expectations of rejection. *American Sociological Review, 52,* 96–112.

Link, B. G., Cullen, F., Struening, E., Shrout, P., & Dohrenwend, B. (1989). A modified labeling theory approach in the area of the mental disorders: An empirical assessment. *American Sociological Review, 54,* 400–423.

Link, B. G., & Phelan, J. C. (2001). Conceptualizing stigma. *Annual Review of Sociology, 27,* 363–385.

Link, B. G., Struening, E., Neese-Todd, S., Asmussen, S., & Phelan, J. (2001). The consequences of stigma for the self-esteem of people with mental illnesses. *Psychiatric Services, 52,* 1621–1626.

Link, B. G., Yang, L., Phelan, J., & Collins, P. (2004). Measuring mental illness stigma *Schizophrenia Bulletin, 30,* 511–541.

Murray, C. E., Crowe, A., & Akers, W. (2016). How can we end the stigma surrounding domestic and sexual violence? A modified Delphi study with national advocacy leaders. *Journal of Family Violence, 31* (3), 271–287. DOI: 10.1007/s10896-015-9768-9.

Murray, C. E., Crowe, A., & Brinkley, J. (2015). The stigma surrounding intimate partner violence: A cluster analysis study. *Partner Abuse, 6,* 320–336.

Murray, C. E., & Graves, K. N. (2012). *Responding to family violence.* New York: Routledge.

Overstreet, N. M., & Quinn, D. M. (2013). The intimate partner violence stigmatization model and barriers to help seeking. *Basic and Applied Social Psychology, 35,* 109–122.

Perlick, D., Rosenheck, R., Clarkin, J., Sirey, J., Salahi, J., Struening, E., & Link, B. (2001). Adverse effects of perceived stigma on social adaptation of persons diagnosed with bipolar affective disorder. *Psychiatric Services, 52,* 1627–1632.

Scheff, T. J. (1974). The labelling theory of mental illness. *American Sociological Review, 39,* 444–452.

Sirey, J., Bruce, M., Alexopoulos, G., Perlick, D., Friedman, S., & Meyers, B. (2001). Perceived stigma and patient-rated severity of illness as predictors of antidepressant drug adherence. *Psychiatric Services, 52,* 1615–1620.

Smith, A. L., & Cashwell, C. S. (2010). Stigma and mental illness: Investigating attitudes of mental health and non mental health professionals and trainees. *Journal of Humanistic Counseling, Education, & Development, 49,* 189–202.

Smith, A. L., & Cashwell, C. S. (2011). Social distance and mental illness: Attitudes among mental health and non-mental health professionals and trainees. *Professional Counselor, 1 (1),* 13–20

Socall, D., & Holtgraves, T. (1992). Attitudes toward the mentally ill: The effects of labels and beliefs. *The Sociological Quarterly, 33,* 435–445.

Wingfield, D. A., & Blocker, L. S. (1998). Development of a certificate training curriculum for domestic violence counseling. *Journal of Addictions and Offender Counseling, 18,* 86–94.

Wuest, J., & Merritt-Gray, M. (2001). Beyond survival: Reclaiming self after leaving an abusive male partner. *Canadian Journal of Nursing Research, 32,* 79–94.

Chapter Twelve

Essential Elements for an Effective Treatment Model of Domestic Violence in a Complex World

Lenore E. A. Walker and Tara Jungersen

WHAT ARE TRAUMA-INFORMED SERVICES?

Trauma-informed services are those interventions that are delivered in a culture in which everyone understands the incidence and prevalence of trauma, the psychological impact of trauma, the intersection of trauma with other patient issues, and the complex paths to healing and recovery from trauma. Within this culture, there is a conscious effort to avoid retraumatization of those who seek services, and to prevent the vicarious traumatization of those who are on the staff, whether or not they deliver services: "Safety First" is the credo of anyone providing trauma-informed services. Regardless of whether or not trauma-specific treatment models are used, both the structure and the function of service delivery attend to the issues known to be of importance to trauma survivors. All service providers in this trauma-informed culture make the effort to "do no harm."

Trauma-specific services differ from trauma-informed services in that they have the primary task to address the impact of trauma directly, to focus on its impact, and to facilitate trauma recovery. Usually trauma-specific services address Posttraumatic Stress Disorder (PTSD) and other mental health consequences of trauma. While some trauma-specific services focus on a particular type of trauma (e.g., domestic violence and sexual assault), others intersect with a complex system of factors, including gender, sexual orientation, transgender and gender non-conforming issues, substance abuse, severe mental illness, racism, classism, poverty and other social issues, and legal involvement.

In the late twentieth century, as community-based agencies began to learn about the incidence and prevalence of trauma in the persons they served, many attempted to create a new culture that incorporated the trauma-informed philosophy. Harris and Fallot (2001) described a program to produce what they called "culture shift" in agencies. Taking an average of two years to finalize the shift, they suggested implementation in stages by persuading the administration and the staff mental health practitioners to agree to accept five core values: (1) safety, (2) trustworthiness, (3) choice, (4) collaboration, and (5) empowerment. Most of the time, developing a culture shift within an organization is much more difficult than within an individual. In an agency it is necessary to get either a knowledgeable champion to lead the implementation or an external consultant to educate all employees at once. In either case, the trauma-informed organizational culture shift occurs across time and will not likely develop after just one or two training sessions. Furthermore, all departments of the agency must abide by these principles—from the scheduler handling an appointment request to the security personnel displaying visible weapons.

The individual working to develop a trauma-informed philosophy has many opportunities. Options exist to attend trauma workshops and conferences and to peruse both the professional and research literature, as well as to adopt already developed change models. While time-consuming given professionals' busy schedules, these efforts are easier when others are on the same change trajectory. Nonetheless, better understanding of trauma survivors' needs, strengths, and challenges can improve service delivery in a variety of expected and unintended ways. Before beginning any trauma-specific program, it is important to check that your own environment and program meets a trauma-informed services model to avoid re-traumatization.

Trauma-Informed Care Basics

Providers must ensure that *physical and emotional safety* are maintained, so that trauma survivors feel safe in disclosing and re-experiencing their trauma. It may be important to re-examine: How secure is the area where services are delivered? Are there people around? How is security handled? Does your own office have a "welcoming" feel to it? Is it personalized with pictures, paintings, and other décor? Is it respectful of the variety of cultures of the patients who will enter? Are the restrooms clean and secure? In group settings, is there sufficient personal space for different patients? Is the staff attentive to uneasiness or discomfort of the patients and concerned with respecting privacy? Do you, as the provider, feel safe and secure when working with certain populations (e.g., with domestic violence survivors or their abusers)?

Mutual goal-setting with patients is already a good step toward *trustworthiness*. Task clarity, consistency, and respecting boundaries are all important features of trustworthiness in a relationship. Providers avoid multiple relationships and clarify boundaries when they are unavoidable in order to keep the professional relationship inviolate. Informed consent is required when beginning new areas together, along with clarification that consent can be revoked at any time. This helps keep these mutual goals in mind. Providers must explain the patient's privilege along with willingness to keep everything confidential within certain legal and ethical exceptions (i.e., responding to legal subpoenas, making child/elder abuse reports, or taking some action if you think the patient is going to harm him or herself or others). It is also important to clarify the role as the provider to make it clear what you can and cannot do in the relationship. A clear explanation of the risks and benefits, as well as consequences, of certain actions all contribute to rebuilding trust. This trust-building is critical, especially since most trauma survivors have felt betrayed by their family, partners, or even by their own expectations.

How much *choice* do you and/or your patients have about what happens in therapy? If you are conducting groups in a closed setting, like a hospital or jail, do you give participants some choices, like whether to do a particular exercise or skill, or talk about a particular topic? If your program is quite regimented, can you give an individual or group choice about how much time to spend on a particular topic area? Are the therapy services a privilege, a right, or even a responsibility? What, if any, are the consequences for not following the rules and are they arbitrary or punitive? What choices do you, as the therapist, feel you have in delivering the services? Most trauma survivors, especially those who have experienced domestic violence, have had their choices taken away from them by controlling partners, so helping them even be willing to make a small choice can be therapeutic.

How can you maximize *collaboration* and sharing of power? While it is understood that the therapist has more power than the patient in knowledge or training about recovery, is the patient's knowledge about her or his own experiences acknowledged and willingly shared in its importance? Does the treatment program foster collaboration between the patient and the therapist? Can there be some advance planning in which the patient does collaborate? Does the administration in a group setting permit collaboration with the therapist and support the staff in decisions around various issues? Domestic violence survivors have had their power taken away, so helping them regain power in a variety of situations is an important part of trauma work.

The process of *empowerment* helps patients feel important and able to perform the skills that they need to function again and is a critical area for trauma recovery. Strength-based interventions often assist to rebuild the self-confidence and self-esteem that trauma survivors need to heal and return to wellness. Staff needs to feel engaged and empowered also, so they can continue to empower their patients. Keeping a positive and affirming attitude is an important part of empowerment. Therapists need to feel that they are helping their patients, but their source of self-esteem should come from within themselves and supportive consultants and supervisors, not their clients.

GENDER VIOLENCE AND DOMESTIC VIOLENCE

When designing effective treatment programs for domestic violence survivors, it is important to understand that most victims, although not all, are women and most of their abusers, although not all, are men. Given these data, it is important to recognize that when working with battered women survivors, other intersecting issues may make any intervention more complex. Gender violence includes acts such as child physical and sexual abuse, sexual assault and rape, sex trafficking, sexual exploitation between authority figures and patient/client, and sexual harassment in the university or workplace. In some of these forms of abuse, the victims may also be boys or men, but the perpetrators are overwhelmingly male. Many battered women have experienced these other forms of gender violence in addition to having been abused by an intimate partner. Some, although not many, have had more than one partner who abused them. The battered women for whom we provide services also have other non-gendered experiences that may intersect with their trauma responses such as racism, sexism, ageism, discrimination because of their immigration status, sexual orientation, and transgender and gender non-conforming behavior (Walker, 2017).

Couples Therapy

Early on within the domestic violence treatment movement, couples therapy was seen as problematic in relationships where violence was present. First, and perhaps most importantly, the abuser needs to take full responsibility for the abuse of power and control and the use of violence. There may be many components of the relationship that are unhealthy, but it is the person's choice to use violence, and only the person can stop the domestic violence. The goal is to be violence-free, not to fix the relationship to adapt to the abuse. While it is true that many people in domestic violence relationships have dependency issues, these must be confronted and dealt with separately and not together. Interfering with the system that has violated the boundaries through the use of physical, sexual, and psychological violence to get power and control may escalate out of control and further hurt, or even kill, the participants. This is especially true when the couple is on the verge of or already has separated, which is the most dangerous time in domestic violence relationships. In traditional couples' therapy, the therapist listens to both sides of the participants' stories; in domestic violence relationships the abuse is always worse than either party can describe verbally. Further, trauma victims usually lose the ability to perceive objectivity and neutrality; if the system's therapist is not seen as objective and fair, this type of treatment will not be successful (Walker, 2017). They are less likely to develop trust that the therapist will believe and support them, especially if the therapist tries to explain the abusers' point of view. An analysis of a domestic violence relationship cannot share blame for the abuse, even indirectly; it is the responsibility of the abuser not to use violence no matter what the behavior of the other party unless it is necessary in self-defense.

Adaptation to Other Groups

The STEP program described below was originally designed to be used with battered women whose partners were also involved in offender-specific counseling to assist in stopping their violent behavior. When STEP's use expanded into a variety of settings outside of independent practice, such as in community agencies and the jails and prisons, most participants were found to have had multiple trauma experiences. Interestingly, we tried modifying the program for intervention with adolescent girls; however, an explicit focus on trauma was not productive. The most important modification for this group required embedding the trauma work within a focus on positive and developmentally appropriate growth. When we modified the program for men, we found the opposite; they loved the program and very little modification was needed. This is probably because so many men who later use violence in their lives were also directly abused or were exposed to domestic violence as children (Hotaling & Sugarman, 1986).

SURVIVOR THERAPY EMPOWERMENT PROGRAM (STEP)

Philosophy and Theory

The Survivor Therapy Empowerment Program (STEP) was originally developed to be a companion program for women whose violent partners were attending batterer intervention programs. At the time the program was originally developed, in the mid 1990s, it was necessary for women to learn what the men were learning, so that men could not use their new knowledge to further terrorize or intimidate the women (Walker, 2017). The program was based on both feminist and trauma theories.

Principles of feminist theory focus on the fact that women and men are not yet treated as equals in the world, which then causes oppression and lack of choices for women if forced into behaving in sex role socialization patterns. Research found that men are more likely to be at risk to perpetrate violence while women are more likely to be at risk to become victims of different types of violence (Walker, 1999). Although domestic violence is also found in LGBTQ couples, the gendered aspect of need for power and control remain a dominant part of the abuse. If the therapist is less authoritative and more authentic about sharing the power in the therapy session, by valuing the patient's experiences as much as her or his psychology knowledge, then the power issues that are replicated in therapy relationships can be examined and modified. The feminist slogan, "The personal is political" suggests that what happens to one woman will have an impact on all women. Validation, supporting strengths, and empowerment are key ways to reverse the impact of trauma and work toward new levels of wellness and resilience.

Principles of trauma therapy focus on the fact that exposure to danger and trauma can cause psychological problems in healthy or clinical populations, and that verbal psychotherapy can reduce or ameliorate these problems. However, trauma exposure may result in some resiliency loss, so it will be important to build in pathways to wellness beyond just resolving trauma symptoms. Trauma theory suggests that safety and stability are critical for healing as are respect, positive regard, and courage to heal. An optimistic attitude about life, as expressed within different cultures, is also a factor in helping trauma survivors heal. Re-empowerment and moving toward growth with a focus on building self-efficacy through strengths is also part of the trauma philosophy.

Both the feminist and trauma theories borrowed techniques from other therapy theories as their development started at about the same time. It is probably not surprising that many of the techniques utilized are similar given that the goals are so similar. For example, Briere, who developed one of the earliest interventions on healing from trauma, emphasized the identification of trauma triggers that caused the continued re-experiencing of trauma as an important treatment focus (Briere & Scott, 2015). Once it was understood that the trauma response impacted emotions, which then triggered anxiety responses, use of developed behavioral techniques (e.g., deep muscle relaxation, visual imagery, breathing, relaxation training, approximate desensitization, and thought stopping) began to be adapted for trauma-specific treatment. Feminist techniques, such as reviewing all the "shoulds" that came from sex role socialization and recognition of choice of how a person behaved, also began to be implemented during therapy. Assertiveness training was adapted to assist women in taking back their power in a less threatening way (Alberti & Emmons, 2008). Gold (2008) expanded the focus to include all the other areas of the person's life in which the trauma interfered, especially the disruption of the usual developmental path for adults traumatized as children. Foa, Rothbaum, Riggs and Murdock's (1991) prolonged exposure and breathing techniques were also adapted for those battered women for whom they were helpful. Teaching battered women the cycle of violence and how to break the patterns (Walker, 2009) has also been found to be useful in healing.

TRIPARTITE MODEL

With the above cited theories in mind, the first iteration of the STEP program began with 12 sessions, with each session divided into three parts. Later it became clear that some sessions needed more than time, so the 12 "sessions" became 12 "units," divided into as many sessions as were needed (Jungersen, Walker, Black, Kennedy, & Groth, in review). Each unit, then, has the three components. First, facilitators lead an educational segment about a particular issue common to trauma survivors. Next, participants discuss and process what was just presented, and finally, participants learn a skill to reinforce the particular topic presented. The STEP program offers therapists the chance to review and hone their group facilitation skills, especially techniques that encourage sharing the "talk" time and redirect group members who may attempt to monopolize the group. The tripartite model also allows facilitators to structure the sessions based on the needs of the individual group or agency.

Reinforcement of Trauma Healing Skills

Clients/patients undergoing trauma-focused interventions benefit from reinforcement of information and skills outside of the face-to-face sessions. Therefore, handouts were developed within the STEP program in order to review both the educational and skill-building components. Participants are provided handouts that review key components of the educational portion of each unit, as well as handouts outlining the skills to be practiced in between sessions. These skills are also assigned as an exercise to practice before the next session and are reviewed at the beginning of the next session. Both handouts attempt to address the probability that PTSD symptoms of anxiety, distractibility, and inability to concentrate could have interfered with the participant's understanding all that was discussed in the session.

The original STEP program was developed for women to complete sequentially, in closed groups, partly to overcome some of the isolation often associated with domestic violence. However, later, when the program was introduced in the jails, it became impossible to control the number of participants or expect that each participant would attend sequentially. Therefore, each STEP unit was redesigned to stand alone. This makes it possible to use STEP concurrently with individual therapy, as a unit may be introduced as needed when a particular issue arises. For example, if a woman was trying to develop cognitive clarity in therapy, the unit dealing with common myths or ways battered women typically avoid thinking about the abuse can be used in individual therapy. Or the unit that deals with identification and descriptions of various forms of intimate partner violence can be used in safety planning whenever that need arises. As will be described later, the program efficacy research demonstrates that the order in which the units were presented and the settings where STEP was used accounted for less variance toward trauma healing than did the number of units attended. That is, the more of the 12 units attended, the lower the anxiety and satisfaction experienced (Jungersen et al., in review).

Modification for Use in Jails, Prisons, or Hospital Settings

The traditional group setting, with the same 8 to 12 members who meet for approximately 1½ to 2 hours each week, required modification for use of STEP in the local jails or any setting that required open groups with strict time limits. Anywhere between 20 and 45 women could show up at the jail groups and some members could not attend consistently because of court appearances or other mandatory activities. It became necessary to have three or four group leaders present to assist in managing the group process parts of the program. One of the requirements of the jail was to permit attendance by anyone who self-identified as having had trauma experiences and wished to come. Given that broad definition, initially women who had traumatic experiences other than domestic violence also came and participated. In some cases, these women began to identify as having been abused in former relationships after listening to the descriptions of domestic violence. In other cases, women who had not experienced intimate partner abuse kept coming to the groups because they found the information and skill building interesting and helpful to heal from other traumatic experiences, such as physical and sexual child abuse, sex trafficking and other forms of exploitation and harassment. Several STEP groups were conducted in the general jail population and in specialized units (e.g., women with substance abuse or domestic violence charges). Other groups were conducted in mental health units. The evidence-based research found that the site of the program did not make a difference in STEP's efficacy; all women's anxiety was reduced and satisfaction levels increased. The magnitude of the change was directly related to how many of the 12 units the women attended (Jungersen et al., in review).

When STEP was modified to use in the juvenile detention center with girls, it was found that many of the topics utilized in the adult program were not of as much interest to them. A different program, Girl Talk, was developed using many of the same principles and skills training, but the educational component was embedded in areas such as urban/hip-hop music, choosing the right person to date, and other teenage interests. STEP was also modified for working with men who were housed in the mental health unit of a local jail and had experienced trauma. They were also assessed for program efficacy and like the women, they were both satisfied and had reductions in anxiety measured (Jungersen et al., in review). Table 12.1 describes the 12 units of the STEP Program.

Table 12.1. Sample Step Program

Outline of Topics and Skills in STEP program		
Unit	**Topic Area**	**Skill**
Unit 1	What Is Violence?	Create Personal Safety Plan
Unit 2	Reducing Stress	Relaxation Training
Unit 3	Changing How We Think	Thought Journal
Unit 4	Boundaries, Assertiveness, and Communication	Role Plays and an Assertiveness Log
Unit 5	Cycle of Violence	Identify Own Cycle
Unit 6	Psychological Effects of Violence/Trauma (PTSD)	Identifying Trauma Symptoms & Triggers
Unit 7	Numbing Behaviors (substances, cutting, denial, minimization)	Identifying & Reducing Own Numbing Behavior
Unit 8	Self Esteem, Empathy, Mindfulness Training & Re-regulating Emotions	
Unit 9	Impact on Children	Developing Support & "No Hitting" rules
Unit 10	Dealing with Legal Issues	Protective Actions & Legal Terminology
Unit 11	Grieving & Letting Go	5 stages of Grief & How to Say Good-bye
Unit 12	Wellness	Redesigning Your Life

SAMPLE CHAPTER 3

Material for the Group Leader/Therapist and Handouts for Participants

Thinking, Feeling, and Actions

Thinking is what we do with our minds.

- The ability to think and solve problems logically is called our cognitive abilities.

- We use our cognitive abilities to learn new things, to change old ideas, to do our work, and to solve our problems. How we think about something also affects our feelings, and how we feel affects our thinking.

Feeling is what we do inside our mind and body and express as emotions.

- We have many different kinds of feelings that express our mood at a particular time. Sometimes we have more feelings than we can express verbally.
- Sometimes our feelings are controlled by how we think about things.
- Sometimes certain feelings become regularly associated with something because of patterns that have been established.

Behavior or how we act is outside our mind and body.

- Your behavior is often an expression of how you feel or what you think. You have control over your behavior.
- Sometimes you can change your behavior before you are able to change how you think or feel about something.
- However, these behavioral changes usually won't last unless they are consistent with your thoughts, feelings, and beliefs.

Thoughts—Impact Feelings—Impact Behaviors and vice versa!

Psychological Effects of Violence on Thoughts

Women who are abused often distort their thinking in order to control their scared feelings. For example, women may use:

Minimization: Downplaying the danger of your partner's abuse. Example: "It could have been worse."

Denial: You unconsciously believe that something did not happen, when it really did.

Repression: You unconsciously store a bad memory deep down where it is hard to access.

Dissociation: You mentally leave a dangerous situation so you don't feel anything during the violent acts. Example: Like floating above and watching what is happening, like an "out of body" experience.

EDUCATIONAL FACT SHEET FOR PARTICIPANTS

3 Types of Faulty Thinking:

1. Negative Thoughts about Self or Others

These include global core beliefs about yourself or others. For example:

—I am not capable of having a successful relationship.
—I am not capable of being happy without my partner.
—I am not capable of changing.
—I am a worthless person.
—I am stupid.
—If I tell someone how I feel they will use it against me.
—If I let someone get close to me I will be eventually abandoned.

2. Escalating or Exacerbating thoughts

These thoughts support negative beliefs about yourself and others, and tend to make negative thoughts worse. Sometimes, they make things seem like a catastrophe. For example:

—He will take custody of the kids if I don't reconcile with him. *Becomes . . .*
—If my kids have fun during their visits with him, then he is manipulating them for control. *Becomes . . .*
—He will, therefore, take the children to live in another state.

3. Irrational Thought Patterns

This type of dysfunctional thinking reflects an unrealistic appraisal of yourself or someone else because what you think about that person is colored by your feelings. Sometimes irrational beliefs can be identified by their all-or-nothing quality, and can be signified by using words such as *always, never, forever, nothing,* or *everything.* For example:

—I'm depressed, therefore things will *never* get better.
—My life is over. I will *never* fall in love again.
—Things are not that bad that I need to change.
—*Nothing* is going right in my life.
—I'm stupid, or —You're crazy.
—I *shouldn't* have left him.
—He will *always* hate me for what I have done.
—Only I can make him understand and change.

Breaking Dysfunctional Thought Patterns

If you observe the following list of rules, you will be able to challenge your negative thought patterns and turn them into more positive and hopeful ones. When you challenge your dysfunctional beliefs:

1. Be specific.

- Frequently we make blanket statements about ourselves, others, or our situations that are not accurate reflections of reality. When you make a statement like, —I'll never get over this loss, do you mean this year, in the next few years, or forever?
- Maybe it is true that you probably won't be feeling better for a while. But forever is a long time, and history proves that things change whether we like it or not. It would be more specific, and accurate, to say, —I will be feeling this loss for quite a while.

2. Take a look at the evidence.

- Where is the evidence that he is going to hurt or leave you if you do not do what he demands? Are you being a mind reader or do you have evidence? Does he have a particular pattern of behavior that he engages in before a battering incident begins to escalate. Does he stalk you and watch your every move? Does he escalate when he talks about a particular topic? Can you read his facial cues that he is getting angrier? Do you have good evidence that he is not controlling himself at that time? Although it is not your responsibility to control his anger, can you do something to de-escalate his anger so that you can stay safe or leave? Is he asking you to do something that is illegal? If you do it, you may protect yourself from his anger but you may end up in jail while your partner gets on with his life. The important point here is to learn how to stop and think about the evidence before you act impulsively.

3. Question your beliefs.

- Just because you do not like yourself or he tries to make you think you are a bad person, doesn't make it so. Have you no redeeming qualities? You are just human with imperfections like the rest of us. Start to think more about your good qualities, the things you like about yourself. Now you have an opportunity to better yourself—are you going to take it?

4. Get input from others.

- Share your thoughts about yourself, your partner, and the situation with the other people in your session.
- Talking with others is a good way of gaining perspective on yourself and your situation. Frequently, we see ourselves in a much more negative light than others. You may be your own worst critic. Talking with friends can help us develop a more balanced view of ourselves.
- Talking with others also helps us to become more accountable for our actions—so that we are not acting within a vacuum.

5. Learn to laugh at yourself.

- If we can see the irrational, outrageous, and even ridiculous side of ourselves, and can laugh at it, then we are certainly ahead of the game. Most importantly, keeping your sense of humor in a difficult time can mean the difference between pain and suffering and a little less pain and suffering.

6. Learn the origin of your patterns.

- Where did you learn your dysfunctional thought patterns? Was it from an abusive father who constantly criticized you and blamed you for the problems in his life? Was it the neglectful mother who made you feel unworthy because she neglected you emotionally?
- Understanding these origins helps give you perspective on yourself. These thoughts just didn't come out of nowhere but were instilled within you at an early age. Sometimes the thoughts can be the exact words of an abusive parent.

THOUGHT JOURNAL

Instructions: Every day you have many thoughts that give rise to feelings and actions that you probably do not pay attention to. Every day, at least once per day, write down at least one thought you experience about yourself or the situation with your partner. Chances are you will experience these thoughts when you purposely think about your partner, family, or situation. Sometimes these thoughts may just pop into your head spontaneously. After you write down the thought (or thoughts), try to see if it fits into any of the three categories described in the boxes below. Table 12.2 is an example of a "thought Journal" chart.

- Is it a thought that is negative about yourself or others?
- Is it a thought that leads to more escalated thinking or catastrophizing?
- Is it an irrational thought?

Table 12.2.

Date	What were your thoughts about your relationship today?	Were these dysfunctional thoughts that reflected negative beliefs about yourself or your partner?	Were these dysfunctional thoughts that escalated uncomfortable feelings?	Were these irrational thoughts that escalated uncomfortable feelings?	How did these thoughts affect your feelings and behaviors?	How did you challenge these dysfunctional thoughts?
Example: 1/7	I should be a better wife.	Yes, I think I am a bad wife because I want a divorce.	Not sure.	Yes.	I felt guilty and angry at myself	I want a divorce so my kids and I can be safe. It has nothing to do with how good of a wife I am.

SAMPLE CHAPTER 5

Educational Fact Sheet

The Cycle of Violence

Understanding the cycle of violence will better help you begin to understand the impact abuse has had on you, your partner, and other family members. It is this cycle, in part, that provides the reinforcement that has kept your relationship together. The cycle is divided into three phases: Tension Building Stage, Acute Battering Incident, and Loving and Contrition Stage

Phase I—Tension Building Stage: Verbal abuse, put downs, tension increases. You give in to minor demands to keep things from getting worse. This is the longest phase.

Phase II—Acute Battering Incident: The batterer discharges the tension in a rapid explosion. Each time an acute battering incident occurs, the violence increases and becomes more and more dangerous. This is the shortest phase.

Phase III—Loving Contrition Stage: The batterer tries to make amends, and may be extremely loving and kind, or there is an absence of tension. This may remind you of who he was when you were first dating. He may become puzzled as to why his apology doesn't result in immediate and total forgiveness. This lays the groundwork for a new building up of tension as he starts to think and verbalize, "Look at all I've done and she's still not satisfied" or "What do I have to do before she'll forgive me?"

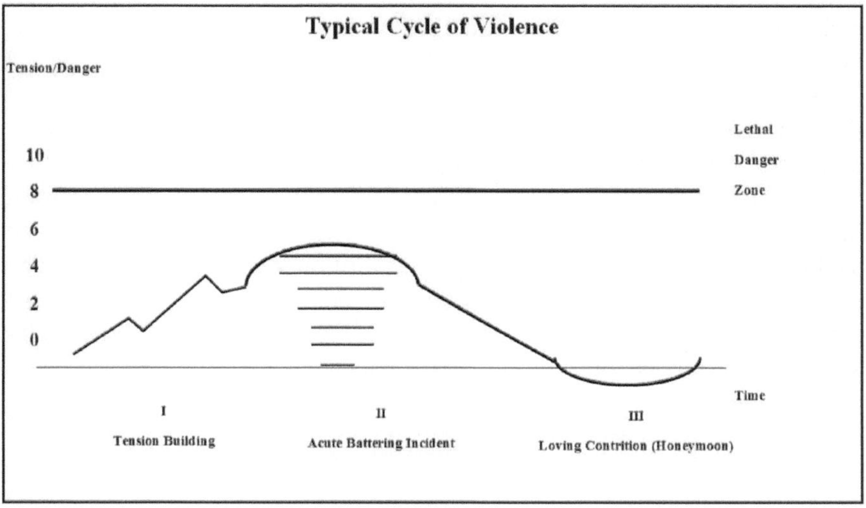

Figure 12.1.

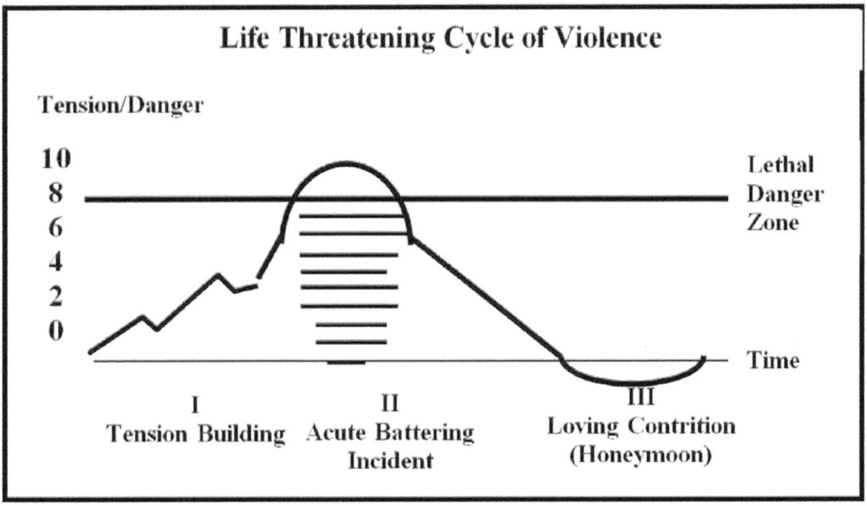

Figure 12.2.

SAMPLE EXERCISE: IDENTIFY YOUR CYCLE OF VIOLENCE

To do this exercise, you will need to remember three specific battering incidents: (1) The first one you can remember, (2) a typical battering incident, and (3) the worst or one of the worst ones. Describe in detail, to yourself or to the group, the first battering incident you can remember. What led up to it? Did you notice any tension before it occurred? What was the worst part of the incident? What happened afterward? Did he say he was sorry, in some way, even if not in words? What did he do? What did you do? About how long did it take for this incident to occur? What was the longest part? What was the shortest part? Go back to the abuse history check-list that we worked on in Step 1 and check off each act that happened during this first incident.

Now, try to draw the incident with the first part representing the tension rising, the second part representing how bad the abuse felt at the time, and the third part being how good the loving-contrition stage felt at the time. The scale we are using starts with zero tension and rises to level ten, the most serious violence that can result in your possible death. Remember, the tension will probably be lower during this first incident than later on.

IDENTIFYING CYCLE OF ABUSE

Now, review these three battering incidents you selected. Try to remember the details you used to describe the tension-building stage, the acute battering

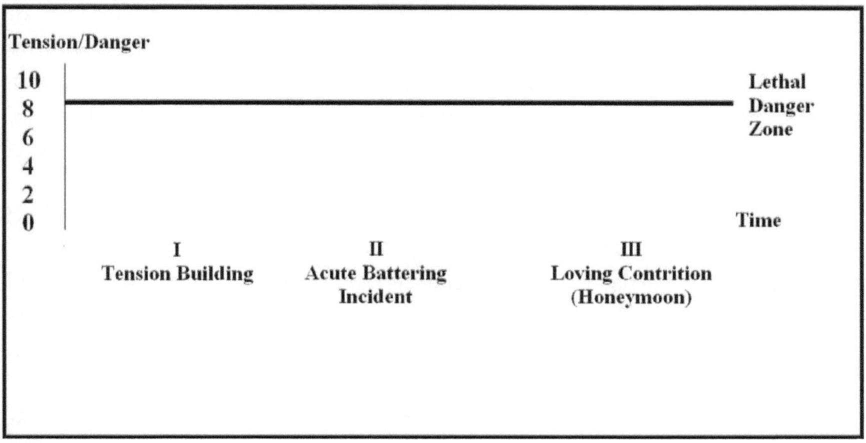

Figure 12.3. My Typical Cycle of Violence Created by the authors

incident and the loving-contrition stage. Were you able to focus on what actually happened, rather than on why you think you or your partner did whatever? Were you making excuses and justifying your partner's choice of using abuse? Did you use minimization or denial as you began your descriptions? How was your memory? What were you feeling during each stage? Were your thoughts clear and not confused? What were your dysfunctional thought patterns in each stage? What were your behaviors in each stage? Continue working in your Thought Journal but use an extra sheet to record dysfunctional thinking patterns you recognize as you go over these three incidents in your mind. Then, change them to positive thoughts. If you can't think of any in these incidents, try to remember another bad one that stands out in your mind and repeat this exercise for that one, too.

MEASURING EFFECTIVENESS OF THE PROGRAM

Given the emphasis on evidence-based treatment, the STEP program has been evaluated using several different types of data over the past five years (Jungersen et al., in review). As each STEP unit needed to stand on its own, given people being able to come and go throughout the 12 or more weeks the program is offered, measures were administered before and after each unit. This included both the Beck Anxiety Inventory (BAI; Beck, Epstein, Brown, & Steer, 1988) a standardized test to assess for anxiety, and a simple Subjective Units of Distress Scale (SUDS; Wolpe, 1958) from 1 to 100. Efficacy was found across all settings with the more sessions attended, the lower the anxiety and higher satisfaction with the program. The one unit where distress continued to be at a high level resulted from the discussion of children. This was not surprising given the lack of adequate protection for children or women from abusive homes, especially in the family courts (Kleinman & Walker, 2014; Walker, Cummings, & Cummings, 2012). Additionally, many of the women reported feeling maternal guilt for exposing their children to their abusers, which exacerbated the anxiety from the already present trauma histories.

Prior to the STEP unit on PTSD, the Trauma Symptom Inventory (TSI; Breire, 1995) and the Detailed Assessment of Posttraumatic Stress (DAPS; Breire, 2001) are usually administered. These are fairly short, standardized tests measuring PTSD and the participants found it useful to know the areas in which they had significant problems as compared with the standardized sample. While it would be better for research purposes to administer these two assessments before and after the STEP program itself (e.g., pretest-posttest), given the fact that the participants are not in a closed-group, this proved difficult. In some cases, the Personality Assessment Inventory (PAI) and a substance abuse measure were also administered prior to entering the group. However, it was found that the additional testing was not particularly useful to the purpose and efficacy of the STEP program itself.

CONCLUSION

In conclusion, survivors of domestic violence benefit from a trauma-informed model that integrates feminist and trauma theories with awareness and reinforcement of the knowledge and skills to promote healing. One example of such a model is the STEP program. Originally designed to reduce trauma symptoms in battered women, an unintended positive consequence found that other trauma-exposed women and men benefited from the program. STEP's goals of trauma reduction, re-empowerment, and movement toward wellness and, perhaps, happiness, were met in a variety of treatment settings. STEP's evidence-based treatment has been used in independent clinical practices, clinics, and jail settings.

The manual contains information for the facilitator/therapist to use during the educational section, ideas for the discussion or process section, and materials to facilitate the skill-building portion of the unit. The program is flexible so that participants can complete the unit in one or more sessions or even integrate a particular unit into individual psychotherapy where appropriate. In addition to the STEP program itself, the importance of creating a trauma-informed environment in which to conduct the program is of cucial importance.

DISCUSSION QUESTIONS

1. What are some ways to maximize collaboration between therapist and patient? What are some risks involved?
2. What are the most important factors to consider in designing effective treatment programs for domestic violence survivors?
3. How might non-gendered experiences interact with trauma responses?
4. What is the goal of couples therapy where domestic violence is present, and how is this different from individual therapeutic dynamics?
5. Describe the Survivor Therapy Empowerment Program (STEP) from a theoretical perspective. How has this program been adapted for use in jail settings?

REFERENCES

Alberti, R. E., & Emmons, M. L. (2008). *Your perfect right: Assertiveness and equality in your life and relationships* (9th Ed.). Atscadero, CA: Impact Publishers.

Beck, A. T., Epstein, N., Brown, G., & Steer, R. A. (1988). An inventory for measuring clinical anxiety: Psychometric properties. *Journal of Consulting and Clinical Psychology, 56*, 893–897. doi: 10.1037/0022-006X.56.6.893.

Briere, J. (1995). *Trauma Symptom Inventory professional manual*. Odessa, FL: Psychological Assessment Resources.

Briere, J. (2001). *Detailed Assessment of Posttraumatic Stress (DAPS)*. Odessa, FL: Psychological Assessment Resources.

Briere, J. N., & Scott, C. (2015). *Principals of trauma therapy: A guide to symptoms, evaluation & treatment (2nd ed., DSM-5 Update)*. Thousand Oaks, CA: Sage.

Foa, E., Keane, T. M., Friedman, M. J., & Cohen, J. A. (Eds.). (2009). *Effective treatments for PTSD: Practice guidelines from the International Society for Traumatic Stress Studies*. New York: The Guilford Press.

Foa, E. B., Rothbaum, B. O., Riggs, D. S., & Murdock, T. B. (1991). Treatment of posttraumatic stress disorder in rape victims: A comparison between cognitive-behavioral procedures and counseling. *Journal of Consulting and Clinical Psychology, 59* (5), 715-723. DOI: 10.1037/0022-006X.59.5.715

Gold, S. N. (2008). Benefits of a contextual approach to understanding and treating complex trauma. *Journal of Trauma & Dissociation, 9*, 269–292. doi: 10.1080/15299730802048819.

Harris M., & Fallot, R. (Eds.). (2001). *Using trauma theory to design service systems: New directions for mental health services*. San Francisco, CA: Jossey-Bass.

Hotaling, G. T., & Sugarman, D. B. (1986). An analysis of risk markers in husband to wife violence: The current state of knowledge. *Violence and Victims, 1*, 101–124.

Jungersen, T., Walker, L., Black R., Kennedy, T., & Groth, C. (in review). Trauma treatment for intimate partner violence in incarcerated populations.

Kleinman, T. G., & Walker, L. E. (2014). Protecting psychotherapy clients from the shadow of the law: A call for the revision of the Association of Family and Conciliation Courts (AFCC) guidelines for court-involved therapy. *Journal Of Child Custody, 11*, 335–362. doi:10.1080/15379418.2014.992563.

Walker, L. E. A. (1979). *The battered woman*. New York: Harper & Row.

Walker, L. E. A. (1999). Psychology and domestic violence around the world. *American Psychologist, 54*, 21–29.

Walker, L. E. A. (2017). *The battered woman syndrome* (4th ed.). New York: Springer.

Walker, L. E., Cummings, D. M., & Cummings, N. A. (2012). *Our broken family court system.* Dryden, NY: Ithaca Press.

Wolpe, J. (1958). *Psychotherapy by reciprocal inhibition.* Stanford, CA: Stanford University Press.

IV

Conclusion

In the course of this book we engaged in an exploration of the many important challenges in understanding and assessing domestic violence. Addressed in this book is the fact that domestic violence cannot be seen as only affecting certain societies or members of those societies; it is a condition whose impact reverberates throughout the lives of many individuals and communities around the world. It is that reality that is challenging the traditional view in favor of a view where men and women, whatever their gender orientations, religious and political persuasions, and racial and cultural backgrounds, are seen as possible victims and/or perpetrators of DV. In the end, this new perspective is forcing treatment interventions that are more sensitive to all these different dimensions and hence more likely to be effective. In this final chapter, we summarize the major points made in the book in this regard and provide additional analysis about the factors making the eradication of domestic violence so challenging. In this context, the issue of trauma is discussed further and a list of treatment recommendations is provided, meant to facilitate designing interventions that are more relevant to and in keeping with what the clients are looking for when seeking our assistance.

Chapter Thirteen

The Complex Nature of Domestic Violence

Possible Causes and Solutions

Rafael Art. Javier, William G. Herron, and Michelle Yakobson

The preparation of this book was guided by five basic and interconnected considerations: The first one is the growing recognition of the need to expand the definition of the traditional family to include more nontraditional families, such as those formed by members of the Lesbian Gay Bisexual Transgender (LGBT) community and those formed as a result of national and/or international adoption (Institute of Medicine, 2011). Such realization is compelling social and behavioral scientists and professionals interested in working with these groups to pay more attention to the unique ways in which domestic violence incidents are to be described, understood, and addressed in the context of the different family configurations and intersectionality.

The second consideration is that we no longer can afford to speak about the "traditional family" without considering the growing appreciation of the impact of cultural, racial, and ethnic contexts that now characterize various members of our society. Data from our 2010 U. S. Census on America's Diversity (2010/2011) have already described a society that is growing more culturally, linguistically, racially, and ethnically diverse. Such data are forcing a different conversation with regard to the understanding of domestic violence and the development of more appropriate assessment and intervention tools to be used with these individuals.

The third consideration is the growing recognition of the impact of technological advances (Internet, Facebook, Twitter, etc.) that now seem to play an increasingly major role in everyday transactions of our traditional and nontraditional families. We are cognizant that these new technologies are now more likely to be incorporated as part of the repertoire used by the abuser (e.g., domestic cyberbullying) to exert control over the abused (Javier & Dillon, 2013a, 2013b).

The fourth related issue is the fact that we live in a global society. The impact of this globalization in our families can be seen in the fact that cultural borders that once clearly defined the parameters of the family traditions and cultural norms are now continuously being challenged by external and global influences. The greatest impact of globalization is usually felt among younger populations, particularly with regard to the development of their self-definition (Arnett, 2002). This globalization, which provides access to other cultures, traditions, and customs through the use of the Internet, Facebook, Twitter, and similar technology, has resulted in the breakdown of those boundaries usually relied upon by the traditional family to provide guidance and monitor the behavior of its members. Since our families are now more likely to be part of and influenced by the global community that is also impacting individuals and families all over the world and in the United States (Arnett, 2002; Bullock, 2006), it is important to look at issues of domestic family violence through a national and international lens.

Finally, while much has been described in terms of the physical, psychological, and economic consequences of domestic violence, there are other types of injuries suffered by the victims of domestic violence that can initially become undetected but that could have insidious consequences on those affected. There may be a wider range of injuries on the victims of domestic violence than first observed. It is important to widen the scope of inquiry into the extent of damage that may accompany incidents of domestic violence; and it is our view that any evaluation related to domestic violence should include a discussion of more subtle injuries (such as subtle traumatic brain injury). For that, it requires an expansion in our line of inquiry regarding what can occur to the individual when submitted to frequent and repeated injuries to the face and head without any apparent sign of physical trauma (see chapter 10 in this book). This issue was most recently highlighted by Murray, Lundgreen, Olson, and Hunnicutt (2016), who provide specific guidelines to assist the professional in recognizing the possible presence of such a condition. These types of injuries may remain hidden from those responsible for assessing the immediate and long-term impact of injuries suffered during domestic violence incidents, while still creating havoc in the lives of those affected.

What emerges from all the material we cover in this book is the fact that domestic violence is complex and multifaceted, where a single incident of domestic violence is imbued with a great deal of meaningful and contributing factors. It is that involvement of multiplicity of factors that makes understanding of the phenomenon and finding adequate solutions more challenging. One of the challenges is to determine which contributing factor is the most important one to focus on at a particular time that will address the most crucial issue of the specific domestic violence incident.

A NEED FOR A PARADIGM SHIFT IN THE ASSESSMENT/ INTERVENTION OF DOMESTIC VIOLENCE AND ITS CONSEQUENCES

A shift is the need to reconsider treatment approaches to address issues of domestic violence that are more systemic and multiphasic in scope. Stith and colleagues (2012) provide a comprehensive analysis of relevant findings from outcome studies to support their contention that a more systematic approach (particularly with regard to IPV) is called for. Although the urgent call made by these authors for such an approach focuses primarily on IPV, it is clearly relevant to domestic violence in general, considering the theme throughout this book.

In figure 13.1, we attempt to provide an overview and the different pathways discussed in this volume that could impact an individual, such as constitutional characteristics, the condition of the family environment, and the socioeconomic and sociopolitical context at the time the individual enters into that family. The quality of the family dynamic becomes instrumental in the individual's development, providing the necessary context for self-definition and one's unique personal scripts that then come into play when creating his own family with spouses and children. It can become a vicious cycle if changes to these scripts are not made, which can only occur by an intentional act on the part of the individuals involved. In this context, consider the following themes to keep in mind and explore when evaluating and treating individuals in the midst of domestic violence. We offer these suggestions with the understanding that the sources of whatever happens in that situation did not start then and there.

RELEVANCE OF EARLY EXPERIENCE FACTORS

Although we are emphasizing the development and operation of scripts in terms of its evolutionary value, development is an interactive process. What happens with the individual in the environmental context where one is born, develops, and operates could have a tremendously influential impact on that individual (see figure 13.1). We recognize that scripts and their neurological connections can become further fixed and solidified in the person's repertoire, or altered, as a function of the peculiarity of the experience in one's environment, particularly the interpersonal environment (Solms & Turnbull,

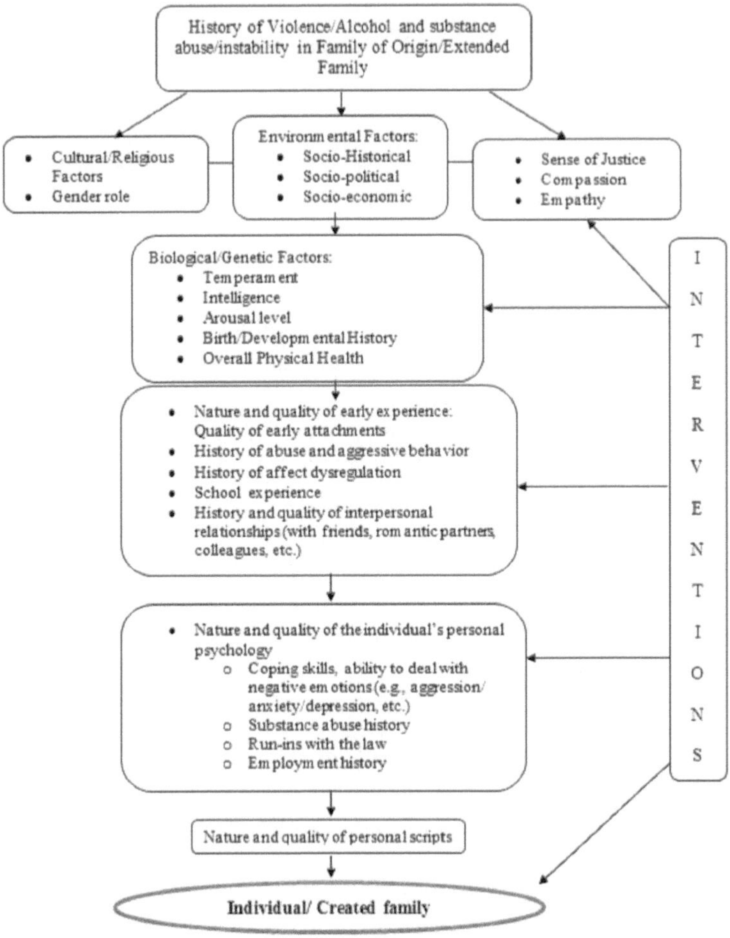

Figure 13.1. Important Factors in Assessment/Treatment of Domestic Violence: A Working Mode Created by the authors

2002). It is more likely that one's scripts can become fixed when the individual comes from an environment with the following characteristics:

a. A family context with an intergenerational history characterized by socioeconomic and emotional instability, poor coping skills, and the view that corporal punishment, fear, coercion, and intimidation are essential parts of imparting values of respect and good behavior on children (Javier & Yussef, 1998);
b. A family context with the view that one of the spouses (whatever the gender orientation) will have the ultimate control for the family

atmosphere, an expectation reinforced with physical (at times severe) and emotional coercion and abuse (Kraft, Menatti, & Gidycz, 2014).

c. A society where the legal system also follows these same standards in applying the law and ultimately ignore pleas for protection from family members/intimate partners who are trying to escape abusive situations at home. Such a condition is likely to bring about another layer of oppression for these individuals and add to the resulting trauma.
d. Religious and educational institutions that tacitly or more openly condone physical punishment as part of the family responsibility (Gruenbaum, 2006; Johnson, 2007; United Nations Population Fund, 2015; World Health Organization, 2013); such an attitude is seen as important in producing an upstanding member of the society/community with high moral standards, which can include killing its members so as not to shame the family and protect its honor (Kristof & Wudunn, 2009);
e. The use of alcohol and other substances is an acceptable strategy to deal with stress and conflict (Korvo, 2014; Weiss, Duke, & Sullivan, 2014).

Based on the material presented in this book, the resulting scripts that allow individuals to survive these conditions are more likely to become fixed to their overall behavioral repertoire, the longer the individual is subjected to these types of experiences. The more fixed the resulting personal scripts emerging from these conditions, the more likely they will be deployed and put into operation without much mentation.

However, not everybody subjected to these experiences ends up as a victim and/or perpetrator of domestic violence. Something else has to be at play, as amply described in the various chapters of this book, particularly in chapters 3 by Herron and Javier and 4 by Warburton and Anderson. The nature and quality of early attachment experience have been found to be implicated in this context (Smith & Stover, 2016).

CRUCIAL COMPONENT OF INTERVENTION IN DOMESTIC VIOLENCE

What has become clear from the material covered in this book is the fact that an intervention approach that does not consider the multiplicity of factors involved in domestic violent incidents is likely to miss the mark. We recognize that the personal scripts that keep us involved in relationships where domestic violence predominates are difficult to eradicate, but we also know that it is possible to soften their grip and reduce their effects in the way we operate. What is required is for the individuals involved (victims and perpetrators) to remain actively and consistently vigilant to the emergence of these personal scripts/strategies and to ensure that our behavior and reaction to these events become mediated by mentation. According to Solms and Turnbull (2002), this occurs when the individual develops the capacity for inhibiting "the outward manifestations of fear-anxiety reactions" (p. 136) so that the person is not at the mercy of fear-anxiety and its impulsive demand for action.

Some strategies that, when applied in concert with other interventions, have been found to be effective. Some of these strategies were amply discussed in several chapters of this book. The reason why a treatment approach that does not consider the larger picture as it is dealing with a specific violence incident (e.g., by ensuring the victim safety) is likely to fail eventually is because the conditions that may have made the situation possible are not properly addressed. The perspectives on treatment suggested by Warburton and Anderson, by Walker and Jorgensen in this book, by Stith and colleagues (2012), and Courtois (2016; Courtois & Ford, 2009) are helpful and the reader is strongly recommended to become familiar with these approaches.

One crucial consideration strongly endorsed in this book is the importance of a change in paradigm in the intervention process to include (1) a more comprehensive view of victims and perpetrators of violence (not just a male problem or traditional family units); (2) to distinguish the extent to which we are dealing with a characterological-based violent or situational perpetrator; and (3) to include a more careful analysis of how types of violence may have different consequences in their victims.

Under the best of circumstances, we are suggesting that an intervention for domestic violence incidents should include the following elements:

1. Look at the issue in its present context:

One of the first concerns should be the issue of safety. It should involve an immediate assessment of the current situation, including a safety assessment to ensure protection of the victim(s). This may involve engaging law enforcement and safe-haven agencies (see list of resources in appendix A). Special care should be taken when children are involved, as how one intervenes may worsen an already traumatic situation and add to the children's trauma. The issue of safety should also be considered for the violent perpetrator, with the understanding that using a humane approach may soften the blow of the traumatic event for everyone concerned. This is particularly important in cases where children are involved for whom the abusing situation may have caused tremendous confusion around loyalty. Making sure the safety of the victims and the perpetrators are secured may go a long way in reducing these children's traumatic responses.

An important issue to keep in mind at this juncture is that we should expect some level of resistance and defensiveness. This is particularly the case if the intervention is not the result of a voluntary decision but mandated as part of a legal procedure. We know, for instance, that revealing details of domestic violence in the family may be quite challenging. In fact, in a study assessing that dimension it was found that only 6% of women seeking counseling reported domestic abuse, whereas 53% reported physical violence in their marital relationship when the question of abuse was inquired about directly via a standardized questionnaire (O'Leary, Vivian, & Malone, 1992). The situation is even more problematic when assessing incidents of IPV among members of the LGBTQ populations or among culturally diverse populations or among the illegal immigrants (Ard & Makadon, 2011; Family Prevention Fund, 2009; WHO, 2005, 2013). Embarrassment and retribution by their spouse are likely reasons for not reporting an abusive relationship (Stith, McCollum, Rosen, Locke, & Goldberg, 2005). Other reasons given by members of multiple gender identities, particularly transgender individuals, are fear of further rejection and stigmatization for revealing one's gender orientations to a society that has not shown sufficient empathy to their plights (Ark & Makadon, 2011; Ristock, 2005). We recognize that although assessing abuse is a difficult task, conducting the assessment in a way that minimizes blame and focuses on the relationship dynamics is the best way to gain accurate information. The information that is gathered is likely to provide the therapist with an understanding of what changes may be amenable to intervention and what interventions may be most appropriate (Gladding, 2005).

The concept of neutrality is relevant in this regard. We cannot emphasize strongly enough that the therapist maintains a neutral stand and avoid making judgments of who is at fault; this basic outlook is particularly important at the data gathering stage; at the same time the therapist should make sure that the victim's safety is unquestionably ensured. One may be able to accomplish that by (1) recognizing that there are at least two people involved; (2) that the reason why the violence occurred is not totally and immediately known to the one intervening; and (3) that one's function is to find out from individuals who may be willingly or unwillingly seeking your services.

The issue of victims/perpetrators' concern about the stigma associated with reporting or acknowledgement of domestic violence (See chapter 11 by Murray and Crowe) may militate against being open to provide full disclosure of violence incidents in both parties. Such a maneuver will likely seriously curtail the scope, extent, and effectiveness of the assessment and treatment intervention. Overstreet and Quinn's (2013) IPV Stigmatization Model proposes three stigma components to consider: (a) anticipated stigma; (b) stigma internalization; and (c) cultural stigma. According to these authors, each of these components represents the different levels at which IPV stigmatization can occur (e.g., individual, interpersonal, and cultural) that we should keep in mind in our dealing with domestic violence; we should also keep in mind the implications of each component on IPV victims' help-seeking behaviors, or the extent to which survivors seek help from others to support them in handling various consequences of their abuse.

2. Look at the issue in terms of the individual context (including biological/personality characteristics).

A careful analysis of the victims and perpetrators' feelings and behaviors prior, during, and following the domestic violence incident can provide important information about factors that tend to trigger and escalate the situation. It also may provide important information about personal motivations for the parties involved that may have influenced the specific event. In this context, it is important to explore relevant medical history, substance abuse usage at the time and historical, and so on. In the end, we need to ascertain the extent to which we are dealing with someone with difficulty in controlling anger, who gets easily irritated and explosive, and with low frustration tolerance; we need to know the extent to which that situation worsens under certain condition (e.g., alcohol and/or drugs, including those taken for medical condition) and if it happens only at home with a spouse and/or children and/or at other settings.

3. Look at the issue in terms of its relevant historical and early family context.

It is also important to assess the history of abuse and violence in both the victims and the perpetrators' backgrounds and their families. In this context, an assessment of previous romantic and non-romantic relationships, including during adolescence, should be explored. What we are looking for here is whether or not we are dealing with a pattern of a long family history and how long this pattern has been part of these individuals' behavioral repertoire.

4. Look at the issue in terms of its socioeconomic/sociopolitical/cultural context.

The evaluation of the socioeconomic conditions of both the victims and perpetrators, including employment history, should also be explored, as well as the family's perspective on the use of violence, corporal punishment, and the role of religion in this context. Cultural issues related to gender roles and gender and race differences on the effect of domestic violence should also be explored. This information is particularly important in terms of making sure that the intervention provided consider these factors and utilize what has been helpful for these individuals in the context of their cultural, socioeconomic, and religious beliefs

5. Ethical traps to avoid

Confidentiality is the most important ethical issue when treating couples and families in which there is domestic abuse or violence. For victims of abuse, confidentiality fosters a trusting relationship that allows them to talk about the abusive relationship and develop plans to ensure their safety. However, when used inappropriately, emphasizing confidentiality can work in favor of an abusive individual. Woody and Woody (2001) emphasize that "a therapist who agrees that all individual disclosures will be kept confidential may find herself or himself in the unconscionable position of maintaining secrets that support intimate violence or abuse" (p. 139). It is especially important for professionals who treat couples and families where there is domestic violence or abuse to clarify the limits of confidentiality, including danger to others, at the beginning of therapy, both verbally and in writing as part of the informed consent process. In cases where the therapist's practice includes occasionally seeing one or more of the family members individually, it is crucial that the therapist clarifies whether the policy is to keep information from these individual sessions confidential from other family members. If this is not discussed in advance, clients are likely to assume confidentiality is an option.

Domestic abuse situations highlight the dangers of promising complete confidentiality of information learned from individuals when providing couple or family therapy. Even when therapists do protect the confidentiality of information learned from individuals in couple or family therapy, they may need to break confidentiality if there is a danger to self or others. These possibilities highlight the importance for the professional to keep the individuals informed of the limitation to confidentiality not only at the beginning of the process but throughout the different stages of intervention.

STAGES OF INTERVENTION

Courtois' (2016) suggested specific stages to follow when working with complex posttraumatic conditions that can be an important framework to follow with domestic violence cases. As it is the case with any clinical situation, the recommended sequences of stages are to be considered as flexible guidelines, particularly once the early stages are satisfied. The particular domestic violence situation may require the therapist to emphasize components of an intervention assumed to have been previously accomplished.

Keeping that in mind and in keeping with Courtois' (2016) recommendations, we suggest the following process:

- *A pre-treatment assessment*. In this context, a brief assessment of the violent incidents, what happened, how it happened, who said/did what to whom, antecedents, the nature of the physical and/or psychological injury, if there is an issue with children's safety, and so forth. The professional should assess the condition of the victims and whether there is eminent danger of further escalation.
- This is followed by the first stage (*stage 1*) or stage of safety, education, stabilization, skill-building, and development of working alliance. This first stage may include involvement of other agencies and institutions that could be helpful in negotiating a permanent condition of safety for the victim and family; it is also helpful to aid the perpetrator in finding a living condition that will minimize the potential for violent and aggressive behavior toward any member of the family. Courtois (2016) sees this stage as crucial to ensure the development of healthy boundaries, safety planning, emotional regulation, and strategies in minimizing the emotional impact of the domestic violence incident(s). Also in this stage, emphasis on wellness, stress management, and any medical/psychiatric issues (including prescription of medication) should be considered.
- Once that is accomplished, the stage to address the issue(s) of concern more directly can be initiated (*stage 2*). In this stage, there is not only an opportunity to systematically address the various impacts on the victims, but also to conduct a systematic exploration of the conditions/factors that trigger violent behaviors in the perpetrators and the possible contributions by the victims as well. Emphasizing the importance of exploring the victims' contributions to the domestic violent incident is not meant to endorse justification for the abuse. The goal here is (a) for the victims to have an opportunity, individually, to work through the psychological injury/hurt and profound grief normally associated with domestic violent and (b) attempt to contextualize the event in terms of the victims' personal psychology and extended family history. The techniques widely used in trauma work are expected to be helpful in this context (Courtois & Ford, 2009) and the reader is strongly encouraged to become familiar with these techniques. Similar work should also be done with the perpetrator.
- The final stage (*stage 3*) should focus on the solidification of skills and strategies developed during the previous stages. This may include a consolidation of relational skills and reevaluation of the extent to which relationships involved in the domestic violence incident(s) are to be preserved or severed. In the end, the success of this intervention is more likely to be lasting if there is a reconstitution of a new identity and new ways of

affirming one's self-esteem that do not include engaging in violence as victim and/or perpetrator.

CONCLUSION

As we can see, multiple levels of interventions, delivered in a systematic manner, are involved with the goal of addressing the different complexities likely to be present in any incident of domestic violence. The extent to which we can deliver these interventions in an integrated fashion, we may be able to aid those suffering from domestic violence. Our goal is to help these individuals develop different and more effective personal/family scripts where violence against self and others is no longer the norm.

In this book, we emphasized the need to look at domestic violence through the trauma lens because of the consequences reported by victims of domestic violence have all the characteristics we see in individuals suffering from traumatic conditions. In the end, unless we are able to address the core components of the violent experience, our intervention will fall short. Traumatic experiences reverberate in the lives of those affected and leave an indelible mark in their psychic structure. That indelible mark becomes a reference point to other interpersonal activities (Courtois & Ford, 2009). Trauma causes injury (physically and psychologically) that under more severe and persistent abusive conditions, like Steinberg's case discussed in chapter 1, can render an individual helpless and hopeless, crippling the ability to negotiate the traumatic events and their consequences. Part of these consequences is that it affects one's ability to discern appropriate behavior from those we thought cared for us. It leaves one confused about what it means to be loved and how to judge other's motivations. In the end, there is a distortion of one's perception of what is normal because the abuse (especially if it is persistent) is then seen as a normal part of the relationship; this, in turn, is reinforced by specific strategies and mechanisms used by the perpetrator and responded to by the victim (figure 13.1; Meichenbaum, 2007). There is a dance, although not a joyous one, but one characterized by franticness and desperation. The dance is of anxiety-fear-ridden souls who find themselves locked in acting out a personal script that was put in place way before the relationship was established and that may have provided the ingredients for attraction (see chapter 5). As it is often said colloquially, "it takes two to tango," and thus the two dynamics have to be considered as interplaying in order to understand the stubborn difficulty in addressing issues of domestic violence that keep the victim and the perpetrator locked in abusive relationships (Stith et al., 2012). That is, we need to look not only at the effect of the specific traumatic condition and its mechanism on the victim, but also the mechanism that keeps the abuser in that dynamic as well (see chapters 3–6).

This perspective on domestic violence is particularly important in view of the fact that individuals engaged as victims or perpetrators of domestic violence have been found to come into that situation already with personal histories which can be characterized as traumatic in nature (e.g., with a history of child abuse/neglect, abuse between the parents, alcoholism, violent and abusive sibling relations, and history of illegal behavior) (Babcock, 2003; Black et al., 2011; Center for Disease Control and Prevention, 2013; Fanslow, Gulliver, Dixon, & Ayalo, 2014; World Health Organization, 2005). The individual is already in a condition in which abuse and neglect are the expectation in her interpersonal relations; the person has already developed "specific scripts" or organizing cognitive/emotional structures (personal schemas) that are used to process and make sense of the world around her (Tomkins 1962/1978). The operation of these types of scripts is likely to be present and become operational whenever an individual is facing an abuser who the victim fears for the viciousness and relentlessness in the way the psychological and physical assaults are delivered. In this situation, the victim can become submissive and acquiescent to the abuser's demands (where the goal is the neutralization or de-escalation of the threat), or may just refuse to do so. ("I didn't want to make him mad," is on the often-heard comment by victims in these types of situation.) It is this connection with our early history of abuse and trauma from which we have developed our personal schemas (scripts) that needs to be understood more thoroughly, and that tends to result in what Courtois refers to as "complex trauma" with its cumulative effects (Courtois, 2016; Courtois & Ford, 2009). We need to emphasize the affective component of the experience since affect is what is felt and gets mobilized in domestic violence, the intensity and disorganization of which are involved in trauma formation.

Finally, we need to go beyond the components of early trauma experience to include information related to biological and evolutionary markers that are normally involved in influencing/guiding the individual's interaction with the environment (see chapter 4). We included, in this regard, a discussion of the work of Sylvan Tomkins (1962, 1978) and Mark Solms and Oliver Turnbull (2002) because they provide a comprehensive discussion of the motivational forces that guide most human behaviors and negotiation with the world. In the end, it is not enough to say that domestic violence is about power and control (which is true), but that we need to bring to the conversation and to our analysis information related to the specific (biological, physiological, psychological) characteristics of the individuals involved that may have contributed to their current situation.

DISCUSSION QUESTIONS

1. Discuss the various factors that tend to complicate working with domestic violence victims and perpetrators.
2. Provide an assessment of these factors in specific clinical examples where you or someone else may have been involved.
3. Identify stages of intervention that are important to follow to ensure the most ethical and enduring resolution of domestic violence incidents.
4. Delineate what would you do differently if having to intervene with members of the LGBT, particularly transgender, who are the victims or perpetrators of IPV?
5. List the different resources available in your community to assist victims and perpetrators of domestic violence.

REFERENCES

Afifi, T. O., MacMillan, H., Cox, B. J., Asmundson, G. J. G., Stein, M. B., & Sareen, J. (2009). Mental health correlates of intimate partner violence in marital relationships in a nationally representative sample of males and females. *Journal of Interpersonal Violence, 24*(8), 1398–1417.

Anderson, K. L. (2004). Perpetrator or victim? Relationships between intimate partner violence and well-being. *Journal of Marriage and Family, 64*(2), 851–863.

Archer, J. (2000). Sex differences in aggression between heterosexual partners: A meta-analytic review. *Psychological Bulletin, 126*(5), 651–680.

Ard, K. L., & Makadon, H. J. (2011). Addressing intimate partner violence in lesbian, gay, bisexual, and transgender patients. *Journal of General Internal Medicine, 26*(8): 930–933. Published online 2011 Mar 30. doi: 10.1007/s11606-011-1697-6.

Arnett, J. J. (2002). The psychology of globalization. *American Psychologist, 57*(10), 774–783. doi: 10.1037//0003-066X.57.10.774.

Babcock, J. C. (2003). Toward a typology of abusive women: Differences between partner-only and generally violent women in the use of violence. *Psychology of Women Quarterly, 27*(2), 153.

Babcock, J. C., Canady, B. E., Graham, K., & Schart, L. (2007). The evolution of battering interventions: From the dark ages into the scientific ages. In J. Hamel & T. L. Nicholls (Eds.), *Family interventions in domestic violence: A handbook of gender-inclusive theory and treatment* (pp. 215–244). New York: Springer Publishing Company.

Black, M. C., Basile, K. C., Breiding, M. J., Smith, S. G., Walters, M. L., Merrick, M. T., & Spivak, H. R. (2011). *The National Intimate Partner and Sexual Violence Survey (NISVS): 2010 summary report*. Atlanta, GA: National Center for Injury Prevention and Control.

Bullock, M. (2006, May). Toward a global psychology. *Monitor on Psychology, 37*. Retrieved from http://www.apa.org/monitor/may06/ceo.aspx.

Campbell, J. C. (2002). Health consequences of intimate partner violence. *The Lancet, 359*(9314), 1331–1336.

Centers for Disease Control and Prevention. (2003). *Costs of intimate partner violence against women in the United States*. Retrieved from http://www.cdc.gov/violenceprevention/pdf/ipvbook-a.pdf.

Centers for Disease Control and Prevention. (2009). *Injury-Intimate partner violence consequences*. Retrieved from http://www.cdc.gov/violenceprevention/intimatepartnerviolence/consequences.html.

Center for Disease Control and Prevention (2013). *National Intimate Partner and Sexual Violence Survey.* Retrieved from http://www.cdc.gtov/reproductivehealth/global/surveys.htm.

Centers for Disease Control and Prevention. (2014). *Intimate partner violence: Consequences.* Retrieved from http://www.cdc.gov/violenceprevention/intimatepartnerviolence/consequences.html.

Courtois, C. A. (2016). Complex development trauma in adults: Innovation in integrated treatment. Paper presented at the 2016 ABPP Annual Convocation-APA Annual Convention, Denver, Co August 4–7, 2016.

Courtois, C.A. & Ford, J. (Eds.). (2009). *Treating complex traumatic stress disorders: An evidence-based guide.* New York: The Guilford Press.

Demos, E. V. (1988). Differentiating the repetition compulsion from trauma through the lens of Tomkins's script theory: A response to Russell. In J. G. Teicholz & D. Kriegman (Eds.), *Trauma, repetition & affect regulation: The work of Paul Russell* (pp. 67–104). New York: The Other Press.

Family Violence Prevention Fund for the Robert Wood Johnson Foundation (2009). Retrieved September 2, 2017 from https://www.futureswithoutviolence.org/userfiles/file/ImmigrantWomen/IPV_Report_March_2009.pdf.

Fanslow, J., Gulliver, P., Dixon, R., & Ayalo, I. (2014). Exploring factors associated with women's use of physical violence against a violent partner. Paper presented at the International Family Violence and Child Victimization Research Conference, Portsmouth, New Hampshire, July 13–15, 2014.

Garbarino, J. (2015). *Listening to killers: Lessons learned from my twenty years as a psychological expert in murder cases.* Los Angeles: University California Press.

Gladding, S. T. (2005). *Counseling as an art: The creative arts in counseling* (3rd Ed.). Upper Saddle River, NJ: Pearson Education, Inc.

Gruenbaum, E. (2006). Sexuality issues in the movement to abolish female genital cutting in Sudan. *Medical Anthropology Quarterly, 20*, 121.

Institute of Medicine (2011). *The health of lesbian, gay, bisexual, and transgender people: building a foundation for better understanding.* Washington, DC: The National Academies Press. doi: 10.17226/13128.

Javier, R. A., & Dillon, J. (2013a). Bullying and its consequences-Part I. (Guest Editors). *Journal of Social Distress and the Homeless, 22* (1), 1–57.

Javier, R. A., & Dillon, J. (2013b). Bullying and its consequences—Part II. (Guest Editors). *Journal of Social Distress and the Homeless, 22*(2), 59–118.

Javier, R. A., & Yussef, M. B. (1998). A Latino perspective on the role of ethnicity in the development of moral values: Implications for psychoanalytic theory and practice. In R. A. Javier & W. G. Herron (Eds.), *Personality development and psychotherapy in our diverse society: A source book* (pp. 366–382). Northvale, NJ: Jason Aronson, Inc.

Johnson, M. P. (2006). Conflict and control: Gender symmetry and asymmetry in domestic violence. *Violence Against Women, 12*, 1003–1018.

Johnson, M. (2007). Making mandinga or making Muslims? Debating female circumcision, ethnicity, and Islam in Guinea-Bissau and Portugal. In Y. Hernlund & B. Shell-Duncan (Eds.), *Transcultural bodies: female genital cutting in global context* (pp. 202–223). New Brunswick, NJ: Rutgers University Press.

Johnson, M. (2008). *A typology of domestic violence: Intimate terrorism, violence resistance and situational couple violence.* Lebanon, NH: Northeastern University Press.

Johnson, M. P., & Ferraro, K. J. (2000). Research on domestic violence in the 1990s: Making distinctions. *Journal of Marriage and the Family, 62*, 948–963.

Jones, C. (2014). Men who identified as victims of domestic violence. Paper presented at the International Family Violence and Child Victimization Research Conference, Portsmouth, New Hampshire, July 13–15, 2014.

Kaufman, J., Wright, M. O., Allbaugh, L. J., Folger, S. F., & Noll, J. (2014). The impact of child maltreatment on maturing self-regulatory systems and later substance use. Paper presented at the International Family Violence and Child Victimization Research Conference, Portsmouth, New Hampshire, July 13–15, 2014.

Kelly, J., & Johnson, J. (2008). Differentiation among types of intimate partner violence: Research update and implications for intervention. *Family Court Review, 46,* 476–499.

Korvo, K. (2014). The role of executive function deficits in domestic violence perpetration. Paper presented at the International Family Violence and Child Victimization Research Conference, Portsmouth, New Hampshire, July 13–15, 2014.

Kraft, K., Menatti, A., & Gidycz, C. A. (2014). Examining the relationship between interpersonal victimization and emotion dysregulation. Paper presented at the International Family Violence and Child Victimization Research Conference, Portsmouth, New Hampshire, July 13–15, 2014.

Kristof, N. D., & WuDunn, S. (2009, August 17). The women crusade. *The New York Times.* Retrieved from www.nytimes.com/2009/08/23/magazine/23Women-t.html.

Lichtenberg, P., van Beusekom, J., & Gibbons, D. (1997). *Encountering bigotry: Befriending projecting persons in everyday life.* Northvale, NJ: Jason Aronson, Inc.

Meichenbaum, D. (2007). Family violence: Treatment of perpetrators and victims. Retrieved from www.melissainstititute.org

Miller, A. H. (1998). Neuroendocrine and immune system interactions in stress and depression. *Psychiatric Clinics of North America, 21*(2), 443–463.

Murray, C. E., Lundgreen, K., Olson, L., & Hunnicutt, G. (2016). Practice update: What professional who are not brain injury specialists need to know about intimate partner violence-related traumatic brain injury. *Trauma Violence, & Abuse,17*(3), 298–305.

Neal, A., Dixon, C., Edwards, K. M., & Gidycz, C. A. (2014). College women's motives for perpetrating intimate partner violence. Paper presented at the International Family Violence and Child Victimization Research Conference, Portsmouth, New Hampshire, July 13–15, 2014.

O'Leary, K. D., Vivian, D., & Malone, J. (1992). Assessment of physical aggression against women in marriage: The need for multimodal assessment. *Behavioral Assessment, 14*, 5–14.

Overstreet, N. M., & Quinn, D. M. (2013). The intimate partner violence stigmatization model and barriers to help seeking. *Basic and Applied Social Psychology, 35,* 109–122.

Reich, C. M., Blackwell, N., Simmons, C., & Beck, J. G. (2015). Social problem solving strategies and posttraumatic disorder in the aftermath of intimate partner violence. *Journal of Anxiety Disorders, 32*, 31–37.

Richardson, L., Freeh, B. C., & Acierno (2010). Prevalence estimates of combat-related PTSD: A critical review. *Australian and New Zealand Journal of Psychiatry, 44* (1), 4–19.

Ristock, J. (2005). Relationship violence in lesbian/gay/bisexual/transgender/queer [LGBTQ] communities: Moving beyond a gender-based framework. Violence Against Women Online Resources. Retrieved from http://citeseerx.ist.psu.edu/viewdoc/download?doi=10.1.1.208.7282& rep=rep1&type=pdf.

Russell, P. L. (1998). The role of paradox in repetition compulsion. In J. G. Teicholz & D. Kriegman (Eds.), *Trauma, repetition compulsion, and affect regulation: The work of Paul Russell* (pp. 1–22). New York: The Other Press.

Sigurvinsdottir, R., & Ullman, S. E. (2015). Sexual orientation, race, and trauma as predictors of sexual assault recovery. *Journal of Family Violence,* 1–9. doi:10.1007/s10896-015-9793-8.

Smith, C. W., Stover, C., Meadows, A. L., & Kaufman, J. (2009). Interventions for intimate partner violence: Review and implications for evidence-based practice. *Professional Psychology: Research and Practice, 40*, 223–233.

Smith, L. S., & Stover, C. S. (2016). The moderating role of attachment on the relationship between history of trauma and intimate violence victimization. *Violence Against Women, 22*(6), 745–764.

Solms, M., & Turnbull, O. (2002). *The brain and the inner world: An introduction to the neuroscience of subjective experience.* New York: Karnac Books.

Stith, S. M., McCollum, E. E., Amanor-Boadu, Y., & Smith, D. (2012). Systemic perspectives on Intimate Partner Violence treatment. *Journal of Marital and Family Therapy, 38*(1), 220–240.

Stith, S. M., McCollum, E. E., Rosen, K. H., Locke, L., & Goldberg, P. M. (2005). Domestic violence focused couples treatment. In J. Lebow (Ed.), *Handbook of Clinical Family Therapy* (pp. 406–430). New York: John Wiley.

Sullivan, T. P., Weiss, N., & Price, C. (2014). Coping with individual PTSD symptoms: The unique experience of victims. Paper presented at the International Family Violence and Child Victimization Research Conference, Portsmouth, New Hampshire, July 13–15, 2014.

Tjaden, P. (2000). Prevalence and consequences of male-to-female and female-to-male intimate partner violence as measured by the National Violence Against Women Survey. *Violence Against Women, 6*(2), 142.

Tjaden, P., & Thoennes, N. (2000a, July). *Extent, nature and consequences of intimate partner violence: Findings from the National Violence Against Women Survey.* National Institute of Justice, and United States Department of Justice. Retrieved from https://www.ncjrs.gov/pdffiles1/nij/181867.pdf.

Tjaden, P., & Thoennes, N. (2000b, November). *U.S. Department of Justice—Full report of the prevalence, incidence and consequences of violence against women: Findings from the national violence against women survey.* National Institute of Justice and United States Department of Justice. Retrieved from https://www.ncjrs.gov/pdffiles1/nij/183781.pdf

Tomkins, S. (1962). *Affect, imagery, consciousness (vol. 1): The positive affects.* New York: Springer.

Tomkins, S. (1978). Script theory: Differential magnification of affects. In H. E. Howe, Jr. & R. A. Dunstbier (Eds.), *Nebraska Symposium on Motivation* (pp. 201–236). Lincoln: University of Nebraska Press.

Ullman, S., Petter-Hagene, L. C., & Relyea, M. (2014). Coping, emotion regulation, and self-blame as mediator of sexual abuse and psychological symptoms in adult sexual assault. *Journal of Child Sex Abuse, 23*(1): doi:10.1080/10538721.2014.864747.

United Nations Population Fund (2015). *Female genital mutilation (FGM) frequently asked questions.* Retrieved from http://www.unfpa.org/sources/female-genital-mutilation-fgm-frequently-asked-questions.

U.S. Census Bureau (2010). Retrieved 9/1/2016 www.census.gov/2010census/data.

U.S. Census Bureau (2011). 2010 Census shows America's diversity. Retrieved from http://www.census.gov/newroom/releases/archives/2010_census/cb11-cn125.html.

Veterans and PTSD Statistics (2016). Retrieved from www.veteransandptsd.com/PTSD-statistics.html.

Wadhwa, P. D., Entinger, S., Buss, C., & Lu, M. C. (2011). The contribution of maternal stress to preterm birth: issues and considerations. *Clinical Perinatology, 39,* 351–384.

Walter, M. L., Chen, J., & Breiding, M. J. (2013). *The national intimate partner and sexual violence survey (NISVS): 2010 findings on victimization by sexual orientation.* National Center for Injury Prevention and Control, Centers for Disease Control and Prevention, Atlanta, GA.

Weiss, N., Duke, A. A., & Sullivan, T. P. (2014). Posttraumatic stress disorder and women's use of aggression in intimate relationships: The moderating role of alcohol dependence. Paper presented at the International Family Violence and Child Victimization Research Conference, Portsmouth, New Hampshire, July 13–15, 2014.

Whitaker, D. J., Haileyesus, T., Swahn, M., & Saltzman, L. S. (2007). Differences in frequency of violence and reported injury between relationships with reciprocal and nonreciprocal intimate partner violence. *American Journal of Public Health, 97*(5), 941–947.

Woody, R. H., & Woody, J. D. (Eds.). (2001). *Ethics in marriage and family therapy.* Washington, DC: American Association for Marriage and Family Therapy.

World Health Organization. (2005). *Summary report: Multi-country study on women's health and domestic violence against women. Initial results on prevalence, health outcomes and women's responses.* Geneva, Switzerland: World Health Organization.

World Health Organization (2013). *Global and regional estimates of violence against women: Prevalence and health effects of intimate partner violence and non-partner sexual violence.* Geneva, Switzerland: World Health Organization. Retrieved from www.who.int/reproductivehealth.

Glossary

5-HT serotonin transporter gene—Affects neural circuits connecting the amygdala and the cingulate as well as stress, depression, and anxiety generation.
Acculturation—The process of adopting the cultural traits or social patterns of another group.
Ackerman-Banks Neuropsychological Rehabilitation Battery—Addresses how neuropsychological functions impacts safety. It has many domains, specifying weaknesses and interpersonal difficulties that a victim is experiencing, strengths that can be used in treatment, and recommendations for referral to targeted treatment.
Affective incompetence—Denial of an illness due to clinical conditions.
Ambitendency—An inclination to act in opposite ways or directions in situations of conflict and under the influence of opposing motivational forces.
Anticipated stigma—Survivors' beliefs that others will treat them in stigmatizing ways when they reach out to them for help.
Antisocial Personality Disorder—Characterized by a long-standing pattern of disregard for other people's rights, often crossing the line and violating those rights. A person with this disorder often feels little or no empathy toward other people, and doesn't see the problem in bending or breaking the law for their own needs or wants. The disorder usually begins in childhood or as a teen and continues into a person's adult life.
Associative conditioning—Reflexive or automatic type of learning in which a stimulus acquires the capacity to evoke a response that was originally evoked by another stimulus. Caused by a new association between events in the environment.
Attachment theory—States that a strong emotional and physical attachment to at least one primary caregiver is critical to giving a sense of stability and

security necessary to take risks, branch out, and grow and develop as a personality.

Autonomic responses—Immediate response to stressor exposure via the sympathetic and parasympathetic arms of the autonomic nervous system that provoke rapid alterations in physiological states.

Bidirectional aggression—In which either member of a dyad is considered perpetrator and/or victim.

Borderline Personality Disorder—Difficulty in regulating emotion. This difficulty leads to severe, unstable mood swings, impulsivity and instability, poor self-image, and stormy personal relationships.

Centro de Capacitación para Erradicar la Violencia Intrafamiliar Masculina (CECEVIM)—The Training Center to Eradicate Masculine Intrafamily Violence is a program that is theoretically based on feminist gender analysis, ecology, and ancient native spiritual concepts. Program objectives are for Latino men who have been perpetrators of domestic violence to learn how and why they are violent in the home and develop strategies to stop being abusive and learn how to create intimate, cooperative, supportive, equal, democratic, and nonviolent relationships.

Clitoridectomy—Surgical removal of the clitoris; a form of female circumcision, especially practiced as a religious or ethnic rite.

Coercive control—A course of oppressive behavior that involves depriving women of their rights and liberties and establishing a regime of domination in personal life by limiting access to money and other basic resources.

Cognitive biases—A systematic error in thinking that affects the decisions and judgments that people make. Sometimes these biases are related to memory. The way one remembers an event may be biased for a number of reasons and that in turn can lead to biased thinking and decision-making.

Cognitive Neo-Association Theory (CNT)—Postulates that unpleasant events result in the linking of aggressive thoughts, feelings, and behaviors in an associative memory structure likely to be reactivated in similar situations.

Collective individuality—In which a person is accomplished and has a clear sense of self, identity, meaning, and frame as he or she exists through others and in relationship to the group and community—but not floating completely alone without any anchor point or mutually shared reference.

Common couple violence—One or at most two incidents of violence not used as part of a pattern of behavior to control the partner.

Comorbidity—The simultaneous presence of two chronic diseases or conditions in a patient.

Confabulation—A disturbance of memory, defined as the production of fabricated, distorted, or misinterpreted memories about oneself or the world, without the conscious intention to deceive.

Cultural stigma—Stigmatizing beliefs that are perpetuated by larger social forces, such as organizational policies or traditions and the media.

Cycle of Violence—Involves the Tension Building Stage (verbal abuse, put downs, tension increases; longest phase involves giving in to minor demands to prevent escalation); an Acute Battering Incident (the batterer discharges the tension in a rapid explosion; each time an acute battering incident occurs, the violence increases and becomes more and more dangerous—this is the shortest phase); and a Loving Contrition Stage (the batterer tries to make amends, and may be extremely loving and kind, or there is an absence of tension; this sets the stage for further strife).

Delphi methodology—A forecasting method based on the results of questionnaires sent to a panel of experts. Several rounds of questionnaires are sent out, and the anonymous responses are aggregated and shared with the group after each round.

Disinhibition—A lack of restraint manifested in disregard for social conventions, impulsivity, and poor risk assessment.

Dissociation—The process of separating out of the memory things that are undesirable or cannot be dealt with.

Domestic violence syndrome—Develops in victims of serious, long-term domestic abuse. It is dangerous primarily because it can lead to a state of "learned helplessness" or psychological paralysis in which a victim becomes so depressed, defeated, and passive that he/she is incapable of leaving the abusive situation.

Drive models—Asserts that drives motivate people to reduce desires by choosing responses that will most effectively do so. Results in increased arousal and internal motivation to reach a particular goal.

Dysthymia—Also known as persistent depressive disorder, this is a continuous long-term (chronic) form of depression. You may lose interest in normal daily activities, feel hopeless, lack productivity, and have low self-esteem and an overall feeling of inadequacy. These feelings last for years and may significantly interfere with relationships, work, and daily activities.

Early maladaptive schemas—Comprises a constellation of unhelpful beliefs, attitudes, and feelings about key aspects of life.

Environmental, cultural, and ecological mapping (ECEM)—Examines the experience of domestic violence within a social-political context to fully understand the many factors that have an impact on the individual. These are ecological factors embedded in program implementation, social/emotional stressors, political stressors, personal strengths/resilience, point of contact with the human service provider, and ecological factors in the provision of future support.

Emotionally labile—Refers to rapid, often exaggerated changes in mood, where strong emotions or feelings occur due to a physical problem with the brain.

Epigenetic—Referring to biological mechanisms that will switch genes on and off, resulting in a change in phenotype without a change in genotype.

Excision. [SEE CLITORIDECTOMY]

Excitation Transfer Theory of Aggression—Uses the idea that physiological arousal dissolves slowly, so in the case of anger, once felt, it may be still present for another situation through the transfer of excitation.

Familism—A strong commitment or focus to one's family.

Female-to-male partner violence perpetration (FMPV)—Domestic abuse where a female acts as the batterer.

General Aggression Model (GAM)—A model supported by a large body of evidence explaining domestic violence and formulating practical remedies for it. It incorporates both theories of neural connectivity/behavior and aggression.

General Learning Model (GLM)—A modification of the GAM that emphasizes that exactly the same processes ensure that prosocial person factors interact with cues and triggers to activate prosocial cognitions and feelings, and ultimately prosocial behaviors.

Honor crime/killing—In certain cultures, the killing of a relative, especially a girl or woman, who is perceived to have brought dishonor on the family.

Idiographic—Pertaining to aspects which make human beings unique from one another.

Indirect aggression—Nonphysical forms of aggression that are as harmful and elicit the same physiological pain.

Infantilization—To treat or condescend to as if still a young child thereby reducing to an infantile state or condition.

Infibulation—The practice of excising the clitoris and labia of a girl or woman and stitching together the edges of the vulva to prevent sexual intercourse. It is traditional in some northeastern African cultures but is highly controversial.

Institutional racism—A pattern of social institutions—such as governmental organizations, schools, banks, and courts of law—giving negative treatment to a group of people based on their race.

Institutionalized violence—A form of violence wherein some social structure or social institution may harm people by preventing them from meeting their basic needs; any institutional condition, action or policy that emotionally or physically dominates, diminishes, dehumanizes another group.

Instrumental conditioning—A learning process in which behavior is modified by the reinforcing or inhibiting effects of the resulting consequences.

Internalization—The integration of attitudes, values, standards and the opinions of others into one's own identity or sense of self. In psychoanalytic theory, internalization is a process involving the formation of the super ego.

Internalized stigma—Survivors internalizing and coming to believe negative views of themselves in relation to the IPV they experienced.

Intersubjectivity—A process of continuous and reciprocal interactions and exchanges typical of human beings in which they come to know each other's minds; the psychological relation between people.
Intimate Partner Violence (IPV)—Domestic violence by a spouse or partner in an intimate relationship against the other spouse or partner. It can include a current or former intimate partner, and can take a number of forms, including physical, verbal, emotional, economic, and sexual abuse.
Intimate terrorism—A pattern of ongoing use of physical, emotional, economic, and sexual forms of violence to exert control over the victims. This term is to be distinguished from violence exerted in self-defense.
Kinesiotherapy—The application of scientifically based exercise principles adapted to enhance the strength, endurance, and mobility of individuals with functional limitations or those requiring extended physical conditioning.
Latinx—A term is used to capture the range of geographical, sociohistorical, political, and intersectionality variables that span the Hispanic community. Specifically, it relates to people of Latin American origin or descent (used as a gender-neutral or non-binary alternative to Latino or Latina).
Machismo—A male Latino cultural concept/role. This involves positive forms taking care of the family, showing valor amongst peers, working hard to support one's family, and taking pride in raising one's children. Negative forms include violence toward women and other men, alcoholism, and having sexual partners other than one's wife.
Male-to-female partner violence perpetration (MFPV)—Domestic abuse in which the male acts as the batterer.
Marianismo—The cultural counterpart to *machismo* for Latinas that refers to women's cultural and gender role whereby they sacrifice their own needs and desires, putting those of family before their own. Key components include self-sacrifice, submissiveness to men, and being passive. While this provides women with a valued role within their cultural context, this position is devalued through a domestic violence experience where the woman suffers partner abuse.
Mentalization—The process by which we make sense of each other and ourselves, implicitly and explicitly, in terms of subjective states and mental processes. It is a profoundly social construct in the sense that we are attentive to the mental states of those we are with, physically or psychologically.
Microaggressions—Everyday verbal, nonverbal, and environmental slights, snubs, or insults, whether intentional or unintentional, which communicate hostile, derogatory, or negative messages to target persons based solely upon their marginalized group membership.
Minimization—A type of deception involving denial coupled with rationalization in situations where complete denial is implausible. Can also involve downplaying the significance of an event or emotion—is a common strategy in dealing with feelings of guilt.

Model Minority—The stereotype of a demographic group whose members are perceived to achieve a higher degree of socioeconomic success than the population average.
Monoamine oxidase A gene (MAOA)—One of two neighboring gene family members that encode mitochondrial enzymes that catalyze neurotransmitters that modify cognitive function.
Mutual violent control—A rare type of intimate partner violence occurring when both partners act in a violent manner, battling for control.
Narcissistic injury—A perceived threat or blow to a narcissist's self-esteem or self-worth. It is such that due to reparative ineffectiveness it is not healed, and often instead it is reinforced as a negative self-representation.
National Alliance on Mental Illness (NAMI)—A nationwide grassroots advocacy group, representing families and people affected by mental illness in the United States.
Negative affectivity [SEE NEUROTICISM].
Neural plasticity—The brain's ability to reorganize itself by forming new neural connections throughout life. Neuroplasticity allows the neurons (nerve cells) in the brain to compensate for injury and disease and to adjust their activities in response to new situations or to changes in their environment.
Neuropsychology—The study of the structure and function of the brain as they relate to specific psychological processes and behaviors.
Neuroticism—A long-term tendency to be in a negative emotional state. People with neuroticism tend to have more depressed moods—they suffer from feelings of guilt, envy, anger, and anxiety more frequently and more severely than other individuals.
Nonsuicidal self-injurious (NSSI) behaviors—Deliberate, often impulsive, repetitive non-lethal harming of one's body to cope with and relieve painful feelings which is prevalent among adolescents, especially adolescent females, and young adults.
Patient Protection and Affordable Care Act (ACA)—Provides support for access to health care insurance for victims of domestic violence, including women with disabilities.
Physical aggression—A harmful act in which harm inflicted is through physically hurting another.
Physiological arousal—Features of arousal reflected by physiological reactions, like escalations in blood pressure and rate of respiration and lessened activity of the gastrointestinal system.
Polymorphism—The condition of occurring in several different forms.
Postpartum period—Also known as the postnatal, it begins immediately after the birth of a child and extends for about six weeks.
Predatory violence—Involves documented planning and preparation for days to months, sometimes recorded by the perpetrators and typically ob-

served by others and the absence of emotion in the offender during the commission of the event.

Proactive aggression—Planful and goal-oriented aggression motivated by external reward.

Psychodynamic theory—A view that explains personality in terms of conscious and unconscious forces, such as unconscious desires and beliefs. It describes that personality consists of the id (responsible for instincts and pleasure-seeking), the superego (which attempts to obey the rules of parents and society), and the ego (which mediates between them according to the demands of reality).

Psychological abuse—A mental form of abuse, characterized by a person subjecting, or exposing, another person to behavior that may result in psychological trauma, including anxiety, chronic depression, or post-traumatic stress disorder.

Reactive aggression—Refers to aggressive responses to others' behavior that is perceived to be threatening and/or intentional.

Relational aggression—A behavior hurting one's interactions with those close to him/her.

Relational theory—Refers to dysfunctions and disconnections within a dyad as relational violations which constitute "the relational paradox": trying to keep out of a relationship so that [one] can stay in it.

Schemas—Patterns of connections that develop from experience. These are discrete entities that come from multiple nodes arranged into a complex network of stable links called knowledge structures. Schemas contain strongly linked thoughts, feelings, concepts and memories related to specific aspects of experience that have in the past occurred regularly and played out similarly. They typically include knowledge about a particular facet of experience, related attitudes, beliefs, expectations and memories, links to typical feelings, and scripts for how to behave.

Script theory—Provides the patterns of learned aggression that have been conceptualized and coded in memory and are available for activation.

Self-recrimination—The act or an instance of blaming or censuring oneself.

Semantic Memory—The portion of long-term memory that processes ideas and concepts that are not drawn from personal experience. This includes things that are common knowledge, such as the names of colors, the sounds of letters, the capitals of countries, and other basic facts acquired over a lifetime.

Sensorimotor skills—Involves the process of receiving a sensory input and producing a motor output.

Sexual minority stress (SMS)—Includes distal experiences of violence, harassment, and discrimination, and proximal stressors related to concealment of sexual identity and negative feelings about being a part of a minority sexually.

Sexual violence—A sexual act committed against someone without that person's freely given consent, usually committed through use of force.
Situational couple violence—Violence that is not motivated by control but is in response to a particular situation. Most prevalent type in the general population and in couples seeking conjoint therapy, where the core problem is communication skill deficiencies, which gets compensated with verbal aggression and violence.
Social abuse [SEE CONTROLLING BEHAVIORS].
Social cognitive theory—Posits that learning occurs in a social context with a dynamic and reciprocal interaction of the person, environment, and behavior. The unique feature of this theory is the emphasis on social influence and its emphasis on external and internal social reinforcement.
Social Information Processing (SIP) Model—Emphasizes the way people perceive the behavior of others and make attributions about their motives. It posits a progression of steps in processing and interpreting cues from the environment. A key construct in SIP theory is the hostile attribution bias—a tendency to interpret ambiguous events as being motivated by hostile intent.
Social interaction theory—An explanation of language development with an emphasis on the role of social interaction between the developing child and linguistically knowledgeable adults.
Social learning theory—Posits that people learn from one another, via observation, imitation, and modeling. It acts as a bridge between behaviorist and cognitive learning theories because it encompasses attention, memory, and motivation.
Sociodemographic—Involving factors such as age, race, ethnicity, and language.
Sociopsychological—Pertains to how people's thoughts, feelings, and behaviors are influenced by the actual, imagined, or implied presence of others.
Somatoform disorders—A form of mental illness that causes one or more bodily symptoms, including pain. A person with this type of disorder will experience various symptoms, such as physical pain, for which there is no clear medical reason.
Stalking—A pattern of behavior that makes you feel afraid, nervous, harassed, or in danger. It is when someone repeatedly contacts you, follows you, sends you things, talks to you when you don't want them to, or threatens you.
Stockholm Syndrome—Psychological response wherein a captive begins to identify closely with his or her captors, as well as with their agenda and demands.
Subjective Units of Distress Scale (SUDS)—A standardized test to assess for anxiety measured on a scale from one to one hundred.
Superego distortions—Result when individuals demand an unachievable level of self-perfection, and experience extremely harsh self-criticism when

they inevitably fall short of this impossibly high standard. They become overly harsh and charged with self-destructive intent. Self-attack may range from guilt-ridden self-loathing to physical assault on the body.

Survivor Therapy Empowerment Program (STEP)—A companion program for women whose violent partners were attending batterer intervention programs. Re-empowerment and moving toward growth with a focus on building self-efficacy through strengths is also part of the trauma philosophy.

Teleological—Pertaining to a reason or explanation for something in function of its end, purpose or goal.

Teratogenicity—The extent to which an agent that can disturb the development of the embryo or fetus. Teratogens halt the pregnancy or produce a congenital malformation (a birth defect). Classes of teratogens include radiation, maternal infections, chemicals, and drugs.

Traumatic brain injury—An often acute event that results in stretching or tearing of brain tissue.

Uni-directional aggression—Involves one perpetrator and one victim.

Verbal aggression—The act of harming another using one's words.

Appendix A

Resources for Domestic Violence Intervention

Many of these resources offer safe escape options for those in danger. Some of these resources offer services in different languages, as well as for the deaf and the physically handicapped.

GENERAL RESOURCES

National Resource Center on Domestic Violence

• http://www.nrcdv.org/

• Those in need are encouraged to call the National Domestic Violence Hotline at 1-800-799-7233 and for the deaf, hard of hearing, or speech impaired, 1-800-787-3224.

• A comprehensive source of information for those wanting to educate themselves and help others on the many issues related to domestic violence through special projects and key initiatives.

• Offices in Harrisburg, Pennsylvania, and Washington, DC

• The center produces many publications and podcasts, and in addition to these, distributes newsletters to highlight new resources, those in development, announcements, and events.

The National Domestic Violence Hotline

• This organization works to provide help to all those affected by domestic abuse. The website explains what characterizes a healthy relationship and what constitutes abuse.

• Information is also provided for abusive partners to identify red flags, as The Hotline is available 24/7 at 1-800-799-SAFE (7233) or at 1-800-787-3224 for the deaf, hard of hearing, or speech impaired.

• Many articles are featured on the website about the options and rights for victims/survivors. Outlines are available for the creation of a safety plan for most situations.

American Bar Association Commission on Domestic Violence

• 1-202-662-1000
• www.abanet.org/domviol

National Center on Domestic Violence, Trauma, & Mental Health

• 312-726-7020

Partners in Prevention

• Survivor success and/or tips with the program are available for free via email. The website, http://www.enddomesticabuse.org/domestic_violence_trt.php, provides many solutions, including eBooks.

• Central program, Intimate Partner Abuse Treatment Program, treats both abusers and victims/survivors both individually as well as with their partner as a couple.

• The primary focus of the Intimate Partner Abuse Treatment Program for the abuser is becoming aware of and accountable for their experience, their behavior, and the impact of their actions on others.

• The victim's process is parallel and collaborative to their partner's treatment, while individually transformative. The focus of their intervention is healing from the impact of abuse and interrupting the abuse dynamic.

• The site highlights case studies to highlight core issues and provide further resources for understanding.

• Therapy occurs over the telephone or via Skype in about 26 individual sessions, with additional sessions being available for partners. The cost range is $175–$250 per consultation.

GoodTherapy.org

• 1-888-563-2112

• Provides background as to what battering is and describes the many forms it may take. This website also explains in depth Batterer Intervention Programs, its criticisms, and the role psychotherapy plays in the process.

• Above all, this is an outlet for finding therapy options either by browsing the website's directory.

The Joyful Heart Foundation

• A national organization with hubs of service in New York, Los Angeles, and Honolulu, their vision is a world free of sexual assault, domestic violence, and child abuse.

• New York Resources include:

• Violence Intervention Program: 1-800-664-5880 (bilingual, Spanish and English) |www.vipmujeres.org

• Sakhi for South Asian Women: 212-868-6741 |www.sakhi.org

• California Resources include:

• California Partnership to End Domestic Violence: 1-800-524-4765 orwww.cpedv.org

• Peace Over Violence: 310-392-8381

• Hawaii Resources include:

• Hawai'i State Coalition Against Domestic Violence: 1-808-832-9316 |www.hscadv.org

• Sex Abuse Treatment Center: 1-808-524-7273 |www.satchawaii.com

ACCESS TO SHELTERS

Center Against Domestic Violence

• http://www.cadvny.org/ , also available in Spanish.

• The Center encourages those in need to call the 24-hour hotline at 718-439-1000.

• Offers support, shelter, and education through counseling, safe houses, and school programs for teens year-round.

• Three shelters within New York City provide lifesaving emergency housing for women and children who are fleeing abusive homes. These shelters work to equip these victims with all the tools needed to start a new life.

• Men who are victims of domestic abuse can call the same domestic violence hotlines as female victims: New York City Domestic Violence Hotline 1-800-621-HOPE (4673). Shelters are available through The Center as well. Gay and Transgender men can access a full range of domestic violence services by calling the New York City Gay and Lesbian Anti-Violence Project Hotline at 212-714-1141.

Safe Horizon

• Domestic Violence Hotline for access to shelters at: 1-800-621-HOPE (4673) (Also available in Spanish). Outside of NYC call the National Domestic Violence Hotline: 1-800-799-7233.

• Similar help is available from Safe Housing Partnerships http://safehousingpartnerships.org/

• Safe Horizon's mission is to provide support, prevent violence, and promote justice for victims of crime and abuse, their families, and communities.

RELIGION-BASED RESOURCES

Christianity/Catholicism

United States Conference of Catholic Bishops

• http://www.usccb.org/issues-and-action/marriage-and-family/marriage/domestic-violence/when-i-call-for-help.cfm

• This organization asserts that violence of any kind within a relationship is sinful and explains what dioceses and parishes can do to provide aid.

• It is also elaborated on the psychological bedrock for why spouses would turn to abuse or choose to stay in the relationship, giving many resources for those in need. It addresses men who abuse, women who are abused, and offers a prayer that may be used as a source of healing.

• When I Call For Help: A Pastoral Response to Domestic Violence Against Women

Mending the Soul: Healing Life's Deepest Hurts

• This article, *A Biblical Response to the Abused Wife*, by Renee M. Malina references the Bible to console, provide options, and make sense of domestic abuse.

• This site in itself offers more resources such as sample sermons, presentations, books, and research articles: https://mendingthesoul.org/research-and-resources/research-and-articles/a-biblical-response-to-the-abused-wife/

• Esta pagina en Español: https://mendingthesoul.org/spanish/

Domestic Violence and Abuse in Catholic Marriages

• Cites the Bible to give insight and points to reflect upon: http://www.acatholic.org/domestic-violence-and-abuse-in-catholic-marriages/

Judaism

Domestic Violence in Jewish Law

• https://jwa.org/encyclopedia/article/wifebeating-in-jewish-tradition
• http://www.myjewishlearning.com/article/domestic-violence-in-jewish-law/
• This article by Naomi Graetz addresses the significance of domestic abuse within Jewish communities, specifically in Israel and the Diaspora. It quotes the Talmud among other sources of Rabbinic literature to explore the issue from a pre-modern and modern Ashkenazi perspective.
• The next entry is an extended article by the same author that cites a greater scope of perspectives and time periods

American Orthodox Jewish Women and Domestic Violence: An Intervention Design

• Discusses women and the Orthodoxy, how to create an intervention, and Project S.A.R.A.H.: http://ssa.uchicago.edu/american-orthodox-jewish-women-and-domestic-violence-intervention-design
• For more on Project S.A.R.A.H., operating chiefly in New Jersey to Stop Abusive Relationships At Home by giving extensive educational and prevention programs for the personal safety of children, go to: https://www.jofa.org/education-jofa-journal/preventing-abuse-our-jewish-communities-fall-2015-winter-2016/project-sarahwww.ProjectSARAH.org or call (973) 777-7638

Islam

The Islamic Solution to Stop Domestic Violence

• This article by Qasim Rashid rebukes the misconception that Islam encourages domestic abuse by referring to Quran verses and establishing pre-emptive deterrence as the key to solving this issue: http://www.huffingtonpost.com/qasim-rashid/islamic-solution-to-end-domestic-violence_b_1307305.html

Islamic Perspectives on Domestic Violence

• Provides an overview of Islamic Law for a critical look into domestic abuse and how partners can uphold their Muslim values: https://yaqeeninstitute.org/en/tesneem-alkiek/islam-and-violence-against-women/

Domestic Violence: Islamic Perspectives

• By Dr. Zainab Alwani: http://karamah.org/wp-content/uploads/2012/07/Domestic-violence-Islamic-Perspective-FINAL.pdf

Buddhism

The Buddhist Perspective on Women's Rights Part IV: Preventing Abusive Relationships

• http://hsingyun.org/womens-rights/

Quotes both the *Sutra of Yuye* as well as the *Srigalaka Sutra* in the context of today's world as well as incorporates aspects of Humanistic Buddhism to get to the core of the problem of domestic abuse.

Hinduism

Change Comes From Within Our Communities: Hindus United Against Domestic Violence

• http://www.huffingtonpost.com/anju-bhargava/change-comes-from-within-our-communities-hindus-united-against-domestic-violence_b_3136322.html

• https://docs.google.com/file/d/0Bwlxj5pIr0I-TXRsbjNPSGxQaE0/edit

SERVICES FOR CHILDREN

Childhood Domestic Violence Association

• https://cdv.org/

• Provides options to those who have experienced CDV and for loved ones of those impacted. The association offers free online training to those willing to help children affected, defines CDV in its many forms, and has compiled leading research in the field.

Domestic Violence Roundtable

• http://www.domesticviolenceroundtable.org/effect-on-children.html

• Multiple resources and information about what constitutes domestic violence, the cycle that occurs, warning signs, how it affects children, and much more.

Help Is Available

• If you or someone you know needs child witness to violence information or resources, you may want to contact one or more of the following programs:

• AWAKE (Advocacy for Women and Kids in Emergency)
Children's Hospital
300 Longwood Avenue
Gardner House 812
Boston, MA
617-355-4760

• The Child Witness to Violence Project
Boston Medical Center
One Boston Medical Center place
Boston, MA
617-414-4244

• The Children's Charter
77 Rumford Avenue
Waltham, MA
781-894-4307

• Wayside Youth and Family Support Network
Child Violence Intervention Project
88 Lincoln Street
Framingham, MA 01701
Contact: Jack Hagenbuch
508-620-0010 ext. 204
jackhagenbuch@wayside.org

Reading Resources:

• *When Dad Hurts Mom: Helping Your Children Heal the Wounds of Witnessing Abuse* by Lundy Bancroft (Putnam Adult, 2004)

• *The Batterer as Parent* by Lundy Bancroft and Jay G. Silverman (Sage Publications, Inc. 2002)

The National Child Traumatic Stress Network

• http://www.nctsn.org/content/children-and-domestic-violence

• Discusses how children are exposed in many ways to domestic violence and the various effects of domestic violence on these children (both short-term and long-term).

• Offers a wide range of treatment types.

SERVICES ALSO FOR MEN

Center against Domestic Violence

• Offers support, shelter, and education through counseling, safe houses, and school programs for teens year-round.

• Their website is http://www.cadvny.org/, also available in Spanish.

• Three shelters within New York City provide lifesaving emergency housing for women and children who are fleeing abusive homes. These shelters work to equip these victims with all the tools needed to start a new life. The center encourages those in need to call the 24-hour hotline at 718-439-1000.

• Men who are victims of domestic abuse can call the same domestic violence hotlines as female victims: New York City Domestic Violence Hotline 1-800-621-HOPE (4673). Shelters are available through The Center as well. Gay and Transgender men can access a full range of domestic violence services by calling the New York City Gay and Lesbian Anti-Violence Project Hotline at (212) 714-1141.

Gay Men's Domestic Violence Project Hotline

• 1-800-832-1901

Men Stopping Violence

• 1-866-717-9317
• www.menstoppingviolence.org

SERVICES FOR SENIORS

National Clearinghouse on Abuse in Later Life

• 1-608-255-0539
• www.ncall.us

National Committee for the Prevention of Elder Abuse

• Helps to identify the perpetrators of elder abuse, who may be at risk, and warning signs to aid in prevention.
• http://www.preventelderabuse.org/elderabuse/domestic.html

Pennsylvania Coalition against Domestic Violence

• http://www.pcadv.org/Learn-More/Domestic-Violence-Topics/Elder-Abuse/
• Works to increase safety and access to services for older victims of domestic abuse.
• Features statistics related to elder abuse and instructs on what to do if you suspect an older person may be a victim.

SERVICES WITH FOCUS ON RACE, CULTURE, ETHNICITY, DISABILITIES, AND MULTIPLE GENDER IDENTITIES (AVAILABLE THROUGH THE NATIONAL COALITION AGAINST DOMESTIC VIOLENCE)

FaithTrust Institute: Working Together to End Sexual and Domestic Violence

• A national, multi-faith, multicultural training organization with global reach.
• http://www.faithtrustinstitute.org/
• The website offers FAQs, articles, statistics, DVD programs, awareness brochures, educational materials for congregations, and news concerning domestic abuse, healthy boundaries, child abuse, sexual violence, and healthy teen relationships in a host of languages beyond English including Chinese, Spanish, Korean, and Laotian.
• Based in Seattle, WA:
2414 SW Andover St, Suite D208
Seattle, WA 98106
206-634-1903 (Telephone)
206-634-0115 (Fax)

Narika: Changing the Way We Live—Violence Free

• Call Narika at (510) 444-6068, 1-800-215-7308, or email narika@narika.org
• This group is most active in California's bay area and founded by immigrant women, is always striving to promote women's independence,

economic empowerment, and well-being by helping domestic violence survivors with advocacy, support, and education.

• This website is available in over 60 languages.

• The Self-Empowerment & Economic Development (SEED) program is designed to foster economic independence and self-reliance among survivors of domestic violence, human trafficking, and even new immigrant population that are particularly vulnerable to abuse and exploitation. Their comprehensive program offers instruction on 4 core topics: ESL, financial literacy, basic computer literacy, and career development training. To create a holistic approach, these core learnings are supplemented with talks and workshops on other critical soft skills that impact self-confidence: such as yoga, hygiene, personal health, self-assertiveness, awareness of basic employee rights, self-defense, art, and even grooming etiquette. Upon completion of a full SEED session, participants are in a position to think about and articulate next steps towards becoming economically and financially independent.

• SEED classes are offered on a modular basis, allowing students to choose topics of learning they feel are most appropriate for their personal and professional needs. Throughout the whole SEED session, free childcare is also provided so children can travel with their parents. Many of these children have experienced family violence as well and need to be supported, just as their mothers are healing from traumatic past. They are in the process of expanding the SEED program to be able to offer these children trauma-informed services as well, focusing on mental health, healthy conflict resolution, and school success. SEED sessions may be offered as a comprehensive 12-week session or as individual modules teaching financial literacy, computer literacy or career development training.

Northwest Network of Bisexual, Trans, Lesbian & Gay Survivors of Abuse

• 1-206-568-7777
• www.nwnetwork.org

Gay Men's Domestic Violence Project Hotline

• 1-800-832-1901

Human Rights Campaign: Sexual Assault and the LGBTQ Community

• https://www.hrc.org/resources/sexual-assault-and-the-lgbt-community

Love is Respect Hotline

- 1-866-331-99474 (24/7) or text "loveis" to 22522

The Anti-Violence Project

- Serves the LGBTQ community. Their hotline is 212-714-1124, which is bilingual and open 24/7.

The Network La Red

- Survivor-led organizing to end partner abuse, serves LGBTQ, poly, and kink/BDSM survivors of abuse; bilingual.
- Their hotline is 617-742-4911
- http://tnlr.org/en/

FORGE

- Contact them at 414-559-2123 or http://forge-forward.org/
- A national transgender anti-violence organization, founded in 1994. Federally funded to provide direct services to transgender, gender non-conforming and gender non-binary survivors of sexual assault. Since 2011, FORGE has served as the only transgender-focused organization federally funded to provide training and technical assistance to providers around the country who work with transgender survivors of sexual assault, domestic and dating violence, and stalking. Their role as a technical assistance provider has allowed them to directly see key continued and emerging challenges many agencies are experiencing in serving sexual assault survivors of all genders.

Domestic Violence Initiative for the Differently Abled

- (303) 839-5510, (877) 839-5510
www.dviforwomen.org

Deaf Abused Women's Network (DAWN)

- Email: Hotline@deafdawn.org
- VP: 202-559-5366
- www.deafdawn.org

Asian and Pacific Islander Institute on Domestic Violence

- 1-415-954-9988
- www.apiidv.org

Domestic Violence and Child Advocacy Center

• Provides child abuse, domestic violence, and teen dating violence help in English and Spanish.

• https://dvcac.org/african-american-women

• Based in Cleveland, Ohio, the Center may be contacted at (216) 229-2420 or (216) 391-HELP (4357) for 24 hour help

• For the deaf community, resources as well as interpretative services are available upon request. Contact Aileen Vasquez at avasquez@dvcac.org or text 216-469-4579.

• Also offers crisis intervention, safety planning, emergency shelter, justice system advocacy, support groups, educational classes, and individual therapy.

• Has a great focus on African American women and Latina/Immigrant women:

• The Ujima program has helped more than 900 African American women and relates back to the church to help victims. If you would like a list of churches or information about Ujima, please call (216) 229-2420

• The Latina Domestic Violence Program helps women to identify what qualifies as domestic abuse and accordingly address it. Their free, 24-hour confidential hotline is at 216-391-4357. All services are bilingual. For more information about the Latina Project services or outreach, please contact: Vanessa Rivera (Spanish), Latina Project Coordinator, Phone: (216) 229-2420, Email: vrivera@dvcac.org

• Legal remedies for battered immigrants. If you are an immigrant who is being abused by an intimate partner it is crucial that you speak with an immigration attorney or an advocate experienced in immigration issues about your rights, especially before going to an immigration hearing or interview. For a list of referrals, please contact 216-391-4357. Options include:

• The VAWA self-petition, which enables battered spouses and their children to obtain lawful immigration status without the abuser's knowledge or permission since it is a confidential petition.

• The U Visa is for unmarried women or women married to someone undocumented. The U Visa was created to assist immigrant crime victims. This legal remedy is for noncitizens who have suffered substantial physical or mental abuse resulting from a wide range of criminal activity (domestic violence, child abuse, sexual assault, kidnapping, and other crimes). The victims must collaborate with the investigation or prosecution of the crime. The U Visa provides eligible immigrants with authorized stay in the United States and employment authorization.

• The T Visa is specifically for immigrants trafficked into the United States for commercial sex or labor. The perpetrator's status and relationship to the victim are irrelevant in the U Visa and T Visa, however both visas require cooperation with the criminal system.

Institute on Domestic Violence in the African American Community

• 1-877-643-8222
• www.dvinstitute.org

Deaf World against Violence Everywhere

• Based in Ohio, their mission is to promote the empowerment of and equality for Ohio's diverse deaf, deaf-blind, and hard of hearing communities by offering culturally affirmative advocacy and education, while inspiring community accountability, in response to oppression and relationship and sexual violence.

• Information at dwaveohio.org or at 614-678-5476.

• Involvement in the cause is welcome through serving on a committee, volunteering locally, or donations.

End Abuse of People with Disabilities

• Help to foster accountability, create inclusion, strengthen prevention, and raise awareness: https://www.endabusepwd.org/

Sakhi for South Asian Women

• 212-868-6741 | www.sakhi.org

Women against Violence Europe

• https://www.wave-network.org/

Asian Americans for Community Involvement

• Based in California, AACI Asian Women's Home believes that everyone deserves to live healthy and safe lives. They offer vital life-saving services to individuals and families affected by domestic violence, those who might have nowhere else to go due to cultural and linguistic barriers. They provide quality care to meet the unique needs of the clients we serve, including emergency shelter, legal and social services advocacy, and a 24-hour hotline. Their prevention work includes media outreach; educational training workshops for professional, paraprofessionals and community groups; and a first-of-its-kind multilingual (English, simplified and traditional Chinese, and Vietnamese) website with information and resources for victims of domestic violence: dv.aaci.org

- AACI Asian Women's Home 24-hour hotline: 408-975-2739.
- For workshops, brochures, information tables or media inquiries please e-mail us at dvcomed@aaci.org.

Asian Task Force against Domestic Violence

- https://www.atask.org/site/
- 24-hour multilingual hotline: 617-338-2355
- Primarily serving immigrants and refugees from East Asian, South, and Southeast Asian in the New England region.

LITERATURE AND TEXT RESOURCES

Domestic Violence Literature

- https://mpdc.dc.gov/page/domestic-violence-literature
- Domestic violence crosses all barriers of age and gender and results in serious illness and even death. Help them save lives by making yourself aware of the risks and warning signs!
- This department based in Washington, DC, offers printable, informative brochures in PDF format that address every facet of domestic abuse within the United States.

The Truth about Domestic Violence: Literature Review (Psychology in Action)

- https://www.psychologyinaction.org/psychology-in-action-1/2013/03/28/the-truth-about-domestic-violence-literature-review
- Provides statistics and demographics related to domestic violence as well as useful terminology related to the issue.

Appendix B

Legal Precedents

UNITED STATES SUPREME COURT

Voisine v. United States (2016)

In 2003 and 2005, Stephen Voisine was convicted of assaulting a woman (with whom he was in a domestic relationship) under a Maine state statute that establishes that a person is guilty of assault if that person "knowingly, intentionally, or recklessly causes bodily injury or offensive physical contact to another person." A violation of that statute is misdemeanor domestic violence assault if the victim is a family or household member.

Question: Does a misdemeanor crime that requires only a showing of recklessness qualify as a misdemeanor crime of domestic violence?

Conclusion: A reckless domestic violence assault qualifies as a misdemeanor crime of domestic violence. The Court held that the relevant statutory text—"us[ing] force"—does not rule out an interpretation that encompasses an act of force carried out recklessly, or with a conscious disregard of the substantial risk of causing harm. Although the statutory language does not apply to true accidents, it certainly does to reckless conduct.

https://www.oyez.org/cases/2015/14-10154

Elonis v. United States (2015)

Anthony Elonis was convicted under Title 18 of the United States Code for posting threats to injure his coworkers, his wife, the police, a kindergarten class, and a Federal Bureau of Investigation agent on Facebook.

Question: Does a conviction of threatening another person require proof of the defendant's subjective intent to threaten?

Conclusion: Yes. Chief Justice John G. Roberts Jr. delivered the opinion for the 8–1 majority. The Court held that the prosecution needed to show that Elonis intended the posts to be threats, and therefore that there was a subjective intent to threaten. An objective reasonable person standard does not go far enough to separate innocent, accidental conduct from purposeful, wrongful acts.

https://www.oyez.org/cases/2014/13-983

Ohio v. Clark (2015)

On March 17, 2010, a preschool teacher noticed some facial injuries on one of her three-year-old students. When the teacher inquired about the injuries, the student indicated that his mother's boyfriend, Darius Clark, caused them. The teacher forwarded her concerns to a child-abuse hotline, which resulted in the arrest of Clark for child abuse.

Question: Does an individual's obligation to report suspected child abuse make that individual an agent of law enforcement for purposes of the Confrontation Clause? Do a child's out-of-court statements to a teacher in response to the teacher's concerns about potential child abuse qualify as "testimonial" statements subject to the Confrontation Clause?

Conclusion: No and no. The Court held that the child's statements to his teachers were non-testimonial because the totality of the circumstances indicated that the primary purpose of the conversation was not to create an out-of-court substitute for trial testimony. In this case, there was an ongoing emergency because the child, who had visible injuries, could have been released into the hands of his abuser, and therefore the primary purpose of the teachers' questions was most likely to protect the child. Moreover, a very young child who does not understand the details of the criminal justice system is unlikely to be speaking for the purpose of creating evidence. Finally, the Court held that a mandatory reporting statute does not convert a conversation between a concerned teacher and a student into a law enforcement mission aimed primarily at gathering evidence for a prosecution.

https://www.oyez.org/cases/2014/13-1352

Lozano v. Alvarez (2014)

Diana Alvarez and Manuel Lozano, two native Colombians, met while living in London and had a daughter together. At trial Alvarez testified that, from 2005 until 2008, Lozano was abusing and threatening to rape her. Lozano denied these allegations and claimed that, although they had normal couple problems, they were generally "very happy together." In November 2008, Alvarez took the child and, after a stay at a women's shelter, moved to her sister's home in New York.

Question: Does the one-year statute of limitations on a petition to return an abducted child under the Hague Convention stay in effect when one parent has deliberately concealed the child's whereabouts from the other parent?

Conclusion: The one-year period is not subject to equitable tolling; the Supreme Court held that the policy of equitable tolling, which pauses the running of a statute of limitations when a litigant has diligently pursued his rights, does not apply to the Hague Convention's provision on international child abduction.

https://www.oyez.org/cases/2013/12-820

United States v. Hayes (2009)

Question: Under the Gun Control Act of 1968, does a conviction for misdemeanor battery constitute a "misdemeanor crime of domestic violence" when the victim was the offender's wife and the predicate offense statute did not designate a "domestic relationship" between aggressor and victim as an element of the crime?

Conclusion: The Court reasoned that the language of the Gun Control Act suggested that the predicate offense statute need only include "the use of force" as an element of the crime and need not include a "domestic relationship" as an additional element.

https://www.oyez.org/cases/2008/07-608

Giles v. California (2008)

Question: Are a batterer's rights violated when the common law "forfeiture by wrongdoing" doctrine is applied to allow out-of-court statements made by a witness, absent due to the defendant's own conduct, into evidence without giving defendant an opportunity to cross-examine the absent witness?

Conclusion: Yes, the Court held that the forfeiture by wrongdoing exception only applies to situations where the defendant causes the witness' absence with the intention of preventing that witness from testifying at trial. A majority of the justices agreed that a history of domestic violence is a meaningful indication of the defendant's "intent to silence" the victim when he killed her. The multiple opinions demonstrated a remarkable understanding of domestic violence as a form of silencing of the victim.

https://www.oyez.org/cases/2007/07-6053

DISTRICT OF COLUMBIA COURT OF APPEALS

Carrell v. United States (2013)

This case deals with the intent standard required to be proven for misdemeanor threats in DC in light of the U.S. Supreme Court's decision in *Elonis v. U.S.*, which rejected an objective (negligence) standard for the federal felony threats statute. It contested if the DC Court of Appeals should uphold its current standard (an objective approach) or adopt, at most, a requirement that the government prove that the government prove the defendant acted recklessly. It emphasizes the impact requiring proof of the speaker's subjective intent would have on domestic violence victims, for whom threats by abusers often cause extreme harm.

http://www.dvleap.org/Portals/dvleap/Carrell%20v%20US.pdf?ver=2017-06-30-190841-773

Salvaterra v. Ramirez (2014)

Dealt with equal protections to victims of unrelated sexual assault as are provided to victims of domestic violence. A perpetrator of sexual abuse was ordered to vacate his own home, which he did not share with the victim, a remedy could not be ordered under the vacate provision that is limited to parties sharing a home. The victim and perpetrator both lived in a small rental building; she had to walk by his apartment to enter and leave the building and was often victimized as she did so. The Court of Appeals decision resoundingly affirms this rule and establishes that a perpetrator may be ordered out of his own home under the statute's "catch-all" provision, when that is necessary to effectuate a stay-away order.

http://www.dvleap.org/Portals/dvleap/Salvattera%20v.%20Ramirez%20Opinion.pdf?ver=2017-06-30-190841-773

Index

About the Contributors

Naji Abi-Hashem, MDiv, PhD is a clinical and cultural psychologist and has taught at several institutions, universities, and seminaries in the United States, the Middle East, Europe, and Asia. Dr. Abi-Hashem specializes in cross-cultural psychotherapy, with emphases on the psychology of refugees, immigration, and spirituality.

Craig A. Anderson, PhD is Distinguished Professor of Psychology at Iowa State University; director at the Center for the Study of Violence; and past-president of the International Society for Research on Aggression. His General Aggression Model has been applied to clinical, social, personality and developmental psychology, pediatrics, criminology, war, and climate change, among other fields.

Martha E. Banks, PhD is a research neuropsychologist in the Research & Development Division of ABackans DCP, Inc., in Akron, Ohio, and an adjunct professor of psychology at Kent University. Dr. Bank's specialties include the psychology of women and gender, psychology of peoples of color, trauma, and health care.

June F. Chisholm, PhD is a licensed clinical psychologist who received her doctorate from the University of Massachusetts at Amherst. She is a professor of psychology at Pace University and studies community psychology, gender, issues in the psychological treatment of women of color, multicultural psychology, prejudice, parenting, cyber-bullying, and school violence.

Caroline S. Clauss-Ehlers, PhD is associate professor, and program coordinator at Rutgers' School Counseling and Counseling Psychology Departments. Dr. Clauss-Ehler's research focuses on how culture and environment foster resilience in children. She is a licensed psychologist.

Allison Crowe, PhD is associate professor of Counselor Education at East Carolina University and teaches graduate-level courses on helping skills, clinical mental health counseling, and research. Dr. Crowe researches stigma to intimate partner violence and mental illness, in addition to creative approaches in counselor education.

Jennifer De Mucci, MA holds a degree in school psychology from St. John's University. Her main areas of interests focus on international and cross-cultural psychology and the impact of generational transmission of trauma, particularly on young children.

Fatima El-Jamil, PhD is clinical assistant professor of psychology at the American University of Beirut in Beirut, Lebanon. She has authored and co-authored several chapters on applying Western psychotherapy models in the Arab Middle East. She is a New York–licensed psychologist.

Tara Jungersen, PhD, LMHC, CCMHC, NCC is chair and associate professor of the Department of Counseling at Nova Southeastern University. She is a licensed mental health counselor whose work includes directing a clinic with a high volume domestic violence cases.

Fred Millán, PhD, ABPP, NCC is professor of psychology at SUNY Old Westbury and Director of the Graduate Mental Health Counseling Program. He is a licensed counseling psychologist and maintains a part-time private practice in Spanish and English. He also provides clinical supervision to clinical trainees.

Christine E. Murray, PhD is associate professor and coordinator of the Couple and Family Counseling Track in the UNCG Department of Counseling and Educational Development. Dr. Murray's primary research interest relates to the bridging the gap between research and practice in the area of domestic violence.

Gerald A. Pantoja, MA is a doctoral candidate in clinical psychology at St. John's University. He is interested in how dynamic processes are defined and ultimately, how they affect clinical presentation and outcomes.

Lenore E. A. Walker, PhD is a clinical forensic psychologist who testifies in cases across the United States. Well recognized in the field, her work and research interest focus on the exploration of various forms of gender violence, especially battered women, sexual assault, sexual harassment, sex and human trafficking, false confessions of women, and child abuse.

Wayne Warburton, PhD is senior lecturer in psychology at Macquarie University and a registered psychologist with experience working with victims of domestic violence. His research interests primarily center around aggressive behavior and media impacts, with a particular focus on aggressive schema, violent and pro-social media, family violence, and screen addiction.

Carolyn M. West, PhD is professor of psychology and the Division Chair of Social, Behavioral, and Human Sciences in the School of Interdisciplinary Arts and Sciences at the University of Washington. Her research focuses on intimate partner violence and sexual assault, with a special focus on violence in the lives of women of color.

Michelle Yacobson, MA is a PhD candidate in clinical psychology at St. John's University in New York. Her research and clinical interests span ageing and development, neuropsychology, and the brain, and health psychology.

Clare Jinzhao Zhao, MEd is a fourth-year doctoral student in counseling psychology at University of Denver. Her primary clinical and research interests are multicultural counseling and identity development.

About the Editors

William G. Herron, PhD, ABPP was a professor at St. John's University for more than 35 years and served as the director of both the School of Psychology and Clinical Psychology programs. He earned his PhD from Fordham University. He has been on the faculty, supervisor, and training analyst at two analytic institutes and published 12 books. The most recent was *Specialty Competencies in Psychoanalysis* in 2015. He practices in New Jersey and is a supervisor in the psychiatric residency program at New Bridge Medical Center.

Rafael Art. Javier, PhD, ABPP is professor of psychology and the director of Inter-agencies Training and Research Initiatives, director of the Post-Graduate Professional Development Programs, and director of the Postdoctoral Certificate Programs in Forensic Psychology at St. John's University. He is also a faculty member at the Object Relations Institute. Dr. Javier has presented at national and international conferences on topics ranging from domestic violence, forensic psychology, psycholinguistics, psychotherapy, and cultural and ethnic issues. He is the editor-in-chief for the *Journal of Psycholinguistic Research* and the past coeditor of the *Journal of Social Distress and the Homeless*. His current research activities include issues of violence and moral development, suicide in adolescents and young adults, and bilingualism.

www.ingramcontent.com/pod-product-compliance
Ingram Content Group UK Ltd.
Pitfield, Milton Keynes, MK11 3LW, UK
UKHW041128071026
15587UKWH00009B/292

9 780765 709530